Internalized Oppression

E. J. R. David, PhD, was born in the Philippines to Kapampangan parents and was raised in Pasay, Las Piñas, Makati, and Barrow, Alaska. He received his MA and PhD in Clinical Community Psychology from the University of Illinois at Urbana-Champaign. Dr. David is currently an assistant professor at the University of Alaska, Anchorage, in the Joint PhD Program in Clinical Community Psychology that has a cultural and indigenous emphasis, where he also serves as the director of the Alaska Native Community Advancement in Psychology Program. His research program on the psychological effects of internalized oppression as experienced by different ethnic and cultural groups started while he was in graduate school and led the American Psychological Association (APA) Division 45 to give him the Distinguished Doctoral Student Research Award "for his significant contribution in psychological research related to ethnic minority populations." In 2012, Dr. David was honored by the APA Minority Fellowship Program with the Early Career Award in Research for Distinguished Contributions to the Field of Racial and Ethnic Minority Psychology, citing his "outstanding scientific contributions and the application of this knowledge toward the improved mental and physical well-being of people of color." In 2013, the Asian American Psychological Association presented him with the Early Career Award for Distinguished Contributions to Research. Dr. David is also the author of *Brown Skin, White Minds: Filipino -/ American Postcolonial Psychology*.

Internalized Oppression
The Psychology of Marginalized Groups

E. J. R. David, PhD
Editor

SPRINGER PUBLISHING COMPANY
NEW YORK

Springer Publishing Company, LLC
11 West 42nd Street
New York, NY 10036
www.springerpub.com

Acquisitions Editor: Stephanie Drew
Production Editor: Shelby Peak
Composition: diacriTech

ISBN: 978-0-8261-9925-6
e-book ISBN: 978-0-8261-9926-3

13 14 15 16 / 5 4 3 2 1

The author and the publisher of this Work have made every effort to use sources believed to be reliable to provide information that is accurate and compatible with the standards generally accepted at the time of publication. The author and publisher shall not be liable for any special, consequential, or exemplary damages resulting, in whole or in part, from the readers' use of, or reliance on, the information contained in this book. The publisher has no responsibility for the persistence or accuracy of URLs for external or third-party Internet websites referred to in this publication and does not guarantee that any content on such websites is, or will remain, accurate or appropriate.

Library of Congress Cataloging-in-Publication Data

Internalized oppression: the psychology of marginalized groups / edited by E.J.R. David, Ph.D.
  pages cm
Includes index.
ISBN 978-0-8261-9925-6
1. Marginality, Social—Psychological aspects. 2. Oppression (Psychology)
3. Minorities. 4. Intergroup relations. I. David, E. J. R. (Eric John Ramos)
HM1136.I65 2014
305—dc23
              2013034826

Printed in the United States of America by Edwards Brothers Malloy.

This book is dedicated to Malakas, Kalayaan, Kaluguran, and the other children of the world. May you love all parts of your selves, and may your generation be free of internalized oppression.

Contents

Contributors

James Allen, PhD
Professor of Biobehavioral Health & Population Sciences
University of Minnesota Medical School, Duluth Campus
Center for Alaska Native Health Research, University of Alaska Fairbanks
Fairbanks, Alaska

Alvin N. Alvarez, PhD
Professor of Counseling
Associate Dean, College of Health & Social Sciences
San Francisco State University
San Francisco, California

Marielle Amrhein, MA
Group Facilitator
Interchange Counseling Institute
San Francisco, California

Teresa I. Baca, MS
Downey High School
Downey, California

Tamba-Kuii M. Bailey, PhD
Assistant Professor of Counseling Psychology and Community Services
University of North Dakota
Grand Forks, North Dakota

Twyla Baker-Demaray, PhD
Mandan, Hidatsa, & Arikara Nation
Vice President of Student Services
Fort Berthold Community College
New Town, North Dakota

Steve Bearman, PhD
Founder
Interchange Counseling Institute
San Francisco, California

E. J. R. David, PhD
Assistant Professor of Psychology
University of Alaska Joint PhD Program in Clinical-Community Psychology
University of Alaska Anchorage
Anchorage, Alaska

Annie O. Derthick, MA, MS
University of Alaska Joint PhD Program in Clinical-Community Psychology
University of Alaska Anchorage
Anchorage, Alaska

Eduardo Duran, PhD
Private Practice
7th Direction Psychotherapy, Assessment, and Consulting
Bozeman, Montana

Brian Favors, MEd, MSEd
Co-Founder and Director
Sankofa Community Empowerment Inc.
Brooklyn, New York

Elizabeth Fleagle
Inupiaq
Fairbanks, Alaska

Stephany Gallegos Payan, MS
California State University, Long Beach
Long Beach, California

John Gonzalez, PhD
White Earth Anishinaabe Nation
Associate Professor of Psychology
Bemidji State University
Bemidji, Minnesota

Tristan Görgens
Policy Researcher
Isandla Institute
Cape Town, Republic of South Africa

Carlos P. Hipolito-Delgado, PhD
Associate Professor of Counseling
University of Colorado Denver
Denver, Colorado

Chase Iron Eyes
Standing Rock Lakota Nation
Co-founder of Last Real Indians, Inc.

James M. Jones, PhD
Professor of Psychology and Director of the Center for the Study
of Diversity
University of Delaware
Newark, Delaware

Poka Laenui
Executive Director
Wai`anae Coast Community Mental Health Center
Wai`anae, Hawai'i

Jordan Lewis, MSW, PhD
Aleut
University of Washington School of Social Work
Indigenous Wellness Research Institute
Seattle, Washington

RJ Mendoza
APICHA Community Health Center
New York, New York

James B. Millan, MA, MS
Progress Foundation
San Francisco, California

Kevin L. Nadal, PhD
Associate Professor of Psychology
John Jay College of Criminal Justice, City University of New York
New York, New York

Michael Salzman, PhD
Professor of Educational Psychology
University of Hawai'i at Manoa
Honolulu, Hawai'i

Estelle Simard, MSW
Couchiching First Nation
Executive Director of the Institute for Culturally Restorative Practices
Fort Frances, Ontario, Canada

Brian Watermeyer, PhD
Research Fellow
Department of Psychology
University of Stellenbosch
Stellenbosch, Republic of South Africa

Wendi S. Williams, PhD
Assistant Professor of Counseling and School Psychology
Long Island University—Brooklyn
Brooklyn, New York

Foreword

It is a great honor to be asked to write the Foreword to such an important book edited by E. J. R. David, filled with contributions from leading and emerging psychological scholars on internalized oppression. Nearly two decades have passed since the publication of *Native American Postcolonial Psychology* (Duran & Duran, 1995), in which historical trauma and its negative consequences among America's First Peoples were extensively discussed. Historical trauma and its effects are becoming well known in many of our communities of color and other devalued social groups. Communities have gone through a spiritual and psychological shift of consciousness as we have become aware that many of the problems that visit our individuals, families, and collectives have a historical context. Through the process of understanding the historical context, we become liberated to heal historical trauma and to begin a new narrative of wellness.

Within the emerging narrative of well-being, a new awareness is being subjected to conscious investigation. An understanding of how trauma can become part of the psycho-spiritual internal fabric of human beings is taking the story to a new level of discourse. The fact that trauma deeply impacts the psyche and can then become part of the psychological makeup of the person will continue to create symptoms, which may exceed those brought on by the initial trauma. Internalizing the oppressor or identifying with the aggressor—the topic of this book—are ideas that are at least a half century old and need to be revisited in the process of healing intergenerational trauma in our communities.

Psychological ideas, theory, and prescribed practice abound in the area of trauma and internalized trauma. Because there is a plethora of work already done from a Western perspective, many of which are covered in this book's chapters, I am privileged in this Foreword to present theory from an indigenous perspective. I realize that there is no essential indigenous perspective and it may appear that I am falling into the common trap of cultural glossing. Therefore, I need to clarify where the perspective is coming from. After several decades of working with indigenous communities from many tribes, ideas and theory have crystallized in my psyche and I believe that there are threads that tie indigenous and marginalized communities from all over the world. This book is an example of the thread that ties our communities together in a manner that transcends the colonial mindset that has become part of our collective history. It is from these similar experiences and teachings that the traditional theoretical implications I will discuss next have arisen.

During my early years working with Native people who had been subjected to historical and personal trauma, I found that it was very difficult to treat the persistent symptoms that caused so much suffering. Also, I found that many of the people I was treating were suffering from an underlying feeling of guilt. The guilt made no rational sense because the person feeling the guilt was the victim and not the perpetrator. The difficulty of getting the person to heal, along with the feelings of guilt, led me to rethink trauma theory from the Western mindset toward an indigenous psycho-spiritual one.

When a perpetrator allows the arising of intent in his or her heart-mind to cause harm and suffering toward another person, there are several factors that must be understood. In Western models, trauma occurs at the physical and psychological layers of the person. The people I was treating were getting these aspects treated by medical and mental health providers. Yet in some cases, symptoms persisted well into old age. The fact that symptoms persisted despite treatment led me to believe that there is another aspect to trauma that we in the West were oblivious to.

After discussion with my root teacher from a Native tradition, it became obvious to me that the missing piece was "spirit." When a victim is traumatized, in addition to the emotional and physical assault, there is also a spiritual assault. Therefore, the perpetrator passes on physical, emotional, and spiritual energy to the victim. The fact that spiritual energy is "shot" (projected) at the victim makes the traumatic encounter one that is best understood by victims as an act of sorcery or spiritual intrusion. I became aware that the spirit of the perpetrator going into the victim brings with it the symptoms of the perpetrator, such as guilt and the lineage of trauma that has been the historical trauma legacy of the perpetrator. It is important to understand that the trauma or sorcery can be at an individual and/or collective level.

What does all of this look like in the day-to-day or century-to-century context? When we consider the extent of trauma that has been inflicted on our communities in this country via genocide, slavery, racism, sexism, and other intolerant forms of violence, we can begin to understand that the injury where blood does not flow (i.e., posttraumatic stress disorder) continues to afflict our communities, families, and individuals in the present. Trauma becomes internalized very quickly and the victim becomes a perpetrator as an act of survival, as illustrated in the case of Stockholm syndrome or analyzed through theoretical descriptions described as identification with the aggressor. An eloquent image was given by Stephen Biko: "The most potent weapon in the hands of the colonizer are the minds of the colonized."

For example, when working with a Native community where there is a high level of violence, it is critical to bring historical context to the issue. I usually pursue Freirean questions of the simplest kind. I ask: "Did you have a domestic violence program in your community 200 years ago? Why not? What happened that you need one now?" This type of questioning allows people to change the narrative of pathology that has been imposed on them and to begin to change the storyline into one that includes history. The inclusion of the historical context is liberating to the people and community because now they can change the ending of the story, by starting the story at the time before they were pathologized by Western medical model ideas of how dysfunctional the community has become. In essence, the community can trace the infliction or projection of the spirit of the perpetrator to a point in time that has since affected the community in a manner that is not congruent to the original instructions given to the community by the Great Mystery.

Another example can be taken by a question that is asked of me by inner-city community workers involved with preventing violence. I answer the question by facilitating the community worker in tracing the beginning of the violence to its source at a point in historical time. If the issue involves African American–on–African American violence in their communities, it is important to make the individuals involved in the violence aware of where the violence originated. The horrendous violence encountered during slavery was a profound act of collective sorcery projected toward our African relatives. The violence that was perpetrated on our African elders through the holocaust of slavery continues to express itself in the ongoing historical trauma impacting our communities. The violence was internalized and now the plantation owner continues to perpetrate violence on his community through the people he possessed. This narrative becomes very challenging to the present perpetrator in that he or she is being asked to understand that the violence does not belong to him or her. Instead, the violence continues to be the spirit of violence that was perpetrated as a form of spiritual violence on our African ancestors. A most difficult issue is to be compared to the plantation owner. As insulting as this is, the present day perpetrator of violence must understand that he or she has internalized the plantation owner and, more than that, has become him. This new narrative has a direct impact on the profound spiritual understanding of the individual, and the last thing he or she wants to be is the plantation owner.

The examples can be tailored to fit any community that is struggling with internalized oppression, many of which are focused on within specific chapters in this book. Facilitating an understanding of history and leading the person to the source of the violence is liberating, but it also facilitates forgiveness toward the individual and community. It is only through awareness that the person involved in the dysfunctional destructive behavior can begin to realize that the narrative handed to him or her by history is the wrong one, and only he or she can correct this narrative by developing a new story.

Therefore, as the reader goes through the chapters in this book, it would be advantageous to keep in mind the lineage of history. Simple Freirean questions must be asked about all the scenarios and illustrations presented by the contributing authors. Speaking of the authors, it is remarkable that in this book the community voice is included. Each chapter has a coauthor who is a member of the community discussed in the particular chapter. Equally important is the fact that the community voice is not being heard as a voice of academia, which gives life to the narrative on internalized oppression in a manner that is real and not simply theoretical. I am not saying that community voices are not theoretical. They most certainly are, but the theoretical analysis is from an indigenous community point of view and has not been filtered through Western logical positivism, as is usually the case in most of the literature being written about our communities. One of the best features of the book, in my opinion, is that the chapter authors (if they are a part of the community they are writing about) are allowed to share their own personal experiences and that such experiences are regarded as just as valid and legitimate as the "theories" and "empirical studies" that they review. This feature of the book may also serve as an opportunity for academicians to also express their lived realities, which may serve as a demonstration that we can write with both our minds and our hearts.

Because of the real stories and "heart" contained in each chapter, as a reader of this text, I would see my task as not just reading words for the sake of reading and analyzing. Instead, I would approach the material with the intent of wondering how this story will assist me in facilitating liberation in my immediate life-world. I have discussed psychological ideas from a perspective that is in keeping with the root metaphor of the word "psychology." If we are to address some of the historical sicknesses that have been imposed on our communities through the brutality of history, I believe that this can only be done through the study of soul (*psychology* in Greek). If we have the courage to see with the eyes of our ancestors and through their understanding of the world of soul, we can ensure that our descendants will not have to struggle in the same manner as we have for many generations. Instead of a historical trauma legacy, we can leave them with a historical healing way of being in the life-world.

Eduardo Duran, PhD
7th Direction Therapy, Assessment, and Consulting
Author of Healing the Soul Wound
Coauthor of Native American Postcolonial Psychology

Preface

"Stop. Collaborate and listen."

—Vanilla Ice

Of course Vanilla Ice was referring to something unrelated to psychology and the topic of this book, and perhaps using a quote from this rapper may be "cheesy." However, the literalness of these lyrics completely captures what I believe the field of psychology needs to do to better understand and serve the majority of people in our world. The popularity and simplicity of these lyrics may also help the field to easily remember what it needs to do when conducting research, providing services, or developing programs. Yes, I believe psychology needs to literally *stop, collaborate*, and *listen*. Here is why.

MY ABBREVIATED JOURNEY

There were many moments in my early life when I questioned my thoughts, attitudes, emotions, and behaviors, especially those that pertained to my heritage. I asked myself questions such as: "Why do I think that anything made in the United States is better than anything made in my motherland of the Philippines?" "Why do I believe that speaking fluent English without a Filipino accent is a marker of intelligence and higher social status?" "Why do I feel ashamed and embarrassed to admit that I am proficient in Tagalog and that I am Filipino?" and "Why do I stay away from the sun and use skin-whitening products to make my skin lighter?" In fact, these questions that I now know are signs of internalized oppression—the topic of this book—were the reasons I became fascinated with the field of psychology, as it is the scientific study of human thoughts, emotions, and behaviors. When I was young, these questions were left unanswered because there was not enough available information about them, or at least there was no easily accessible information that could potentially address them. What was most easily accessible, however, was information that led me to the conclusion that it was just all in my head—that it was just all me. Thus, I was often left blaming myself and wondering about what was wrong with me. Why am I so weird? Many times, I felt alone.

Fast forward to my college years, when I was fortunate enough to be given the opportunity to access information that allowed me to realize that, no, I am not alone and I am not weird. Most of this information was from outside the field of psychology, which made me quickly realize that the majority of our scientific psychological knowledge was developed for, conducted with, and intended to capture the experiences of people who are not like me. I also heard similar stories from people who are like me—people who are parts of various marginalized communities—showing me that my confusion and struggles are very common. Indeed, there are many other Filipinos in the Philippines, Filipinos in the United States, and people of other races and ethnicities all over the world who are asking the same questions about their heritage. Given this realization, the next questions for me were: "Why are all of these very different groups of people—with different cultures, geographic locations, and histories—experiencing the same thing?" "As different as all of these peoples are, what makes them similar?" and "What makes them different from the dominant White, Western group that does not seem to be asking these inferiorizing questions about their heritage?" This common thread among various groups of people is oppression, one that was mostly experienced under the dominant White, Western, patriarchal, and heterosexual worldview that permeates our world.

So when I got to graduate school, I embarked on bringing these questions about oppression into the psychological community, a community that had very few answers for them. Why is it that my and many other peoples' experiences—something very real to us—are not given much attention and value in psychology? Recently, a quick search on *PsycINFO*—the largest database for psychology literature—revealed 3,812 hits for the term "oppression," suggesting that psychology has paid a good amount of attention to oppression and its many forms (e.g., racism, sexism, heterosexism). However, the term "internalized oppression" returned only 110 hits (only 23 when "internalized oppression" was searched as a keyword). Even more contemporary forms of oppression called "microaggressions," a term which did not become popularized until 2006, produced more results at 163 than internalized oppression. These numbers reveal that although oppression and its many forms have been increasingly explored by the field of psychology, the internalization of such experiences of oppression—perhaps its most insidious and harmful consequence—continues to be understudied.

Now that I am in my early career in this field, psychology's (dis)regard of this topic has not changed much. For example, when I submitted research grant proposals to study internalized oppression, the scientific merit and rigor was well-received (I received good scores), but the phenomenon of interest was not, as it did not fit into the funding organizations' "research priorities." When I submitted my first book about internalized oppression, *Brown Skin, White Minds: Filipino -/ American Postcolonial Psychology* (2013), for publishers to consider, the most common feedback I received along with the rejections was that it was well-written and interesting, but the market was too small for the book because very few people experience and care about the phenomenon. It is still definitely difficult to convince people—especially those in power—that these experiences are real, valid, legitimate, widespread, and important. Why is psychology not listening? It is no wonder, therefore, that many racial and ethnic minorities, and other folks who are members of socially marginalized groups, commonly feel that their experiences—their lived realities—are not reflected and captured by psychological works (theory, research, and services). No wonder they feel marginalized and unheard.

That is why I am very excited about this book, because it may contribute to regarding internalized oppression as real, important, and widespread so that we can spend less time convincing people of its legitimacy and more time actually doing research and providing services to better understand and address it. Just as importantly, the book may serve as one avenue for socially devalued and marginalized communities to share their experiences, have their voices heard, and have their lived realities be regarded as equally valid and legitimate as dominant "theories" and "scientific knowledge." This book is a demonstration of how psychology can *stop*, or at least pause, its standard operating procedures and do something different. This book may serve as one example of how psychology can *collaborate* with and *listen* to the people whom the field is purporting to serve. This book is a demonstration of how psychology can produce works that are more reflective of the lived realities of many socially devalued and marginalized groups, people whose voices have been unheard and whose experiences have been ignored. It is time to hear their voices, regard their concerns as legitimate, and validate their experiences. It is time to let people know that they are not alone in their struggles.

INTERNALIZED OPPRESSION: THE PSYCHOLOGY OF MARGINALIZED GROUPS

There are some other books on internalized oppression, but they are all focused on one particular racial, cultural, or social group. Furthermore, all other texts on internalized oppression have approached the topic from a sociological, historical, or ethnic studies perspective, and not one has explored the phenomenon from a psychological or mental health standpoint. Moreover, no existing book on internalized oppression provides recommendations for how it may be addressed in clinical and community settings for specific groups. This book addresses the limitations of the current literature and significantly contributes to research and practice, because it is the first book to cover the common manifestations of internalized oppression, its mental and behavioral health consequences, and promising clinical and community programs to address internalized oppression for various social groups. This is the first book to highlight the universality of internalized oppression, but at the same time acknowledge its unique manifestations and implications for various communities.

The book is organized into four parts. Part I contains one chapter that provides an overview of internalized oppression, its historical development, and contemporary conceptualization. Part II is dedicated to the experiences of indigenous peoples in the United States—American Indians, Alaska Natives, and Native Hawaiians and other Pacific Islanders. Part III contains chapters on the other racial and ethnic minority groups in the United States—African Americans, Latina/o Americans, and Asian Americans. This does not mean, however, that members of these racial and ethnic groups do not have multiracial/multiethnic or indigenous identities, and many of their experiences may be similar to those discussed in the other chapters in both Parts II and III. Finally, Part IV focuses on other socially marginalized groups—women; the lesbian, gay, bisexual, and transgender (LGBT) community; and people with disabilities. Of course, members of these marginalized groups may also identify with the social groups covered in the other chapters as well. Indeed, multiple and intersecting minority identities within individuals are very common in our highly diverse world.

Each chapter is co-written by leading or emerging psychology scholars who study internalized oppresiion, and these authors bring their own styles in discussing the experiences of the communities they write about. One of the similarities between the chapters, however, is that the chapter authors were encouraged to share their own personal experiences and that such experiences are regarded to be just as valid and legitimate as the "theoretical and scientific literature" that they reviewed. Each chapter also includes a "community voice" coauthor, which is one of my favorite features of the book. Having "community voice" coauthors is an attempt, albeit a small one, to incorporate "real-world" experiences into what would otherwise be another purely academic discourse. In a way, this is an attempt to "bring the concepts to life," and one way to demonstrate community collaboration in that the chapters really are the products of collaborating with a community or, at least in this case, collaborating with a community member. This exhibits collaboration between "academics" and the community they are purporting to serve, a collaboration that is sorely needed in our field. Consistent with community psychology principles, this book is an example of how we can "give psychology away."

Finally, it is important to acknowledge that this book does not contain a chapter on all marginalized and oppressed groups in the world, primarily because of feasibility. However, the chapters do touch on the experiences shared by various peoples throughout the world. The chapters focusing on American racial and ethnic minorities (i.e., African Americans, Latinas/os, Asian Americans), for example, also discuss the oppression and colonization of various countries in Africa, Latin America, and Asia. Even the chapters on the indigenous peoples of the United States cover topics that are pertinent to the experiences of other indigenous peoples in the world. Furthermore, it is obvious that there are women, LGBT pepole, and people with disabilities all over the world as well. Thus, I hope that people from outside the United States can still find something in this book that is relevant and meaningful to their lives. To this end, it is my hope that this book may remind very different people of their similarities and connections, and that, essentially, we are all one.

Maraming salamat (many thanks) and I hope you find this book worthwhile.

E. J. R. David

Acknowledgments

First and foremost, I want to sincerely thank my Koyukon Athabascan wife—Margaret—and our three Filibascan children—Malakas, Kalayaan, and Kaluguran. *Maraming Salamat, dakal a salamat, enaa' baasee'* for understanding why I had to spend so much time working, and for listening to me talk about oppression almost endlessly.

Second, I want to extend genuine gratitude to all the chapter authors for putting up with my feedback, edits, suggestions, and annoying persistence, but most especially for sharing their knowledge and hearts in this book; Drs. Eduardo Duran and James M. Jones for seeing the value in this book, for sharing their wisdom, and for writing the Foreword and Afterword, respectively; Dr. Sumie Okazaki for taking a risk by accepting me into graduate school back in 2002—for this, I am eternally grateful; Dr. Kevin Nadal for being a brother and a role model; Drs. Matthew R. Lee, Noriel Lim, and Anne Saw for listening to my undeveloped thoughts about this topic when we were in graduate school; the American Psychological Association (APA) Division 45, the APA Minority Fellowship Program, and the Asian American Psychological Association for being my professional families; Anissa Hauser and the rest of the Department of Psychology at the University of Alaska Anchorage; and Stephanie Drew, Kathryn Corasaniti, and the rest of Springer Publishing Company for believing in me and appreciating the need for this book.

Last, but definitely not least, I want to acknowledge my Nanay, Tatay, Ate Ellen, Bonz, Jass, and Alex for always being there for me; the Vinas, Ebue, Concepcion, Rochon, Danner, Morse, Olin, Hoffman, Shaw, David, Clemente, Pangilinan, Ocampo, Dimson, De Leon, and Abad families for being my family; my Alaska and Busko Boys for always having my back; the Nageak, Harcharek, Fuller, and Baksis families for seeing something valuable in me when no one else did; and the Barrow High School Whalers and the entire community of Barrow, Alaska for giving a lost boy a chance and some direction.

Maraming salamat, dakal a salamat, enaa' baasee', quyanaqpak, many thanks, and *mabuhay kayong lahat!*

What Is Internalized Oppression, and So What?

E. J. R. David and Annie O. Derthick

A large proportion of non-European women—approximately 77% in Nigeria, 59% in Togo, 50% in the Philippines, 45% in Hong Kong, 41% in Malaysia, 37% in Taiwan, 28% in Korea, and 27% in Senegal—use skin-whitening products (see Mercury Policy Project, 2010). The World Health Organization (WHO, 2011) considers this a worldwide health concern, focusing primarily on physical health consequences. The WHO linked skin-whitening products, especially those with dangerous amounts of mercury, to scarring, skin rashes, and kidney failure, as well as to psychological disorders such as anxiety and depression. Consequently, the WHO called for policy changes to control the amount of mercury in these products. Although these are troubling health concerns, and although the policies were necessary, framing the problem this way is limited and problematic. This limited conceptualization hides the fact that an important contributor to the problem is oppression and internalized oppression, phenomena women, men, and children throughout the world experience.

Conceptualizing the phenomenon as a "mercury problem" calls for a simplified solution to eliminate mercury from skin-whitening products. It is implied that desiring to look more White is acceptable as long as it is done without mercury or other substances that may negatively affect health. By keeping oppression out of the conversation, it makes it appear as though the problem and the blame belong completely to the individuals (e.g., they are not satisfied with self, and they are consuming harmful chemicals). Alternatively, if we frame the problem as oppression, then we

1

necessarily must look for factors outside of the individual—historical and contemporary sociopolitical factors—that may influence the use of such products. Furthermore, it will become clear that the problem is more than just racial oppression, but also cultural oppression and its other forms (e.g., sexism, heterosexism). Hence, the problem will be viewed as more than just a desire to have lighter skin but a desire and preference for Western culture and worldview. By framing the problem as internalized oppression, it will become clear that the problem also involves a devaluation or inferiorization of one's self and one's group. It will also become clear that the health implications go far beyond just physical health, to also include mental health. Thus, by conceptualizing the problem more broadly and more accurately as internalized oppression and *not* mercury exposure, it becomes clear that this is an even larger worldwide health concern. It is not just a "mercury problem," and it is not just a concern among peoples who happen to have darker skin. It is about oppression and internalized oppression, and it is a concern for many oppressed, marginalized, and devalued groups throughout the world.

The omission of oppression and internalized oppression when conceptualizing peoples' experiences, as relayed in the example above, is not a new or unique occurrence. In the field of psychology, as in many other scientific disciplines, there has been a long-standing bias to look for factors within individuals to explain phenomena (e.g., biological or physiological factors; Keller, 2005). Acknowledging that factors outside individuals—such as neighborhoods, organizations, and institutions—play important roles in various phenomena raises the possibility that social change may be necessary to adequately and appropriately address these problems (e.g., Albee, 1986). Conceptualizing the problem more broadly and more accurately may indicate that those in power may need to change their values and ways of doing things. However, as is the case for many of us, it is easier to blame individuals for problems and to make them change than it is to change ourselves (Ryan, 1971), or to change the institutions we are parts of and their deeply seeded values and conventions that permeate our environment and, thus, ourselves. In other words, if we limit the conceptualization of a problem to show that very few people experience it, combined with our tendency to overvalue intra-individual explanations, then it is easier to conclude that the problem resides within individuals.

Just because it is simpler to ignore larger sociopolitical factors when conceptualizing phenomena, however, does not mean that it is the most beneficial—especially to those who are experiencing the phenomena. When it comes to non-Western, non-White, nonmale, and nonheterosexual people, who collectively compose the majority of our world, oppression is perhaps the most important sociopolitical factor that influences the entire range of their psychological experiences (David, 2013). Indeed, oppression in one form or another continues to exist in both interpersonal and institutional levels (Jones, 1997). Because of its pervasiveness, oppression can also become internalized—the hidden injury of oppression that is often ignored or minimized (Pyke, 2010). To this end, this chapter will discuss oppression in its many forms, followed by how internalized oppression is perhaps the most insidious consequence of oppression, and a brief overview of internalized oppression as experienced by various groups. Classic and more contemporary conceptualizations of internalized oppression will be presented, and first-person narratives from the authors will be inserted in select parts to serve as examples of the concepts discussed. We will end the chapter with a partial list of the characteristics of internalized oppression—"partial" because there is plenty still to be learned about this phenomenon. Along with the other chapters in this book, it is our intention to offer a more complete conceptualization of the psychological experiences of various groups, a conceptualization that incorporates historical and contemporary sociopolitical factors, so that the field can better understand and ultimately serve the majority of people in our highly diverse world.

OPPRESSION AND ITS MANY FORMS

Oppression occurs when one group has more access to power and privilege than another group, and when that power and privilege is used to maintain the status quo (i.e., domination of one group over another). Thus, oppression is both a state and a process, with the state of oppression being unequal group access to power and privilege, and the process of oppression being the ways in which inequality between groups is maintained (Prilleltensky & Laurier, 1996). Oppression, therefore, results in the differentiation of people into groups (e.g., dominant/dominated, powerful/powerless, superior/inferior, oppressor/oppressed), and group membership determines the degree to which an individual has power or the opportunity and ability to access resources. Differentiating people into groups can be done in many ways (e.g., race, sex, sexual orientation, abilities) and, thus, oppression based on group membership also comes in various forms (e.g., racism, sexism, heterosexism, ableism).

Oppressors, or those who are dominant or in power, use their access to power and privilege to impose their worldviews on the oppressed and justify and enforce the social, political, and systematic denial of resources to the oppressed. Indeed, oppression can take the form of imposition and deprivation. According to Hanna, Talley, and Guindon (2000), oppression by imposition or force is "the act of imposing on . . . others . . . a label, role experience, or set of living conditions that is unwanted, needlessly painful, and detracts from physical or psychological well-being . . . [such as] demeaning hard labor, degrading job roles, ridicule, and negative media images and messages that foster and maintain distorted beliefs" (p. 431). On the other hand, oppression by deprivation "involves depriving people of desired jobs, an education, healthcare, or living conditions necessary for physical and mental well-being . . . [such as] food, clothing, shelter, love, respect, social support, or self-dignity" (Sue, 2010, p. 7). In the case of heterosexism, for example, heterosexuals hold power and privilege over nonheterosexuals (i.e., heterosexuals are more likely to be in positions of power), and that position is used to maintain power and privilege (e.g., imposing a certain belief about acceptable expressions of love and partnership, while refusing to support anti-discrimination policies and laws, which would make it more likely for nonheterosexuals to make themselves visible and attempt to secure positions of power). This justification is often based on the supposed superiority of one group over another. Again, in the case of heterosexism, heterosexuals deny access to resources based on the argument that nonheterosexuals are abnormal, deviant, pathological, and are abominations—inferiorizing labels and perceptions imposed onto them by the dominant group.

Oppression can also occur at the institutional or systemic levels, such as with laws, policies, and "normative" practices that marginalize and inferiorize groups of people (Jones, 1997). Institutionalized oppression can be seen through laws (e.g., voter identification laws), policies (e.g., requiring food stamp recipients to announce in front of other customers how they are paying), physical environments (e.g., having diaper changing stations only in the women's restrooms), and social norms and conventions (e.g., the standard use of "he" as the default pronoun for neutral or unidentified gender). Another example of institutional oppression includes universities frequently having buildings dedicated to White, heterosexual men, subtly conveying to People of Color, nonheterosexuals, and women that it is not typical for people like them to succeed in this particular setting. In addition to institutional oppression, oppression also occurs at the interpersonal level between individuals (e.g., a White person clutches a purse when a Person of Color walks by), between groups (e.g., able-bodied individuals refer to dysfunctional, deviant, and substandard things as "retarded"), and within groups (e.g., American-born Asians refer to newly arrived immigrants as "FOB"—fresh off the boat).

In addition to oppression being present in multiple levels, oppression may also be overt or subtle, with contemporary forms of oppression being not as blatant as oppression of the past (Sue et al., 2007). Given that oppression today is not as overt or obvious as before, it is necessary to understand how more modern and subtle forms of oppression affect the psychological experiences of oppressed groups (Dovidio, Gaertner, Kawakami, & Hodson, 2002; Pierce, Carew, Pierce-Gonzalez, & Willis, 1978; Sears, 1988; Sue et al., 2007; Thompson & Neville, 1999). The contemporary reality of oppression is particularly precarious for oppressed individuals because modern forms of oppression occur at a subtle, often unconscious level (such as the examples provided in the previous paragraph). Sue and colleagues (2007) outlined a taxonomy of microaggressions—subtle, everyday communications of discrimination and prejudice. According to their conceptualization, microaggressions often occur outside of the conscious awareness of the victim. Consequently, victims of microaggressions experience "attributional ambiguity," which is the absence of a clearly identifiable source of oppression and discrimination (Sue et al., 2007). In other words, because microaggressions are perpetrated and experienced subtly and often unconsciously, the victim often questions the reality of oppression. Thus, victims of microaggressions frequently blame themselves for being "overly sensitive" or "crazy" and dismiss the behavior of the perpetrators. Nevertheless, microaggressions produce equally distressing psychological consequences as overt oppression and discrimination, perhaps even more so, because of the lack of a distinguishable target to which one can direct anger (Sue, 2010). When one is denied an opportunity to confront the source of oppression, the anger is directed inwardly at those who remind the oppressed individual of him- or herself. In this way, microaggressions contribute to internalized oppression and work to perpetuate oppression.

Annie, a lesbian, shares some of her experiences with microaggressions:

> Recently, I was engaged in a conversation with a colleague about an upcoming event. My colleague, whom I respect and value, said, "I'm not even sure if I want to go. The whole thing sounds pretty gay to me." I immediately felt exposed, self-conscious, and confused. Here was my colleague, my friend, equating a fundamental piece of my identity with something that was undesirable, and doing so in a dismissive, frivolous way. I walked away from the conversation knowing intellectually that my colleague did not mean that the way it sounded, but ever since then, I have questioned the extent to which she actually accepts me for who I am—really accepts me. It feels lonely.

Annie went on to share a microaggressive act against her as a woman:

> Last year, I was teaching Community Psychology. In the spirit of the subject, I met with each of my students individually to assess their level of comfort with the material and how I could help them meet their goals. One of my students, a White, heterosexual male asked me during his meeting if I was a doctoral student. I confirmed that I indeed was. His response was to inform me that another one of his instructors that semester was also a doctoral student (who also happens to be female). He followed by stating, "You girls are doing a great job." In that small statement, my student informed me that the fact that I was about 15 years older than him did not

matter, nor did the fact that I have two Master's degrees. To him, I was an insignificant *girl*, who, on some level, needed his approval to feel good about myself. I did not feel good about myself. I felt ashamed.

E.J., a Filipino American man, shared one of his experiences that touches on various forms of oppression, taken from his journal while attending graduate school in the Midwest:

I was waiting at the bus stop one day with other people. There was me, a Filipino dude whose loved ones are all away. In addition to the discrimination I face for being an immigrant, colored man in this society, I'm a guy who misses people daily. There was a young Black man, who is probably aware of all the racism that he and other Black men face. It is probably something that is constantly on his mind. He was probably thinking, "I wonder what kind of racism I will face today. Will it be in my job, in the grocery store, in the school, or by some random people in the streets? Will I be accused of something I did not do today? Will people be suspicious of me and follow me around like a criminal as I go shopping?" There was an elderly Black woman, who is probably old enough to remember and personally experience racial segregation. She probably has a long list of racist experiences, both explicit and implicit ones. There was a very old White woman, who uses a cane to help her stand and walk around. Although she probably never experienced racism in her life, she probably experienced discrimination of some sort, especially now with her old age. Also, she was probably old enough to have experienced blatant sex discrimination, like when women were simply regarded as inferior to men. The thought of death has probably passed through her mind. Then there was a White man, probably in his mid-thirties. Out of the five people in the bus stop, he was the one who represented the privileged group. Out of all of us, I thought that he was probably the one with the fewest problems . . . until he talked.

At first, he was just mumbling, then his speech became much clearer, until he began somewhat yelling. He said, "Jesus, can you give me a jet with the speed of a Mach-3?" Then, he looked at me and the Black man and said, "You see, if you want something, you need to ask Jesus. Like, Jesus, can you give me a Mercedes? Can you give me a Trailblazer? Or what about, Jesus, can you please stop the war on Iraq?" "Ask Jesus, not your bogus God." Then he got distracted by the cars passing by us, as he said "People with cars suck." A few more minutes went by, and his topic changed. He looked at me and the Black man and asked, "What are you guys thinking about?" Then he began answering his own question. "Are you thinking about leaving this town? I have been stuck in this town for 10 years. It's like there's a fence around this town that keeps me from leaving. This town sucks!" He continued by saying, "Are you guys thinking about girls? Girls in this town are easy." He looked at me and asked, "Are you thinking about taking more jobs away from me?" He looked at the Black man and asked, "Are you thinking about making more money? Legally, I hope." A BMW passed by and he said, "There's another rich man." He kept saying this to all the cars that passed by, until he saw another BMW and said, "There's another rich man . . . oh wait, he's a drug dealer . . . it's easy to detect a drug dealer . . . it's like it's written right there on the license plate." As this BMW was passing by us, I noticed that the driver of the car was a Black man.

This White man, who talks to himself. A White man who is probably struggling to make ends meet. A White man who probably has more problems than me, the Black man, the Black woman, and the elderly White woman. A White man who I thought had more important things in his life to deal with, yet he still had time and found time to be racist, sexist, and whatever else. With all the problems he had to deal with, all the things that are bothering his heart and his mind, he still found space for prejudice and bigotry.

It is clear that many forms of oppression remain highly ubiquitous, they can be overt or subtle, and they can operate in institutional, interpersonal, and internalized levels. Relative to the other types of oppression, however, internalized oppression has not been as extensively studied (Pyke, 2010), a disturbing reality given that overcoming internalized oppression is a prerequisite for overcoming oppression (Itzen, 1985). Therefore, we will now turn to a discussion of internalized oppression, beginning with Fanon's (1965) classic framework on colonialism. Although Fanon's model focuses on the oppression of racial or ethnic groups, it should be noted that this framework may also be applied to the oppression of women (e.g., Comas-Diaz, 2010), sexual minorities (e.g., Hawley, 2001), and people with disabilities (e.g., Kumari Campbell, 2008; see Part IV for chapters specifically on these groups), which may result in specific forms of internalized oppression such as internalized sexism, internalized heterosexism, and internalized ableism. Indeed, as Poupart (2003) stated, "as many expressions of internalized oppression exist as experiences of oppression" (p. 90).

COLONIALISM, OPPRESSION, AND INTERNALIZED OPPRESSION

Fanon's (1965) four-phase colonial model is the classic framework for understanding oppression and internalized oppression. The first phase of colonialism is the forced entry of a foreign group into a territory to exploit its natural resources, including its inhabitants (e.g., slaves, cheap labor). The second phase is when the colonizer imposes its culture, disintegrates the indigenous culture, and recreates the indigenous culture as defined by the colonizer. This transformation of the indigenous culture differentiates the colonizer's supposedly more civilized ways of life and the colonized people's supposedly inferior or savage ways. Once the society has clearly contrasted the colonizer and the colonized, the third phase begins, as the colonized are portrayed as wild, savage, and uncivilized peoples who the colonizer has to nobly monitor, tame, and civilize. Thus, the third phase essentially conveys that tyranny and domination, and hence oppression, are necessary. The completion of the first three phases leads to the fourth phase—the establishment of a society where the political, social, and economic institutions are designed to benefit and maintain the superiority of the colonizer while simultaneously subjugating the colonized. The fourth phase can be clearly seen in established institutions (e.g., churches, boarding schools) in colonized lands that reward those who assimilate into the colonizers' ways, while punishing those who do not. Thus, colonialism is a specific form of oppression (see Part II for chapters specifically on indigenous groups with histories of colonization).

Based on Fanon's (1965) model, it is clear that "there is enormous social, psychological, and infrastructural work in producing the colonized person" (Okazaki, David, & Abelman, 2007, p. 96). Extending this conclusion based on the discussion of the various forms of oppression in the previous section, there is plenty of work necessary to create the oppressed person. So, how does such an oppressive context influence oppressed individuals? Postcolonial scholars (e.g., Fanon, 1965; Freire, 1970; Memmi, 1965) argue that internalized oppression, or specifically, internalized colonialism, is the major psychological effect of colonialism. Fanon argued that the sustained denigration and injustice that the colonized are subjected to often lead to self-doubt, identity confusion, and feelings of inferiority among the colonized. Memmi added that the colonized may eventually believe the inferiority of one's indigenous identity. Freire further contended that because of the inferiority attached to their indigenous identities, the colonized might develop a desire to rid oneself of such identities and to emulate the colonizer because their ways are seen as superior. Further, the colonized may eventually feel a sense of gratitude and indebtedness toward the colonizer for civilizing and enlightening the colonized (Rimonte, 1997).

Based on postcolonial theory, experiencing oppression over lifetimes and generations can lead individuals to internalize the messages of inferiority they receive about their group membership. In fact, internalizing the alleged inferiority and undesirability of one's social group can begin at a very young age (Clark & Clark, 1947). Over time, internalized oppression can become an unconscious, involuntary (Batts, 1983; David & Okazaki, 2010) response to oppression in which members of oppressed groups internalize the negative stereotypes (Amaro & Raj, 2000; Bailey, Chung,

Williams, Singh, & Terrell, 2011; Brown, 1986; Hill, 1999; David & Okazaki, 2006a; Pheterson, 1986; Rosenwasser, 2002) and expectations (Brown, 1986) of their group based on messages they have received from the oppressor. Internalized oppression may even lead to active self-fulfilling prophecies as oppressed individuals begin to act out negative stereotypes (Thomas, Speight, & Witherspoon, 2005). Using Lipsky's (1987) definition, internalized oppression is the "turning upon ourselves, upon our families, and upon our own people the distress patterns that result from the . . . oppression of the (dominant) society" (p. 6).

Not only is internalized oppression the result of oppression and exploitation (Brown, 1986; Itzin, 1985; Moreau, 1990; Padilla, 2001; Prilleltensky & Laurier, 1996; Ramos-Diaz, 1985), it also perpetuates oppression (Duran & Duran, 1995; Hill, 1999). Thus, as previously alluded to, internalized oppression is a component of oppression, whereby oppressors maintain domination over the oppressed. Duran and Duran (1995) argued that internalized oppression operates on an individual as well as a group level to maintain power structures that benefit the oppressors. Individuals, for example, having internalized hatred, develop unhealthy relationships with drugs and alcohol, while communities redirect anger toward the oppressor at those who remind the oppressed of him- or herself through domestic violence, homicide, and sexual assault (Duran & Duran, 1995; Poupart, 2003). Another example is the case of internalized homophobia, where nonheterosexuals are subjected to distorted images of sexuality (Brown, 1986), inferiorizing and dehumanizing labels (e.g., "abomination"), and the denial of power and privilege (e.g., the former Don't Ask/Don't Tell policy, marriage). These messages and experiences are incorporated into one's understanding of oneself based on membership to an "inferior" group. As a result, nonheterosexuals may try to outwit the oppressive system by "passing" as a heterosexual (Perez, 2005) or self-concealment (Hill, 1999; Pheterson, 1986), but to do so means a denial of one's authentic identity. Consistent with this, Neville, Coleman, Falconer, and Holmes (2005) found a negative relationship between internalized oppression and the degree to which individuals endorse the existence of racism. That is, the more oppressed an individual is, the more denial the individual has about his or her own reality as an oppressed person, effectively fragmenting the individual's experience of him- or herself and the world.

Internalized oppression also leads to intragroup fragmentation (Pyke & Dang, 2003). It prevents group members from connecting with one another (Gainor, 1992; Kanuha, 1990) and causes intragroup conflict (Norrington-Sands, 2002; Pyke & Dang, 2003). Oppressed group members may begin to discriminate against one another (David & Okazaki, 2006a; Itzin, 1985; Neallani, 1992) and choose to emulate and identify with oppressors (Hill, 1999; Lipsky, 1977; Padilla, 2001). This is not surprising, because in systems in which the oppressed is consistently, aggressively, and systematically devalued and dehumanized, the oppressor becomes the model of acceptable humanity (Freire, 1970). To effectively emulate the oppressor, the oppressed must devalue his or her own group membership (Padilla, 2001) and reject his or her culture (Bailey et al., 2011; David & Okazaki, 2006a; Rosenwasser, 2005). Further, internalized oppression reinforces oppression because it generates mistrust and criticism of emerging leaders (Lipsky, 1977; Padilla, 2004), creating unrealistic expectations for possible leaders and resulting in burnout and abandonment of a vision of liberation (Lipsky, 1977).

Finally, perhaps the most devastating collective consequence of internalized oppression is intragroup (i.e., horizontal) violence (Amaro & Raj, 2000; Bailey et al., 2011; Freire, 1970; Lipsky, 1977; Padilla, 2001; Tappan, 2006). Fellow group members are viewed as inferior and as less of a threat than the dominant group, at whom the real anger is directed, so violence is sublimated or redirected to members of one's group (Artz, 1996). Additionally, the oppressed participates in his or her own oppression through self-destruction and violence toward self (Hill, 1999; Padilla, 2001), self-denigration (David & Okazaki, 2006a), substance abuse, and suicide (Duran & Duran, 1995). Furthermore, internalized oppression may cause oppressed groups to victimize each other. A logical extension of horizontal violence is intergroup violence between oppressed groups. Similar to intragroup violence, anger toward the oppressor is redirected to those who are equally (or perhaps more) vulnerable. Consequently, we see a striking disunity between historically oppressed groups in this country. For example, anti-gay sentiment among People of Color is common (Greene, 2009; Ochs, 1996), and bi-directional tensions between African Americans and Asian Americans (e.g., African Americans resenting Asian American-owned businesses in historically Black neighborhoods, and Asian Americans resenting Affirmative Action; Tawa, Suyemoto, & Tauriac, 2013) speak to this intergroup conflict between oppressed groups. Even more insidious, however, is that internalized oppression results in the incorporation of negative stereotypes into cultural values and traditions (i.e., "that's just the way we are"; Lipsky, 1977, p. 5), so that oppression becomes a cultural norm and transmitted across generations.

Below, Annie shared some of her experiences that touch on various manifestations of internalized oppression, both as a woman and as a lesbian:

> I remember watching a TV show with my grandmother once. One of the characters was a female police detective. Her character was what I would describe as "no-nonsense" and strong. She did not let anyone push her around. At one point, my grandmother snarled at the TV and said, "I don't like when women act like that." "Like what," I asked. "Like men." I realized three things in that moment: (1) my grandmother had been taught to

devalue the part of her femininity that has the capacity for strength and power, (2) that is so very sad, and (3) there was only one, rigid and limited way be an acceptable female in my grandmother's eyes, and in the world. There was an invisible barrier between us, placed there by a society that only values passivity and submissiveness in women. She had learned to accept this contrived image of women, to strive for it, and to devalue members of her own feminine tribe who deviated from it. To this day, I have moments in my life when I hear my grandmother's voice in my mind, and I have a moment of insecurity about my own femininity, followed by a longer moment of sadness. I wonder, if she was still alive, if she would understand and appreciate the woman I have become. I wonder if I understand and appreciate the woman I have become.

I consider myself to be a proud lesbian woman. I am actively involved in the LGBT [lesbian, gay, bisexual, transgender] community, and I support gender equality personally and publically. However, I still experience a twinge of discomfort when I am associated with the LGBT community or my gender. For example, I "googled" myself a few years ago. One of the first links to appear said, "GAY PRIDE" and had my name listed as a contributor to an LGBT conference. My immediate reaction was panic and to think, "Who has seen this? What will they think!"Even though I consistently and actively engage and embrace my community, I have moments of dread and shame that the world will actually realize I am gay, and in the moments when I am being completely honest with myself, I understand that there is a part of me that does not want to the world to know, because then they won't like me . . . because according to them, it's not ok to be who I am. So, I suppose it is ironic that seeing my name linked to Gay PRIDE induced feelings of shame.

INTERNALIZED OPPRESSION AMONG VARIOUS GROUPS

Now that we have described internalized oppression, let us now turn to a brief overview of how common this phenomenon is among various groups, focusing on some oppressed groups in the United States. As previously discussed, the racial climate in the United States is consistent with oppression because "the opportunities [in the country] are not randomly [or equally] distributed across race . . . and social structures are not equally supportive for minorities" (Trickett, 1991, pp. 213–214; see Part III for chapters on specific racial groups). Again, such inequalities extend beyond race to also include sex, sexual orientation, people with disabilities, and other social groups. Thus, using Fanon's (1965) classic framework, the historical and contemporary oppression faced by dominated groups in the United States is one of *internal colonialism*. Although there is no recent forceful entry by a foreign group, internal colonialism is analogous to classic colonialism in that the society is characterized by social inequalities, cultural or worldview imposition of the dominant group, disintegration or devaluation of oppressed groups' cultures or worldviews, and stereotypical recreation of oppressed groups' identities by the dominant group. In terms of its consequences, Rudkin (2003) stated that the oppression of American minority groups "leads to self-debasement, alienation, loss of cultural identity, dependency, and internally-directed hostility" (p. 290), similar to the effects of colonialism provided by postcolonial scholars (Fanon, 1965; Freire, 1970; Memmi, 1965).

Harrell's (1999) discussion of the psychological consequences of oppression among African Americans is an excellent example of the applicability of the classic colonial model in describing the experiences of oppressed American minority groups. In his analyses, Harrell used Fanon's (1965) term—Manichean—to argue that American society is one that is essentially based on incompatible opposites such as good versus evil, light versus dark, white versus black. In a Manichean society, anything of the dominated group, including language, physical traits, and cultural values and traditions, is ascribed with inferior, undesirable, or negative characteristics. Concurrently, anything of the dominant group is attached with superiority and desirability. Further, this society also involves the destruction and reinterpretation of the history and culture of the oppressed through the eyes of the dominant group. Consequently, a Manichean society creates conditions that lead African Americans to develop self-hatred and to behave in self-destructive ways. Internalized racism, a form of internalized oppression, among African Americans leads to identity confusion and to the development of an inferiorized identity (Thomas, 1971). The Black Identity Development Model proposed by Cross, Parham, and Helms (1991) also argued that internalized oppression may lead African Americans to highly value the dominant culture and simultaneously devalue their own, leading many African Americans to hold anti-Black sentiments or have Black self-hate (see Chapter 6 on African Americans).

Another oppressed group within the United States are Native Americans or American Indians, whose experiences involve both classical and internal colonialism. McBride (2002) argued that these historical and contemporary experiences of oppression led many Native Americans or American Indians to lose their cultural identity and spirituality. Duran and Duran (1995) and Brave Heart (1998) also argued that internalized oppression is passed on intergenerationally by continued oppression, lack of opportunities to critically and accurately understand history, and forced Americanization—contemporary forms of oppression that may be seen as internal colonialism (see Chapter 2 on Native Americans). Internalized oppression and its intergenerational transmission are also salient among Alaska Native Peoples, and are argued to contribute to the high rates of depression, suicide, domestic violence, and substance use among Alaska

Native Peoples today (Napoleon, 1996; see Chapter 3 on Alaska Native Peoples).

Internalized oppression is also salient among Hispanic or Latina/o Americans. Hall (1994) argued that colonization and oppression—both historically and contemporarily—lead many Hispanic or Latina/o Americans to believe that light skin is advantageous, attractive, and desirable. The internalization of such a skin-color ideal results in a desire to become as white as possible in order for social mobility or acceptance, leading many Hispanic or Latina/o Americans to use "beauty" creams and other products such as bleach in order to whiten their skin (Hall, 1994). Indeed, according to Hall, many Hispanic or Latina/o Americans "will value and internalize all aspects of the mainstream culture—including the idealizations of light skin color—at the expense of their [heritage] culture" (p. 310; see Chapter 5 on Latina/o Americans).

Among a specific Hispanic or Latina/o American ethnic group—Puerto Ricans—the effects of centuries of Spanish and American colonialism include (a) identity confusion, (b) feelings of shame regarding their ethnic and cultural identity, (c) feelings of inferiority about being Puerto Rican, (d) discriminating against less-Americanized individuals, and (e) not having national pride (Varas-Diaz & Serrano-Garcia, 2003). Similar experiences of internalized oppression have also been observed among the indigenous Chamorros in Guam, a United States colony just like Puerto Rico (Perez, 2005; see Chapter 4 on Pacific Islanders).

As previously discussed, internalized oppression also goes beyond racial oppression to also include oppression of women (i.e., internalized sexism; Bearman, Korobov, & Thorne, 2009), people with disabilities (i.e., internalized ableism; Kumari Campbell, 2008), and lesbian, gay, bisexual, and transgender individuals (LGBT; i.e., internalized heterosexism; Szymanski, Kashubeck-West, & Meyer, 2008). For example, in his minority stress model for lesbian, gay, and bisexual (LGB) individuals, Meyer (2003) argued that discrimination negatively influences LGB individuals' mental health. Perhaps the worst consequence of this form of discrimination is internalized homophobia—a specific form of internalized oppression in which LGB individuals eventually redirect negative homophobic societal attitudes toward themselves (e.g., I do not deserve equal rights). It is another form of self-hate due to experiences oppression (see Chapter 9 on LGBT individuals).

CONTEMPORARY CONCEPTUALIZATIONS OF INTERNALIZED OPPRESSION

Although internalized oppression is a common experience among various social groups, this phenomenon continues to be understudied and underappreciated, and thus, largely unknown to the field of psychology. Perhaps one reason for this is that most of the literature on internalized oppression is framed using postcolonial theory, instead of theoretical frameworks that are more familiar with and, thus, more palatable to psychological professionals. Therefore, although based on and still consistent with postcolonial theories, a more contemporary conceptualization of internalized oppression has been proposed (David, 2009) using the principles and concepts of cognitive behavioral theory (CBT), a theory that is familiar to and popular with psychological professionals. In general, CBT considers five components to any phenomenon: (1) cognitions (thoughts); (2) moods or affects (emotions); (3) physiological reactions (e.g., increased heart rate); (4) behaviors; and (5) environment (Padesky & Greenburger, 1995). CBT posits that individuals' environmental contexts, such as how they were raised and what messages about the world, about themselves, and about others they constantly receive, can lead to the development of general patterns of thinking (mental schemas). These general patterns of thinking are highly influential in producing the automatic thoughts or cognitions that individuals have as they interact with the world. In turn, CBT argues that a person's thoughts or cognitions influence that person's mood, behavior, and physical sensations in response to his or her environmental context. Thoughts or cognitions that are distorted, inaccurate, or false may lead to unhealthy or maladaptive moods, behaviors, or physical sensations, whereas thoughts or cognitions that are accurate, true, or realistic contribute to healthy and adaptive moods, behaviors, and physical sensations (Beck, 1995).

Using CBT principles and concepts, internalized oppression may be conceptualized as a set of self-defeating cognitions, attitudes, and behaviors that were developed as one consistently experiences an oppressive environment. Further, internalized oppression may be conceptualized as a distorted view of one's self and of others that is a consequence of how one experiences his or her environment. One of the most basic tenets of CBT is that thoughts that occur most frequently and are most easily accessible in memory are the ones we tend to believe. Historically, oppressed groups have been, both in subtle and overt ways, consistently receiving the message that they are inferior to the dominant group. Eventually, members of oppressed groups may no longer need the dominant group to perpetuate such inferiorizing messages, because they begin inferiorizing themselves in overt and subtle (and automatic) ways (David, 2009).

Consistent with CBT, another way to conceptualize internalized oppression is to use the empirical literature on learning and cognition, memory, priming, spreading activation theory, and the dynamic constructivist approach to culture and cognition (Hong, Morris, Chiu, & Benet-Martinez, 2000). Based on this body of literature, members of oppressed groups may internalize the oppression they experience in such a deep way that it creates within them a knowledge system that is characterized by automatic negative cognitions and perceptions of their social group. Using methods such as the word-completion task, implicit association test, and the lexical decision priming task among multiple samples of Filipino Americans (David & Okazaki, 2010; David, 2010)—the second largest Asian American ethnic group in the United States and a population for whom internalized oppression is highly salient—empirical evidence was found to support the notion that many (approximately 55%) members of this group have automatically associated undesirable, unpleasant, and negative thoughts with the Filipino culture, and desirable, pleasant, and positive thoughts with the American culture. These findings suggest that oppression has been internalized deeply enough by members of this group for a distorted cognitive system to be developed and automatically operate (see Chapter 7 on Asian Americans).

Thus, based on these series of studies (David, 2010; David & Okazaki, 2010)—the literature on learning and cognition, priming, spreading activation, the dynamic constructivist approach to culture and cognition, CBT, and internalized oppression among various groups—four conclusions may be made concerning the cognitive operation of internalized oppression. First, oppression may be deeply internalized by members of oppressed groups such that their cultural knowledge systems reflect internalized oppression. Second, internalized oppression is an individual differences variable in that not all members of oppressed groups experience it. Third, internalized oppression may be activated using priming techniques typically used in the areas of social cognition and memory. Lastly, oppression may be deeply internalized such that stimuli that are related to one's own group are automatically associated with ideas of unpleasantness or inferiority and stimuli that are related to the dominant group are automatically associated with ideas of pleasantness or superiority (David & Okazaki, 2010).

E.J. provides an example of how internalized oppression may automatically influence one's perceptions, attitudes, and behaviors outside of awareness or control:

> As much time as I've spent thinking deeply about internalized oppression, and as aware of it as I am, I am sure I still have it and my daily life is still affected by it, whether I am aware of it or not, and even if I don't want it to. For example, I still find myself laughing at FOB jokes until I remind myself of how wrong it is. I still have a tendency to feel embarrassed whenever I hear other Filipinos speak English with a thick Filipino accent. I still find myself ignoring the opinions of Filipinos who are not very Americanized. It is even very likely that my initial attraction to my wife, who I met when we were in 8th grade, was driven by my tendency to regard lighter skin as more beautiful. Today, I'm probably on the high end when it comes to having pride in my Filipino heritage, but there are still some times when I feel

embarrassed and ashamed of some aspects of it that, when I think about it more deeply, are just things that are different and there's nothing about them that should really embarrass or shame me. It's like my automatic responses to some Filipino things are negative, until I catch myself, think more, then reconsider.

SO WHAT? MENTAL HEALTH IMPLICATIONS OF INTERNALIZED OPPRESSION

Following the use of CBT to discuss internalized oppression in the previous section, and consistent with CBT's conceptualization of how psychological disorders develop (e.g., Beck, Rush, Emery, & Shaw, 1979), underlying automatic thoughts (e.g., "men are strong, women are weak") or behaviors (e.g., deferring to men to do heavy "manual" labor) are maladaptive general beliefs or mental schemas (e.g., "men are stronger than women") that have been developed from previous experiences (e.g., socialization that "manual" labor is for men and women are the "weaker" sex). Such thoughts and beliefs contribute to the creation of dysfunctional self-schemas (e.g., "I am a woman, so I am weak") that may lead to psychological distress and disorders (David, 2009; see Chapter 8 on Women). For historically and contemporarily oppressed groups, years of subjugation may have created a general belief that their social groups are inferior to the dominant group. Such a belief may underlie the automatic self-deprecating thoughts and behaviors that many members of oppressed groups display today. Such automatic negative cognitions, attitudes, and related behaviors are likely damaging to peoples' self-esteem and may contribute to the development of various forms of mental health concerns. Figure 1.1 is a representation of how internalized oppression may operate and lead to psychological distress and psychopathology using CBT concepts.

Acculturation and Ethnic Identity

Beyond a CBT explanation, the literature on ethnic minority psychology also provides other ways in which the mental health and psychological well-being of oppressed groups may be influenced by internalized oppression. One way is through acculturation—the extent to which an individual does or does not stay connected with one's heritage culture and the degree to which an individual connects or does not connect with another culture (David, 2006). Many factors can influence acculturation, including larger sociopolitical factors such as the economy, immigration status, and oppression. As they navigate through various sociopolitical factors, acculturating individuals may acculturate in four different ways: assimilation (high

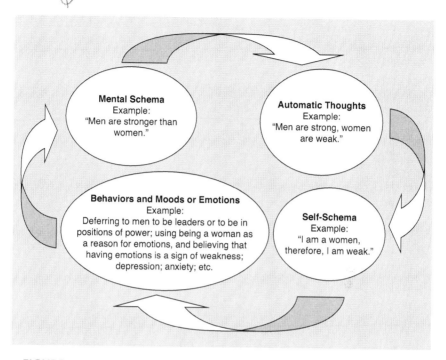

FIGURE 1.1 Conceptualizing internalized oppression using cognitive behavioral theory.

adherence to dominant culture and low adherence to heritage culture), integration (high adherence to both cultures), separation (low adherence to dominant culture and high adherence to heritage culture), and marginalization (low adherence to both cultures; Berry, 2003). Although there is no consensus as to which is the most beneficial (Rudmin, 2003), high levels of enculturation (i.e., the extent to which one adheres to one's heritage culture), either alone (i.e., separation) or in combination with dominant culture adherence (i.e., integration), often contribute to better well-being and mental health (e.g., David, Okazaki, & Saw, 2009; LaFromboise, Coleman, & Gerton, 1993; Tsai, Chentsova-Dutton, & Wong, 2002; Ying, 1995). Enculturation is theorized to lead toward the development of a positive ethnic identity—the extent to which members of an ethnic group positively value their heritage—which is associated with psychological well-being (e.g., Gong, Takeuchi, Agbayani-Siewart, & Tacata, 2003; Phinney, Chavira, & Williamson, 1992).

Among various oppressed racial groups, there is evidence suggesting that internalized oppression is related to lower levels of enculturation and higher levels of assimilation (e.g., David, 2008; David, 2010; David & Okazaki, 2006b; Walker, Wingate, Obasi, & Joiner, 2008). These studies also show that internalized oppression is related to lower levels of ethnic

Enculturation = adherence to heritage culture ⟹ ↑ psych well-being

identity development. The stress associated with cultural adaptation (i.e., acculturative stress, which includes racism; Berry, 2003) has been found to be associated with depression among African Americans (Walker et al., 2008). Furthermore, Walker and colleagues (2008) also found acculturative stress and ethnic identity moderate the link between depression and suicide, in that depressed African Americans who do not positively regard their heritage are more likely to think about suicide. Among Latinas/os, Codina and Montalvo (1994) also found that darker skin color and loss of Spanish culture were associated with higher levels of depression, suggesting that oppression and assimilation negatively affect Hispanic or Latino/a Americans' mental health through assimilation and low levels of ethnic identity.

Self-Esteem

Another way for internalized oppression to influence the mental health and psychological well-being of oppressed groups is through self-esteem. Most of our understanding of the self is focused on the personal aspect or personal self-esteem (i.e., how positively we evaluate our personal characteristics). Developing a positive collective self and having a positive collective self-esteem (i.e., how positively we evaluate the social groups to which we belong), however, is also vital for mental health (Crocker & Luhtanen, 1990; Crocker, Luhtanen, Blaine, & Broadnax, 1994; Tajfel & Turner, 1986). Indeed, our self-concept is composed of both a personal and a collective component and each can be associated with either positive (or pleasant) or negative (or unpleasant) attributes (Tajfel & Turner, 1986). The manner in which we associate positive or negative attributes to our personal characteristics (e.g., being tall, having blonde hair) and the characteristics of our social groups (e.g., "people with disabilities, like myself, are a burden") is influenced by our experiences and what we have been taught (see Chapter 10 on People With Disabilities). If personal self-esteem is the extent to which individuals evaluate their personal selves positively, collective self-esteem is the extent to which individuals evaluate positively the social groups to which they belong (Crocker & Luhtanen, 1990; Crocker et al., 1994). Thus, how positively we evaluate the characteristics of our social groups is an important contributor to our mental health. For historically and contemporarily oppressed groups, their experiences may have resulted into internalized oppression, which may negatively influence their collective self-esteem. Empirically, internalized oppression is related to lower levels of personal and collective self-esteem (e.g., Bailey, 2009; David & Okazaki, 2006b; David, 2008; David, 2010; Frame, 1999; Norrington-Sands, 2002). Not surprisingly, because of its influence on self-esteem, internalized oppression has also been linked to poor body image

(Bailey, et al., 2011; Lehman, 2009; Parmer, Arnold, Natt, & Janson, 2004) and eating disorders (Frame, 1999; Harris, 1997; Nakamura, 2006).

Depression

As discussed above, ethnic minority psychology literature suggests that constructs that are especially salient to minorities (e.g., enculturation, ethnic identity, collective self-esteem) are important contributors to their mental health, specifically depression (see solid variables and paths in Figure 1.2). Research also suggests that such constructs may be influenced by internalized oppression (e.g., David & Okazaki, 2006b; David, 2010; Walker et al., 2008). Further, studies also suggest that internalized oppression may be related to depression (Majied, 2003; Thomas et al., 2005; Ross, Doctor, Dimito, Kuehl, & Armstrong, 2007) and other negative emotions that are related to depression such as feelings of inferiority (Gainor, 1992; Pheterson, 1986; Prilleltensky & Laurier, 1996), resignation and powerlessness (Pheterson, 1986), learned helplessness (Prilleltensky & Laurier, 1996), shame (Rosenwasser, 2005), and humiliation (Rosenwasser, 2002). Interestingly, levels of depression have been shown to decrease when internalized oppression is a central focus of therapy (Ross et al., 2007),

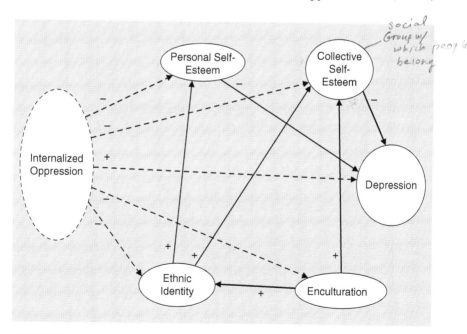

FIGURE 1.2 Internalized oppression and its mental health implications.
Source: David (2008).

further suggesting that internalized oppression is an important factor to consider when conceptualizing depression as experienced by members of oppressed groups. Thus, internalized oppression may also be related to depression through enculturation, ethnic identity, and collective self-esteem (see dashed lines in Figure 1.2). Using structural equation modeling with data obtained from a Filipino American sample, a model of depression that included internalized oppression was tested versus a model that did not include it, and the results showed that the internalized oppression-model better captured depression, that the model accounted for a large percentage of the variance in depression, and that internalized oppression had a direct and significant effect on depression above and beyond the effects of the other important variables (David, 2008). Thus, internalized oppression can significantly contribute to the depression symptoms that many members of oppressed groups experience.

Other Mental and Behavioral Health Implications

Given internalized oppression's documented relationships with variables such as personal and collective self-esteem and depression symptoms, it is not surprising that internalized oppression may also be negatively related to other mental health concerns facing various oppressed groups, primarily because low self-esteem and depression typically go hand-in-hand or co-occur with other problem behaviors and conditions (e.g., Clark, Watson, & Reynolds, 1995; Owens, 2001). Indeed, as an example, it has been shown that internalized homophobia is related to negative mental health outcomes (Hatzenbuehler, 2009; Williamson, 2000), with recent research suggesting that experiences of oppression may lead oppressed individuals to experience maladaptive emotional and cognitive states such as rumination, emotional avoidance, negative self-schemas, and feelings of hopelessness in response to such experiences, all of which may increase the likelihood for oppressed individuals to develop clinically diagnosable disorders or for them to engage in high-risk behaviors (Hatzenbuehler, 2009). Furthermore, having low levels of enculturation and not positively identifying with one's social group can lead one to become avoided and, thus, marginalized, even by others who are important characters in the person's life (e.g., family, relatives, friends). Indeed, internalized oppression has been linked to isolation (Gainor, 1992; Pheterson, 1986; Rosenwasser, 2002, 2005). Not having a strong and positive social support system may lead to many high-risk and problematic behaviors such as alcohol and drug use, unprotected sex, delinquency, and school drop-outs (e.g., Kim & Goto, 2000; Pierce, Frone, Russell, Cooper, & Mudar, 2000; Solomon & Liefeld, 1998; Steptoe, Wardle, Pollard, Canaan, & Davies, 1996).

The psychological literature on various oppressed groups such as African Americans, Alaska Natives, and American Indians also suggest that internalized oppression is related to domestic violence and other violent crimes, substance use and abuse, school drop-out rates, and high-risk behaviors that may lead to sexually transmitted diseases and teen pregnancies (e.g., Duran & Duran, 1995; Frame, 1999; Harrell, 1999; McBride, 2002; Tatum, 1994). Tatum (1994) proposed that colonialism, or more specifically, internal colonialism/oppression, is another explanation for the high rates of crime and delinquency among African Americans. She argued that crime and delinquency may be seen as the self-destructive behavioral responses to a society wherein opportunities for social mobility are limited because of one's race. The internalization of such historical and contemporary forms of oppression is also argued to contribute to cultural isolation, vocational stresses, and problematic behaviors such as substance abuse and domestic violence among American Indians (McBride, 2002). Furthermore, using the colonial model and the theories of postcolonial scholars Fanon (1965), Freire (1970), and Memmi (1965), among others, Duran and Duran (1995), Brave Heart (1998), and McBride (2002) also argued that colonialism and contemporary forms of oppression that continue to send inferiorizing messages about American Indian and Alaska Native identity may contribute to the high rates of suicide, alcoholism, and domestic violence among America's First Peoples. Thus, although there are various factors that may contribute to such problematic and health-risk behaviors, and internalized oppression may also be one of such important factors that may contribute to the development of behavioral and mental health concerns. Combined with findings that internalized oppression keeps individuals from seeking help (Kanuha, 1990), suggesting that they are at greater risk for developing severe pathology (Bailey, 2009; Szymanski & Gupta, 2009; Szymanski & Kashubeck-West, 2008; Szymanski & Stewart, 2010), increased attention to this highly salient but severely understudied phenomenon is desperately needed.

Below is an example of how internalized oppression made Annie feel about herself, and how this affected her well-being and mental health:

> Sometimes I wish I did not know about internalized oppression. Because I do, I am forced to confront the artifacts of oppression in my own life, as well as the ways I perpetrate oppression on others. However, I am aware of internalized oppression, and I want to be a good steward of that knowledge, so I try to cultivate an intentional, focused practice of self-reflection. In the moments when I am aware enough to recognize the forces of internalized oppression in my life, I take a moment to survey my thoughts and feelings. What I find is not always pretty.
>
> I have learned that I have a quiet shame that lurks in the corners of my psyche. It colors and influences the way I interact with the world, form

relationships, and understand myself. It operates by causing me to second guess myself when I know I'm right; It makes me select a male name from the phonebook when I am looking for a doctor and feel immediately embarrassed when I realize what I am doing; It makes me resent other LBGT individuals who "talk about gay stuff all the time," which is something I recently found myself saying to my girlfriend. Before I go any further, I would like to note that internalized oppression is at work even as I write this, as I originally wrote the last sentence as: "something I recently found myself saying to a friend, conditioned to deny real pieces of myself." For me, these forces, this shame, it is a catch-22 because no matter how hard I try, I cannot be without shame. I am ashamed of my shame. I hate that there is a part of me that hates a part of me.

SUMMARY AND CONCLUSION

In addition to having a clearer understanding of internalized oppression, it should now also be evident why it is important to better understand and address internalized oppression. Although we present a great deal of information here, this chapter is by no means comprehensive. Instead, it is only a general overview of the wide range of oppressive experiences and even wider range of internalized oppression manifestations and consequences faced by various groups throughout the world. The rest of the chapters in this book provide more in-depth coverage and analyses of internalized oppression as experienced by specific groups, further illuminating and bringing to life the losses, pains, and struggles faced by these communities. As a summary of the literature discussed in this chapter, and as an accessible guide as the reader proceeds with the rest of the book and beyond, we present a partial list of the characteristics of internalized oppression in Table 1.1.

In closing, there is no doubt that internalized oppression is a salient experience among various groups throughout the world, and empirical evidence is emerging to suggest that internalized oppression has immense negative mental and behavioral health consequences. Thus, in our efforts to better serve the majority of the people in our world, we need to incorporate larger sociopolitical factors (i.e., oppression) and its consequences (i.e., internalized oppression) in our conceptualizations of their psychological experiences. This broader, more complete, and more accurate conceptualization of the psychological experiences of socially marginalized groups will necessitate a change in the manner in which the field develops, conducts, and implements its research and service activities. This chapter, along with the rest of the chapters in this book, hopes to help facilitate this change.

TABLE 1.1
A Partial List of the Characteristics of Internalized Oppression

- Internalized oppression is an uncritical devaluation of one's own group and valuation of another.
- The devaluation of one's own group may or may not occur simultaneously with the valuation of another group.
- It is commonly experienced by members of various oppressed groups.
- It is an individual differences variable in that some members of oppressed groups experience it while other members may not.
- It is an individual differences variable in that the severity of it may vary between individuals and between groups.
- It is an individual differences variable in that the manifestations and implications may vary between individuals and between groups.
- It may be passed on from generation to generation or from one person to the next through socialization and continued experiences of oppression.
- It can develop at a very young age and last a lifetime.
- It may exist and operate automatically, outside of awareness, intention, or control.
- It is both the result of oppression and a perpetuating force of oppression, in that it works to maintain power structures that benefit the dominant group disproportionately to the dominated group.
- It engages the oppressed in the work of their own oppression through intrapersonal and intragroup violence and destruction.
- It influences how people think and feel about themselves, as well as how people behave.
- It influences how people think and feel about, as well as behave toward, other members of their group and other oppressed groups.
- It influences how people think and feel about, as well as behave toward, the dominant group.
- It has serious consequences for behavioral and mental health.
- The devaluation of one's own group, and the valuation of another group, are results of learning and conditioning experiences; people are not born with internalized oppression—it is learned.
- Because internalized oppression is learned, it can be unlearned. People can learn to value their own group just as much as they value other groups.

REFERENCES

Albee, G. W. (1986). Toward a just society: Lessons from observations on the primary prevention of psychopathology. *American Psychologist, 41*, 891–897. doi:10.1037/003-066X.41.8.891

Amaro, H., & Raj, A. (2000). On the margin: Power and women's HIV risk reduction strategies. *Sex Roles, 42*, 723–749. doi:10.1023/A:1007059708789

Artz, S. U. (1996). On becoming an object. *Journal of Child and Youth Care, 11*(2), 17–37.

Bailey, T.-K. M. (2009). Construct validity of the internalized racial oppression scale. *Dissertation Abstracts International: Section A: Humanities and Social Sciences, 17*(3-A), 773.

Bailey, T.-K. M., Chung, Y. B., Williams, W. S., Singh, A. A., & Terrell, H. K. (2011). Development and validation of the internalized racial oppression scale for Black individuals. *Journal of Counseling Psychology, 58*, 481–493. doi:10.1037/90023585

Batts, V. A. (1983). Knowing and changing the cultural script component of racism. *Transactional Analysis Journal, 13*(4), 255–257.

Bearman, S., Korobov, N., & Thorne, A. (2009). The fabric of internalized sexism. *Journal of Integrated Social Sciences, 1*(1), 10–47.

Beck, A. T., Rush, A. J., Emery, G., & Shaw, B. F. (1979). *Cognitive therapy of depression*. New York, NY: Guilford.

Beck, J. S., (1995). *Cognitive therapy: Basics and beyond*. New York, NY: Guilford.

Berry, J. W. (2003). Conceptual approaches to acculturation. In K. M. Chun, P. Balls-Organista, & G. Marin (Eds.), *Acculturation: Advances in theory, measurement, and applied research*. Washington, DC: American Psychological Association.

Brave Heart, M. Y. H. (1998). The return to the sacred path: Healing the historical trauma and historical unresolved grief response among the Lakota. *Smith College Studies in Social Work, 68*(3), 287–305.

Brown, L. S. (1986). Confronting internalized oppression in sex therapy with lesbians. *Journal of Homosexuality, 12*, 99–107. doi:10.1300/J082v12n03_09

Clark, K. B., & Clark, M. P. (1947). Racial identification and preference among negro children. In E. L. Hartley (Ed.), *Readings in social psychology*. New York, NY: Holt, Reinhart, and Winston.

Clark, L. A., Watson, D., & Reynolds, S. (1995). Diagnosis and classification of psychopathology: Challenges to the current system and future directions. *Annual Review of Psychology, 46*, 121–153. doi:10.1097/AJP.0b013e318261c9f9

Codina, G. E., & Montalvo, F. F. (1994). Chicano phenotype and depression. *Hispanic Journal of Behavioral Sciences, 16*, 296–306. doi: 10.1177/07399863940163007

Comas-Diaz, L. (2010). LatiNegra: Mental health issues of African Latinas. *Journal of Feminist Family Therapy, 5*, 35–74. doi:10.1300/J086v05n03_03

Crocker, J., & Luhtanen, R. (1990). Collective self-esteem and in-group bias. *Journal of Personality and Social Psychology, 58*, 60–67. doi:10.1037/0022-3514.58.1.60

Crocker, J., Luhtanen, R., Blaine, B., & Broadnax, S. (1994). Collective self-esteem and psychological well-being among White, Black, and Asian college students. *Personality and Social Psychology Bulletin, 20*, 503–513. doi:10.1177/00146167294205007

Cross, W. E., Parham, T. A., & Helms, J. E. (1991). The stages of Black identity development: Nigrescence models. In R. L. Jones (Ed.), *Black psychology* (3rd ed., pp. 319–338). Berkeley, CA: Cobb & Henry Publishers.

David, E. J. R. (2006). Biculturalism. In Y. Jackson (Ed.), *Encyclopedia of multicultural psychology* (pp. 66–68). Thousand Oaks, CA: Sage.

David, E. J. R. (2008). A colonial mentality model of depression for Filipino Americans. *Cultural Diversity and Ethnic Minority Psychology, 14*, 118–127. doi:1031037/1099-9809.14.2.118

David, E. J. R. (2009). Internalized oppression, psychopathology, and cognitive behavioral therapy among historically oppressed groups. *Journal of Psychological Practice, 15*(1), 71–103.

David, E. J. R. (2010). Testing the validity of the colonial mentality implicit association test (CMIAT) and the interactive effects of covert and overt colonial mentality on Filipino American mental health. *Asian American Journal of Psychology, 1*, 31–45. doi:10.1037/a0018820

David, E. J. R. (2013). *Brown skin, White minds: Filipino -/ American postcolonial psychology (with commentaries).* Charlotte, NC: Information Age Publishing.

David, E. J. R., & Okazaki, S. (2006a). Colonial mentality: A review and recommendation for Filipino American psychology. *Cultural Diversity and Ethnic Minority Psychology, 12*, 1–16. doi:10.1037/1099-9809.12.1.1

David, E. J. R., & Okazaki, S. (2006b). The colonial mentality scale for Filipino Americans: Scale construction and psychological implications. *Journal of Counseling Psychology, 53*, 241–252. doi:10.1037/0022-0167.53.2.241

David, E. J. R., & Okazaki, S. (2010). Activation and automaticity of colonial mentality. *Journal of Applied Social Psychology, 40*, 850–887. doi:10.1111/j.1559-1816.2010.00601.x

David, E. J. R., Okazaki, S., & Saw, A. (2009). Bicultural self-efficacy among college students: Initial scale development and mental health correlates. *Journal of Counseling Psychology, 56*, 211–226. doi:10.1037/a0015419

Dovidio, J. F., Gaertner, S. L., Kawakami, K., & Hodson, G. (2002). Why can't we just get along? Interpersonal biases and interracial distrust. *Cultural Diversity & Ethnic Minority Psychology 8*, 88–102. doi:10.1037/1099-9809.8.2.88

Duran, E., & Duran, B. (1995). *Native American post-colonial psychology.* Albany, NY: State University of New York.

Fanon, F. (1965). *The wretched of the earth.* New York, NY: Grove.

Frame, M. W. (1999). Balm in Gilead: Spiritual dimensions in counseling African American women. *Journal of Multicultural Counseling and Development, 27*, 182–192. doi:10.1002/j.2161-1912.1999tb0034x

Freire, P. (1970). *Pedagogy of the oppressed.* New York, NY: Continuum.

Gainor, K. A. (1992). Internalized oppression as a barrier to effective group work with Black women. *The Journal for Specialists in Group Work, 17*, 235–242. doi:10.1080/01933929208414355

Gong, F., Takeuchi, D. T., Agbayani-Siewart, P., & Tacata, L. (2003). Acculturation, distress, and alcohol use: Investigating the effects of ethnic identity and religiosity. In K. M. Chun, P. Balls-Organista, & G. Marin (Eds.), *Acculturation: Advances in theory, measurement, and applied research* (pp. 189–206). Washington, DC: American Psychological Association.

Greene, B. (2009). The use and abuse of religious beliefs in dividing and conquering between socially marginalized groups: The same-sex marriage debate. *American Psychologist, 64*, 698–708. doi:10.1037/0003-066X.64.8.698

Hall, R. E. (1994). The "bleaching syndrome": Implications of light skin for Hispanic American assimilation. *Hispanic Journal of Behavioral Sciences, 16,* 307–314. doi:10.1177/07399863940163008

Hanna, F. J., Talley, W. B., & Guindon, M. H. (2000). The power of perception: Toward a model of cultural oppression and liberation. *Journal of Counseling and Development, 78,* 430–446. doi:10.1002/j.1556-6676.2000. tb01926.x

Harrell, C. J. P. (1999). *Manichean psychology: Racism and the minds of people of African descent.* Washington, DC: Howard University Press.

Harris, D. J. (1997). Ethnocultural identity and eating disorders in women of color. *Professional Psychology: Research and Practice, 28,* 341–347. doi:10.1037/0735-7028.28.4.341

Hatzenbuehler, M. L. (2009). How does sexual minority stigma "Get under the skin" A psychological mediation framework. *Psychological Bulletin, 135*(5), 707–730.

Hawley, J. C. (2001). *Postcolonial, queer: Theoretical intersections.* Albany, NY: State University of New York Press.

Hill, S. M. (1999). Does race matter: A study of the role on the identity process of incarcerated Black women. *Dissertation Abstracts International: Section A: Humanities and Social Sciences, 60*(6-A), 2235.

Hong, Y., Morris, M. W., Chiu, C., & Benet-Martinez, V. (2000). Multicultural minds: A dynamic constructivist approach to culture and cognition. *American Psychologist, 55,* 709–720. doi:10.1037/0003-066X.55.7.709

Itzen, C. (1985). Margaret Thatcher is my sister: Counseling on divisions between women. *Women's Studies International Forum, 8,* 73–83. doi: 10-1016/0277-5395(85)90036-6

Jones, J. M. (1997). *Prejudice and racism* (2nd ed.). New York, NY: McGraw-Hill.

Kanuha, V. (1990). Compounding the triple jeopardy: Battering in lesbian of color relationships. *Women and Therapy, 9,* 169–184. doi:10.1300/ J015v09n01_10

Keller, J. (2005). In genes we trust: The biological component of psychological essentialism and its relationship to mechanisms of motivated social cognition. *Journal of Personality and Social Psychology, 88,* 686–702. doi:10.1037/0022-3514.88.4.686

Kumari Campbell, F. (2008). Exploring internalised ableism using critical race theory. *Disability and Society, 23*(2), 151–162.

LaFromboise, T., Coleman, H. L. K., & Gerton, J. (1993). Psychological impact of biculturalism: Evidence and theory. *Psychological Bulletin, 114,* 395–412. doi:10.1037/0033-2909.114.3.395

Lehman, J. D. (2009). The effects of internalized oppression and family influence on body image in Filipina American women. *Dissertation Abstracts International: Section B: Science and Engineering, 69*(7-B), 4430.

Lipsky, S. (1977). Internalized oppression. *Black Re-emergence, 2*(1–3), 5–10.

Lipsky, S. (1987). *Internalized racism.* Seattle, WA: Rational Island Publishers.

Majied, K. F. (2003). The impact of racism and homophobia on depression. *Dissertation Abstracts International: Section A: Humanities and Social Sciences, 64*(5-A), 1849.

McBride, B. A. (2002). Aspects of community healing: Experiences of the Sault Sainte Marie Tribe of Chippewa Indians. *American Indian and Alaska Native Mental Health Research: The Journal of the National Center, 11,* 67–68. doi:10.5820/aian.1101.2003.67

Memmi, A. (1965). *The colonizer and the colonized.* Boston, MA: Beacon.

Mercury Policy Project. (2010). *Factsheet: Mercury in skin lightening cosmetics.* Montpelier, VT: Author. Retrieved from http://mercurypolicy.org/wp-content/uploads/2010/06/skincreamhgfactsheet_may31_final.pdf

Meyer, I. H. (2003). Prejudice, social stress, and mental health in lesbian, gay, and bisexual populations: Conceptual issues and research evidence. *Psychological Bulletin, 129,* 674–697. doi:10.1037/0033-2909.129.5.674

Moreau, M. J. (1990). Empowerment through advocacy and consciousness-raising: Implications of a structural approach to social work. *Journal of Sociology and Social Welfare, 17*(2), 53–67.

Nakamura, K. (2006). Struggles among Japanese women with conservative gender roles flooded with 'ideal' feminine images through commercialism. *Psychotherapy and Politics International, 4,* 55–61. doi:10.1002/ppi.42

Napoleon, H. (1996). *Yuuyaraq: The way of the human being.* Fairbanks, AK: The Alaska Native Knowledge Network.

Neallani, S. (1992). Women of colour in the legal profession: Facing the familiar barriers of race and sex. *Canadian Journal of Women and the Law, 5*(1), 148–165.

Neville, H. A., Coleman, M. N., Falconer, J. W., & Holmes, D. (2005). Color-blind racial ideology and psychologically false consciousness among African Americans. *Journal of Black Psychology, 31,* 27–45. doi:10.1177-095798404268287

Norrington-Sands, K. (2002). Sister-to-sister: The influences of family socialization messages, personal self-esteem, and collective self-esteem on social-comparison jealousy between African American women. *Dissertation Abstracts International: Section B: Sciences and Engineering, 63*(2-B), 1040.

Ochs, R. (1996). Biphobia: It goes both ways. In B. A. Firestein (Ed.) *Bisexuality: The psychology and politics of an invisible minority.* Thousand Oaks, CA: Sage.

Okazaki, S., David, E. J. R., & Abelman, N. (2007). Colonialism and the psychology of culture. *Social and Personality Psychology Compass, 1,* 90–106. doi:10.1111/j.1751-9004.2007.00046.c

Owens, T. J. (2001). *Extending self-esteem: Theory and research.* Cambridge, MA: Harvard University Press.

Padesky, C. A., & Greenburger, D. (1995). *Clinician's guide to mind over mood.* New York, NY: Guilford Press.

Padilla, L. M. (2001). 'But you're not a dirty Mexican': Internalized oppression, Latinos, and law. *Texas Hispanic Journal of Law and Policy, 7*(1), 58–113.

Padilla, L. M. (2004). Internalized oppression and Latino/as. *Diversity Factor, 12*(3), 15–21.

Parmer, T., Arnold, M. S., Natt, T., & Jansen, C. (2004). Physical attractiveness as a process of internalized oppression and multigenerational transmission in African American families. *The Family Journal, 12*, 230–242. doi:10.1177/1066480704264931

Perez, A. (2005). Internalized oppression: How it affects members of the LGBT community. *Diversity Factor, 13*(1), 25–29.

Perez, M. P. (2005). Colonialism, Americanization, and indigenous identity: A research note on Chamorro identity in Guam. *Sociological Spectrum, 25*(5), 571–591.

Pheterson, G. (1986). Alliances between women: Overcoming internalized oppression and internalized domination. *Signs: Journal of Women in Culture and Society, 12*, 146–160. doi:10.1086/494302

Phinney, J., Chavira, V., & Williamson, L. (1992). Acculturation attitudes and self-esteem among high school and college students. *Youth & Society, 23*, 299–312. doi:10.1177/0044118X92023003002

Pierce, C., Carew, J., Pierce-Conzalez, D., & Willis, D. (1978). An experiment in racism: TV commercials. In C. Pierce (Ed.), *Television and education* (pp. 62–88). Beverly Hills, CA: Sage.

Pierce, R., Frone, M., Russell, M., Cooper, M., & Mudar, P. (2000). A longitudinal model of social contact, social support, depression, and alcohol use. *Health Psychology, 19*(1), 28–38.

Poupart, L. M. (2003). The familiar face of genocide: Internalized oppression among American Indians. *Hypatia, 18*, 86–101. doi:10.2979/HYP.2003.18.2.86

Prilleltensky, I., & Laurier, W. (1996). Polities change, oppression remains: On the psychology and politics of oppression. *Political Psychology, 17*, 127–148. doi:10.2307/3791946

Pyke, K., & Dang, T. (2003). 'FOB' and 'Whitewashed': Identity and internalized racism among second-generation Asian Americans. *Qualitative Sociology, 26*(2), 147–193.

Pyke, K. D. (2010). What is internalized racial oppression and why don't we study it: Acknowledging racism's hidden injuries. *Sociological Perspectives, 53*, 551–572. doi: 10.1525/sop.2010.53.4.551.

Ramos-Diaz, E. I. (1985). Re-evaluation counseling as a tool to overcome internalized oppression of an exploitative society: A case study of Third World women in the United States. *Dissertation Abstracts International: Section B: Sciences and Engineering, 46*(3-A), 655.

Rimonte, R. (1997). Colonialism's legacy: The inferiorizing of the Filipino. In M. P. P. Root (Ed.), *Filipino Americans: Transformation and identity* (pp. 39–61). Thousand Oaks, CA: Sage.

Rosenwasser, P. (2002). Exploring internalized oppression and healing strategies. *New Directions for Adult and Continuing Education, 94*, 53–61. doi:10.1002/ace.59

Rosenwasser, P. (2005). Exploring, resisting, and healing from internalized Jewish oppression: Activist women's cooperative inquiry. *Dissertation Abstracts International: Section A: Humanities and Social Sciences, 66*(5-A), 1975.

Ross, L. E., Doctor, F., Dimito, A., Kuehl, D., & Armstrong, M. S. (2007). Can talking about oppression reduce depression: Modified CBT group treatment for LGBT people with depression. *Journal of Gay and Lesbian Studies, 19,* 1–15. doi:10.1300/J041v19n01_01

Rudkin, J. K. (2003). *Community psychology: Guiding principles and orienting concepts.* Upper Saddle River, NJ: Pearson.

Rudmin, F. W. (2003). Critical history of the acculturation psychology of assimilation, separation, integration, and marginalization. *Review of General Psychology, 7,* 3–37. doi:10.1037/1089-2680.7.1.3

Ryan, W. (1971). *Blaming the victim.* New York, NY: Vintage Books.

Sears, D. O. (1988). Symbolic racism. In P. Katz & D. Taylor (Eds.), *Eliminating racism: Profiles in controversy* (pp. 53–84). New York, NY: Plenum Press.

Solomon, R., & Liefeld, C. P. (1998). Effectiveness of a family support-center approach to adolescent mothers: Repeat pregnancy and school drop-out rates. *Family Relations, 47,* 139–144. doi:10.2307/585617

Steptoe, A., Wardle, J., Pollard, T. M., Canaan, J., Davies, G. J. (1996). Stress, social support, and health-related behavior: A study of smoking, alcohol consumption and physical exercise. *Journal of Psychosomatic Research, 41,* 171–180. doi:10.1016/0022-3999(96)00095-5

Sue, D. W. (Ed.). (2010). *Microaggressions and marginality: Manifestations, dynamics, and impact.* Hoboken, NJ: John Wiley and Sons.

Sue, D. W., Capodilupo, C. M., Torino, G. L., Bucceri, J. M., Holder, A. M. B., Nadal, K. L., & Esquilin, M. (2007). Racial microaggressions in everyday life. *American Psychologist, 62,* 271–286. doi:10.103770003-066X.624.271

Szymanski, D. M., & Gupta, A. (2009). Examining the relationships between multiple oppressions and Asian American sexual minority person's psychological distress. *Journal of Gay and Lesbian Social Services, 21,* 267–281. doi:10.1080/10538720902772212

Szymanski, D., & Kashubeck-West, S. (2008). Mediators of the relationship between internalized oppressions and lesbian and bisexual women's psychological distress. *The Counseling Psychologist, 36,* 575–594. doi:10.1177/0011000007309490

Szymanski, D. M., Kashubeck-West, S., & Meyer, J. (2008). Internalized heterosexism: A historical and theoretical overview. *The Counseling Psychologist, 36,* 510–524. doi:10.1177/0011000007309488

Tajfel, H., & Turner, J. C. (1986). The social identity theory of intergroup behavior. In S. Worchel & W. Austin (Eds.), *Psychology of intergroup relations.* Chicago, IL: Nelson-Hall.

Tappan, M. B. (2006). Reframing internalized oppression and internalized domination: From the psychological to the sociocultural. *Teachers College Record, 108,* 2115–2144. doi:10.1111/j.1467-9620.2006.00776.x

Tatum, B. (1994). The colonial model as a theoretical explanation of crime and delinquency. In A. T. Sulton (Ed.), *African American perspectives on crime, causation, criminal justice administration, and crime prevention* (pp. 33–52). Woburn, MA: Butterworth-Heinemann.

Tawa, J. Suyemoto, K. L., & Tauriac, J. J. (2013). Triangulated threat: A model of Black and Asian relations in a context of White dominance. In S. O. Pinder

(Ed.) *American multicultural studies: Diversity of race, ethnicity, gender, and sexuality.* Thousand Oaks, CA: Sage.

Thomas, A. J., Speight, S. L., & Witherspoon, K. M. (2005). Internalized oppression among Black women. In J. L. Chin (Ed.), *The psychology of prejudice and discrimination: Bias based on gender and sexual orientation* (Vol. 3., pp. 113–132). Westport, CT: Praeger Publishers/Greenwood.

Thomas, C. W. (1971). *Boys no more: A Black psychologist's view of community.* Beverly Hills, CA: Glencoe.

Thompson, C. E., & Neville, H. A. (1999). Racism, mental health, and mental health practice. *The Counseling Psychologist, 27,* 155–223. doi:10.1177/0011000099272001

Trickett, E. J. (1991). *Living an idea: Empowerment and the evolution of an alternative high school.* Boston, MA: Brookline Books.

Tsai, J. L., Chentsova-Dutton, Y., & Wong, Y. (2002). Why and how researchers should study ethnic identity, acculturation, and cultural orientation. In G. C. N. Hall & S. Okazaki (Eds.), *Asian American psychology: The science of lives in context* (pp. 41–66). Washington, DC: American Psychological Association.

Varas-Diaz, N., & Serrano-Garcia, I. (2003). The challenge of a positive self-image in a colonial context: A psychology of liberation for the Puerto Rican experience. *American Journal of Community Psychology, 31*(1–2), 103–115.

Walker, R. L., Wingate, L. R., Obasi, E. M., & Joiner, T. E. (2008). An empirical investigation of acculturative stress and ethnic identity as moderators for depression and suicidal ideation in college students. *Cultural Diversity and Ethnic Minority Psychology, 14*(1), 75–82.

Williamson, I. (2000). Internalized homophobia and health issues affecting lesbians and gay men. *Health Education Research, 15,* 97–107. doi:10.1093/her/15.1.97

World Health Organization (2011). *Mercury in skin lightening products.* Geneva, Switzerland: Author. Retrieved from http://www.who.int/ipcs/assessment/public_health/mercury_flyer.pdf

Ying, Y.-W. (1995). Cultural orientation and psychological well-being in Chinese Americans. *American Journal of Community Psychology, 23,* 893–911. doi:10.1007/BF02507020

The Internalized Oppression of North American Indigenous Peoples

John Gonzalez, Estelle Simard, Twyla Baker-Demaray, and Chase Iron Eyes

Are we really oppressed? Shall we just forget about the past, shall we just move on? Isn't it time to heal? Why can't we all just return to humble greatness? There is no easy answer. Why do we live the way we do? Asking these questions will get you hours upon hours of intense discussion and research about colonization, imposed poverty culture, loss of language, intergenerational historical trauma, lateral oppression, genocide, holocaust, boarding schools, Church-perpetrated sexual abuse, massacres, diseases, loss of lands,

Author Note

John Gonzalez is a member of the White Earth Anishinaabe Nation and an Associate Professor of Psychology at Bemidji State University. Estelle Simard is a member of Couchiching First Nation and Executive Director of the Institute for Culturally Restorative Practices in Fort Frances, Ontario, Canada. Twyla Baker-Demaray is a member of the Mandan, Hidatsa, & Arikara Nation and Vice President of Student Services at Fort Berthold Community College in New Town, North Dakota. Chase Iron Eyes is a member of the Standing Rock Lakota Nation and the co-founder of Last Real Indians Inc. Each of us authors are deeply connected and involved in our respective communities. As a result, the narrative flows between third person and first person quite often as we discuss internalized oppression. When possible, we attempt to delineate who is speaking with the initials of the author. However, all of our voices can be heard throughout the paper, as well as the voices of our communities and the spirits of our ancestors.

loss of bundles, loss of sacred sites, and on and on. Indeed, those of us who operate within the oppression complex, permanently or fleetingly, can make a life attempting to dissect and grow out of the oppression we have either internalized, are unaware of, or just want to ignore.

—Chase Iron Eyes

To talk about internalized oppression among indigenous Peoples is to tell a story, many stories. Stories about loss. Stories about suffering. Stories about pain. Stories of genocide and destruction. But there are also stories of survival. Stories about resilience. Stories about pride. And yes, stories about healing. We hope to share some of these stories of cultural restoration, which have thrived from the lived experiences that exist in our memories, transmitted from our parents, grandparents, and our communities. In our worldview, an indigenous worldview, we strive for balance as we try to recount these stories that still affect us today. We will honor our ancestors, our families, and community members whose spirits are still wounded and show the struggle that exists in the construct of internalized oppression. To talk about internalized oppression among our peoples can invoke shame and guilt because of the long historical effect associated with colonization. We do not wish to cast blame or imply weakness within our peoples, as this is a manifestation of internalized oppression. Instead, we want to talk about who we are, where we came from, and the great traumas that we have survived and continue to face so that we can learn to heal together. In order to heal from this trauma, we also need to acknowledge and recognize how this trauma affects and influences ourselves, so we do not further perpetuate the oppression among our own people. That is the story of internalized oppression.

One of the most destructive and insidious consequences of colonialism happens when the colonized begin to think, feel, and act like the colonizer, particularly as it relates to the stereotypes and prejudices of themselves and their own people. This manifestation of thoughts, emotions, and behaviors has been referred to by many names, including, but not limited to: "internalized oppression," "internalized racial oppression," "internalized racism," "internalized whiteness," "colonial mentality," and even "racial self-hatred." Some of the earliest writings on this concept come from Du Bois (1903/1989) as he described a "double-consciousness" of looking at one's self and measuring one's worth through the eyes of others. Since Du Bois's time, there have been numerous studies and papers illustrating the effects of internalized oppression on People of Color (Clark & Clark, 1939, 1952; David, 2011; David & Okazaki, 2006; Padilla, 2001; Pyke & Dang, 2003). In *Pedagogy of the Oppressed*, Paulo Freire (1971) provided one of the most powerful and eloquent discussions of how the oppressed comes to identify with the oppressor, even as they struggle for liberation. Freire delineated many reasons for this process and the forms it takes. He stated there is a struggle to be human, to be free, but the oppressed have internalized the image of themselves from the oppressor. Thus, they come to believe that to be free means to act and think like the oppressor, and, consequently, subjugate themselves and their people to afflictions they themselves have experienced (Freire, 1971). This is the crux of the dilemma for the marginalized, the oppressed, and those who desire liberation.

For Native Peoples of North America, the literature and research is virtually nonexistent and is sparse at best. Some of the first and most well-known writings about internalized oppression with Native Peoples come from Maria Yellow Horse Brave Heart, Lemrya DeBruyn, and Eduardo and Bonnie Duran (Brave Heart, 1998, 1999; Brave Heart & DeBruyn, 1998; Duran & Duran, 1995). In addition, there is a growing body of literature and its subsequent liberation movement that focuses on the decolonization processes of indigenous Peoples in North America and around the world (Smith, 1999; Unsettling Minnesota, 2009; Wilson & Yellow Bird, 2005; Zig-Zag, 2006). Brave Heart (1998) brought forth and discussed the concept of historical trauma response and unresolved grief as a result of the tremendous trauma experienced by Native Peoples. She went on to discuss how this has led to many of the challenges that contemporary Native Peoples face today (Brave Heart, 1998). Duran and Duran (1995) also discussed this trauma and its effects, calling the grief a "soul wound" that continues to affect the colonial psychology of Native Peoples today.

Poupart (2003) also discussed internalized oppression and the expressions of internalized oppression about North American indigenous Peoples. Internalized oppression exists in self-defeating thoughts, the lack of connectedness to ancestral family, the spirit, the self, the family, the extended family, the community, the nation, the environment, and many others. Internalized oppression is the belief systems etched in negative stereotyping of indigenous Peoples. It is buying into the negative stories we have been told about ourselves since childhood: *they are bums, they are lazy, they don't work, they are drunks, they are uneducated, they are unhealthy, they are on drugs, they don't care for their kids, they are corrupt, they are wagon-burners, they are squaws, they are dependent on the government, or they can't hold jobs.* It is internalizing the "not as good as" mentality because of either the indirect or direct messages given by society to "conform" into the melting pot of society. As a result, we begin to act like all is okay in an effort to build the façade. Poupart (2003) stated, "American Indians have been socially constructed as incapable of experiencing emotional response to pain and suffering [. . .], the stoic and the savage [. . .], and this belief system intimates that Indians had no capacity to mourn and subsequently, no need or right to grieve" (p. 89). Acknowledgement of this history and present-day latent consequences calls for an understanding of its internal influence on us as a people. Media has propagated and sensationalized the lived experience of indigenous Peoples, further reinforcing an account of lies and misrepresentation designed to support an ideology to suppress and oppress the indigenous experience. Thus, our experiences—your experiences—are invalidated, unsupported, unacknowledged, and placated by society at large.

When understanding the concept of internalized oppression, we attempt to shed light on the issue from a holistic account. Internalized oppression always begins with the understanding of historical trauma associated with the mass colonial experience of indigenous Peoples of North America. What is the collective history that we have been through as a people and how did it impact us individually? What is colonization? How does colonization continue to erode cultural identity and the indigenous cultures' life-giving structures that promote indigenous authentication or indigenous self-actualization? We are coming to understand that internalized oppression is the result of colonization and its subsequent identifier as marginalized peoples once again taking it out on each other. For those of us who are a part of and live in Indian Country, we have experienced and witnessed the forms and symptoms of internalized oppression. Some of these characteristics include alcohol and substance abuse, domestic abuse and violence in our communities, high levels of anxiety and mental health problems, the diabetes epidemic, suicide epidemics, tribal politics, and infighting. In the most treacherous of forms, we begin to believe the systematic oppression and turn our backs on our own indigenous cultures or its structures that guide our values, ethics, and inherent mechanisms to attach to our cultural ways as indigenous Peoples. All of these historic and contemporary issues can be linked to internalized oppression (Brave Heart & DeBruyn, 1998; Simard & Blight, 2011). As we tell the stories of who we are, where we come from, and where we are going, the links will be clear. To aid our effort to share some of the experiences of North American indigenous Peoples, narratives from each of the authors are inserted in select parts throughout this chapter.

WHO WE ARE AND WHERE WE COME FROM:
NATIVE PEOPLE YESTERDAY AND TODAY

"Hey you, Hey Indian! Who are you?" (Means, 1993, track 16). This seems like an easy question. However, there is not an easy answer for individuals or for indigenous Peoples as a whole. Historically, indigenous People were an extraordinarily diverse group of cultures that lived in every area of

Turtle Island (North America). These indigenous Nations had unique cultural structures and socialization processes that supported the collective and holistic development of the people (Simard & Blight, 2011). The idiosyncratic nature of cultural structures allowed for societies to flourish and live harmoniously within their Nations. Further, these cultural structures of indigenous Nations allowed for interdependence among other Nations of people throughout Turtle Island. It is estimated that the population of Native People living in North America prior to European contact was as high as 100 million and as low as 2 million (Page, 2003).

Currently, Native People live in every state in the United States with nearly 50% living in urban settings. There are 565 federally recognized tribes (Nations) in the United States alone, with 335 reservations and 617 "legal" areas in which census data is collected. The population of Native People is currently 5.2 million in the United States, and as of 2010 2.9 million self-identified as Native only and another 2.3 million identified as one or more races (U.S. Census Bureau, 2011). Previous data shows the American Indian population to be as low as 550,000 in the 1960 census. In Canada, there are over 633 recognized First Nation communities. Census data indicates that there are four distinct population groups documented by the federal government: First Nation (60%), Metis (33%), Inuit (4%), and Multiple/Other (3%). This grouping makes up 1,172,785, or 3.8% of Canada's total population. Of this population, there is an estimated 48% who are under the age of 24 and 62% under the age of 34. According to Statistics Canada (2008), 40% of this total population lives on reserves, while 60% of the population lives off reserves in rural or urban areas.

HISTORICAL OPPRESSION:
COLONIALISM AND GOVERNMENT POLICIES

Ask an indigenous person today whether or not he or she celebrates Columbus Day, and the answer may come back surprising to some. For many indigenous Peoples in the Americas, Columbus Day is less a day of celebration or the odd day off from work, and more a day of remembrance, demonstration, education, and even mourning. Asking an indigenous person to acknowledge Columbus's arrival in the Americas is akin to asking a Jewish person to pick a day to acknowledge the rise of the Third Reich in Germany. One does not celebrate the advent of the physical and cultural genocide of his or her people. As vexing as the celebration of Columbus Day can prove for many indigenous People, there has been in years past a growing movement calling for the end of this national holiday, or perhaps a recognition of the genocide that took place on American soil.

It should be noted that prior to Western contact, life in the Americas was far from a Utopian existence. Like anywhere else on the globe, tribal nations rose and fell, made war, made peace, intermingled, broke apart, crossed continents, and readily traded with each other, whether it was goods, cultural practices, or even languages. In other words, the colonists who arrived on Turtle Island were not stepping foot onto unknown, uncivilized lands—far from it. Economies, empires, and dynasties had already been in existence here for hundreds of years prior to contact. From initial contact to today's modern context, colonialism and the policies of assimilation echo their impacts in our current existence time and time again. One need not delve too deeply into the history of the American government and its relationship with its first People to know that it is strained at best, and devastating and destructive at worst. Groups once oppressed by outside forces have begun internalizing the attitudes and ideas of the oppressor, and oftentimes willingly continue the colonists' work of systematically deconstructing, devaluing, and destroying their own social and cultural structures.

Some of the most well-known destructive and devastating effects of colonialism and government policies were forced removal and relocation, such as the trail of tears, the establishment of reservations, and the assimilation policies that included outlawing spiritual and ceremonial practices, the establishment of boarding schools, and the allotment act. Embedded within each of these policies are countless stories of genocide and oppression that had profound effects on indigenous Peoples. As JG shared:

> This is what my people experienced on the White Earth Indian Reservation. The story of White Earth is not that unique, only one that has been thoroughly documented and one that I know from stories shared to me by my relatives. The establishment of the White Earth reservation was the result of one of the last treaties signed by the Ojibwe of Minnesota, the Mississippi band in particular, in 1867. Initially, it was conceived as a way to reduce the land base of the previously established reservations in Minnesota with plans to relocate indigenous people from those reservations to White Earth. My grandmother, Angela Charette, and her parents were one of those families that were relocated from the Lake Superior region. The geography of White Earth is unique in that half of the reservation is pristine farmland at the edge of the plains and the other half is made of forest and lakes, which include the headwaters of the Mississippi River. As such, it was believed this would be ideal to make us Ojibwe farmers and allow us to continue to hunt and gather.

Soon after the establishment of the reservation at White Earth, a series of events unfolded that were tragic for the people of White Earth, which has present-day effects on the internalized oppression of the Ojibwe people.

Like elsewhere, spiritual and ceremonial practices were outlawed and missionaries quickly moved in to convert the people. As JG continued:

> The boarding school policy took hold in the federal government and children were removed from their homes and families. In 1890, the Dawes Act, better known as the general allotment act, was passed. This act forced the tribes throughout the United States to parcel the land to be property of individual families instead of held by the tribes as a whole. In addition to this, it stated that Indians could not sell their land unless they had at least one drop of White blood quantum, thus began one of the most notoriously devised plans to divide and conquer indigenous Peoples. Government officials swooped in and began to attempt to determine who was a full-blooded Indian and who was not. Stories are still told today about the abuses that took place and the unscientific methods that were used. For example, my grandmother was born a full blood, but somehow died a half-breed. As you can imagine, once over half the people were "identified" as not being full-blooded, thus eligible to sell their individual allotments, White settlers and forestry and logging companies all rushed in to buy this prestigious farmland and forest for pennies on the dollar. As a result, most of the land on my reservation does not belong to the tribe or to Ojibwe families. Over the decades we found ourselves confined to the villages on the reservations and pushed further and further into poverty, with little to no resources or opportunities to change the situation.

Though we may have moved beyond policies of premeditated murder, enslavement, rape, reckless endangerment with depraved indifference, cruelty, and biological warfare that were committed during the time of Columbus, the colonist policy and mindset lives on in the form of various educational, religious, and health policies extant today. Whether it is education systems, economic development, environmental issues, cultural and belief systems, or sovereignty and Nation building, the indigenous person in the United States is the most legislated individual in the nation. In the State, local, tribal, or federal levels, indigenous Peoples have been micromanaged nearly to the point of oblivion—quite literally, in some cases. Arguably, no other ethnic group in the United States has had to attempt to survive with such an explicit policy of assimilation or extermination leveled at them as the indigenous People of the United States. In a nation ostensibly founded upon the principle of "freedom of religion," ours was the only religion or belief system to be outlawed; it is little wonder that after such a long, determined, *silently insidious* battle, the first Peoples of Turtle Island began to turn on themselves.

CONTEMPORARY OPPRESSION: INDIAN LIFE IS TOUGH; IT'S HARD TO BE INDIAN

JG shares a recent experience he had while reading Vine Deloria's *Custer Died for Your Sins* (1969) in an airplane:

> Although I have read this book many times, I still enjoy listening to Vine tell me how it was, how it is, and how it will be, from time to time. Yes, deep down, part of me also enjoys seeing the look on White peoples' faces as they glance over and see the title of the book. Every now and then, a few of them even ask, "That looks interesting. What is that book about?" On this flight, it happened in earnest. As I gave my summary of Vine's manifesto, the White woman's facial expressions fluctuated between astonishment, disbelief, anger, denial, and even a few I could not identify. She seemed amazed that Native and White relations occurred as they did; shocked that her beloved government treated the indigenous People so unfairly and with such cruelty; and almost refused to accept that such treatment continues in the 21st century. There was an irony in all of this; she was a nurse, who was going to start a new job in a rural Native village in Alaska. Chapter 4 of Deloria's book was talking about her; a professional do-gooder, who "knew" about Indians and Indian problems. She "knew" that Indians were alcoholics. She "knew" that Indians had diabetes. She "knew" that Indians were obese. She "knew" that Indians were poor. She "knew" that Indians were unemployed. But, she just didn't know how "they" got that way and why, for goodness sake, they couldn't get themselves out of those "desperate circumstances." As you can imagine, the 3-hour flight from Washington, DC to Minneapolis was a fun-filled evening in which the passengers in row 10, seats A and B (and maybe E, F and G) received a lesson in contemporary Indian Education.

Much of this education outlined the several ways in which the oppression of indigenous Peoples continues in North America—oppression that is woven into the fabric of all areas of life. The problem is that Whites have a hard time seeing it, because they are blinded by their privilege and colonialist status. But for Natives and other People of Color, we see it all around us. We see it in the tremendous disparities that exist in education, economic opportunities, unemployment, poverty, incarceration rates, disease and access to health care, suicide and other accidental deaths, exposure to toxins, and many others. These disparities exist not only because of the legacy of genocide and racism, but they are perpetuated by social policies and private actions. Nationally, there is disparity in education rates. In Minnesota, for example, we have one of the largest education disparities between Students of Color and Whites. For American Indians, the high school graduation rate is 41%, compared to 80% for Whites (MMEP, 2009). This is particularly troubling given that there are 11 federally recognized tribes and we have one of the largest Native populations in the country. One would think that Indian education and education about Indians would be important. However, there is no requirement in K-12 education for American Indian history. Schools and school districts that serve American Indian students and communities are severely underfunded. There are little to no systematic efforts to train American Indian teachers. These are all specific policy issues that result in the un-education, and miseducation, of American Indian youth. In addition, there is little private action by Whites to learn about and understand their Indian neighbors.

In Canada, Indian education fell under the most notorious colonial tool that continues to exist—The Indian Act. This Act allowed for a pluralism of education across Canada, a distinct curriculum for non-Indian people and an acculturation curriculum for Indian students. These residential schools began in the late 1800s and continued until the last school closed in 1996. In the 1920s it was law for all First Nation children to attend residential school, and to not do so, parents would be incarcerated. In 1907, Dr. Peter Bryce first documented the atrocities that existed in residential schools when he discussed the deliberate infection of First Nation children with diseases like tuberculosis (Sproule-Jones, 1996). Spiritual, emotional, sexual, and physical abuses go hand in hand with the residential school experience. Thus, a long history of cultural genocide is the backdrop to understanding the current educational issues facing the indigenous Peoples of Turtle Island.

The criminal justice system is where we can see other examples of contemporary oppression faced by Native Peoples. American Indians are jailed or imprisoned 38% more often than Whites. When we look at it by state, the links between policies and systems of oppression become even clearer. For example, in South Dakota, American Indians make up 10% of the population but are 21% of all inmates. In North Dakota, American Indians are 6% of the population but constitute 19% of those jailed. In Minnesota, Native youth are 4% of the population but they are nearly 47% of those in detention centers or treatment facilities. Contrast this with states like Arizona and Oklahoma, two of the top five American Indian populated states, where the incarceration disparity does not exist. It is argued that this is the result of American Indian reservations and spaces being policed by tribal authorities and litigated in tribal courts in these states (DOJ, 2011, 2012; Rave, 2009; Smith, 2008). Again, this suggests that there are policies and private actions behind the disproportionate incarceration rates in many states.

Similarly, in Canada, we are seeing an over-representation of First Nation People within the justice system. According to the report on Aboriginal Peoples in the Canadian criminal justice system (Canadian Criminal Justice Association, 2000):

- Aboriginal accused are more likely to be denied bail;
- More time is spent in pre-trial detention by Aboriginal People;

- Aboriginal accused are more likely to be charged with multiple offences, and often for crimes against the system;
- Aboriginal People are more likely not to have legal representation at court proceedings;
- Aboriginal clients, especially in northern communities where the court party flies in the day of the hearing, spend less time with their lawyers;
- As court schedules in remote areas are poorly planned, judges may have limited time to spend in the community;
- Aboriginal offenders are more than twice as likely to be incarcerated than non-Aboriginal offenders;
- Aboriginal Elders, who are also spiritual leaders, are not given the same status as prison priests and chaplains in all institutions, and
- Aboriginal People often plead guilty because they are intimidated by the court and simply want to get the proceedings over with (para. 3).

Health disparities between American Indians and Whites suggest another aspect of systematic oppression that exists in our society. American Indians die from preventable diseases and conditions at exceptionally higher rates than the general population: 500% higher for tuberculosis; 177% higher for diabetes; 82% higher for suicide; and 514% higher for alcoholism (U.S. Department of Health and Human Services, 2011). As cancer death rates decrease for Whites they are increasing for American Indians. This same inverse relationship is true for overall health status as well. How can it be that such startling numbers exist in the "richest and most powerful" country in the world? Many have argued it is the social determinants of health largely linked to policies that determine who receives access to care, what types of care are available, the types of goods and services that are available in communities, and the social and economic conditions of certain communities. Probably the most powerful example is the diabetes epidemic affecting Indian country and the story of the Pima and Tohono O'odham tribes of southern Arizona. They appear to have the highest rates of diabetes in the entire world, with half the adults afflicted by this disease (Pavkov et al., 2007; Schulz et al., 2006). This is a very recent phenomenon, as less than a century ago diabetes was unheard of in this community.

Many have assumed that it must be genetic or some other medical explanation. However, we only need to look to the Gila River to understand what happened. During the late 19th and early 20th centuries, water stopped coming down the Gila River. Dams and other water projects diverted the river for White farmers, ranchers, and mining interests, leaving the Pima with none. In 1930, the Coolidge Dam was opened and President Calvin Coolidge promised the Pima access to water, but it never came. To the Pima, Maricopa, and Tribal Peoples everywhere, water is life. This virtually destroyed their way of life and ability to provide for themselves. The Pima and other Southwest tribes were master farmers and engineers of the water. Once that way of life was gone, many died, initially from starvation and eventually from diseases such as diabetes. They soon became dependent on commodity foods: white flour, cheese, lard, and canned foods, which created and eventually killed the diabetic. Only recently have the Pima and other tribes in southern Arizona won their water rights back, but the damage has been done and is severe. Over half the Pima on the reservation live in poverty, with little access to fresh foods and resources to fight diabetes (California Newsreel, 2008; Smith-Morris, 2008). The Pima's story is extreme, but it is a similar one that plays out in many American Indian spaces and communities.

Beyond systemic and policy-level examples, there are many other ways American Indians continue to be oppressed today. This can be seen in the way American Indians are portrayed in society and the effect this has on creating and maintaining stereotypes. These images include sports team mascots, clothing lines, beer and liquor brands, Halloween costumes, Thanksgiving Day literature and decorations, children's toys, and film and television portrayals. It is also evident in the national discourse and language that is used in reference to American Indians. When someone is not acting in accordance to the group or social norm, he or she is considered to be "off the reservation." A very famous incident involved the use of Geronimo as the code name for Osama Bin Laden. JG relates a story about how subtle microaggressions can be identified in everyday life, told to him by a friend and colleague who works in a health care setting:

> I was sitting in my office one morning, getting ready for the day, and another Native coworker stopped in to visit. So, there we were just visiting for a few minutes and a White male coworker came by to give me some paperwork. As he peaked in the door he saw us two Native women visiting and he says, "Hey, are we having a powwow here today?" I was sort of shocked and didn't know how to react or respond. But after I thought about it I was offended. Powwows are important to us Native People, and even sacred to some. The regalia that people wear and the feathers we carry are sacred to us, and for him to try and make a funny comment made me angry.

It is clear from the narrative above that the image of the American Indian is forever cast as living in the past or as socially and culturally deviant in some way. These types of portrayals and interactions are really modern forms of discrimination based on the legacy of genocide, oppression, and racism and are referred to as microaggressions. Microaggressions are subtle verbal, behavioral, or environmental insults (Pierce, Carew, Pierce-Gonzalez,

& Willis, 1977; Sue et al., 2007). These insults and indignities are often unintentional but send a clear message that demeans and/or invalidates the persons existence as a member of a marginalized group. Recent research has documented the occurrence of microaggressions with nearly all marginalized groups (Sue, 2010), including American Indians (Gonzalez et al., 2012; Hill, Lee, & Williams, 2010). There is also evidence that experiencing microaggressions produces physiological responses similar to other chronic stressors (Gonzalez et al., 2013). It is within the context of both the historical and contemporary forms of oppression—in systemic and interpersonal levels—that American Indians struggle for a sense of voice, identity, and liberation that internalized oppression begins to manifest.

MANIFESTATIONS OF INTERNALIZED OPPRESSION: DO YOU WANT TO BE A WHITE MAN?

"That's life on the Rez." Many a native brother and sister have said this— no doubt, each of the authors has probably said this upon occasion. The use of this phrase, in fact, is a manifestation of internalized oppression. Why? This phrase is often used in the context of normalizing problems experienced on Indian reservations and communities. It is said when a motor vehicle accident occurs, when an abusive situation occurs, when a child is neglected and removed from the home, when a drunk driving offense occurs, or when a tribal politician abuses power against his or her own people. It also includes whether or not our own people, our story tellers, content creators, professors, lawyers, doctors, scholars, engineers, scientists, teachers, intercessors, community leaders, councilpersons, and so on maliciously laugh at, make fun of, criticize, speak ill of, or degrade even for the slightest moment in their own mental process, any spiritual practice, or expressive natures of our own indigenous practices. To illustrate the meaning of this idea, think of the thing we Indians do to ourselves. We make humor of, or with ill intent vocalize to others, the practice of wearing long hair, speaking with a rez slang or accent, looking Indian because you have an "Indian" nose, giving each other a pass due to "Indian time," "commod bods," learning your own language, looking down on those of us not educated in Western institutions, and negatively judging those of us without material wealth and ways. On the surface it appears to be a benign coping strategy—a way to deal with this oppression of who we are as people, with our biting humor, with our projected machismo, by internally adopting the West's standard of aesthetic beauty. We say to ourselves, "This is a new time, I am free to adapt and adopt these foreign cultural norms as I please." Certainly, that previous sentence does raise these important questions: Is this not how indigenous People survive? Did we not adapt with the

English language, written languages, horses, guns, pots, pans, religions, and other foreign entities?

However, this "coping strategy" of saying, "That's life on the Rez" and the other acts mentioned above raise a potentially deeper, more insidious implication. In one sense it implies that we have come to accept these situations and incidents as part of who we are as indigenous People, as part of what it means to be Indian. We have internalized the stereotypes and images that have been created about us. In addition, it may also be a way for some Natives to distance themselves from other Natives they see as "rugged Indians." This is similar to the Asian who has assimilated into American culture and refers to other Asians who speak with an accent or maintain their traditional ways as "fresh off the boat." While the Native or Asian feels liberated or is in the process of liberating him- or herself, he or she has unfortunately fallen into the trap that Freire (1971) posited— identifying with the oppressor and seeing his or her own people as the oppressor sees them.

Yellow Bird (2004) discussed this identification with the oppressor as it related to the cowboys and Indians narrative that runs deep in American culture. He recalled memories of his childhood and how the imposed norms of dressing and "acting" like cowboys was preferred. Boys and men were supposed to be "tough," cut their hair, and wear cowboy boots. To do anything else was to be weak and confirm the narrative that Indians were inferior to cowboys. A contemporary vestige of accepting the oppressor's image can be seen in the Native sports mascot and nickname controversy. The fact that it remains a controversy is fueled, in part, by the acceptance and endorsement of some American Indians. However, the endorsement by some Natives is surely a form of internalized oppression. Whites, the oppressor, created the American Indian images and nicknames used by sports teams. They are fictionalized, romanticized, stereotyped caricatures that live only in the minds of the oppressor. These mascots and nicknames were created at a time when Native People had no voice or political power—they were offered as an honor to "our country's" indigenous Peoples. This is an example of what Virgilio Enriquez (1992) describes as surface accommodation/tokenism and transformation/exploitation. As an example at the University of North Dakota (UND), this played out in very dramatic fashion for decades. UND officials, athletics, and alumni always claimed they were honoring the state's indigenous People. They were always quick to tout the number of "Indian" programs and so-called support the University provided. The oppressors would always "hold-up" and point to the few Natives who were supportive of the use of the Fighting Sioux.

Manifestations of internalized oppression also present through the *robbing/losing of one's identity* as an indigenous person—Anishinaabe,

Mohawk, Lakota, Blackfeet, or Navajo, and so on. The robbing of identity is diabolically completed though a systematic process that exists within education, child welfare, mental health, justice, or health systems to deal with issues with only one specific way of knowing—the White way. It is not acknowledging that there was a system of education unique to the Mohawk People or the Anishinaabe People. It is not acknowledging that as indigenous People we have our own unique ways and cultural structures that support education, child welfare, mental health, justice, or health care. It is the shunning of our belief system and cutting off the opportunities to attach to our cultural strengths in a manner that promotes efficacy. By cutting off these very life-giving opportunities, we decrease the opportunities to instill cultural pride and resiliency. JG shares a story from his own identity loss:

> I remember growing up on White Earth in the 70s. My dad, Jim "Ironlegs" Weaver taught us how to sing and dance—we went to powwows every summer. We had sweats behind our house. But, back then, hardly anybody was doing sweats or ceremonies, it seemed like nobody was singing or dancing and going to powwows, except our family and maybe a few others. I looked around the Rez and started to wonder why. When I would go hang out with cousins and friends, they would tease me. I started to question my own identity. Instead of going to powwows and doing ceremonies, it seemed like being Indian meant partying and doing drugs. I strayed from the sacred Circle. I wanted to be like the other Indians on the Rez. I had to go through some rough times and learn the hard way before I freed myself and found my way back to our Anishinaabe ways so that I could heal.

Because of oppression and its subsequent influences on the internalized process of oppression, we are left as wounded people. The problem is that we think this only applies to us as adults, we think that our children do not feel the influences of oppression or experience the construct of internalized oppression—but they do. The children feel internalized oppression as well; however, they are worse off than us as adults because at least we have outlets and mechanisms to heal or not to heal. Children, on the other hand, are powerless at the hands of internalized oppression, which results in a deeper call for us as indigenous parents, aunties, uncles, and grandparents, to solve this problem together. For nothing in this world hurts a family member more than seeing the light lost from a child's eyes.

> One of my (JG) sisters was not as fortunate as I and still struggled with internalized oppression. As we grew older we had children and,

of course, raised them in the teachings that we know. Our children would play together when my nieces and nephews would come to my house. I would tell them stories about Wenaboozhoo, about the spirits all around us, about our travels to powwows in places near and far. It was painful to see the doubt in their eyes and to hear the way they would question and not believe me. What I was telling them was not what they "knew" about what it meant to be Indian. It reminded me of my own youth and how my cousins also questioned me. This cycle was repeating itself in another generation. As they grew up, some of them found the Anishinaabe way, but sadly, some of them have not.

Internalized oppression also exists when indigenous people are *immobilized* and cannot be all that they want to be. This includes fulfilling their purpose in life. This purpose can be seen as their sacred role to be a protector or a provider. In a contemporary context, it is one's inability to sustain one's family, and the truly devastating feelings this situation leaves on that person. It is the *powerlessness* when they cannot buy their child a winter jacket or boots because of the cut-backs to tribal or First Nation welfare programs. It is the *fear* a mother feels when she welcomes her baby into the world, because she knows the reality of child welfare. She knows the child welfare history and subsequent systematic racism and institutional power they have wielded over our indigenous children for centuries. It is the *deep longing* and *loneliness* our grandparents and parents have felt in their boarding/residential school experience. Through our relationship the *deep sense of disconnect* passed on to us inter-generationally. It is the *sense of great loss* we felt in trying to connect to our family when at times that door was closed due to child welfare separations, alcoholism, abuse, violence, neglect, or death. At times, our internalized oppression is the *pain* and *anger* we feel about our situation in life: *We might not have a job, we are dependent on the reserve to make jobs, they give the jobs to non-natives, they have no job training programs, and so on*—all of which negatively exasperate a person's worth as a man or a woman, often falling short of the "ideal" of what it means to be a provider/protector in these contemporary White times. In the end, internalized oppression is the *profound despair* one feels when choosing suicide as the only option.

MENTAL AND BEHAVIORAL HEALTH IMPLICATIONS OF INTERNALIZED OPPRESSION: WOUNDED SPIRITS

Like any cultural group trying to live in the modern world, keeping the balance between tradition and contemporary values can result in challenges for community members. Native Peoples, however, face a particularly difficult set of circumstances and challenges as a result of living in a Fourth World Context. This Fourth World Context occurs when an indigenous population exists in a nation where a colonizing majority holds institutional power and privilege (Browne & Fiske, 2001; O'Neil, 1986). The historical and contemporary oppression discussed earlier has resulted in an extraordinary amount of trauma within the Native population. Two separate sets of seminal writings and research began to tell this story of trauma and its effects on Native Peoples today (i.e., Brave Heart, 1998, 1999; Duran & Duran, 1995). Historical trauma is the cumulative emotional and psychological wounding, over the life span and across generations, emanating from massive group trauma experiences (Brave Heart, 1999). Historical unresolved grief is defined as intergenerational emotional and/or psychological injury resulting from a legacy of genocide (Brave Heart, 1998, 1999). Brave Heart contends the high rates of suicide, depression, alcohol abuse, violence, and physical abuse in Native spaces is attributable to the processes of internalized oppression. While this may seem like a very bold and profound statement, her work and subsequent research in this area lends support to this assertion. For example, in her work with Lakota Peoples, Brave Heart documented the high rates of social problems and traced these problems to the cultural genocide and oppression Native Peoples have experienced. Through clinical work, mainly incorporating traditional American Indian healing methods, significant improvements were demonstrated in the participants' psychosocial well-being and sobriety. The concept of historical loss and grief was further supported in the work of Les Whitbeck and colleagues (Whitbeck, Adams, Hoyt, & Chen, 2004), where they identified negative emotions such as depression, shame, anger, anxiety, and distrust of White people as associated with the historical and contemporary experiences of oppression faced by American Indians.

Poupart (2003) discussed the *expressions of internalized oppression* to being physical, emotional, verbal, and sexual assaults that exists within First Nation communities. The expression of internalized oppression is manifested by conditioning an indigenous person to either do nothing or to be destructive. This dichotomy is designed to keep indigenous People separate, for if we are fighting ourselves, or fighting with each other, there is no way that we can gather together to stand against the oppressor— because we become the oppressor.

Expressions of internalized oppression further exist in cultural discontinuity (Kirmayer, Brass, & Tait, 2000). Cultural discontinuity is simply the disarray that exists in our tribal communities. It is the backstabbing, mistrust, infighting, and lack of safety this creates for the community. It is the violence in all forms: lateral violence, sexual violence, physical violence, emotional or character assassination, bullying, intimidating, and so on. Cultural discontinuity exists in the social ills within all tribal communities across Turtle Island. It is the problems with alcoholism, prescription drug addiction, domestic violence, and plain old band politics. It is the assaults to our sovereignty through mass acculturation processes, designed from a capitalist ideology. As Kirmayer and colleagues stated, "Cultural discontinuity is the experience of rapid culture change, marginalization, and absorption into a global economy that has little regard for their (us) autonomy" (p. 607). The expressions of internalized oppression exist because there is no outlet to discuss why we feel the way we do about our situation. Often times, we might not understand or have the words to describe the oppression and this contributes to the overall frustration of internalized oppression.

Expressions of internalized oppression exist in the blind acceptance of the White world, without the acknowledgement first and foremost of our own inherent indigenous ways of knowing. It is internalizing White patriarchy and power, constructs of gender and gender differences, structures of power and its subsequent privilege, constructs of women and women's roles or constructs of children, hierarchies, and the subsequent violence that evolves through these non-indigenous structures (Poupart, 2003). Expressions of internalized oppression exist when we adopt other ideologies as our own, especially when we begin to perpetrate these ideologies on each other. When we begin to think we have power and privilege, we become the abuser, we shame each other. More importantly, however, we cut each other off from our own spiritual development. Twyla Baker-Demaray (TBD) shares a story:

> I had an incident of a student who, when invited to sweat and other ceremonial and cultural doings upon arriving on campus, couldn't have been more excited and pleased. This student expressed that he had been doing some soul searching of late, and was very interested in exploring who he was as an indigenous person. Much of this side of himself had been kept from him growing up, as he came from a strongly Christian background. Time passed and this student stopped coming to our regular gatherings, or even responding to messages inviting him. When I ran into him some time later, and asked as to whether he'd be coming to sweat that weekend, he broke down. He told me that he'd shared with his family members that he'd gone to some of our gatherings, and had been told in no uncertain terms by close family members that our way of life was "demonic," "evil," and that he should no longer associate with us. He was deeply confused, and felt ashamed, both of avoiding me and of his family's reaction.

This is how the cycle of internalized oppression evolves. TBD continues:

> Our way of life doesn't allow for judgment calls such as the ones his family had made, and I simply advised him that I was not angry, nor

did I feel betrayed or hurt. I did feel badly for him in that he had been experiencing such anguish and that he could still talk to me about other things, if he felt he didn't want to talk about indigenous lifeways. I see this happen from time to time, with young people coming into their own, still deeply and quite naturally influenced by the input of their families and loved ones. Sometimes they come back to ceremony. Sometimes they don't. I make a point of advising them that neither I nor anyone else within our circle is here to proselytize. What we share is made available to those who would choose it. Therein lies a primary difference between the indigenous and Western worldview.

CLINICAL AND COMMUNITY PROGRAMS FOR INTERNALIZED OPPRESSION: HEALING AND THE SEVENTH GENERATION

If there is any one truism for all indigenous Peoples, it surely must be that *everything is related*. This not only applies to our spiritual, physical, and mental processes, but also to the social issues we experience and the environments in which they occur. As previously discussed, the manifestations of internalized oppression are widespread and the spiritual, physical, and mental health consequences far reaching. Thus, any attempt to heal from internalized oppression must include this core worldview of interrelatedness—for individuals and communities. By many accounts, this kind of healing is occurring for many indigenous People and communities. Many have suggested that we are in the 7th Generation—an Anishinaabe as well as other tribal nations' prophecy that states a great rebirth and healing will come in this numbered generation after the contact with Europeans and the accompanying trauma. Amazing efforts and results are happening in Indian Country in a variety of forms and can be referred to as decolonization.

For example, language revitalization such as Waadookodaading Ojibwe Immersion Charter School in Lac Courte Orielles Wisconsin, Fort Berthold Community College Tribal Language Mentor Project in North Dakota, Fond Du Lac Community College Teacher Training and Language Immersion Camp in Minnesota, Lakota Language Immersion Nest in Sitting Bull College in North Dakota, and many others (Hermes, 2007; Reyhner, 2008, 2010; Treuer, 2012). Substance abuse and trauma healing efforts by national programs/movements such as the White Bison, Wellbriety, and the Longest Walk Movements also exemplify decolonization. Similarly, there are coordinated mental and behavioral health research and service efforts with the establishment of centers and institutes led and directed by indigenous Peoples such as the National Center for American Indian and Alaska Native Mental Health at the

University of Colorado, the indigenous Wellness Research Institute at the University of Washington, the Center for Alaska Native Health Research at the University of Alaska Fairbanks, the National Resource Center on Native American Aging and the Seven Generations Center of Excellence in Native Behavioral Health at UND, the Research for indigenous Community Health Center at the University of Minnesota—Duluth, and many others. Of particular importance among these research and service efforts is the use of local indigenous knowledge systems and people to promote health and well-being.

Decolonization can also be seen in the many community grassroots land recovery and treaty rights efforts such as the White Earth Land Recovery Project founded by Winona LaDuke and the Last Real Indians (LRI) co-founded by community co-author Chase Iron Eyes (CIE). LRI is a unique organization founded in 2012. The mission of LRI is to give voice to the indigenous community through an indigenous perspective. This voice is expressed primarily in writings, but can also be heard in the presence of community events and activities that LRI members organize. JG shares the following to describe some of his experiences with CIE and LRI events, to serve as an example of what Native individuals and communities can do to address historical trauma, cultural loss, and internalized oppression:

> While Chase will not say this publicly, because he is truly a humble being, I see him demonstrating how to be a 21st indigenous warrior who is grounded and centered by his culture and identity—that is decolonization. LRI and CIE are using modern day tools of social media such as Facebook, Tumblr, and Twitter to inspire and at the same time are embedded within the community and can be seen on the ground, literally running with the Wounded Knee runners, sitting and conversing with the Elders at language camps and conferences—they don't just talk, but also walk the talk. They do all this, not because they are the LRI, but rather so that we all don't become the LRI. They are showing the current generation that we don't have to accept the images, the stereotypes, and the way of life that has disempowered our people for so long.

CIE further shares some of his experiences with LRI that demonstrate specific ways in which American Indian communities can be decolonized and empowered:

> During the past year we (CIE) have been truly blessed at LRI to be involved in, and a part of, a spiritual reawakening all across Turtle Island. Perhaps one of the most significant activities we were a part of was the purchasing of Pe'sla—the spiritual center of the Lakota Nation located at the center of the sacred Black Hills. This event of

being able to have Pe'Sla back in Lakota control is empowering and sends a message of hope to all oppressed peoples everywhere. The efforts of all the individuals and tribes who came together to make this a reality also shows us that we are much more than the "broken Indian" and fallen warriors that much of White America, that our own people see us as.

The Institute for Culturally Restorative Practices (ICRP) is another example of an organization designed to deal with the internalized oppression of our people by bringing education and healing to the programs and services designed to work with our indigenous children, youth, families, and communities. ICRP works within a culturally restorative framework that promotes healing within our natural protective networks. The natural protective network principle is composed of themes that may be used for understanding our inter-relatedness within our communities. These principles are the core mechanisms to healing, and are depicted in Figure 2.1.

Historically and in some contemporary situations, structures have existed that promoted the natural protective network. For example, across Turtle Island there are distinct languages, ceremonies, customs, and practices indigenous to a Nations' land base. These communities built relationships through these land-based activities, and they etched the holistic belief systems that existed within our families and communities. Roles and responsibilities existed through the natural protective network, as

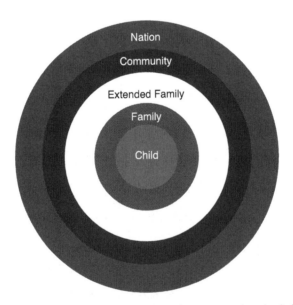

FIGURE 2.1 The natural protective network principle.
Source: Simard (2009).

did teachings and life-giving properties on human development across the life span. These activities are instilled and fostered by ICRP activities:

- Through our tribal government and their leadership abilities
- Through our elders and their cultural knowledge, their spiritual guidance, their access to our historic generational window, their ability to provide life span wisdom and knowledge, their promotion or revitalization of values, systems, and structures, and their collective strengthening of our community ways
- Through our men and their gift in protecting and securing our society, and
- Through our women and their roles in social and family matters

Working with "practice-based" evidence curriculum and instruction, ICRP works with individual practitioners and organizations to produce better outcomes for our people.

One of the authors (Estelle Simard [ES]), who is also one of the developers of the natural protective factor principle described above, shares her own personal journey from internalized oppression to decolonization:

> After years of inter-city living (aka, colonialism and acculturation), continuous disconnect from the life-sustaining teachings of my culture, and the effects of alcoholism, abandonment, family violence, and abuse, led to a crippled identity as an indigenous woman. I realize today that I will probably never comprehend the full impacts of my own internalized oppression; however, today I accept these experiences as a part of my identity. As an adult, I did not understand anything about my culture until I met my spiritual advisor—Dave Gehue. Today I appreciate the worldview this man gave to me. He changed my life and brought to me what I now call "cultural attachment."

Cultural attachment is a philosophy, which encapsulates how an individual bonds to his or her culture. Cultural attachment creates a direct spiritual force, where the bond begins, develops, and evolves for the individual. In Anishinaabemowin, cultural attachment is expressed as *wiidamaagowiziwinan*. This means the deep connection between the individual and the spiritual connection to his or her Creator via access to cultural structures. Cultural attachment is a life-giving philosophy, as it instills life force energy into an individual (Simard & Blight, 2011, p. 39). ES continued to describe her decolonization journey below:

> Cultural attachment was the answer to my internalized oppression. The more opportunities I had to heal my spirit wounds through ceremonies, the more I found out who I was. In the White psychological constructs of

attachment we only look at the attachment to significant others—mom, dad, caregivers, etc. In an indigenous approach to cultural attachment theory, attachment is promoted by access to all cultural structures that exists within an indigenous Nation. These activities of cultural attachment theory gave me my identity as an Anishinaabekwe. They gave me the opportunity to heal the spiritual and emotional wounding of internalized oppression. These activities are my toolkit for surviving in this world dominated by a worldview different from my own, one that has historically lied and cheated me from the truth of my own family, my own community, my own Nation, and you—my brothers and sisters. In my efforts of healing, I have come to understand the traumas that existed in my own natural protective network. I began to understand the traumas of the racism, the poverty, the separatisms of colonialism, and the residential and training school scenarios perpetrated on my parents. However, through the reconciliatory efforts involved in ceremonial activities, we have built strong family values, and through that my sense of loss, isolation, and abandonment I once felt . . . is gone.

FUTURE DIRECTIONS: THE NEXT GENERATION

The dreams of our ancestors will not die with us. In order to "resist" oppression we must live. We must learn our languages, sing our songs, practice our ceremonies, treat each other as relatives, clear our minds, cleanse our bodies, and bless our spirits. Oppression is not a discourse among those living within the "oppressed" culture. One would be hard-pressed to find one of our spiritual leaders, for instance, speak about decolonization, neocolonialism, oppression, or any other derivation of the invader-invaded complex. Yet, they are shedding the yoke of oppression simply by living in the ceremonies, respecting our kin or clan relationships to each other and the natural environment.

At stake is our own existence, our own place on this earth in this day and age, our own spiritual health, and self-esteem. Since we lost control of our spiritual self-determination, due to the overwhelming forces of European/American influence, it has been extremely difficult for our children to learn that their esteem already exists within them—for so long we have been taught that we were less than, we were uncivilized, we were primitive, superstitious, and impediments to progress. Native culture and ways of life are fluid and adaptable, which lends to their beauty. This is part of the reason our ways survived, and, in turn, our people have as well. As the needs of the people change, so does the culture; this is the way it has been since time immemorial. At some point in time, the songs sung today, which many Native People would consider traditional, were sung for the first time somewhere. Someone composed those songs, and passed that knowledge on to someone else, and they, in turn, did the same on down the line. This traditional knowledge, or "medicine," as it is commonly referred to in Native communities, is increasingly being adapted into systems of education, curricula, treatment and prevention programs, language and cultural revitalization, mental health and youth programming, and expressions of decolonization throughout Indian Country.

Let us close with a powerful and inspiring example of this decolonization with a story about the Idle No More movement that is occurring at the time of this writing. As a result of culturally oppressive policies against First Nations Peoples and Mother Earth by the Harper administration in Canada, four women took a stand, calling for repeal of Omnibus Bill C-45, which eliminated protections for most of Canada's water ways and ignored the treaty rights of First Nations. Each of these strong women contributed to the movement in unique ways—eloquently written statements, grassroots organizing of local communities, and a hunger strike by Chief Theresa Spence of the Attawapiskat First Nation. They called for peaceful demonstrations and the people answered. In fact, thousands of indigenous People answered—marching and demonstrating on the Canadian parliament and other government locations across Canada. Others began to organize and conduct flashmob round dances at shopping malls and other public spaces, using some of those medicines discussed above—song, dance, and prayer. Through the use of social media, and the traditional moccasin telegraph, word spread of this movement worldwide. Flashmob round dances were organized and conducted throughout the United States. Soon, other types of flashmobs and demonstrations began occurring in Central and South America, Pacific Islands, Australia, New Zealand, Africa, and Asia. Indigenous Peoples all around the world are rising up to let their voices be heard in support of Idle No More, but also in support of decolonization. The 7th generation is now— and the White minds of the Brown Nations are showing their true colors.

REFERENCES

Brave Heart, M. (1998). The return to the sacred path: Healing the historical trauma response among the Lakota. *Smith College Studies in Social Work, 68*(3), 287–305.

Brave Heart, M. Y. H., & DeBruyn, L. M. (1998). The American Indian Holocaust: Healing historical unresolved grief. *American Indian Alaska Native Mental Health Research, 8*(2), 60–82.

Brave Heart, M. Y. H. (1999). Oyate Ptayela: Rebuilding the Lakota Nation through addressing historical trauma among Lakota parents. *Journal of Human Behavior and the Social Environment, 2*(1/2), 109–126.

Browne, A. J., & Fiske, J. (2001). First Nations women's encounters with mainstream health care services. *Western Journal of Nursing Research, 23*(2), 126–147.

Bureau of Justice Statistics. (2011). *Jails in Indian Country, 2010.* (DOJ Publication No. NCJ 236073). Washington, DC: US Government Printing Office.

Bureau of Justice Statistics. (2012). *Jails in Indian Country, 2011.* (DOJ Publication No. NCJ 238978). Washington, DC: US Government Printing Office.

California Newsreel. (Producer). (2008). *Bad sugar* [Documentary]. United States: Vital Pictures.

Clark, K. B., & Clark, M. P. (1939). The development of consciousness of self and the emergence of racial identification in Negro preschool children. *Journal of Social Psychology, 10*(4), 591–599.

Clark, K. B., & Clark, M. P. (1952). Racial identification and preference in Negro children. In G. Swanson, T. Newcomb, & E. Hartley (Eds.), *Readings in social psychology* (pp. 551–560). New York, NY: Hold.

Canadian Criminal Justice Association. (2000). *Aboriginal Peoples and the Criminal Justice Association.* Retrieved from http://www.ccja-acjp.ca/en/aborit.html.

David, E. J. R., & Okazaki, S. (2006). The colonial mentality scale for Filipino Americans: Scale construction and psychological implications. *Journal of Counseling Psychology, 53*(2), 241–252.

David, E. J. R. (2011). *Filipino -/ American postcolonial psychology: Oppression, colonial mentality, and decolonization.* Bloomington, IN: ArthorHouse.

Deloria, V. (1969). *Custer died for your sins: An Indian Manifesto.* New York, NY: Macmillan Publishing Company.

Du Bois, W. E. B. (1903). *The souls of Black folk.* New York, NY: Penguin. (Original work published 1989)

Duran, E., & Duran, B. (1995). *Native American postcolonial psychology.* Albany, NY: SUNY Press.

Enriquez, V. (1992). *From colonial to liberation psychology: The Philippine experience.* Honolulu, HI: University of Hawaii Press.

Freire, P. (1971). *Pedagogy of the oppressed.* New York, NY: Continuum.

Gonzalez, J., Brodeur, S., Cramer, C., Goughnour, C., Magoon, C., Ronich, J., . . . Wheelhouse, E. (2013, January). *An Indian in the room: Microaggressions in the classroom.* Poster presented at the 2013 National Multicultural Conference and Summit. Houston, TX.

Gonzalez, J., Erickson, C., Hall, E., Lundquist, C., Showers, A., & Zamora, I. (2012, August). *Microaggressions experiences and the American Indian college student.* Poster presented at the 120th American Psychological Association Convention, Orlando, FL.

Hermes, M. (2007). Moving toward the language: Reflections on teaching in an Indigenous-immersion school. *Journal of American Indian Education, 46,* 54–71.

Hill, J. S., Kim, S., & Williams, C. D. (2010). The context of racial microaggression against Indigenous peoples: Same old racism or something new? In D. W. Sue (Ed.), *Microaggressions and marginality: Manifestations, dynamics, and impact* (pp. 105–122). Hoboken, NJ: Wiley.

Kirmayer, L. J., Brass, G. M., & Tait, C. L. (2000). The mental health of Aboriginal peoples: Transformation of identity and community. *Journal of Canadian Psychiatry, 45*(7), 607–616.

Means, R. (1993). *Hey you, Hey Indian. On Electric Warrior: The Sound of Indian America.* [CD]. Warrior Records.

Minnesota Minority Education Partnership. (2009). *State of students of color & American Indian students.* Retrieved from www.mmep.org

O'Neil, J. (1986). The politics of health in the fourth world: A northern Canadian example. *Human Organization, 45*, 119–128.

Padilla, L. (2001). "But you're not a Dirty Mexican: Internalized oppression, Latinos and the law." *Texas Hispanic Journal of Law and Policy, 7*(1), 59–113.

Page, J. (2003). *In the hands of the Great Spirit: The 20,000 year history of American Indians.* New York, NY: Free Press.

Pavkov, M. E., Hanson, R. L., Knowler, W. C., Bennet, P. H., Krakoff, J., & Nelson, R. G. (2007). Changing patterns of type 2 diabetes incidence among Pima Indians. *Daibetes Care, 30*, 1758–1763.

Pierce, C. M., Carew, J. V., Pierce-Gonzalez, D., & Wills, D. (1977). An experiment in Racism: TV commercials. *Education and Urban Society, 10*(1), 61–87.

Poupart, L. (2003). The familiar face of genocide: Internalized oppression among American Indians. *Hypatia, 18*(6), 87–100.

Pyke, K., & Dang, T. (2003). "FOB" and "Whitewashed": Identity and internalized racism among second generation Asian Americans. *Qualitative Sociology, 26*(2), 147–172.

Rave, J. (2009, February 6). Percent of American Indians in jail is high. *Bismarck Tribune.* Retrieved from http://bismarcktribune.com/news/state-and-regional/percent-of-american-indians-in-jail-is-high/article_3de882e7-003a-5785-81aa-4eaed3da4be6.html

Reyhner, J. (2008). Promoting human rights through Indigenous language revitalization. *Intercultural Human Rights Law Review, 3*, 152–189.

Reyhner, J. (2010). Indigenous language immersion schools for strong Indigenous identities. *Heritage Language Journal, 7*, 138–152.

Schulz, L. O., Bennett, P. H., Ravussin, E., Kidd, J. R., Kidd, K. K., Esparza, J., & Valencia, M. E. (2006). Effects of traditional and Western environments on prevalence of type 2 diabetes in Pima Indians in Mexico and the U.S. *Diabetes Care, 29*, 1866–1871.

Simard, E. (2009). Culturally restorative child welfare practice—A special emphasis on cultural attachment theory. *First Peoples Child Family Review, 4(2)*, 44–61.

Simard, E., & Blight, S. (2011). Developing a culturally restorative approach to Aboriginal child and youth development: Transitions to adulthood. *First Peoples Child & Family Review, 6*(1), 28–55.

Smith, F. (2008). *Incarceration of Native Americans and private prisons.* Retrieved from http://www.lenapeprograms.info/Articles/Prison.htm

Smith, L. T. (1999). *Decolonizing methodologies: Research and indigenous peoples.* Dunedin, New Zealand: University of Otago Press.

Smith-Morris, C. (2008). *Diabetes among the Pima: Stories of survival.* Tucson, AZ: University of Arizona Press.

Sproule-Jones, M. (1996). Crusading for the forgotten: Dr. Peter Bryce, Public Health, and the Prairie Native Residential Schools. *Canadian Bulletin of Medical History, 13*(2), 199–224.

Statistics Canada. (2008, January). Aboriginal Peoples Highlight Table, 2006 Census. (Catelogue No. 97-558-XWE2006002). Retrieved from http://www12.statcan.ca/census-recensement/2006/dp-pd/hlt/97-558/index.cfm?Lang=E

Sue, D. W., Capodilupo, C. M., Torino, G. C., Bucceri, J. M., Holder, A. M. B., Nadal, K. L., & Esquilin, M. (2007). Racial microaggressions in everyday life: Implications for clinical practice. *American Psychologist, 62*(4), 271–286.

Sue, D. W. (2010). *Microaggressions and marginality: Manifestations, dynamics, and impact.* Hoboken, NJ: Wiley.

Treuer, A. (2012). *Everything you wanted to know about Indians but were afraid to ask.* St Paul, MN: Minnesota Historical Society Press.

U.S. Census Bureau. (2011). *The American Indian and Alaska native population 2010: 2010 census briefs.* Washington, DC: U. S. Government Printing Office.

U.S. Department of Health and Human Services. (2011). *Indian health service fact sheet.* Retrieved from http://www.ihs.gov/PublicAffairs/IHSBrochure/Disparities.asp

Unsettling Minnesota. (2009). *Unsettling ourselves: Reflections and resources for deconstructing colonial mentality.* Retrieved from www.unsettlingminnesota.org

Whitbeck, L. B., Adams, G. W., Hoyt, D. R., & Chen, X. (2004). Conceptualizing and measuring historical trauma among American Indian people. *American Journal of Community Psychology, 33*(3–4), 119–130.

Wilson, W. A., & Yellow Bird, M. (Eds.). (2005). *For indigenous eyes only: A decolonization handbook.* Santa Fe, NM: School of American Research Press.

Yellow Bird, M. (2004). Cowboys and Indians: Toys of genocide, icons of American colonialism. *Wicazo Sa Review, 19*(2), 33–48.

Zig-Zag. (2006). *Colonization and decolonization: A manual for indigenous liberation in the 21st century.* Salish Territory: Warrior Publications.

Internalized Oppression and Alaska Native Peoples: "We Have to Go Through the Problem"

Jordan Lewis, James Allen, and Elizabeth Fleagle

We can't go over it or pass over it. We can't leave it the way it is. We have to go through the problem and come out the other side of it and go on from there.

In beginning this chapter, along with each subsequent chapter section, we feature a quote from coauthor Elizabeth Fleagle, an Inupiaq Elder and a descendant of the Inupiaq leader and healer Manilaq. We chose each of these quotations because they express, simply and with clarity, a truth about the oppression of Alaska Native people, as well as about how oppression is internalized and what its consequences are. This first quote provides a perspective that in many ways embodies the resilient response of Alaska Native people to historical and contemporary circumstances that might have otherwise engulfed them.

Alaska Native people constitute an extremely diverse set of cultural groups. However, amidst their significant diversity, Alaska Native people also share a common legacy of colonial contact and oppression. Rapid social change, attended by oppressive colonial and disenfranchising intrusions, has resulted in both significant social and behavioral health problems as well as considerable impact on the individual sense of self of Alaska Native people. One of the more substantial impacts of enduring historical and contemporary oppressive intrusion upon the sense of self is associated with the process by which oppression can become internalized. With respect to Alaska Native people, any examination of internalized oppression must begin with the ongoing and lingering impacts of colonization. This experience includes historical and contemporary examples of marginalization, exclusion, cultural suppression, forced assimilation (e.g., removal of children to residential boarding schools), and outright extermination.

Coupled with this legacy are ongoing practices of racism and discrimination. These practices include demeaning portrayals of Alaska Native people in popular media and social discourse. They extend to contemporary social policies that have widespread impact on Alaska Native people's sense of connection to their land and their coinhabitants. The end result are numerous negative impacts upon identity—both at the level of the individual, and, equally important, as an element of understanding internalized oppression among Alaska Native people, on collective identity—as the historical process associated with colonization and its accompanying oppression has created patterns of persistent internalizations of this experience. These patterns are carried forward to the present day through contemporary expressions of exclusion and prejudice.

Oppression is generally understood as the domination of subordinate groups in society by a more powerful group, where power can be based politically, socially, economically, or culturally (Mullaly, 2010). Numerous in forms, oppression can range from microaggressions to genocide, and can span exploitation, marginalization, powerlessness, cultural imperialism, and violence. Oppression can also include various forms of discrimination that may occur at any one of three levels: the personal or individual, the cultural, and the institutional or structural level. These three levels of oppression directly influence each another; they are interconnected. The focus of this chapter is on internalized oppression, defined in one of its earliest definitions as the "turning upon ourselves, upon our families, and upon our own people the distress patterns that result from the racism and oppression of the majority society" (Lipsky, 1977, p. 6). The implications of this definition are that those who are oppressed identify with and, as a result, can even emulate actions of their oppressors (Fanon, 1963; Freire, 2007). Further, Padilla (2001) suggests these behaviors associated with internalized oppression occur outside of awareness, and can include acceptance of negative group stereotypes that feed notions of inferiority. However, we must always bear in mind the interconnection of internalized oppression at the individual level with oppression at other levels.

In this chapter, we open with a brief overview of the broad diversity of Alaska Native cultural groups. We then outline basic elements of historical and contemporary oppression of Alaska Native people, with attention to phenomenon variously described as historical trauma and as disruptions to cultural continuity. We describe common manifestations of internalized oppression, including behavioral health implications, identifying these manifestations as providing an important dimension in an understanding of factors in suicide and alcohol risk among Alaska Native people. However, we also focus equally upon the positive, noting the important role of personal and collective response to internalized oppression played out through numerous efforts constituting individual and community-level resilience processes. These efforts support cultural continuity and invigorate personal and collective identity, reclaim symbolic culture for healing, life narrative and meaning, and the future transmission of heritage. We then describe program efforts that address internalized oppression through these modalities as part of their work. These include efforts that advance family relations, oral traditions and storytelling, connection to the land, traditional healing practices, and spirituality and ceremony. They also involve work that fosters cultural identity, knowledge, and continuity, and, finally, collective and political agency. We conclude with suggestions for future research directions with Alaska Native people on internalized oppression.

It is important to note at this point that Alaska Native people are a resilient and determined people, having overcome numerous social, political, economic, and personal challenges over the course of recent history. Alaska Native people are also blessed with an optimistic outlook on life; as one of the authors notes, his own Native Elders always shared with him that "tomorrow will be a better day." Despite challenges and barriers that have devastated their families, communities, and cultures, Alaska Native people have overcome adversity and remain determined to make this world a better place for their grandchildren, and for the seventh generation. Thus, although this chapter will highlight the historical and contemporary oppression experienced by Alaska Natives, it will also present solutions developed from a strengths-based perspective. While this chapter deals with difficult topics, we need to learn from our Elders that Native people can overcome these challenges, remain optimistic and resilient, and continue to be proud as Native peoples.

A DEMOGRAPHIC PROFILE OF ALASKA NATIVE PEOPLE

The State of Alaska is home to over 700,000 people, of whom 15% identify as Alaska Native (U.S. Census Bureau State & County Quick Facts, 2011). The term Alaska Native is itself an ethnic gloss (Trimble, 1991), encompassing several quite distinct cultural linguistic groups. These groups are often divided into five major groupings (Langdon, 1989), including the Aleut/Alutiq (Southwestern Aleutians), Athabascan (Interior Indians), Inupiat (Northern Eskimos), Yup'ik (Southern Eskimos), and Tlingit/Haida/Tsimshian (Southeastern Coastal Indians). Each of these groups are culturally distinct through important differences in a myriad of cultural practices, including variation in complex kinship networks; developed subsistence hunting and gathering practices and technologies; and unique languages, belief systems, art, music, storytelling, spirituality, and dance traditions (Roderick, 2010). At the same time, Roderick also details a number of important commonalities among the Alaska Native cultural groups, by emphasizing their relationship and connection to the environment and to each other. The groups all honor both the land and waters upon which their lives depend, have respect for the fish and animals, and value community over individuality, sharing with each other over amassing personal possessions, and respecting and learning from their Elders.

Aleut/Alutiq

The Aleut/Alutiq are the smallest Alaska Native group. For centuries, they have made their living from the rich seas that surround their home on the Aleutian Islands, Alaska Peninsula, and Kodiak Archipelago. Their culture was heavily influenced by the Russian expansion beginning in the 18th century. The Russian Orthodox Church remains a major influence to this day, and Russian words now are part of the vocabulary of the indigenous language. The Aleuts/Alutiq are distinctive among the world's people for their remarkably successful maritime adaptations; they paddled hundreds of miles in skin-covered baidarkas (kayaks) to trade, visit, hunt, and stage daring raids on enemy villages. Food, clothing, shelter, heat, and tools came from animals and resources living in the ocean or along its shorelines. Ducks, otters, whales, and fish were among the animals used by the Aleuts, and they continue to be a main staple of their diets today.

Athabascan

The Athabascan people live in Interior Alaska in a region that stretches south of the Brooks Mountain Range all the way to the Kenai Peninsula. Traditionally they lived along five major river ways: the Yukon, the Tanana, the Susitna, the Kuskokwim, and the Copper Rivers. There are eleven Athabascan linguistic groups in Alaska, along with numerous local dialects; these linguistic groups are close relatives to the Navajo and Apache. The Athabascans were known as accomplished hunters who followed the herds of caribou and tracked moose for long distances. They also fished for salmon and other river fish, and gathered roots, berries, and other edible plants in order to survive in a harsh and often difficult environment. Their fringed and beaded skin garments were highly prized by other Natives. These garments, along with furs and other items, were often traded with neighboring Tlingit, Yup'ik Eskimo, and Inupiat peoples.

Inupiat

The Inupiat settled along the northern and northwest coast of Alaska, where they hunted, fished, and gathered the berries and roots that grew during the brief, cool summers. Today, they continue this tradition of hunting and gathering societies that subsist on the land and sea, while also being increasingly part of the cash economy, driven by the discovery of oil in their region. To the people of the North, the extreme climate and environment are not a barrier, but instead the gift of a natural realm for a wide variety of mammals, birds, and fish upon which they have historically depended for survival. Contingent on location and the time of the year, the Inupiat harvest walrus, whale, seal, polar bear, and caribou while also directing a complex economy based upon mineral extraction.

Yup'ik

The Yup'ik settled along the coast and river regions of southwest Alaska, where they constitute the largest and most linguistically intact of the Alaska Native cultural groups (Fienup-Riordan, 1995, 2003). Subsistence hunting, fishing, and gathering remain to this day a dominant economic activity. Historically, the Yup'ik people were very mobile, traveling with the migration of game and fish. Families came together and dispersed according to the seasons. Similar to the other Alaska Native cultural groups, Yup'ik Eskimo social culture and behavior were geared toward survival and social harmony among extended kinship groups (Langdon, 1989). Day-to-day life continues to be organized by the seasonal patterns of the plants and animals they hunt and gather, along with a pride in and protection of their cultural practices, including language and local control over their communities.

Tlingit/Haida/Tsimshian

The Tlingit/Haida/Tsimshian live in southeast Alaska amidst lush forests, mild climate, and abundant fish, game, and plants. This cultural linguistic group is one part of a larger Northwest Coastal culture extending south throughout the Pacific Northwest. The Tlingit, Haida, and Tsimshian possess important differences in language and a complex social system consisting of moieties, phratries, and clans—the Tlingit and Haida identify through membership in moieties, while the Tsimshian social systems are organized through phratries (Langdon, 1989). The people in this region have long depended on the ocean and rivers for their food and travel. The environment in southeast Alaska is a temperate rain forest. Their homes, totem poles, boats, daily utensils, storage and cooking boxes, transportation, celebration garments, and clothing were traditionally made from wood or wood products, and to this day represent a high form of art and craftsmanship.

Summary: A Strong and Present Diversity of Native Peoples

Alaska's diverse Native peoples retain a strong presence in the state, and continue to steadfastly practice their Native culture in the face of assimilationist and colonial pressures. In many regions, and especially in rural communities, Alaska Native people still hunt, fish, and gather the same plants and animals they have over the centuries, practicing their traditional culture as passed down to younger generations through the stories, teachings, and life example of their Elders. In some communities, subsistence foods make upwards of 50% of the diet; even for Alaska Native people living in the urban centers of Anchorage and Fairbanks, connections to relatives in rural Alaska supply them with Native foods. It is common to see traditional cultural celebrations and ceremonies practiced in communities, and many of the Elders make a concerted effort to pass on their knowledge of traditional activities such as hunting, gathering, survival skills, ivory and wood carving, beadwork, and kayak building to the younger generations.

HISTORICAL OPPRESSION

You can really get disconnected. That's what I realize when I heal. I was so disconnected . . . Just like I was not even me.

These adverse events began with the Russian expansion in the 1700s, intensified soon after Alaska was purchased from Russia by the United States in 1867, and continue to present day. In addition to missionaries and educators, waves of gold miners, whalers, and trappers arrived, together bringing disease and illness to which Alaska Native immune systems had never been exposed. These same diseases had earlier decimated American Indian populations in the lower 48 states; they similarly destroyed communities across Alaska. Within a short period of time, most of the population of Alaska Natives had perished from diseases that included diphtheria, influenza, cholera, smallpox, measles, mumps, chickenpox, and tuberculosis (Fortuine, 1992) in a cataclysm described by Napoleon (1991) as the "great death." As waves of death swept through communities, traditional healers had no experience with and were powerless to cure these new ailments. These devastating illnesses became the first leading cause of historical trauma in Alaska, followed next in rapid succession by government boarding schools and other concerted efforts to assimilate the Native people of Alaska.

Graves, Shavings, Rose, Saylor, and Smith (2007) notes how very little is written on the Alaska Native experience of boarding schools, despite the immense impact this institution has had upon communities. However, there does exist a larger body of literature on the experience among American Indian and Canadian First Nations individuals and communities (Brave Heart & DeBruyn, 1998), describing the impacts of a parallel occurrence to that experienced by Alaska Native people. For an entire generation, most youth were removed from their homes for Western schooling at distant missionary schools. These boarding schools were not in locations near their natal communities, so children were sent all over the United States, from Washington and Oregon to as far east as Pennsylvania and Tennessee, from where they were not permitted to return home for years. The prevailing attitude of the missionaries and educators who came to Alaska focused on work to Christianize and to "civilize" its indigenous inhabitants. Their coercive efforts to adopt White, Euro-American cultural ways entailed wholesale destruction of Alaska Native cultures through forced abandonment of their traditional lifestyle and practices in efforts that constituted cultural genocide. Their works included the obliteration of traditional spirituality, dancing, and extended family structures; children were even punished in boarding schools for speaking their Native language, which was forbidden (Graves et al., 2007). These efforts also included such things as cutting their hair, clothing them in proper Western attire, and forcing them to speak only English while at the same time punishing them for speaking their indigenous language. This was a time in Alaska Native history of great destruction in the social fabric and the communal nature of their societies, reshaping the lives and experiences of Alaska Native people in the course of a single generation. The boarding school experiences further alienated children from their families, communities, and culture, making it very difficult for them to return home after years away, unfamiliar any longer with their own culture and their home surroundings.

It is within this context of destroying culture that the boarding schools can be understood as the second leading cause of historical trauma among Alaska Natives. These boarding schools are still very recent history. The last of these schools closed in the 1970s. Their direct impact is still experienced as trauma felt by thousands of Alaska Natives who are entering Elder status, and who may or may not have healed from their experiences.

In addition to introducing disease and forced assimilation through the missionary and boarding school experience, Westerners also brought with them alcohol. The introduction of this new drug to the cultures of Alaska, at the same time of disease, illness, and cultural genocide, had further devastating effects on individuals, families, and communities that continue to the present day. Much as the Native peoples of Alaska did not have immunity to the new diseases, Alaska Native people had no previous exposure or experience with alcohol, all at a time that their cultural was quite literally under assault. The Alaska Federation of Natives Report, *A Call for Action* (1994), described the disruption to communities and family of alcohol abuse as "the latest epidemic" to hit Alaska Native people. Its introduction and impacts constitute a third source of historical trauma.

These experiences of pain, loss, and frustration are passed down from generation to generation and are experienced to this day in contemporary Alaska Native peoples' lives (Graves et al., 2007). Historical trauma is the "cumulative emotional and psychological wounding both over a life span and across generations, emanating from massive group catastrophes" (Brave Heart, 2003, p. 5), and has affected the psychology of Alaska Native individuals, families, communities, and cultures over time, across generations, to this day. Through colonialism and its attendant assimilative practices, Alaska Natives lost the right to speak their Native languages, sing their traditional songs, engage with their Elders, connect with nature, be actively engaged in their community, and continue practicing their traditional lifestyle and survival skills. The Alaska Native cultural system of joint perspectives, ideals, traditions, conduct, and artifacts were permanently destroyed (Graves et al., 2007) and these experiences have had detrimental effects on the overall health and well-being of Alaska Native peoples, manifesting themselves in unhealthy behaviors such as addiction, abuse, and mental health problems. Persistent and unresolved trauma arising from shared colonial experience has resulted in loss of cultural practices, an assault on individual and collective identities, and disruption of parent-child relationships. This experience is one key element in a constellation of social determinants of the chronic social and health problems many Alaska Natives are experiencing.

Other major historical events that have shaped Alaska Native peoples' lives include Alaska Statehood (1959), the 1964 earthquake and tidal wave, the 1971 Alaska Native Claims Settlement Act (ANCSA), the Molly Hootch Act to establish schools in rural villages in 1975, and the 1989 Exxon Valdez oil spill (Napoleon, 1996). The cultural devastation as a result of illness, depletion of natural foods, destruction of traditional religion, language, and Native roles all contribute to historical trauma and the social and health issues currently facing Alaska Native individuals and communities today (Graves et al., 2007). Substance abuse, suicide, family disruption, community and interpersonal violence, and mental health issues all have links to this destruction of culture (Fortuine, 1992; Freeman, 1965; Haycox, 2000; Napoleon, 1991; Weaver & Postman, 1988). Currently, Alaska Native families and communities continue to experience social and health disparities. Stress process approaches to historical trauma (Walls & Whitbeck, 2012) help us to understand both the historical antecedents of stress exposure and the subsequent emergence of distress and disorder, and the Alaska Native experience constitutes examples of how historical trauma persists to this day as contemporary oppression. This interaction of historical trauma with current trauma has been termed colonial response trauma (Evans-Campbell, 2008; Evans-Campbell & Walters, 2006).

CONTEMPORARY OPPRESSION

My dad drilled into us when we were growing up, he said, "Our culture, we're just so different and different language," he said, "Once you get out and meet the other cultures you're going to treat them the way you want to be treated." He taught us that, he drilled that into my head before I left. "So if you be treated badly, be silent about that and not fight back at it because it's going to make you just like them." I mean he trained us. It was very hard, I went through a lot.

Alaska Natives continue to experience many forms of oppression every day, from racial stereotypes to blatant discrimination. The landmass of the State of Alaska is predominantly rural, and many Alaska Natives originally lived in rural villages and migrated to urban centers, such as Anchorage or Fairbanks, where half the Alaska Native population currently resides. It is common to hear derogatory remarks made about Alaska Natives who visit or move from the villages, and this makes it especially challenging to adjust to new surroundings and to feel accepted. The experience of these new urban dwellers brings into sharp focus a broad array of issues that arise in contemporary Alaska Native experience to create oppressive circumstances. These contemporary forms of oppression surface through such acts as suppression of Native lifestyle preferences and belief systems, and discrimination in housing and employment opportunities.

Duran (2006) organizes these acts under the notion of institutional violence, which directly creates circumstances of maltreatment. For example, in June 2011, the Anchorage Daily News reported a story about one of their Alaska Native employees searching for housing. The employee found a two-bedroom apartment in Anchorage for her family after living with relatives. She received a positive response over the phone and made arrangements to move in, but the mood changed once the landlord met the family.

The property owner's concern was the family's connection to its home rural community, and because of this, the perceived possibility they might break the lease and leave the apartment. The property owner's questioning became more personal, with the landlord eventually rejecting the family for no other apparent reason beyond the family's connections to their village. The employee attempted to rationalize the entire situation in her mind:

> Did we just get discriminated against? Now, if you know me, I am not one to use this word "discriminate" lightly. I tried to rationalize the entire situation over and over, it was just then, I realized that we were discriminated against. ("Housing Discrimination Lives On in Anchorage," 2011)

There are many challenges to living in rural communities in Alaska. These include high costs of food and fuel, very limited employment opportunities, and distance and other access barriers to health care services. Relocation from rural villages to an urban center can be driven by a decision to seek higher education, find a job to support one's family, or the need to escape the extremely high costs of living that make it very difficult to raise a family in rural Alaska. Individuals who relocate not only face the challenge of adjusting to a new environment, they may be leaving behind family members and the home in which they have lived for many years, as well as crucial social support networks. Having to live through such experiences does not make this an easy, or wanted, transition. Denial of something as basic as housing puts incredible strain on the family, as well as the extended family that may be hosting them in the city until they find a home of their own. These experiences have a negative impact on the health and well-being of these individuals, resulting in poorer quality of life. The experiences can also link to and serve as reminders to past historical discrimination in housing and even public places endured by their ancestors, experienced as a continuity of these past practices to the current day.

Many Alaska Natives relocate to urban settings to receive health care services that are not readily available in the rural communities. Oftentimes they are faced with challenges associated with medical care, such as not being eligible for services because they have not lived in Anchorage for a long enough extended period, requiring them to wait months to receive care. These experiences exacerbate their current health status and make it especially challenging to engage in healthy behaviors, take care of their families, find housing, and find secure employment. Duran (2006) notes how this type of "dysfunction in healing institutions is perpetuated by hiring and retaining staff that are not culturally competent and through the implementation of strictly Western models of treatment, which maintain the process of colonization" (p. 25). Because health care systems are operated in this manner, Alaska Natives may continue to suffer from the illnesses that were the primary reason they relocated.

One of the consequences of families relocating from rural villages to urban settings, such as Anchorage, is the large influx of school-age children and a growing need for housing. There have been numerous instances of Alaska Native children not getting to school or missing school completely because their parents are struggling to find housing or they are living in a car. The cities in Alaska are faced with a growing population of Alaska Natives who require housing, health care, education, employment, and other necessities in order to survive. In an effort to address these concerns, programs and services are in development. In the mean time, these families continue to be the topic of headlines in newspaper articles and news stories, and viewed as a social problem, instead of casualties of a larger social problem. As more rural community members continue to relocate, the population will continue to rise and we need to educate our city leaders on how to address these issues in a culturally appropriate manner.

Meanwhile, Alaska newspapers and news articles also contain stories of racial slurs, discrimination, and other adverse events happening to Alaska Natives. The newspapers in Alaska published stories on discrimination and hate crimes against Alaska Natives typically perpetrated for no reason other than the victims are Alaska Native. One example from 2001 is the Anchorage paintball attacks against Alaska Natives. These were a series of premeditated and racially motivated drive-by paintball shootings targeted at Alaska Natives in downtown Anchorage in the evenings. All of the attacks were videotaped by surveillance cameras, which helped the police capture the individuals responsible (Porco, 2001). As result of these attacks, a new report was published by Gov. Tony Knowles's Commission on Tolerance, which listed nearly 100 recommendations for improving race relations (Verhovek, 2001), and condemned the incident as a hate crime. Despite this commission report and attempts as passing State legislation, incidences of discrimination against Alaska Natives continue to occur throughout the State.

In August 2009, the Anchorage Daily News published a story under the headline "Police arrest pair in assault posted online" (Halpin, 2009). In this event, two young adults assaulted and physically and mentally abused an Alaska Native man, accosting him, taunting him, mocking his rural Alaska speech, and kicking him and shoving him around. According to the police, the only apparent motive for the attack was that the man was an Alaska Native. Their actions were unprovoked; he was simply a Native man in the wrong place at the wrong time, the victim of another act of hate.

> The pair threatened the man, threw things at him and used racial slurs, police said. They pushed and kicked the man, police said. He didn't fight back, just asked to be left alone. (Halpin, 2009, p. 1)

Oppression impacts all ages. Children, adults, and Elders alike experience negative events with devastating effects. These experiences are exacerbated by commonly held stereotypes of Alaska Natives as drunks, living on welfare, or being lazy and greedy. The examples described here touch upon all five areas of oppressive experience as described by Young (1990): exploitation that leads to unequal distributions of wealth, marginalization, powerlessness, systemic violence, and cultural imperialism. However, Young noted that it was this final dimension, cultural imperialism, that feeds the channel through which oppression becomes internalized; through cultural imperialism, Alaska Native groups are both stereotyped and made invisible through the assertion of the now dominant immigrant group as being representative of the social norm. The dominant group's stereotypes of Alaska Natives as drunks, living on welfare, lazy, and greedy becomes internalized as group members engage in a search for an identity, and thus oppression becomes internalized as it functions as part of "the normal processes of everyday life" (Young, 1990, p. 41).

COMMON MANIFESTATIONS OF INTERNALIZED OPPRESSION

It was very tough for a while and then my children were in high school and that's when one of my sons got in the wrong crowd and before I know it he committed suicide 'cause I was going through a divorce at the same time. I didn't know how bad off he was, he was living with his dad. He used to come tell me how bad it was and . . . and I started thinking, "Oh boy," and then I blamed myself until an elder told me, "No, it wasn't your fault, he was almost 18 and he made up his own mind." She had to shake me to get me out of it. To not blame me or anybody else for what happened.

Internalized oppression is "pervasive, operating at the interpersonal and institutional levels simultaneously, its effects are cumulative, spanning generations, individuals, time, and place—encompassing much more than discrete acts" (Speight, 2007, pp. 126–127). Duran (2006) describes internalized oppression's insidious effects and its impact upon formal organizations and informal structures within oppressed communities, "Internalized oppression by some leaders is expressed in community and work environments in which administrative subordinates or community members are systematically abused" (p. 25). He portrays its impact upon formal and informal organizational structures as a type of institutional violence, and renders this as a violation that further alienates people from their communities and families, thereby isolating them from their own society, which further heightens their vulnerability to be more readily victimized by oppressive forces.

In the recent past, internalized oppression has emerged through some Alaska Native people's feelings of inferiority about being Native, and adoption of assimilationist attitudes, at times to the point of denying or even ridding oneself of one's cultural heritage. In the extreme, this resulted in episodes of discrimination, against other Natives perceived as being "too Native" and not Western enough, as well as intimidation about standing up against discrimination among Alaska Native people in general. Napoleon (1991) wrote eloquently and tragically about this history:

> Having silently abandoned their own beliefs, the survivors were reinforced in their decision not to talk about them by the missionaries who told them their old beliefs were evil and from the tuunraq, the devil. They learned to sternly tell their grandchildren not to ask them questions about the angalkuq, the old symbol of Yup'ik spiritualism, as if they were ashamed of them and of their old beliefs. They allowed the missionaries and the school teachers to inflict physical punishment on their children; for example, washing their children's mouths with soap if they spoke Yup'ik in school or church. Their children were forbidden, on pain of "serving in hell," from dancing or following the old ways. The parents—the survivors—allowed this. They did not protest. The children were, therefore, led to believe that the ways of their fathers and forefathers were of no value and were evil. (p. 13)

More recently, as overtly racist attitudes about Alaska Native people have become less acceptable within the dominant group in Alaska, internalized oppression has emerged in new, more subtle, and even paradoxical ways that continue to constitute a type of violation alienating people from community and family. Two examples of these more recent attitudinal, emotional, and behavioral expressions of internalized oppression among Alaska Native peoples include the experience of many Alaska Native college students, and the experience of the current generation of Alaska Native youth regarding Alaska Native regional corporation shareholder status. In the book *Brown Skin, White Minds* (2013), Jim LaBelle shared his personal experiences of being caught up in the colonization process as it occurred in Alaska. It began innocently as a child and became more pronounced as he grew up, but he shared a story from his childhood on how it began:

> After watching westerns on Friday nights, we would act out movie roles on the playgrounds and in the Boys dorm. Of course, no one wanted to play the "Indian." Indians were losers; menacing, violent savages. And they always lost . . . I and some others were almost always the white cavalry soldier or the cowboy. We enjoyed killing the Indian on the playground. When it came to a Western education, many of us were captive to the indoctrination. However, the quicker we were able to understand and speak

English proficiently we curried the favor of the teachers, minimized our own punishments, and used that against less able fellow students. Those of us who knew English going into boarding school had somewhat of a leg up . . . We were encouraged to rat on other students for infraction of the rules by matrons who were keen to enforce sanctions. As an 8- and 9-year-old, I became good at telling matrons that so and so was speaking his language . . . To the offender, however, they became subjected to the many punishments meted out for their offenses. Some of the punishments included being spanked by a cat-o'-nine tails, locked into dark closets, running through a strap line gauntlet, and wearing the infamous dunce-cap in front of the classroom . . . In many ways I became one of the kids willing to sell out fellow students for resorting back to speaking Aleut, Yupik, Inupiat, Athabascan, Suqpiaq, Tlinget, and Haida. By the time I was 12 and 13, I began to see my actions in a different light . . . In fact, I was beginning to question why I did not speak Inupiat and the never-ending and senseless beatings we were subjected to, sometimes at the whim of some employees . . . some of us still made fun of those students who struggled with the English language or could only speak Pidgin English. We would mimic their words and laugh at them. We merely added to the shame those students were already experiencing: ridicule and rounds of punishment from the adults there; be it matrons, teachers, health care workers, kitchen staff, and administrative staff.

There is as yet a paucity of internalized oppression literature on Alaska Natives and their first-hand experiences with oppression, therefore, many of the examples in this section will reflect the experiences of one of the authors. Up until quite recently, many Alaska Natives who pursued higher education have been told there is no place for them back in their home community, often by people from their own home community. This was not merely a result of a lack of jobs for people with college degrees in rural Alaska communities, though this certainly is a concern. It also reflects distrust of an individual who has succeeded in higher education, experienced by the recent graduate through overtones that the person had "sold out" on their cultural heritage in order to be successful, and is now removed and disconnected from that culture. The implication was that one had lost something of themselves culturally in order to succeed in higher education, and in some fundamental way, could no longer relate to those back home. This places the recent college graduate in an awkward situation—where to live and work after graduation? These individuals may have experienced instances of dismissal or even ridicule of their accomplishments in higher education, going as far as outright rejection and contempt directed toward the student, and especially toward those who may have attended college outside of Alaska. Often, community reaction can leave students feeling as if they have even betrayed their cultural roots, with some community members reacting negatively to their new vocabulary, way of speaking, and ideas, and sharing intimations with the student that they now act as if they are better than or too good for people back home. The authors have observed several college students who chose to leave Alaska for school encounter difficulties associated with maintaining connections to their home community in the face of these hostile reactions. This experience leaves the student with a heightened sense of vulnerability, lacking crucial supports from back home as they, at the same time, are having to adjust and learn to live in a Western higher education setting.

When it comes to acceptance by other Alaska Native people of one's Alaska Native heritage and identity, part of how this has come to be defined is through association and affiliation with one of the Alaska Native regional corporations. As an alternative to the reservation system elsewhere in the United States, the ANCSA (P.L. 92-203) authorized 200 Alaska Native villages to form 13 regional organizations to share profits related to land claims. These Alaska Native regional corporations hold funds from these claims and the businesses that these funds have spawned. Becoming a shareholder in an Alaska Native regional corporation is directly contingent on having at least ¼ blood quantum, along with being born prior to 1971, and possessing a family connection to a community within the region that the Alaska Native regional corporation is based. Alaska Native corporations and individuals are currently facing a new and unique challenge. Increasingly, parents want to enroll their children born after 1971 as shareholders with their respective Native corporation. However, existing corporation requirements currently do not provide for this and must be altered if they are to allow this. Contemporary Alaska Native youth may not always meet the ¼ blood quantum restriction, or may lack parents who are enrolled shareholders. In these cases, identity status can become contested, as defined by the regional corporation. Native corporations as organizations are changing how Alaska Native people identify as Alaska Native. The ways in which they do or do not redefine their eligibility requirements will inevitably lead to shifts in how each generation define themselves as Alaska Native, as well as what it means to be Alaska Native historically and today.

A second example of a common manifestation of internalized oppression includes the experience of not feeling "Native enough" because one did not grow up living in a rural village year round. This assumes Alaska Native people, to be authentic, must come from the rural village. There are additional pressures related to dialect; only when one speaks with a distinctive accent and uses specific words does one "speak like a Native." Finally, there is the situation of not looking Alaska Native; one may face ostracization because of having blond hair and blue eyes, and not physically look Alaska Native, notwithstanding family and blood heritage.

Despite efforts taken to eliminate oppression and discrimination through education and awareness, this can still occur despite a person's community heritage and background.

While remaining ever vigilant to its broad scope, and ever mindful of the numerous ongoing contemporary manifestations of oppressive experience for Alaska Native people described above, it is also critical to note that the most common manifestation of oppression experienced by Alaska Natives are the daily hassles originally described by Pierce (1974) as microaggressions. Microaggressions take the form of daily slights and insults. For an Alaska Native person, microaggressions are events directed at and experienced solely as a result of the person's membership in their ethnocultural group. Microaggressions can take many forms. They might include interactions such as being treated as if one is a threat to others, or, alternatively, as if one does not exist in a social encounter. Microaggressions, much like more overt forms of racisms and discrimination, constitute a source of stress. As such, they comprise a particularly troubling part of the acculturative stress (Sam & Berry, 2010) that Alaska Native people experience in their cultural contact with the dominant group. Alaska Natives share with other North American indigenous people a unique and unsettling dimension of acculturative contact. Their acculturative experience is forced and involuntary; it is part of the colonial arrangements that characterize their contact with an immigrant culture that has asserted dominance in their home. The actions of microaggressions, in combination with more overt forms of discrimination, create daily oppressive experience that serves as a potent reminder of and carries forward Alaska Native historical trauma to the current day, creating levels of stress, including traumatic stress, that are often at the root of physical and behavioral health problems.

MENTAL AND BEHAVIORAL HEALTH IMPLICATIONS OF INTERNALIZED OPPRESSION

So you both know my story from before—how I was a victim, and how when I start my healing journey I refused to be called a victim anymore because I overcame the feelings that I had before where I had no hope. I became a born-again and got a lot of help on my sobriety and started thinking that no longer will I be a victim and put myself in places where I would be a victim. And after a while I am not a victim anymore.

Akbar (1984) described the concept of self-destructive disorder as representing any type of behavior destructive to the functioning and survival of the individual and the community. Brave Heart and DeBruyn (1998) reported that drug and alcohol abuse and suicide were, in part, due to internalized oppression. Similarly, alcohol and drug abuse allows for the escape from the painful realities of oppression, regardless of the harm caused by their use (Akbar, 1984). Domestic violence (Brave Heart & DeBruyn, 1998) and sexual violence (Poupart, 2003) are also associated with this outward expression of internalized oppression.

Based on this conceptualization, self-destructive behavior is both a component of internalized oppression as well as one of its outcomes. Carter (2007) provides a comprehensive integration of the literature on racism and oppression, stress, and traumatic stress, describing how trauma results from racist, oppressive events. Speight (2007) further extends this thinking on oppression-induced trauma and self-destructive behavior, by accounting for its internalization, with effects that are cumulative across generations, and that result in the acceptance by marginalized groups "of the negative societal beliefs and stereotypes about themselves" (Williams and Williams-Morris, 2000, p. 225).

This chapter has highlighted the historical and contemporary forms of oppression faced by Alaska Native peoples, and how this oppression has come to be internalized. Woods, Zuniga, and David (2011) found associative links of historical trauma with lessened collective self-esteem. Over the years, shame and guilt have plagued Alaska Native peoples related to their inability to heal from past and ongoing experience, and equally importantly, inability of individuals to assist other Native people in their own healing process. The lasting effects of these circumstances have contributed to high levels of trauma disorders, substance abuse, and suicide. Despite numerous strengths in their culture and communities, suicide and alcohol use disorder rates are extremely high among Alaska Native people, and, in particular, among youth and in many rural communities across the state (Allen, Levintova, & Mohatt, 2011).

The tragedy of suicide provides a means for understanding the role of internalized oppression through many of the self-destructive behaviors plaguing Alaska Native people. Chandler and LaLonde (1998), in their work in northern Canada, examined self-continuity and its role as a protective factor against suicide. They note the historical experiences of Native communities, and especially attendant colonial intrusions, have deeply disrupted social and cultural continuity, all as a result of outsiders' efforts to "civilize" Native people. The resulting self-discontinuity represents profound disruptions in the understanding of self, along with one's place in the collective and their community. The authors conclude that focusing attention on the connection between the personal and the cultural change is critical to better understanding of the challenges facing Native communities, and to working toward ameliorating these social issues, including the calamity of suicide plaguing these communities.

On the community level, Chandler and Proulx (2006) quantified a variety of indicators, including linguistic intactness and local control over community affairs. They labeled this composite community-level variable as cultural continuity. Across several First Nations Canadian communities, they found an association between cultural continuity and lower rates of suicide. The implication is Native communities that are able to preserve their cultural past and additionally, able to exert local control over their present and future lives through enhanced self-determination, have significantly lower suicide rates. In order to successfully address and overcome the challenges facing Native communities resulting from trauma, oppression, and internalized oppression, there is a need to develop and integrate the cultural practices that provide for a healthy and stable self-continuity. The need for cultural practices giving members a sense of purpose today and in the future becomes apparent. Equally apparent is the role of these efforts to enhance culture in daily life in combating internalized oppression in order to treat and prevent these behavioral health concerns.

CLINICAL AND COMMUNITY PROGRAMS FOR INTERNALIZED OPPRESSION

> *Yes, my spirituality is my highest point in life. That was the center with our life with my grandparents; their singing and drumming and teaching us; the spiritual food we eat: the seal oil and the frozen fish and all that with them, and then they drum and dance for us. That was so spiritual so I never forget them; they see how much they've done for us. Without a mother they all stepped in.*
>
> *We all have that spiritual connection to the land, to the water, to everything we survived by when we were growing up. Us Elders especially and even the younger generation have a touch of that. They should all have that spirituality in them.*

The past few years have witnessed heightened awareness of historical trauma and oppression among tribal communities across the country, including Alaska. The work that still needs to be done in our communities includes healing from these issues, past and present, as discussed in this chapter. Duran (2006) states that knowledge of the traumas and how they affect the day-to-day life of community members still needs to reach the roots of the community and its leadership. He outlines three steps to engage in community healing from oppression and trauma: (1) raising awareness; (2) devising a plan to continue the healing process; and (3) thoroughly evaluating tribal government administrative systems (pp. 117–118). The primary goal of this process is to achieve some type of positive change, so that the community and its individuals see how not all change is negative. It is also important to note, "Through the healing of individuals, the groundwork can be laid for the greater healing of the community" (p. 123). Healing on a community level takes a long-term commitment and patience, but it also must come from the community itself, starting on the level of its individual members, who then can contribute to collective healing. Several community programs have recently emerged that seek to address the types of oppressive internalizations we have described above in this way; they are representative of the positives and the strengths of Alaska Native communities as they confront internalized oppression and its impacts by promoting individual healing in order to collectively foster community healing and community-level resilience capacities.

Family Wellness Warriors

Family Wellness Warriors (2007), a program of the Southcentral Foundation in Alaska, is a statewide education and training program designed by the Alaska Native people to address domestic violence, child sexual abuse, and child neglect. It provides individuals and communities with culturally appropriate tools, skills, and strategies to prevent domestic violence and child maltreatment. The program trains and works with natural helpers in the community. Training provides an experiential component, modeling how helpers can create an environment for people to identify harmful patterns and gain tools for safe and healthy relationships.

Elders in Training

The University of Alaska Fairbanks, Rural Behavioral Health Training Academy, has developed a statewide program that recruits and mentors individuals to become Elders in their respective communities. This peer-based program works to recruit and train individuals who have the desire to teach and lead their community but are not sure of how to begin their journey. This program provides an opportunity for those wishing to learn how to be effective leaders to share experiences, stories, and lessons as well as serve as a network and support system. This program currently has approximately 20 Elders trained and growing, who are now working in their communities as Elders and leaders to promote health and well-being of their peoples.

Alaska Native Dialogues on Racial Equity

The Alaska Native Policy Center of First Alaskans Institute launched the Alaska Native Dialogues on Racial Equity (ANDORE). Funded by the W. K. Kellogg Foundation, ANDORE seeks to reset the dialogue on race in Alaska by bringing people together to challenge current perceptions. It seeks to raise the level of awareness around race and racism, identify instances of institutional and systemic racism, and advance policy solutions toward racial equity. ANDORE is a statewide project based on indigenous principles and values. It seeks to intentionally reshape the dialogue on racism in Alaska through three distinct work groups. As part of ANDORE, 17 individuals from diverse backgrounds will form the Host Group to host community conversations throughout the state on racism. These conversations, along with planned Indigenized Focus Groups held with specific demographics to capture their perspectives, hold clear potential to empower dialogue participants by raising collective awareness about historical and contemporary racism, including elements of internalized oppression, and by normalizing peoples' experiences with racism. A Visionary Group of 11 culture bearers and leaders will advise the project, while a broad Partnership Circle will form a coalition of projects and organizations that create memorandums of understanding with First Alaskans Institute in pursuit of shared goals and activities on race and racism. By elevating stories and experiences through community conversations, ANDORE seeks to meaningfully engage in communities in conversation across Alaska on race, racism, and racial equity, in order to move people into a place of understanding, healing, and growth (First Alaskans Institute, 2012).

Qungasvik/Elluam Tungiinun Project

Elluam Tungiinun "toward wellness" is a cultural program creating contexts for youth to experience *ellangneq*, or "understanding" (Allen, Mohatt, Fok, Henry, & People Awakening Team, 2009; Allen et al., 2011). It was developed by a local community planning group to build 13 protective factors from suicide and alcohol abuse risk identified through earlier research using a community-based participatory research framework (Allen et al., 2006). Community members, under the supervision of their Elders, deliver the program, which provides youth skills to do important traditional cultural activities including subsistence, survival, and arts skills. These provide protective experiences and training in the cultural values that underlie the activities. *Qasgiq*, or "men's community house," was a structure for sweatbaths, dances, and feasts (Fienup-Riordan, 1995); here, youth receive teachings or hear stories from their Elders (Fienup-Riordan, 2003).

By symbolically recreating this sacred center for learning, teachings are shared and youth learn roles and respectful behavior. As young people move toward wellness in the community, they move closer to greater interconnection in relation to their family, community, and to the land and its animals.

Talking Circles

Talking circles represent a practice many but not all Alaska Native people view as an indigenous practice adapted from outside Alaska. In the talking circle (Morgan & Freeman, 2009) all are in an equal position. The circle calls each person's spirit helpers to assist them to express and release concerns along with negative thoughts and emotions, in order to provide cleansing. The leader of the circle, sometimes an elder, is a person in a position of respect in the community, who can facilitate listening in the circle with respect to experiencing the feelings of others without interruption. The goal of the circle is the development of the emotional, mental, and spiritual strengths in the person; it has become a component of many treatment approaches for alcoholism, domestic violence, and other concerns, including the manifestations of internalized oppression with Alaska Native people.

HOPE FOR THE FUTURE

They're the ones that guided me. They're all Elders that I looked up to that prepared me for who I was going to be. Just give me little hints here and there and I carry it with me. I don't forget what they tell me. That was the way we were taught growing up and still carrying on in my adult life.

Kirmayer, Dandeneau, Marshall, Phillips, and Williamson (2011) and Kirmayer, Sehdev, Whitely, Dandeneau, and Issac (2009) explore structural and functional elements of community resilience. The concept of community resilience provides an important framework for research and future programs that aim to heal individuals from internalized oppression. It provides ways of thinking about and developing efforts that ultimately work on the level of the community to foster collective healing, health, and well-being. For example, the structures of expressive metaphor in ritual and story-telling, and activities such as ceremonies, describe structures of community resilience that counter internalized oppression by promoting cultural pride, connectedness, and collective self-esteem (Woods, Zuniga, & David, 2011), and, in addition, can foster self-regulation through alignment with larger mythical structures. Re-telling traumatic histories can instead emphasize the heroic in collective identity, and reclaim symbolic culture for healing. Other research (Chandler & LaLonde, 2009) suggests linkages between cultural continuity, enculturation, community control, and action as functional community resilience processes that not only foster well-being, but may also prevent suicide and a host of self-destructive disorders associated with internalized oppression. The multilevel factors that community resilience perspectives allow us to consider as healing of internalized oppression include family relations, oral traditions and storytelling, connection to the land, traditional healing practices, and spirituality and ceremony. Such efforts involve and promote cultural identity, knowledge, and continuity, and through this, collective and political agency.

Despite ongoing oppression, Alaska Native peoples have remained resilient. They continue to take control of their health and well-being, and to heal. Alaska Native Elders have witnessed tremendous changes, experiencing a lifetime of oppression and discrimination, yet they have aged well, and have become formidable leaders and role models in their families and communities. As the State of Alaska becomes more diverse in both its rural and urban communities, we will need to seek the wisdom and guidance of Alaska Native Elders and tribal leaders to bring these issues to the forefront and address them in a culturally sensitive manner.

Alaska Native people have come out of a tumultuous history filled with adverse events that include epidemics, boarding schools, the introduction of alcohol, and ongoing racial discrimination. Despite these events, they remain optimistic about their future. The Elders and parents all want the best future for their children, and work to do what they can to ensure this through their thoughts, actions, and leadership. The future of Alaska rests on the shoulders of its youth; we need to ensure all youth have a brighter future free of oppression and discrimination. This can only be done through education and awareness about the role of oppression in our society, including its internalized forms. This is the first step in community and societal change that will allow us to "go through the problem."

REFERENCES

Akbar, N. (1984). *Chains and images of psychological slavery.* Jersey City, NJ: New Mind Productions.

Alaska Federation of Natives. (1994). *A call to action: Taking community responsibility.* Anchorage, AK.

Allen, J., Levintova, M., & Mohatt, G. V. (2011). Suicide and alcohol related disorders in the U.S. Arctic: Boosting research to address a primary determinant of circumpolar health disparities. *International Journal of Circumpolar Health, 70*, 473–487.

Allen, J., Mohatt, G. V., Rasmus, S. M., Hazel, K., Thomas, L., & Lindley, S. (2006). The tools to understand: Community as co-researcher on culture specific protective factors for Alaska Natives. *Journal of Prevention and Intervention in the Community, 32*(1/2), 41–64.

Allen, J., Mohatt, G. V., Fok, C. C. T., Henry, D., & People Awakening Team. (2009). Suicide prevention as a community development process: Understanding circumpolar youth suicide prevention through community level outcomes. *International Journal of Circumpolar Health, 68*, 274–291.

Allen, J., Mohatt, G. V., Rasmus, S. M., Two Dogs, R., Ford, T., Iron Cloud Two Dogs, E., . . . People Awakening Team. (2011). Cultural interventions for American Indian and Alaska native youth: The *Elluam Tungiinun* and *Nagi Kicopi* programs. In P. Spicer, P. Farrell, M. Sarche, & H. E. Fitzgerald (Eds.), *Child psychology and mental health: Cultural and ethno-racial perspectives, American Indian child psychology and mental health, Volume 2: Prevention and treatment.* New York, NY: Praeger Publishers.

Brave Heart, M. (2003). The historical trauma response among natives and its relationship with substance abuse: A Lakota illustration. *Journal of Psychoactive Drugs, 35*, 7–13.

Braveheart, M. Y. H., & DeBruyn, L. M. (1998). The American Indian holocaust: Healing historical unresolved grief. *American Indian and Alaska Native Mental Health Research, 8*(2), 60–82. doi:10.5820/aian.0802.1998.60

Carter, R. T. (2007). Racism and psychological and emotional injury: Recognizing and assessing race-based traumatic stress. *The Counseling Psychologist, 35*, 13–105.

Chandler, M., & Proulx, T. (2006). Changing selves in a changing world: Youth suicide on the fault-lines of colliding cultures. *Archives of Suicide Research, 10*, 125–140.

Chandler, M. J., & Lalonde, C. E. (1998). Cultural continuity as a hedge against suicide in Canada's first nations. *Transcultural Psychiatry, 35*(2), 221–230.

Chandler, M. J., & Lalonde, C. E. (2009). Cultural continuity as a moderator of suicide risk among Canada's first nations. In L. Kirmayer & G. Valaskakis (Eds.), *The mental health of Canadian aboriginal peoples: Transformations, identity and community* (pp. 221–248). Vancouver, BC: University of British Columbia Press.

Duran, E. (2006). *Healing the soul wound: Counseling with American Indians and other Native Peoples.* New York, NY: Teachers College Press.

Evans-Campbell, T. (2008). Historical trauma in American Indian/Native Alaska communities: A multilevel framework for exploring impacts on individuals, families, and communities. *Journal of Interpersonal Violence, 23*(3), 316–338.

Evans-Campbell, T., & Walters, K. (2006). Indigenist practice competencies in child welfare practice: A decolonization framework to address family violence and substance abuse among First Nations peoples. In R. Fong, R. McRoy, & C. Ortiz Hendricks (Eds.), *Intersecting child welfare substance abuse, and family violence: Culturally competent approaches* (pp. 266–290). Washington, DC: CSWE Press.

Family Wellness Warriors Initiative. (2007). Retrieved from http://www .fwwi.org/

Fanon, F. (1963). *The wretched of the earth*. New York, NY: Grove Press.

Fortuine, R. (1992). *Chills and fever: Health and disease in the early history of Alaska*. Fairbanks, AK: University of Alaska Press.

Freire, P. (2007). *Pedagogy of the oppressed* (3rd ed.). New York, NY: Continuum.

Freeman, D. (1965). Anthropology, psychiatry, and the doctrine of cultural relativism. *Man, 65,* 65–67.

Fienup-Riordan, A. (1995). *Boundaries and passages: Rule and ritual in Yup'ik Eskimo oral tradition*. Norman: University of Oklahoma Press.

Fienup-Riordan, A. (Ed.). (2003). *Quilrat qanemcit-llu kinguvarcimalriit—Stories for future generations: The oratory of Yup'ik Eskimo Elder Paul John*. Bethel, AK: Calista Elders Council in Association with University of Washington Press, Seattle.

First Alaskans Institute. (2012). *Alaska Native Dialogues on Racial Equity*. Retrieved from http://www.firstalaskans.org/index.cfm?section=Alaska-Native-Policy-Center&page=Racial-Equity

Graves, K. G., Shavings, L., Rose, C., Saylor, A., & Smith, S. L. (2007). *Boarding school project: Mental health outcome*. Anchorage, AK: National Resource Center for American Indian, Alaska Native, and Native Hawaiian Elders.

Halpin, J. (2009, August 13). Police arrest pair in assault posted online. *Anchorage Daily News*, p. 1. Retrieved from www.adn.com

Haycox, S. (2000). *A resource colony. Anchorage daily news*. Anchorage, AK: K4.

Housing discrimination lives on in Anchorage. (2011, June 1). *Anchorage Daily News*, p. 1. Retrieved from www.adn.com

Kirmayer, L. J., Dandeneau, S., Marshall, E., Phillips, M. K., & Williamson, K. J. (2011). Rethinking resilience from Indigenous perspectives. *Canadian Journal of Psychiatry-Revue Canadienne De Psychiatrie, 56*(2), 84–91.

Kirmayer, L. J., Sehdev, M., Whitely, R., Dandeneau, S. E., & Issac, C. (2009). Community resilience: Models, metaphors and measures. *Journal of Aboriginal Health, 5*(1), 62–117.

LaBelle, J. W. (2013). As indigenous children. In E. J. R. David (Ed.), *Brown skin, White minds: Filipino -/ American postcolonial psychology (with commentaries)* (pp. 267–272). Charlotte, North Carolina: Information Age Publishing.

Langdon, S. J. (1989). *The Native people of Alaska*. Anchorage, AK: Greatland Graphics.

Lipsky, S. (1977). Internalized oppression. *Black Re-Emergence, 2,* 5–10.

Morgan, R., & Freeman, L. (2009). The healing of our people: Substance abuse and historical trauma. *Substance Use & Misuse, 44,* 84–98.

Mullaly, B. (2010). *Challenging oppression and confronting privilege*. Ontario, Canada: Oxford University Press.

Napoleon, H. (1996). *Yuuyaraq: The way of the human being*. Fairbanks, AK: Alaska Native Knowledge Network.

Padilla, L. M. (2001). "But *you're* not a dirty Mexican": Internalized oppression, Latinos and law. *Texas Hispanic Journal of Law & Policy, 7,* 59–113.

Pierce, C. (1974). Psychiatric problems of the Black minority. In S. Arieti (Ed.), *American handbook of psychiatry* (pp. 512–523). New York, NY: Basic Books.

Porco, P. (2001, February 24). 3 teens hunted Natives with paintball guns, police say. *Anchorage Daily News:* p. A1.

Poupart, L. M. (2003). The familiar face of genocide: Internalized oppression among American Indians. *Hypatia, 18*(2), 86–100. doi:10.1111/j.1527-2001.2003.tb00803.x

Roderick, L. (2010). *Alaska native cultures and issues: Responses to frequently asked questions.* Fairbanks, AK: University of Alaska Press.

Sam, D. L., & Berry, J. W. (2010). Acculturation: When individuals and groups of different cultural backgrounds meet. *Perspectives on Psychological Science, 5,* 472–481. doi:10.1177/1745691610373075

Speight, S. L. (2007). Internalized racism: One more piece of the puzzle. *The Counseling Psychologist, 35*(1), 126–134. doi:10.1177/0011000006295119

Trimble, J. E. (1991). Ethnic specification, validation prospects, and the future of drug abuse research. *International Journal of the Addictions, 25,* 149–169.

U.S. Census Bureau. (2011). *State and County Quick Facts.* Data derived from Population Estimates, American Community Survey. Retrieved from http://quickfacts.census.gov/qfd/states/02000.html

Verhovek, S. H. (2001, December 30). Alaska panel has suggestions for improving race relations. *The New York Times,* p. 1A–14.

Walls, M. L., & Whitbeck, L. B. (2012). Advantages of stress process approaches for measuring historical trauma. *American Journal of Drug and Alcohol Abuse, 38*(5), 416–420.

Weaver, H., & Postman, D. (1988). A people in peril. *Anchorage Daily News.* Anchorage, AK: pp. A1–A12, B4. Retrieved from www.adn.com

Williams, D. R., & Williams-Morris, R. (2000). Racism and mental health: The African American experience. *Ethnicity & Health, 5*(3/4), 243–268.

Woods, T. M., Zuniga, R., & David, E. J. R. (2011). A preliminary report on the relationships between collective self-esteem, historical trauma, and mental health among Alaska Native peoples. *Journal of Indigenous Research, 1*(2), Article 1. Retrieved from http://digitalcommons.usu.edu/kicjir/vol1/iss2/1

Young, I. M. (1990). *Justice and the politics of difference.* Princeton, NJ: Princeton University Press.

Internalized Oppression Among Pacific Island Peoples

Michael Salzman and Poka Laenui

No one can make you feel inferior without your consent.
—*Eleanor Roosevelt*

Eleanor Roosevelt's statement is an appreciation of Mana and Ho'omana, (internal or innate power, to worship). The central idea in traditional Hawaiian practice was to recognize the internal strength or power within everything and person. We could create gods and spiritual entities from rocks, trees, and even words, by our knowledge of the ability to transfer or feed these objects mana. This transfer was through "worship" or praying to, or some form of "feeding" that entity. Christians taught us to leave behind those ways; that Jehovah was all that needed to be prayed to. Yet, they also opened the door for a foreign military, economy, language, and political systems, overthrew ours, and have since forced upon us a new form of worship not only to their God, but to their institutions and philosophy, while downgrading ours.
—*Poka Laenui*

The Oxford Encyclopedic English Dictionary (Pearsall & Trumble, 1995) defines *oppression* as "prolonged harsh or cruel treatment or control; mental distress" and *oppress* as to "keep in subservience by coercion; to govern or treat harshly or with cruel injustice and to weigh down with cares or unhappiness" (p. 1019). Oppression may take many forms, and it may be the result of external and/or internal forces. *Internalized oppression* may be the more insidious of the two because we do it to ourselves. Internalized oppression is not the cause of mistreatment; it is a result of mistreatment. Internalized oppression would not exist without the real external oppression that is imposed on the less powerful by the more powerful. It includes the internalized negative self-evaluations and dehumanizations believed to be true by peoples suffering unjust and imposed social conditions such as racism, colonialism, and conquest. It is when members of oppressed groups internalize or come to believe the oppressive and dehumanizing messages they have received from oppressors and the oppressive institutions they control. Internalized oppression influences the thoughts, behaviors, and attitudes toward self, members of one's defined group, and the dominant group. It has consequences for behavioral and mental health (e.g., David, 2008). The phenomenon of internalized oppression and its many consequences are highly salient in the lived realities of Pacific Peoples. Thus, this chapter will focus on the vast Pacific region, its peoples and their similar histories of trauma and colonization, with a particular emphasis on Native Hawaiians primarily because they are the largest Pacific Islander group in the United States and the community voice co-author—Poka Laenui (PL)—is a well-respected Hawaiian leader who is well-grounded and highly knowledgeable about his indigenous community. As such, PL's thoughts and experiences—such as the opening narrative above—will be presented throughout the chapter as we describe the experiences of resistance, rejection, and the paths taken and being taken for psychological and political decolonization and recovery among Pacific Island Peoples.

DEMOGRAPHIC PROFILE

The Pacific Ocean is the largest geographical feature on earth. It has a width of more than 16,000 kilometers, and a distance from the Bering Strait to Antarctica is more than 14,000 kilometers. It contains approximately 25,000 islands that exhibit diverse physical characteristics ranging from high volcanic islands and continental islands to low atolls and raised atolls. The peoples inhabiting this vast area include many who are identified as indigenous, such as Australian Aboriginals (population 548,370; 2011 Australian census), Chamorros of Guam (population 62,135 Native and part Chamorro, or 43% of the population living in Guam; Rapadas, Balajadia, & Rubinstein, 2005), Fijians, (population 880,000; Central Intelligence World Fact Book, 2005), Marshallese (population 57,738; Central Intelligence World Fact Book, 2005), peoples of the Federated States of Micronesia (population 107,000; Federated States of Micronesia, 2010), and Native Hawaiians (population of 401,168 in the United States and 282,667 full or part Native Hawaiians living in the State of Hawai'i; U.S. Census Bureau, 2000). Although this paper indicates many commonalties in the experience of Pacific island peoples such as ocean ecologies and colonization, and although this paper focuses on the experience of Native Hawaiians, one cannot overemphasize that the region is inhabited by numerous Pacific island peoples (e.g., Samoans, Tongans, Maoris, Chukese) who share similarities but also differ in their historical experience and cultures (Ogan, 2005).

It is clear that there is substantial diversity among Pacific Peoples, however, there is considerable similarity in their experiences resulting from contact with Europeans and subsequent colonization attempts. The indigenous peoples that have historically populated this vast region produced cultures that evolved over many centuries. These cultures represent adaptations to a wide range of ecological realities and therefore manifested considerable variability (Howe, Kiste, & Lal, 1994). People developed cultures in response to both ecological demands and psychological necessities. The cultures developed over many centuries by the indigenous peoples of the region placed the individual in a profound interrelationship with nature and the universe. The Australian aboriginal peoples, for example, developed a culture in a harsh and barren country where they established ". . . a perfectly valid way of life that had kept the race alive through unknown centuries of time" (Moorehead, 1966, p. 133). PL's thoughts below, as he refers to the Kumulipo creation chant (Johnson, 1981) speaks to Pacific Peoples' strong connection with their indigenous environment:

The Hawaiian creation chant, the Kumulipo, shares a pattern similar to other Polynesian chants, describing not only traditional Hawaiian perspectives on the environment but a relationship to that environment and the tracing of the environmental elements as our ancestors. The Kumulipo illustrates the deep and enduring differences between Western and traditional Hawaiian ways of relating to and respecting the ocean. More than just an "environment" or a "resource," the ocean is a living being—a home for other living beings and of a living god. The first division of the Kumulipo corresponds with the text of the Wharewananga belonging to the east coast of New Zealand as well as to creation chants found in Tahiti, the Marquesas, and the Tuamotus (Beckwith, 1970, pp. 311–312). The full chant is over 2,000 lines. British explorer Captain James Cooke exclaimed, when he arrived in Hawai'i, that these (Pacific) people formed the largest nation in the world stretching across the vast Pacific he had just visited. In doing so, he acknowledged that in spite of the vastness of the distance among the people, they spoke a language and followed cultural patterns such that he recognized the Polynesians as a single nation.

HISTORICAL OPPRESSION AND ITS EFFECTS

The Pacific Island and Oceanic peoples have experienced similar histories of contact with the West—colonization, depopulation, and its consequences. Smith (2012) asserts that imperialism, its expression through colonialism and its exploitation and subjugation of Native populations frame the indigenous experience in the Pacific. The timeline below presents a brief account of the history of colonization in Hawai'i, which exemplifies the process and its consequences.

Indeed, as Howe et al. (1994) stated, "Everywhere, contact with Europeans had deleterious consequences for Pacific Islanders" (p. 21). Numerous observers and scholars (e.g., Bushnell, 1993; Butlin, 1983; Farnsworth, 1997; Harris, 1990; Stannard, 1989) have reported on the effects of this contact. Initial contact seemed to be invariably followed by the introduction of deadly and horrifying diseases to which islanders had no natural immunity. Although there is some variation of experience, the indigenous peoples of the Pacific have been affected by one or another form of colonialism (Ogan, 2005) and waves of epidemics that decimated and demoralized the population. For example, an epidemic of measles in Fiji in 1875 reduced the population by more than 25%. On Pohnpei, a similar tragedy killed 50% of the population, and in the New Hebrides the indigenous population was almost wiped out (Val, 1994). It was estimated that in 1788 there were about 1,500 aborigines around Sydney. Darwin, in 1836, found only a few hundred remaining, still trying to live their tribal lives among the colonists' farms on the outskirts of the settlement but there were no animals left to hunt. In a few years they too had disappeared and all that was left were a few beggars in the Sydney streets. Darwin wrote, "Wherever the European has trod, death seems to pursue the aboriginal. We may look to the wide extent of the Americas, Polynesia, The Cape of Good Hope and Australia, and we find the same result" (Moorehead, 1966, p. 169).

The example of Micronesia is illustrative of the processes associated with colonization. According to the Director of the Center for Pacific Island Studies at the University of Hawai'i, "violence, domination, exploitation, and racism would all characterize to varying degrees the tenures of each metropolitan power that governed Micronesia at different times between 1886 and the outbreak of World War II" (Hanlon, 1994, p. 93).

Colonization and its consequences has been the subject of much investigation (Fanon, 1968; Memmi, 1965). Fanon, a psychiatrist who studied the processes and effects of both colonization and decolonization, described colonialism as a form of violence, as he observed that, "When the Native is confronted with the colonial order of things he finds he is in a state of permanent tension. The settler's world is a hostile world which spurns the Native" (p. 52). McCubbin and Marsella (2009) note that upon

An Account of the History of Colonization in Hawai'i

500–1000	Estimated migration of the ancestors of Native Hawaiians from Marquesas Islands, Tahiti, and other South Pacific islands
1100	Communal society and culture develops. Kapu system established
1778	Arrival of Captain James Cook Population estimate 400,000–800,000 Native Hawaiians
1802	First Sugar Production starts on Lana'i
1802	First Sugar Production starts on Lana'i
1804	Unknown epidemic diseases decimates Native population. Within 100 years of Cook's arrival it is estimated that less than 10% of the Native Hawaiians remained
1810	Kamehameha "the Great" unifies the Hawaiian Islands. The monarchy is established
1819	Death of Kamehameha and Abolishment of Kapu System
1820	Protestant Missionaries arrive
1823	First Chinese arrive to work on plantations
1826	Missionaries standardizes the Hawaiian language
1838	Mumps epidemic
1848	Great Mahele dispossessing the Hawaiian people of their lands and allows foreigners to own land. Deadly measles epidemic
1852	Chinese migration. Second group
1853	Smallpox epidemic further decimates Hawaiian population
1868	Japanese migration
1878–1886	Portuguese migration
1885	Primary Japanese immigration begins
1887	Bayonet Treaty forced upon and signed by Kalukaua. Kamehemeha Schools are established. United States acquires Pearl Harbor
1893	Overthrow of the Hawaiian monarchy. Native Hawaiian population estimate is 40,000
1895	"Republic of Hawai'i" established by White businessman support by U.S. military. Opposed by President Cleveland, supported by President McKinley
1896	English becomes the official language of Hawai'i
1898	Annexation of Hawai'i to United States
1900	Organic Act & Puerto Rican Migration: Provided for a government for the territory of Hawai'i—provided tariff protection for planters—outlawed penal labor contracts-forbidding indentured labor-pivotal moment in Hawai'i's labor history. Okinawan migration begins, Chinese Exclusion Act

(continued)

An Account of the History of Colonization in Hawai'i (*continued*)

1903	Korean immigration begins
1905	Law is passed forbidding use of Hawaiian language in schools
1906	Filipinos recruited to work on plantations
1907	Gentlemen's Agreement between the United States and Japan halted migration of Japanese Labor. The Sugar industry then turned to the Philippines, a U.S. Colony, for migrant labor. From 1907 to 1924, 57,675 Filipinos arrived in Hawai'i
1909	Major Strike of Japanese sugar workers
1911	Pearl Harbor opens as U.S. Naval Base
1920	Dual union (Japanese and Filipino unions) strike—initial interracial labor cooperation-workers defeated
1924	Strike by only Filipino workers
1927	First Waikiki hotel opens
1931	Massie Case: five "local" men accused of kidnapping and rape of "Haole" woman. Mistrial and defendants freed. Husband kills one and "gets away with murder" of Hawaiiaan defendant. First articulation of "local" people and culture by identifying diverse "local" non-White defendants (as opposed to Haole/Military)
1936	Passenger airline service begins
1937	General Strike of Filipino sugar workers led by Vibora Luviminda was last racial strike a precursor to the interracial movement that followed. National Labor Relations Board arrives (Wagner Act enforced) and opens "space" for labor organizing
1941	Bombing of Pearl Harbor and WWII (note: 1941–1944 martial law suppresses union organizing and worker rights)
1945	International Longshore and Warehouse Union (ILWU) organized plantation workers into first multiracial labor union
1951	Post WWII Samoan immigration
1959	Statehood & Admissions Act
1970s	Reconstruction of "local" identity. Possible to be local Haole, local Japanese, etc.
1970s	Hawaiian (cultural and political) renaissance, Kaho'olawe & Grassroots movements, emergence of the sovereignty movement
1976	Hokule'a sets sail furthering the Hawaiian renaissance
1978	Establishment of the Office of Hawaiian Affairs (OHA) and Hawaiian language is reinstated as an official language

(*continued*)

An Account of the History of Colonization in Hawai'i (*continued*)

1980s	Emergence of hula competitions
1983	Aha Punana Leo (language recovery movement) is organized
1987	Language immersion classes
1990s	Micronesian immigration
1993	100 years since overthrow. Hawaiians demonstrate at Iolani Palace to grieve the overthrow and push for sovereignty. U.S. government apologizes for its actions. President Clinton signs the apology bill acknowledging that Native Hawaiians never relinquished their claim over lands "ceded" to the State of Hawai'i
2000	*Rice v Cayetano* decision of U.S. Supreme Court giving non-Hawaiians same right to vote for trustees of the Office of Hawaiian Affairs representing increasing legal challenges to Native Hawaiian assets
2008	The Hawai'i Supreme Court overturns the lower court's decision and orders the state administration not to sell any "ceded" lands until the claims of Native Hawaiians have been resolved by the Hawai'i legislature. The U.S. Supreme court agrees to the Lingle administration's request for an appeal
2009	In a unanimous opinion, the U.S. Supreme Court overturned the Hawai'i Supreme Court ruling deciding that the Apology Resolution did not provide a legal justification for Native Hawaiian claims over the "ceded" lands and is expected to send the case back to the state Supreme Court. Governor Lingle acknowledged that Native Hawaiians had a moral but not legal claim to these lands and that the State of Hawai'i had the right to develop or sell these lands for all the people of Hawai'i

contact, Captain Cook and his colleagues cultivated numerous stereotypes about Native Hawaiian people. They tended to characterize Native Hawaiians as friendly and hospitable but inclined toward "thievery" (as cited in Lind, 1934) and were "dreadful, mercenary, artful villains." In 1929, Manly as cited in Lind (1934), described Native Hawaiians as "wretched creatures," "savages," with the appearance of half man and half beasts. These stereotypes, and others, support a process of dehumanization that appears to be a prerequisite for atrocity (Salzman, 2012) and allows for the domination, control, and exploitation of a people deemed not quite human and certainly not of equal worth as the colonizers. Smith (2012) describes how research on indigenous peoples systematically followed the imperial project after Cook's initial voyage. Smith notes that Maori people were represented as blood thirsty savages. The imperial descriptions of Maori's and other Pacific peoples were inferiorizing and supported by scientific racism. The "supposed characteristics of primitive peoples was that we could not use our minds or intellects" (p. 26) and that by lacking such virtues and capacities "we were disqualified not just from civilization but from humanity itself" (p. 26). Smith asserts that these and similar inferiorizing descriptions and their internalization represent a challenge to "decolonize our minds" (p. 24). This psychological "decolonization" requires a purging of the internalized oppression represented by such stereotypes that may have been internalized, institutionally reinforced, and believed by the colonized and oppressed.

The denigration of indigenous Pacific cultures and people, supported by military and institutional power and internalized by the colonized, has devastating consequences. The processes of colonization were described by PL (Laenui, 2000) in collaboration with Filipino psychologist and Professor Virgilio Enriquez. It is informative to look at the stages of colonization and note the different forms of violence resident in the various stages and the responses to this process by the subjects of this colonization. The narrative below is also an illustration of what various Pacific Peoples experienced under colonialism.

> Colonization and decolonization are social processes even more than they are political or military processes. Governance over a people changes only after the people themselves have sufficiently changed. The late Virgilio Enriquez, a native son of the Philippines, Professor of Psychology, and advocate for the integrity of native wisdoms, described the process of colonization. Professor Enriquez suggests the following steps in the process of colonization.
>
> First, there's *Denial and Withdrawal.* When a colonial people first come upon an indigenous people, the colonial strangers will immediately look upon the indigenous as a people without culture, no moral values, nothing of any social value to merit kind comment. Thus, the very existence of a culture of any merit among the indigenous people is denied. Indigenous people themselves who develop close relationship with the new-comers, gradually withdraw from their own cultural practices. Some may even join in the ridicule and the denial of the existence of culture among the native people. They may become quickly converted and later lead in the criticism of indigenous societies.
>
> Second, there's *Destruction/Eradication:* The colonists take bolder action in step 2, physically destroying and attempting to eradicate all physical representations of the symbols of indigenous cultures. This may include the burning of their art, their tablets, their god images, the destruction of their sacred sites, etc. At times, the indigenous people themselves may participate in this destruction—some may even lead in the destruction.

Third, there's *Denigration/Belittlement/Insult:* As colonization takes a stronger hold, the new systems which are created within indigenous societies, such as churches, colonial style health delivery systems, and new legal institutions, all join to denigrate, belittle, and insult any continuing practice of the indigenous culture. Churches will style indigenous religious practices as devil worship and condemn the practitioners to physical torture or their souls to hell. Colonially trained medical practitioners will refer to the indigenous doctors as witches if their medicine is successful and ignorant superstitious fools if their medicine fails. The new legal institutions will criminalize the traditional practices, fine the practitioners, and may declare illegal the possession of traditionally sacred or healing materials. In some areas, even their native language is forbidden.

Here, even symbols of evil must be imported by the colonizer in order for evil to gain legitimacy within the society. Thus, we find in many colonized societies the importation of Dracula, Halloween, or other representations of evil through the colonial societies literature or legends, all the while they allude to the indigenous peoples' representations of evil as more ignorant superstitions.

Fourth, there's the *Surface Accommodation/Tokenism:* In this stage of colonization, whatever remnants of culture survived the onslaught of the earlier steps is given surface accommodation. They are tolerated as an exhibition of the colonial regime's sense of leniency to the continuing ignorance of the natives. These practices are called folkloric, as showing respect to the old folks and to tradition. They are given token regard.

Finally, there's *Transformation/Exploitation:* The traditional culture which simply refuses to die or go away is now transformed into the culture of the dominating colonial society. A Christian church may now use an indigenous person as a priest, permitting the priest to use the indigenous language, to incorporate some indigenous terms and practices, within the church's framework of worship. Indigenous art that has survived may gain in popularity and now forms the basis for economic exploitation. Indigenous symbols in print may decorate modern dress. Indigenous musical instruments may be incorporated into modern music. To support indigenous causes within the general colonial structure may become the popular political thing to do so the culture is further exploited. This exploitation may be committed by indigenous as well as non-indigenous peoples.

A Pacific Islander's story from Kanaky (aka, New Caledonia) appears to also ring true for indigenous peoples in many other parts of the Pacific and throughout the indigenous—or what has been known as the 4th—world. This story came to PL by way of Yann Uregei, advocate for the rights of the Kanak people and the independence of Kanaky. Uregei met PL in the mid-1980s in Suva, Fiji at a conference sponsored by the Law Association of Asia and the Pacific. PL recalls Uregei sharing the following story:

The people in my village in Kanaky are very hospitable, taking great joy in welcoming friends and strangers alike. One day, a Kanak man resting on the front porch of his house saw a stranger, a Frenchman, walking down the footpath that crosses the front of his house. When the Frenchman came closer to the house, the Kanak stood up and invited the Frenchman into the house to rest and take some refreshments. The Frenchman accepted this invitation, entered the house, and sat at the table for the refreshments. After the Frenchman was through eating and drinking, he approached the Kanak to pay for the cost of his meal. The Kanak, taken aback, declined any payment, explaining that he had only wanted to share the hospitality of the house by his invitation and sharing of what humble food he had. The Frenchman was happy because he got a free meal. The Kanak was also happy to have been able to have someone appreciate his culture.

The following day, the Frenchman came down the same footpath, bringing along with him two friends. The Kanak was not on the porch this day, so the Frenchman decided that rather than standing on ceremony, he would simply invite himself and his companions into the house, and wait at the table to be served. The Kanak, walking through his house, was surprised to find three Frenchmen in his home, sitting at his table waiting to be served with refreshments, thinking what strange social customs these strangers practice. But his culture of hospitality soon overcomes his astonishment, and he provides these "guests" with refreshments. When they are done with their food and drink, rather than leaving the home, they remain at the table in animated conversation, observing how comfortable this Kanak's house is, built for the particular weather of New Caledonia, and the possibilities for this house. Finally, they approach the Kanak, inquiring how many people live in the home, (two—the Kanak and his wife) and where do they sleep? Again, the Kanak is surprised by the inquiry, but still able to overcome the awkwardness of these strangers' behaviors, he takes them to a small back room and shows them his and his wife's sleeping quarters.

The first Frenchman declared that they liked the room, and they wanted to move into the room. The Kanak, surprised by this declaration, asks, "If you move into my room, where would my wife and I sleep?" The Frenchman suggested they might enjoy the kitchen, or better yet, perhaps the porch! The Kanak takes this as a serious insult, which goes far beyond the boundaries of hospitality. He speaks in a loud, harsh voice, demanding that they get out of his house or he will throw all three of them out. He prepares to fight the Frenchmen and they prepare in kind, but one Frenchman steps between the Kanak and the others, and proclaims, "Let us not resort to violence. Let's act as civilized men. Let us be rational beings. Let us be orderly. Democratic. Let's take a vote!"

The practice of transmigrating the colonizing nation's population into the territories of the indigenous peoples has been common. It is more insidious, more subtle, and more long-lasting than an outright landing and takeover. Whether by a resort to arms, a resort to the ballot box, the destruction of their environment, or the whittling away of indigenous peoples, culture and their robust social structures, the imprint of colonization upon indigenous peoples have been disastrous.

CONTEMPORARY OPPRESSION

As we examine the current manifestations of the colonial dynamic and legacy in Hawai'i, it is useful to consider the "Liturgy" written by the Wai'anae Women's Support Group. The "Liturgy" is read at multitude of churches on a Sunday to reflect on the phenomena of the cross and the flag.

E 'Olelo Kakou, Sisters

(Let Us Speak Together, Sisters)

Sisters and Brothers
Hear our prayer to you,

In the spirit of Aloha which our
gods Bequeathed to us and to
you,
Strong in body, mind and spirit.
Our gods, our ways, our 'aina,
our sea and sky
Provided and nourished us.

But your forefathers came to our
shores
They brought with them the
Cross and
The Flag, and
Disease, and
Alcohol, and
Despair, and

(Let Us Pray Together, Sisters)

We ask you to hear our words
and feel our pain

Long before your Christian
forefathers Came upon our
sacred 'Aina (Land)
We were three hundred thousand strong.
We take sacred nourishment

But they scorned our symbols,
They scorned us. They said,
"Here. With these you will
prosper."
But look at us now, Sisters.
We are the poorest.
We live in cars, tents, on
benches and sidewalks.

Greed, and
Shame for what we were –"lowly
heathens" (I think they said).
They offered, no, demanded
That we accept the Cross and
the Flag
(these Siamese of Power)
And said, "Here, With these you
will prosper."

We tried to put into their hands,
our symbols:
The Kalo (taro) from whose
body
we take sacred nourishment
The Wai and the Kai, (the
inland and sea water) from
whose body

We occupy more jail cells, more
hospital beds, more morgue
slabs and coffins than any other
race in Hawai'i.
Our children are labeled
"DISADVANTAGED" and
can't read
can't write
can't get a job
can't get an education

We are beggars in our own
homeland
But no more.
As we lay down the Cross,
As we lay down the Flag,
We search and have found those
symbols which spring from
this place
this time
this People

In our hands we offer you
a scoop of earth, the 'Aina
a scoop of water from the land and the sea, Life a rainbow, Hope
and Aloha, Love.
But let us be clear
Whether you accept our symbols or not,

We will continue to speak the truth of our history
the truth of our pain
the truth of our oppression
the truth of our colonization.
And through this truth we will be free.
This is our prayer to you, sisters.
Listen to it with you soul, sisters. Amene

The liturgy above demonstrates that native Hawaiians continue to
experience various social inequities today, inequities that are reflections
of the oppression of their indigenous ways. Such social inequities, in turn,
are used to support mythical and inferiorizing perceptions of the native
Hawaiian, stereotypes that continue to maintain, if not fuel, the colonial
practices of the past.

McCubbin and Marsella (2009) noted that Western psychology has contributed to these inferiorizing stereotypes through its deficit perspective of Hawaiian and other Pacific peoples. The deficit perspective is a model that views ethnic "minorities" as having predetermined deficiencies that relegate minorities to inferior status. This "scientific racism" was used to provide empirical evidence of the intellectual capacities of various races that supported the view of the superiority of some races and the inferiority of others. These conclusions, of course, justified colonial domination and exploitation of the colonized.

They also noted that G. Stanley Hall, a founder of organized psychology, referred to Hawaiians as similar to other tropical races as suffering from "weakness of character, idleness and the vices it breeds" (Hall, 1904, p. 658). He described Hawaiians as behaviorally lacking control, morally inert, and sluggish. This characterization of Hawaiians was the predominant view of indigenous people in psychology and these stereotypes strongly influenced "scientific" research and the interpretation of empirical findings (McCubbin & Marsella, 2009). Such is the legacy of early research.

Furthermore, PL's narrative below also speaks to the linkages and similarities between historical colonialism and contemporary oppression as experienced by Native Hawaiians:

> Oppression need not be "harsh or cruel treatment or control" as in the practice of colonization. It may come with the face of benevolence, as an educator, proselytizer, merchant, or politician. It may appear merely to replace or substitute the language of the "civilized people" for one's indigenous language, to bring "high culture" to the community and thus pushing out indigenous cultures, to teach of the scientific approach to medicine, technology, methods of fishing, and so on, all the while pushing out the traditional practices of the indigenous people. These softer forms of oppression are usually accompanied with powerful financial, military, political, and religious forces institutionalized within the community making awareness and rejection of the colonial oppressiveness an almost impossibility. When awareness comes to the fore, challenge or rejection of the intruding colonial practice draws to such protecting individuals the rancor of the oppressor, some of whom now include indigenous collaborators who are now preachers of the foreign ways. The indigenous-colonized are elevated in the colonial institutions. Resistors are kept subservient. Witness the many native Hawaiian judges and prosecutors in the Hawai'i Judiciary who preside over a multitude of criminal charges against native Hawaiians for their refusal to pay homage (they call it taxes) to the colonial government!

COMMON MANIFESTATIONS OF INTERNALIZED OPPRESSION

It is apparent from some of the narratives presented above that the consequences of internalized oppression directly and indirectly impact the physical health, economic conditions, education status, social relationships, and mental health of Pacific Peoples. Fanon (1968), a psychiatrist who worked in colonial Africa, noted that the colonial system has the power to promote the internalization of negative evaluations that become the self-concept of the colonized people. People are strongly motivated to alleviate the aversive state produced by inferiority feelings. What is done is often destructive to self, family, and community, thereby creating more trauma, grief, tragedy, and destructive compensations. The colonial context is defined by inferiority and superiority. Nelson Mandela described the rise of the "Black Consciousness Movement" in apartheid South Africa as filling "a vacuum among young people. Black Consciousness was less a movement than a philosophy and grew out of the idea that blacks must first liberate themselves from the sense of psychological inferiority bred by three centuries of white rule. Only then could the people rise up in confidence and truly liberate themselves from repression" (Mandela, 1995, p. 486).

Memmi (1965) described the colonial situation as one that is based on economic privilege, despite suggestion of more noble goals of religious conversion or civilization. Its key tools are racism and terror. Racism is ingrained in every colonial institution and establishes the "subhumanity" of the colonized, fostering poor self-concepts in the colonized as well.

Inferiority feelings are devastating because they heighten anxiety and promote destructive compensations (i.e., generalized anger expressed in the family) to alleviate this aversive state perhaps by providing a momentary feeling of power and superiority (Ansbacher & Ansbacher, 1946). Manifestations of this dynamic may be reflected in the common social problems affecting indigenous communities across genetic and geographical distances. For example, Austin and Marsella (2005) cited studies indicating that alcohol, drug use, and violence are among the most serious health and social problems facing Native Hawaiians today. Taylor (2005) suggests that, in Fiji, there needs to begin the process of engaging in open discussion on ethnic identity if the negative effects of historical colonialism and globalization are to be avoided. He states, "Fiji citizens need to feel secure in who they are, where they have come from, and where they are going in order to avoid feeling the need to 'drown' their sorrows, sink into a drug-induced oblivion or try to relieve their sense of worthlessness in senseless violence" (p. 128). In Australia's Northern Territories, domestic and family violence is the leading cause of admission to hospitals and that intentional self harm is a major social problem in many indigenous communities and is becoming an unprecedented problem in the traditional indigenous communities in the Northern Territories of Australia (Markey, 1998; Reser, 2000).

The colonial context is defined by inferiority and superiority. Fanon continued that "The settler keeps alive in the Native an anger which he deprives an outlet; the native is trapped in the tight links of the chains of colonialism" (p. 54). He observed that "The colonized man will first manifest this aggressiveness which has been deposited in his bones against his own people" (p. 52). Often, this tension is manifested within families and communities and thereby transmits trauma across generations through such mechanisms as domestic violence and abuse. Memmi (1965), in his classic work, *The Colonizer and the Colonized*, observed that it "is clear that colonization weakens the colonized and all those weaknesses contribute to one another" (p. 115).

Below, PL describes internalized oppression—which is the result of systemic and constant inculcation of the colonized with the colonizer's culture—as experienced by Native Hawaiians. Given that the ways of the colonizer have been deeply internalized, PL fittingly refers to internalized oppression as "deep culture," which contributes to the eradication and devaluation of indigenous ways:

> As time moves on and we are caught in the struggle of the Colonizer and the Colonized, we become swept by a tide of "deep-culture." This culture is so deep that we don't notice its presence, and if we do, we accept it as the normal and natural pattern of human existence. This deep-culture takes over control of all of our formal systems, directing our economic transactions, our social relationships, our style of education, our views on the environment, how we organize our judicial system, the management of our political system, and how we practice national security. If we are not careful, it slips also into our families and our community, even into our deepest sense of spirituality. This deep-culture is controlled by three fundamental pillars, Domination, Individualism, and Exclusion (DIE).

As another example of internalized oppression, the Project Director of the Chuuk Culture and Education Studies Project of the College of Micronesia (J. Peter, personal communication, March 21, 2013) shared the following narrative:

> The oppression of the people of Micronesia is as multi-layered as it is fluid; it has no distinct or tangible beginning or birthdate. Instead, it resides in every corner of the human institutions which perpetuate oppression to the point where it is internalized and normalized. Colonial government and its project of transforming the basic and foundational aspects of people's lives successfully disrupted traditional work, health, and movements. Religion and its conversions through missionization is colonialism's affirmation. Missionaries targeted traditional beliefs and

cultural practices and attacked a wide range of human agency from sexuality to religion and even work. They worked hard to foster a sense of insecurity in the psyche of the islanders.

MENTAL AND BEHAVIORAL HEALTH IMPLICATIONS OF INTERNALIZED OPPRESSION

Salzman (2001), Salzman and Halloran (2004), and Salzman (2005a), informed by current social psychological theory and research, looked at the relationships of culture, self-esteem, and anxiety in the context of the traumatic consequences suffered by indigenous peoples as a result of contact with the West and subsequent colonization. Terror Management Theory (TMT; Greenberg, Solomon, & Pyszynski, 1997) emerged from the field of social psychology and has been broadly supported by hundreds of empirical studies across nations and cultures. These studies point to an essential psychological function of culture and its self-esteem constructing prescriptions for behavior, living, and desirable personality characteristics. TMT proposes that human beings, because of our advanced cognitive abilities, can contemplate the future and become aware of mortality. This has been called existential terror—a "terror" that requires mediation in order to function adaptively in the world with the anxiety or terror managed. Our belief systems and cultural worldviews provide that mediation or "buffer" against this potentially paralyzing human characteristic. Cultural worldviews offer the possibility of transcending our mortal existence by providing for a literal (i.e., religion) or symbolic (cultural) sense of immortality. This cultural worldview serves as an anxiety buffer by making "right action" and "right ways of being available to believers in a particular world view" (Becker, 1971, p. 79). If a person has faith in the cultural worldview and sees him or herself as living up to its standards, the person will achieve what is known as "self- esteem." Self-esteem is that conviction that one is of value in a meaningful world. It is an essential psychological resource because it is inversely related to anxiety and therefore provides for the construction of an anxiety-buffer to the "terror" inherent in human existence that is due to our unique awareness of our mortality. Self-esteem is a cultural construction and is inversely related to anxiety (Greenberg et al., 1997) as well as depression (Sowislo & Orth, 2013).

When a culture is traumatically disrupted, its self-esteem prescribing functions are impaired and the individual or people are flooded with unbuffered anxiety. The cultural trauma is exacerbated by the imposition of colonial systems that are based on the presumed "inferiority" of the colonized and traumatized. Inferiority feelings are inversely related to anxiety. The consequences of contact included the importation of deadly diseases that decimated populations across the Pacific that overpowered traditional sources of meaning and protection. This trauma and the consequent assault on indigenous cultures by colonial powers tore at the fabric of meaning that humans require and is embodied in culture.

Inferiority feelings and low self-esteem among Pacific Peoples have been associated with various indicators of behavioral and mental health (Salzman, 2005a). Alfred Adler, one of the foundational thinkers in psychology, placed "inferiority feelings" and effects and the center of his theory and practice. Adler thought (see Ansbacher & Ansbacher, 1946) that while everyone has a feeling of inferiority, it becomes problematic and even pathological only when the sense of inadequacy overwhelms the individual and, far from stimulating him to useful activity, makes him depressed and incapable of development. He understood drug and alcohol addiction as, in behaviorist terms, negative reinforcement whereby the oppressive feeling of inferiority is temporarily removed (by the substance). The immediate effects of the drug often give the victim a feeling of being unburdened. Adler saw that in all cases of addiction people are seeking alleviation from a certain situation. The colonial situation as noted (Fanon, 1968; Memmi, 1965) is aversive and has the power to promote the internalization of negative evaluations that become the self-concept of the colonized people. Its very foundation is based on notions of inferiority (the colonized) and superiority (the colonizers). This relationship is supported by institutional, military, and religious power. The greater the feeling of inferiority that has been experienced, the more violent the emotional agitation (Ansbacher & Ansbacher, 1946).

PL discusses the various health effects of historical and contemporary oppression—in the individual, community, cultural, and systemic levels—among native Hawaiians below:

> Health impacts resulting from colonization have been extensive, including the genocide-like eradication of native populations by intentional and unintentional introduction of disease and illness, direct slaughter, removal from or destruction of traditional territories, and weapons testing. Other forms of genocide have come through marginalization or eradication of traditional health and cultural patterns, destroying the institutions of traditional health care as well as the traditional health-care givers. Hawai'i's many healing arts through the use of traditional voice technology, the use of ancestor guidance, of group processing, of realignment of an individual's spiritual selves, of an appreciation and integration of the land and sea, of proper diet and herbs, of the traditional forms of massage, of proper child birthing, and many other arts have been pushed into the farthest corners of the community. Some of these practices have been criminalized. If practiced, they generally require a certification or license through the colonial authority.

Behavioral health care has been an area of special attention of the colonial system in Hawai'i. The Hawaii State Department of Health has separated behavioral health from primary health, has separated individual health from family and community health, and has cut apart children and adolescent health care from adult health and addiction health services. The State has further sliced and diced health care into individual compartments of education, judiciary, labor, health (and their myriad sub-compartments), social services, and housing. This is the DIE deep culture of Individualism (including the concept of singularity) at work.

Mental Health Services are under the control of a State-wide system of oversight and control. All community mental health centers originally were controlled by the State. The State determined the academic requirements of practice, and, of course, those academic requirements were only to be met by its colonial institutions. Any indigenous practice of mental health services, if not also abiding by State licensing requirements, would of course incur criminal sanction. Only State-approved services would be approved for reimbursement. This is part of the DIE deep culture of Domination.

By the 1980s, the Wai'anae district of Hawai'i became the most populated of native Hawaiians. This district led Hawai'i and the United States in crystal methamphetamine use, its educational status among the lowest in Hawai'i, its income far below other Hawai'i communities, and its crime, homelessness, and other negative social indicators generally topped all other communities. The behavioral health services there had little relevance to the historical, cultural, or geographic reality of the people being served. A community elder sat in the waiting room for a week, counting how many people were actually served. She counted three!

The consequences of the history and traumas previously described have motivated movements toward political and psychological recovery. Throughout the indigenous world, we see that the recovery of traditional culture, language, and history are central to the efforts of people to overcome the effects of colonization, oppression, and the internalization of these effects. Fanon (1968) asserts that to speak a language is to take on a world and a culture. It follows that to lose a language is to lose a world and a culture that infuses that world with meaning. Humans require a world of meaning to act in ways that enables one to construct a life of value and significance (Salzman, 2008). Therefore, recovery of culture, history, and language are efforts that address essential human needs. We provide further discussion of programs that appear to be successful in addressing the effects of historical and contemporary oppression among Pacific Peoples next.

CULTURE-BASED SCHOOLS AND PROGRAMS FOR CULTURAL RECOVERY

Because colonization has political, cultural, and psychological conse-quences, the remedy (decolonization) must involve these dimensions. Dominant culture-based educational and mental health institutions in a colonial system seek to impose its ideology, version of history, and episte-mology on indigenous and colonized peoples. In a process of decolonization, these institutions must a least accommodate the perspectives, sources of knowledge, and learning styles of the formerly colonized people. The establishment of the Wai'anae Coast Community Mental Health Center, named Hale Na'au Pono (House of Inner Balance), is an example of such a culturally and community-based mental health program. PL, who is the Executive Director of the center, describes it as follows:

> Wai'anae community leaders in the 1980s, outraged with "care" which didn't seem to care, petitioned the State Health Department, inviting it to leave the community and hand over management and control of behavioral health services to the community. In 1986, the Wai'anae Coast Community Mental Health Center was born under the name Hale Na'au Pono (House of Inner Balance), charged with servicing the Wai'anae catchment area of approximately 45,000 people.
>
> Community activists with little or no experience with mental health care (except for being on the receiving end of such care) formed an initial board of directors, incorporated themselves, and in coopera-tion with the University of Hawai'i and funding from the State Health Department, opened its doors.
>
> In its 25 years of recovery from the colonization of its behavioral health practice, Hale Na'au Pono is today the only community mental health center (CMHC) not controlled or operated by the State Department of Health, the only CMHC nationally accredited in Hawai'i, the only CMHC to service Children and Adults under the same roof, the only CMHC to provide more than just behavioral health case management services for the seriously mentally ill, but also chemical addiction services, group home services, psychosocial rehabilitation services, financial management services, and integrated and coordinated services among all these and primary health care of individuals. It also sponsors a "Neighborhood Place," servicing the needs of families facing the crises from alcoholism and drug abuse, to having the electricity and water turned off, to children not having clothes to attend schools. Hale Na'au Pono has amalgamated all of these services within a fiber of aloha, the heartbeat of the native Hawaiian culture. Its practice is informed and

grounded in the predominant native Hawaiian deep cultural principles of 'Olu'olu (compatibility, kindness), Lokahi (unity, togetherness), and Aloha, (love, caring) which brings forth OLA (life, health). This is in contrast to the overwhelming "Westernized" deep cultural practice of Domination, Individualism, and Exclusion (DIE). HNP has achieved the distinction of being the first CMHC in Hawai'i to be nationally accredited by CARF (1995). Today, it is CARF-accredited in more services than any other organization in Hawai'i. In comparison, none of the State-operated CMHCs have any national accreditation. State CMHCs limit their services only to the adult population, and, generally, only for somatic, clinical, and case management services.

It is not unusual to find, embedded within Hale Na'au Pono consumers' Master Recovery Plans, Hawaiian practices of Ho'oponopono as defining family or individual therapy, or see consumers engaged in Hula (traditional dance form), or Lua (traditional art of war), or to see program or organization-wide Aha'Aina (traditional celebrations and feasting), or even Hoe Wa'a (canoe paddling) as part of their recovery methods.

Kanahele (1982) saw the process of recovery and the reconstruction of Hawaiian culture as a psychological renewal, a purging of feelings of alienation and inferiority, as well as a reassertion of dignity. The revalidation of one's culture and its standards for being and living in the world serve to strengthen the essential anxiety-buffering function of the culture. The revival of hula, language study, music, and traditional forms of healing such as Ho'oponopono serve to reconstruct a world of meaning for people to act in and achieve anxiety-buffering self-esteem through the meeting of accessible standards of value defined by a worldview infused with new belief (Salzman, 2005a). Kanahele (1982) also notes similar cultural activism occurring throughout the Pacific Islands. As a result of these efforts to reaffirm and recover the cultural foundations of living and being, "Hawaiians regard themselves, generally speaking, a lot better and with a greater sense of identity, self-assurance, and pride" (p. 7). Self-assurance, pride, and confidence are conditions that make adaptive action more probable in a wide variety of contexts, including those imposed by current conditions. PL describes the importance of addressing and connecting to the traditional "deep culture" of Hawaiians as a part of the process of decolonization (Laenui, 1997):

> In the informal communities of these colonized territories, there still remains a more traditional lifestyle in which we can find a softer and more cooperative deep-culture. In Hawai'i, we call it the OLA ('Olu'olu, describing a comfortable, mellow, relaxed and non-confrontational attitude or circumstance; Lokahi, describing a group or family mindset;

Aloha, to signify an inclusive approach with love, caring, and respect for the dignity of all) deep culture.

In the decolonization discussions of Hawaiian self-determination, independence from the United States, Hawaiian Sovereignty, concern for the deep-culture of Hawai'i is an important part of the dreaming stage of the decolonization process. The argument is simply that we cannot decolonize while we leave the DIE deep-culture in place. Decolonization must root out those very elements which endanger the humanity in each of us. Decolonization must challenge us to take from our informal systems the OLA culture and replace it for the DIE culture of the formal system, bringing a new order of life in which we will be able to sublimate the superiority/inferiority (or dominator/dominated) complex to one of 'Olu'olu, of relating to one another with respect and recognition of the equal dignity of everyone and everything, in which we replace the Individualism/Singularity concept with one of Lokahi, of the togetherness and group relationships, in which we substitute in place of Exclusion, the concept of Aloha.

If we only address a political decolonization process, changing power from one hand to another, yet remain under a pattern of DIE, we will only leave the structure of disaster in place while switching who leads in that disaster. We will need to change that very deep-cultural pattern if there is any hope of real decolonization.

Education has been a focal point in the struggle for self-determination and cultural recovery. The recovery of language and culture, previously suppressed by the forces of colonization, are essential components of psychological and political liberation. This effort has been occurring throughout the indigenous world. The Na Lau Lama (2005) report identified examples of Hawaiian culture-based educational programs. Examples include Hawaiian language medium schools like 'Aha Punauna Leo and Kula Kaiapuni Hawaiian-based charter schools, and the Kamehameha Schools, which began as an instrument of assimilation to address the severe social problems Hawaiians faced in the late 19th century, which was transformed under pressure from the Hawaiian community, alumni, and teachers to become a Hawaiian school for Hawaiians (Reyes, 2012). The strategic plan stated that the Kamehameha Schools will cultivate, nurture, perpetuate, and practice Hawaiian culture, values, history, language, oral traditions, literature, and the significance of cultural and historical places. This is a reflection of the Hawaiian renaissance and the political movement it spawned. Further examples include the Kamehameha Early Education Program that was created, implemented, studied, and modified based on Hawaiian culture for Hawaiian children (Banks & Neisworth, 1995). This is an example of culturally congruent educational programs that affirm and honor indigenous cultures and support the positive evaluation of indigenous identity. Na Pua No'eau (Sing, 1993) is a program created to develop gifted and talented Hawaiian children from kindergarten to twelfth grade. Its philosophical foundations include a consideration of historical, political, and cultural aspects of Native Hawaiians and an integration of Native Hawaiian values as a programmatic foundation and purposefully raising self esteem; thus, contradicting the essential dynamic of internalized oppression and inoculating children against its corrosive effects. 'Aha Punana Leo began with a small group of Hawaiian-speaking educators with federal support. Today, Native Hawaiian children can obtain their entire K-12 education in the Hawaiian language. Community members established Hawaiian immersion schools throughout the Hawaiian Islands from preschool through high school (Reyes, 2012). As PL states:

> There is a difference between colonial education of indigenous peoples and indigenous peoples' education. That difference lies in purpose. Colonial education of indigenous peoples is essentially to fulfill the mantra "school to work." For indigenous peoples, the purpose is to maintain the continuity of indigenous consciousness, found in all of the arts and science, history, language, and humanity of its people.

CONCLUSION

Purging of internalized oppression from the minds and spirit of the previously colonized is a necessary component of decolonization. This process is often associated with anger (Salzman, 2005b). The consequences of contact, disease, depopulation, and colonization across the Pacific that have spawned movements to recover history, culture, language, spirituality, and land are movements inextricably related to the psychological processes of rejecting the negative evaluations imposed by colonial and oppressive systems. Colonization and decolonization are both political and psychological processes. Psychological liberation from the internalized negative evaluations of an external oppressor is a necessary component of the process of decolonization and recovery.

When Bob Dylan picked up an electric guitar and brought the power of rock and the lyricism of poetry together, he was booed and heckled continuously. He was even called "Judas" by purists who were offended by his break with their expectations. His response to the angry crowd was "I DON'T BELIEVE YOU......YOU'RE LIARS!!!!" He went on to change American music and culture. As we opened this chapter, *No one can make you feel inferior without your consent.*

REFERENCES

Ansbacher, H., & Ansbacher, R. (1946). *The individual psychology of Alfred Adler.* New York, NY: Basic Books.

Austin, A., & Marsella, A. J. (2005). Understanding substance use and violent behavior in a Native Hawaiian community. In A. J. Marsella, A. Austin, & Bruce Grant (Eds.), *Social change and psychosocial adaptation in the Pacific Islands: Cultures in transition* (pp. 171–186). New York, NY: Springer.

Banks, S. R., & Neisworth, J. T. (1995). Dynamic assessment in early intervention implications for serving American Indian/Alaska Native families. *Journal of American Indian Education, 45*(3), 25–37.

Becker, E. (1971). *The birth and death of meaning* (2nd ed.). New York, NY: Free Press.

Beckwith, M. (1970). *Hawaiian mythology.* Honolulu, HI: University of Hawaii Press.

Bushnell, O. A. (1993). *The gifts of civilization: Germs and genocide in Hawaii.* Honolulu, HI: University of Hawaii Press.

Butlin, N. G. (1983). *Our original aggression.* Sydney, Australia: Allen & Unwin.

Central Intelligence World Fact Book (2005). Australia-Oceania. Retrieved from http://www.cia.gov/cia/publications/factbookgeos/

David, E. J. R. (2008). A colonial mentality model of depression for Filipino Americans. *Cultural Diversity and Ethnic Minority Psychology, 14*(2), 118–127.

Fanon, F. (1968). *The wretched of the earth.* New York, NY: Grove Press..

Farnsworth, C. M. (1997). Australians resist facing up to legacy of parting aborigines from families. *New York Times,* June 8, 1997, p. 10.

Federated States of Micronesia. (2010). *FSM population estimates and projections.* Retrieved August 13, 2010, from http://www. spc.inc/prism/country/fm/stats/Projections/proj-index.htm

Greenberg, J., Solomon, S., & Pyszczynski, T. (1997). Terror management theory of self-esteem and cultural worldviews: Empirical assessments and conceptual refinements. In M. P. Zanna (Ed.), *Advances in experimental social psychology* (Vol. 29). San Diego, CA: Academic Press, Inc.

Hall, G. S. (1904). *Adolescence: Its psychology and its relations to physiology, anthropology, sociology, sex, crime, religion and education* (Vol. 2). New York, NY: D. Appleton and Company.

Hanlon, D. (1994). Patterns of colonial rule in Micronesia. In K. R. Howe, R. C. Kistes, & B. V. Lal (Eds.), *The tides of history: The Pacific Islands in the twentieth century* (pp. 93–118). Honolulu, HI: University of Hawaii Press.

Harris, J. (1990). *One blood: 200 years of aboriginal encounter with Christianity; a story of hope.* Sutherland, Australia: Albatross Books.

Howe, K. R., Kiste, R. C., & Lal, B. V. (Eds.). (1994). *Tides of history: The Pacific Islands in the twentieth century.* St. Leonards, N.S.W.: Allen & Unwin.

Johnson, R. K. (1981). *Kumulipo Hawaiian Hymn of Creation* (Vol. I). Honolulu, HI: Topgallant Publishing Co., Ltd.

Kanahele, G. S. (1982). *Hawaiian renaissance.* Honolulu, HI: Project WAIAHA.

Laenui, P. (1997). *On Deep Cultures in Hawai'i.* Institute for Zen Studies, May 1997 Newsletter, Honolulu, HI.

Laenui, P. (2000). Processes of decolonization. In M. Battiste (Ed.), *Reclaiming indigenous voice and vision* (pp. 150–160). Vancouver, BC: University of British Columbia Press.

Lind, A. W. (1934). *Modification of Hawaiian* character. New York, NY: McGraw-Hill.

Mandela, N. (1995). *Long walk to freedom.* New York, NY: Little, Brown and Company.

Markey, G. (1998). *The health status of women in the Northern Territory.* Darwin: Territory Health Services Women's Health Strategy Unit.

McCubbin, L. D., & Marsella, A. J. (2009). Native Hawaiians and psychology: The cultural and historical context of indigenous ways of knowing. *Cultural Diversity and Ethnic Minority Psychology, 15*(4), 374–387.

Memmi, A. (1965). *The colonizer and the colonized.* Boston, MA: Beacon Press.

Moorehead, A. (1966). *The fatal impact: An account of the invasion of the South Pacific* (pp. 1767–1840). New York, NY: Harper & Row.

Na Lau Lama Report. (2005). *Culture based education.* Honolulu, HI: Kamahemeha Schools.

Ogan, E. (2005). Social change in the Pacific: Problems old, new, and problems borrowed. In A. J. Marsella, A. A. Austin, & B. Grant (Eds.), *Social change and psychosocial adaptation in the Pacific Islands* (pp. 9–28). Honolulu, HI: Springer.

Pearsall, J., & Trumble, B. (Eds.). (1995). *The Oxford encyclopedic English dictionary* (2nd ed., pp. 1019). New York, NY: Oxford University Press.

Rapadas, J., Balajadiam, M., & Rubinstein, D. (2005). Social change in the Pacific: Problems old, new, and problems borrowed. In A. J. Marsella, A. A. Austin, & B. Grant (Eds.), *Social change and psychosocial adaptation in the Pacific Islands* (pp.145–170). Honolulu, HI: Springer.

Reser, J. P. (2000). Indigenous suicide in cross-cultural context: An overview statement and selective bibliography of sources relevant to Indigenous suicide in Australia, North America and the Pacific. *South Pacific Journal of Psychology, 11*(2), 95–111.

Reyes, K. (2012). *E Ho' ii Ka Piko: Native Hawaiian educators' discourse on Hawaiian education* (Unpublished doctoral dissertation). University of Hawaii at Manoa, Honolulu, HI.

Salzman, M. (2001). Cultural trauma and recovery: Perspectives from terror management theory. *Trauma, Violence & Abuse: A Review Journal, 2*(2), 172–191.

Salzman, M. B., & Halloran, M. J. (2004). Cultural trauma and recovery: Cultural meaning, self-esteem, and the re-construction of the cultural anxiety-buffer. In J. Greenberg, S. L. Koole, & T. Pyszczynski (Eds.), *Handbook of experimental existential psychology* (pp. 231–246). New York, NY: Guilford.

Salzman, M. (2005a). The dynamics of cultural trauma: Implications for the pacific nations. In A. J. Marsella, A. Austin, & B. Grant, (Eds.). *Social change and psychosocial adaptation in the Pacific Islands: Cultures in transition* (pp. 29–52). New York, NY: Springer.

Salzman, M. (2005b). Contextualizing the symptom in multicultural consultation: Anger in the family a cultural-historical context. *Journal of Educational and Psychological Consultation, 16*(3), 223–237.

Salzman, M. B. (2008). Globalization, religious fundamentalism and the need for meaning. *International Journal of Intercultural Relations, 32*(4), 318–327.

Salzman, M. (2012). Dehumanization as a prerequisite of atrocity and killing. In D. J. Christie, & J. E. Pim (Eds.), *Nonkilling psychology.* Honolulu, HI: Global Center for Non-Killing.

Sing, D. K. (1993). *Raising the achievement level of Native Hawaiians in the college classroom through the matching of teaching strategies with student characteristics* (Unpublished doctoral dissertation). Caremont University, CA.

Smith, L. T. (2012). *Decolonizing methodologies: Research and indigenous peoples* (2nd ed.). London & New York: Zen Books.

Sowislo, J. F., & Orth, U. (2013). Does low self-esteem predict depression and anxiety? A meta-analysis of longitudinal studies. *Psychological Bulletin, 139,* 213–240.

Stannard, D. E. (1989). *Before the horror.* Honolulu, HI: University of Hawaii Social Science Research Institute.

Taylor, R. (2005). Fiji's move into the 21st century. In A. J. Marsella, A. A. Austin, & B. Grant (Eds.), *Social change and psychosocial adaptation in the Pacific Islands* (pp.107–132). Honolulu, HI: Springer.

U.S. Census Bureau. (2000). *Census 2000 data for the United States.* Washington, DC: Government Printing Office.

Val, B. V. (1994). The passage out. In K. R. Howe, R. C. Kiste, & B. V. Lai (Eds.), *The tides of history: The Pacific islands in the twentieth century* (pp. 435–461). Honolulu, HI: University of Hawaii Press.

Self-Hatred, Self-Doubt, and Assimilation in Latina/o Communities: Las Consecuencias de Colonización y Opresión

Carlos P. Hipolito-Delgado, Stephany Gallegos Payan, and Teresa I. Baca

Internalized oppression in the Latina/o community is the legacy of the colonial experience and systemic oppression faced by this group. Internalized oppression among Latinas/os has its roots in colonization where, for the purposes of economic gain, European conquerors claimed a position of moral and biological superiority over Native American and African peoples (Chasteen, 2006; Zinn, 2003). Such positions would rationalize the genocide and subjugation of Native Americans and the importation of Africans as slaves (Acuña, 2000; Alaniz & Cornish, 2008). Further, the conquistadors' Eurocentric monocultural ideology led to attempts to eradicate the culture of Native Americans and Africans and to forcefully assimilate these peoples to a European value system (Acuña, 2000; Spring, 2007). Despite the centuries that have passed, Eurocentric values continue to permeate North and South America. Eurocentric monoculturalism to this day infects the minds of Latinas/os, causing them to question their self-worth and the value of their cultural heritage.

Exacerbating the effects of the colonial experience is a history of oppression faced by Latinas/os in the United States. U.S. politicians have used manifest destiny, the Platt amendment, and the Monroe doctrine to justify intervention, occupation, and the destabilization of Latin American countries (Acuña, 2000; Chasteen, 2006; Takaki, 1993). Additionally, the breaking of the treaty of Guadalupe Hidalgo, the implementation of Jim Crow laws, and xenophobic deportation policies crippled Latina/o communities in the United States (Acuña, 2000; Lipsitz, 1998; Spring, 2007; Takaki, 1993). When the historical effects of oppression and the lived experience of poverty, a biased justice system, and inferior schools are hidden by propaganda and the myth of meritocracy, Latinas/os accept the dominant discourse, internalize the oppression they face, and develop learned helplessness.

The lasting legacy of colonization and U.S. oppression for Latinas/os is self-doubt, self-hatred, and assimilation. The psychological consequences of these are diminished coping mechanisms, arrested ethnic identity development, and lowered self-esteem, all of which have important mental and behavioral health implications. To this end, in this chapter we: (1) introduce the reader to the Latina/o community; (2) examine the historical and contemporary origins of internalized oppression; (3) discuss the common manifestations and behavioral health implications of internalized oppression; and (4) introduce programs designed to challenge internalized oppression in Latina/o communities. Personal narratives from the authors, all of whom are part of the Latina/o community, are integrated in select parts of the chapter to bring some of the discussed concepts to life. It is hoped that this chapter will inspire dialogue and increased attention to internalized oppression among Latinas/os.

A DEMOGRAPHIC PROFILE OF LATINAS/OS

Developing a shared identity is a problematic aspect of the Latina/o experience, as a preferred cultural identifier continues to be contested (Gutierrez, 2004). Hispanic, Latina/o, and Chicana/o are examples of the ethnic identity labels endorsed by different segments of this population, but not universally agreed upon. For a more comprehensive discussion of identity labels please see Hipolito-Delgado and Diaz (2013). Though the pan-ethnic term of Latina/o is used in this chapter, it is encouraged that service providers adopt the preferred ethnic label of their clients (Hipolito-Delgado & Diaz, 2013).

Latinas/os are the second largest ethnic group in the United States, comprising 16.7% of the total population and growing by 15.2 million since the last census count in 2000 (Ennis, Rios-Vargas, & Albert, 2011). Geographically, California, New York, and Florida have the highest Latina/o populations (Motel & Pattern, 2012b). However, the South has the highest increase in Latinas/os, experiencing a growth of 57% over a 10-year period (Ennis et al., 2011). The median age for Latinas/os is 25,

12 years younger than the U.S. average (Motel & Pattern, 2012b). The five largest subgroups (comprising 84.4% of the Latina/o population) are Mexican, Puerto Rican, Cuban, Salvadorian, and Dominican. A brief description of these groups follows.

Mexicans

Due to their shared border with the United States and their long history of economic relations, it is no surprise that Mexicans are 63% of the total Latina/o population in the United States (Motel & Pattern, 2012b). Geographically, the majority of Mexicans reside in California. Despite the rhetoric surrounding undocumented immigrants, 73% of Mexicans are U.S. citizens (Motel & Pattern, 2012b). Though Mexicans remain the largest immigrant population in the country, immigration from Mexico has largely come to a standstill due to the economic recession in the United States and increased border enforcement (Passel, Cohn, & Gonzalez-Barrera, 2012). Data from 2005 to 2010 indicate that there is a net zero increase in immigration to and from Mexico (Passel et al., 2012). Migration to the United States has historically been prompted by demand for labor and agreements like the Bracero Program, which was enacted during World War II to authorize the importation of Mexican laborers to fill jobs in the United States that were left vacant by men involved in the war effort. Though Mexicans have one of the highest rates of English proficiency, they have the third lowest college completion rates (9%) among the Latina/o subgroups (Motel & Pattern, 2012b).

Puerto Ricans

Puerto Ricans have a complex sociopolitical and colonial history with the United States. After the War of 1898, the Spanish ceded the island to the United States (Santiago-Valles & Jimenez-Munoz, 2004). Since Puerto Rico is a U.S. colony, residents are granted U.S. citizenship, a unique characteristic from the other Latina/o subgroups. Puerto Ricans are the second largest subgroup, comprising 9.2% of the Latina/o population (Motel & Pattern, 2012b). Many Puerto Ricans identify as Boricuas, deriving from the indigenous name for the island (Santiago & Jiménez-Muñoz, 2004). Puerto Rican laborers, semi-skilled and unskilled, were drawn to the opportunities in the garment industry following WWII and largely migrated to the state of New York (Santiago & Jiménez-Muñoz, 2004). Consequently, the Bronx, New York, is home to the largest concentration of Puerto Ricans in the country.

Cubans

The close proximity and history of commercial ties to the United States make the migration pattern of Cubans particularly unique (Garcia, 2004). A distinguishing characteristic of Cuban migration to the United States is that it happened in waves. The first wave consisted mainly of professionals followed by the working middle classes during the 1960s (Garcia, 2004). Between 1965 and 1970, the second wave was prompted by the Castro regime and allowed those that wanted to leave to freely emigrate. The last wave of emigration occurred during the 1980s and was devised by Castro as a plan to also "rid" Cuba of dissidents and criminals, changing the perception of Cubans in the minds of most Americans (Garcia, 2004). Cubans comprise 3.7% of the Latina/o population in the United states. The average age of Cubans is 40, giving them the highest average age of all Latinas/os (Motel & Pattern, 2012b). In addition, Cubans have the highest rates of homeownership (Motel & Pattern, 2012b). Cubans primarily reside in the South, with the highest concentration being in Florida (Motel & Pattern, 2012b)

Salvadorians

Unlike the previous three subgroups, Salvadorian (3.6% of the Latina/o population) migration to the United States can largely be attributed to political unrest and civil war during the 1980s. Unlike Cubans, Salvadorians were not granted refugee status and the accompanying rights and benefits (Chincilla & Hamilton, 2004). A large majority (64%) of the Salvadorian population arrived to the United States after 1990 (Motel & Pattern, 2012a). Salvadorians are the least likely from the 10 largest Latina/o subgroups to hold a bachelor's degree (7%; Motel & Pattern, 2012b). The largest percentage of Salvadorians are found in the West, with California and Texas having the largest concentrations (Motel & Pattern, 2012b).

Dominicans

Dominican migration to the United States was significantly greater in the 1960s with the fall of the regime of Rafael Leonides Trujillo (Levitt, 2004). Due to the unstable government and subsequent economic decline in the Dominican Republic, thousands of Dominicans immigrated to the United States. Many of those who immigrated hoped to find employment as unskilled laborers; however, the changing labor market in the United States made it difficult for many to find jobs (Levitt, 2004). Dominicans comprise 3% of the Latina/o population and are the fifth largest Latina/o subgroup (Motel & Pattern, 2012b). Dominicans are the least likely of the ten largest Latina/o subgroups to own a home (24%; Motel & Pattern, 2012b). Dominicans are largely concentrated in the East, with 11% of all Dominicans living in New York (Motel & Pattern, 2012b).

EXPERIENCES OF HISTORICAL OPPRESSION

Although the Latina/o subgroups have distinct cultures and histories, they share a common bond of oppression. A thorough examination of the historical oppression faced by Latinas/os is beyond the scope of this chapter. However, to understand the oppression faced by Latinas/os, it is essential to explore the colonial period of Latin American history, the oppression perpetuated by the United States toward Latin America, and the oppression experienced by U.S. Latinas/os during the 19th and 20th centuries. It is also important to clarify at this point that—as alluded to in previous paragraphs—Latinas/os are not a racial group; they are the *mestizo* offspring of various racial groups (Gutierrez, 1998), including Africans, Native Americans, and Europeans. As such, consideration of the Latina/o experience with internalized oppression must consider the colonial experiences of Africans, Native Americans, and Europeans.

Colonial Latin America

The encounters between Europeans, Africans, and Native Americans significantly altered the course of history (Chasteen, 2006), particularly in the continents of North and South America. Europeans came to the Americas with experience dealing with people of diverse cultural origins, battle-hardened from the *reconquista* of the Iberian Peninsula, with superior weapons and armor, and with germs foreign to the Americas—the sum of which provided a significant military advantage over the indigenous population of the Americas (Acuña, 2000; Chasteen, 2006). The European military superiority was used to subjugate or exterminate native communities and to exploit the resources of the Americas (Alaniz & Cornish, 2008).

The conquest and subjugation of various indigenous communities, such as the Mexica (erroneously referred to as Aztecs) and Inca, was facilitated by their sedentary nature and complex social structures (Chasteen, 2006). The Mexica were an advanced society with elaborate cities, well-developed infrastructure, a market economy, educational system, complex agricultural practices, social stratification, and a system of taxation and tribute (Acuña, 2000; Alaniz & Cornish, 2008; Chasteen, 2006). Whereas nonsedentary indigenous tribes were smaller and less tied to land—allowing them to retreat when defeated in battle—the Mexicas, Inca, and other sedentary tribes could not as easily flee (Alaniz & Cornish, 2008). Once the Mexica and Inca was defeated, Spaniards took advantage of existing systems of tribute and taxation by leaving existing labor systems intact, but displaced native nobility so Spaniards would be beneficiaries (Acuña, 2000; Chasteen, 2006; Thorton, 1998). With this model in place, Spaniards were able to obtain precious metals at the expense of indigenous labor—allowing Spain to develop tremendous wealth and relegating native communities to lower social strata (Alaniz & Cornish, 2008; Chasteen, 2006).

The work of subjugating indigenous tribes was completed by the *encomienda* system—where *conquistadores* were "entrusted" the task of Christianizing natives and in exchange received free labor from them (Acuña, 2000; Chasteen, 2006). Through this process, native communities were forced to assimilate by learning Spanish and adopting European values. Part of this assimilation process required reverence for racial purity, which was reinforced through a system known as the *castas*. Pure-blooded Europeans were at the top end of the *castas* and pure-blooded Africans occupied the lowest level (Chasteen, 2006; Montalvo, 2004). The middle rungs of this system became increasingly complex as racial mixing occurred (Chasteen, 2006). Distinct categories existed for *Mulattos*, who had one African and one European parent, and for *Meztizos*, who had one European and one Native parent. Other categories such as *Tente en el aire* (up in the air) and *Salta para atras* (a step back) described more complex racial heritage. Social policy encouraged "whitening" by providing social advantages to those who were on the upper rungs of the *castas*—as such, Africans and Natives sought unions with Spaniards to improve their children's opportunities in life (Montalvo, 2004). The consequence of the *castas* was the idealization of whiteness, which continues to impact Latinas/os today (Montalvo, 2009).

Throughout the Americas, native communities were decimated by disease and European aggression. Native communities were vulnerable to European diseases, which led to a massive number of deaths that facilitated the conquest of many tribes (Acuña, 2000). Additionally, native communities who resisted colonization or who inhabited desirable territories (such as in Brazil, Argentina, Puerto Rico, and Cuba) were exterminated by Europeans (Chasteen, 2006). The eradication of native populations necessitated the importation of African slaves to the Americas (Chasteen, 2006; Thorton, 1998). Africans became the preferred slave of the Americas, as they were immune to many European diseases, had experience tending European cattle and crops, and European policies favored African slavery (Thorton, 1998). African slavery in the Americas and the *castas* system has relegated people of African ancestry to the lowest social and economic strata throughout Latin America.

The U.S. Experience

U.S. foreign and domestic policies continued the legacy of oppression for Latinas/os. The Platt Amendment, which allowed the United States to intervene in Cuba to preserve their independence, and the Monroe doctrine, which protected the Americas from European intervention, were used to rationalize U.S. military interventions in Latin America (Chasteen, 2006; Zinn, 2003). These policies were fueled by racist ideologies that depicted indigenous, Black, and *Mestizo* Latin Americans as inferior to Whites and depicted Latin America as a mischievous younger sibling in need of U.S. discipline (Chasteen, 2006; Zinn, 2003). The effect of these policies on Latin America was to weaken democracies and curtail economic development and independence—allowing the United States to protect its political and economic advantages.

Similarly, Manifest Destiny—the belief that God had destined European Americans to occupy the continent—was used as rationale to invade Mexico and claim the southwest (Acuña, 2000; Takaki, 1993). The treaty of Guadalupe Hidalgo, which ended the Mexican American War, ceded half of Mexico's territory (present day California, Nevada, Arizona, Utah, New Mexico, Texas, and Colorado) to the United States, but guaranteed the Mexicans who remained in the southwest all the rights of U.S. citizens and the ability to maintain their property (Acuña, 2000; Alaniz & Cornish, 2008). Despite this mutually agreed upon treaty, the United States would seize millions of acres of land from Mexicans and would create policy, such as the Greaser Act and the Mexican Miners Tax, that discriminated against people of Mexican ancestry (Acuña, 2000; Alaniz & Cornish, 2008; Takaki, 1993).

U.S. segregation laws also impacted Latinas/os. In 1897, Texas courts ruled that Mexicans were non-White, and in 1930 the California Attorney General categorized Mexicans as Indians; these rulings allowed for the segregation of Latinas/os in social institutions such as schools, public pools, movie theatres, housing, and in employment (Alaniz & Cornish, 2008; Spring, 2007). Despite the Civil Rights Act of 1866 (which granted citizenship for all native-born, non-Native Americans) and the Jones Act of 1917 (which granted citizenship to Puerto Ricans), Latinas/os did not receive full citizenship rights until the Voting Rights Act of 1965 (Spring, 2007). Prior to 1965, Latinas/os were actively and openly discriminated against; they were taken advantage of by the political and justice systems, denied voting rights, segregated in public institutions, and relegated to low-paying manual labor and dangerous working conditions (Acuña, 2000; Alaniz & Cornish, 2008; Spring, 2007). Perhaps the most blatant expression of discrimination came in the repatriation programs of 1930, which led to the deportation of over 400,000 Mexican Americans (Spring, 2007). The United States has a history of importing foreign, often

Latina/o or Mexican, laborers during a time of need and quickly deporting said workers when economic times turn tough. What distinguishes the repatriation acts of the 1930s was the number of U.S. citizens whose civil rights were violated when they were deported.

Through this brief glimpse of Latina's/o's history of oppression, it becomes evident how systemic forces over time have placed Latinas/os at a disadvantage. Next, we examine how this history of oppression has contemporary consequences for Latinas/os in the United States.

EXPERIENCES OF CONTEMPORARY OPPRESSION

The systemic inequalities present in modern U.S. society affect every aspect of the Latina/o experience. These inequities can be seen in the economic, educational, and judicial systems. The following section will briefly highlight examples of contemporary oppression experienced by Latinas/os.

Economic Marginalization and Inequalities

The economic marginalization of Latina/os indicates a troublesome reality. Latina/os comprise 26.6% of those living in poverty (Taylor, Lopez, Velasco, & Motel, 2012). The poverty rates for Latinas/os has increased six percentage points between 2006 and 2010, the largest jump of any ethnic group (DeNavas-Walt, Proctor, & Smith, 2011). Even more troublesome is the fact that for the first time in American history, the largest percentage of children in poverty are not Whites; approximately 32.3% (6.1 million) of all Latina/o children live in poverty, compared to only 17% of White children (Lopez & Velasco, 2011). Living in poverty has a variety of negative implications for Latinas/os, including limited educational resources, high dropout rates, and lack of affordable health care. For instance, Chapman, Laird, Ifill, and KewalRamani (2011) noted that children from low-income families are five times more likely than children from high-income families to drop out of school.

Moreover, recent reports indicate that after the housing market crash and economic downturn in 2008, the wealth gap between racial groups has further widened (Taylor et al., 2012). The percentage of change from 2005 to 2009 in Latina/o household wealth was −66% and represents the largest drop of all racial and ethnic groups—a stark contrast to −16% drop experienced by Whites during that same time period (Kochhar, Fry, & Taylor, 2011). Gaps also exist in median incomes; Latina/o households have a median income of $40,000, which is $9,800 less than the national average (Motel & Pattern, 2012b). It should also be noted that Latinas/os have more persons per household than other ethnic groups, requiring this smaller dollar figure to provide for more people. In addition, 11% of all Latina/os are unemployed, a rate higher than the national average of 8.5% (U.S. Bureau of Labor & Statistics, 2011).

As an example of the difficult realities of many Latinas/os with low socioeconomic standing, the third author (TIB), who is a Latina teacher in a predominantly Latina/o high school, shared her experience working with Latina/o students of low socioeconomic background:

> Working in a community that is largely Latina/o, I see the ways in which poverty directly affects students' educational outcomes. My students often take jobs in order to help support their families. One student worked 30 hours a week to help her family buy groceries. Other students lack proper nutrition. A student once told me that he often went hungry because there was not money to buy groceries. I had another student who lived with his father and was in danger of failing all his classes because he had missed so much school. I learned that this student had to make a 40-minute walk to and from school every day, since his father worked long hours.

Discrimination in the Justice System

Currently, 34.9% of all inmates are Latina/o (Federal Bureau of Prisons, 2012; Mauer & King, 2007) and 40% of all offenders who receive federal prison sentences are Latina/o (Lopez & Light, 2009). Considering that Latinas/os comprise only 16.7% of the general population, one must believe that either Latinas/os are more prone to crime or that ethnic discrimination exists in the U.S. justice system. The latter point becomes more realistic when statistics indicate that Latina/os are incarcerated 1.8 times more than Whites (Mauer & King, 2007). Clearly, Latinas/os are disproportionately represented in the U.S. justice system. The first author (CPH-D), a Chicano professor of Counselor Education, discussed his experience with racial profiling.

> As a young man I had various experiences where I felt I was racially profiled by law enforcement. These include numerous occasions where I was followed or stopped for no apparent reason. As an undergraduate I was once detained for an hour by police officers. The officers explained I was stopped because there had been a number of break-ins in the area and I looked suspicious. I am a dark-skinned Chicano and at the time had a bald head. I lived in a predominantly white, upper

middle class area of LA. It was late evening and I was walking home carrying two bags. The officers called for backup and proceeded to search me and my belongings. At one point I was surrounded by a total of eight police officers. When I was finally released the captain assured me that my civil rights had not been violated, as such it would be pointless to file a complaint. Further, he stated, "You should be more careful when you are out late at night."

Educational Marginalization and Inequalities

The educational system, once thought of as the pathway to social mobility, is not equally serving all students, as Latina/o and African American students are over-represented in special education, remedial education, lower ability groups, and vocational tracks (Potts, 2003; Rothstein, 2004). Students in these groups or tracks do not receive instruction that will promote critical thinking skills (Potts, 2003) or the skills required to be successful in higher education. Additionally, Latina/o students are more likely to attend large, underfunded schools, which limits their access to qualified teachers, professional school counselors, and art, music, and other special programs (Hipolito-Delgado & Lee, 2007). The lack of educational resources negatively impacts the quality and depth of education (Rothstein, 2004).

The lack of quality education for Latinas/os negatively impacts Latina/o students' degree attainment. Despite historical gains, Latinas/os continue to have the lowest rates of high school and postsecondary completion. Data from the U.S. Department of Education (2012b) indicates that Latinas/os have the highest dropout rates among all ethnic groups. Though recent reports indicate a rise in associate's degree attainment among Latina/os, such an attainment do not necessarily lead to bachelor's degree attainment (U.S. Department of Education, 2012a). Latina/o students earn 9% of all bachelor degrees conferred in the United States, a figure that is significantly lower than the proportion of Latinas/os in the country and the 72.9% of Whites holding bachelor degrees (U.S. Department of Education, 2012b).

Additionally, recent battles over ethnic studies in Arizona schools attest to the fact that U.S. society still largely values a Eurocentric monocultural curriculum. This type of pedagogy and curriculum sends the message to Latinas/os and other students of color that the contributions of people of color to U.S. history and society are not valuable and, rather, that only a European American perspective is valid (Loewen, 1995; Spring, 2007). Additionally, Latina/o students are denied knowledge of how centuries of racism and classism have created social and economic privilege for European Americans, and social and economic oppression for Latinas/os (Hipolito-Delgado & Lee, 2007; Lipsitz, 1998). The consequence is that Latina/o students question their ability and the worth of their culture. Subtle messages like these are known as microaggressions—subtle forms of discrimination in the systemic (such as the policies described above) and interpersonal levels that convey negative and degrading messages (Huynh, 2012). Huynh (2012) found that Latinas/os who experienced microaggressions also displayed somatic and depressive symptoms, as well as negative emotions such as anger. While working as a counseling intern at a predominantly White high school, TIB experienced microaggressions in the interpersonal level from both students and staff.

> I vividly remember the first time I experienced a microaggression from a White student. The student was sent to my office by another counselor to talk about the admissions process at Ivy League schools. The student looked confused when he saw me in the office. The student took a step back and went back to the other counselor's office. I overheard the student ask the other counselor if he had made a mistake because he did not think I could help him. He eventually came back to my office, still looking confused and annoyed, and asked me, "Are YOU the counselor that is supposed to help me with my Ivy League applications?" I was in shock and felt that I needed to prove myself by sharing with him my educational background and credentials. I immediately understood that he was judging my abilities based on my appearance—I was the only dark-skinned counselor in the department.

COMMON MANIFESTATIONS OF INTERNALIZED OPPRESSION

It is clear from the discussion thus far that Latinas/os have extensive experiences of systemic and interpersonal oppression. The American ideals of self-sufficiency and the notion of meritocracy are not applicable to all Americans. Systemic inequities make it very difficult for most Latinas/os to climb the socioeconomic ladder. The combined effects of educational, economic, and judicial inequities make the social issues that Latina/os face a systemic issue. When systemic, historical, and contemporary oppression are coupled with a dominant discourse that idealizes rugged individualism and Euro American values, oppression is internalized. When oppression is internalized, Latinas/os accept notions that blame their cultural heritage for their sociopolitical circumstances and for the limited opportunities for social advancement. Although limited literature exists exploring the manifestation of internalized oppression among Latinas/os, it has been our experience that internalized oppression among Latinas/os is often manifested in the extreme acceptance of dominant discourse and propaganda, in full assimilation to Euro American ideals, in lowered academic engagement and achievement, and in learned helplessness.

Dominant Discourse and Assimilation

Dominant discourse in Latin America and in the United States idealizes European values and beliefs, which are often at odds with Latina/o cultural values. For example, Latina/o values of family, humility, community, and cooperation are in contrast with typical American values of rugged individualism, competition, and materialism. Because of the idealization of European values and beliefs, the historical experiences of oppression faced by Latinas/os, and their continued oppression in modern day America as exemplified by the limited recognition of Latina/o contributions to the United States, anti-immigrant sentiments and policies, and English only rhetoric and policies, have created conditions that lead many Latinas/os to feel shame toward their ethnic heritage. As Latinas/os internalize these oppressive notions, they reject their cultural heritage and attempt to assimilate into European American cultural values. According to Berry (1997), assimilation is one acculturation strategy where a person abandons his or her culture heritage and adopts the cultural values of the dominant society. Latinas'/os' experiences of historical and contemporary oppression are important factors promoting many Latinas/os to assimilate to European American cultural values.

An example of this manifestation of internalized oppression is when Latinas/os take action to deny their cultural heritage. CPH-D describes his experiences with many Latina/o high school and university students who deny their heritage and prefer an American identity.

> I have interacted with many Latina/o students who are aggravated when they are called "Latina/o." They believe that they are purely American. Back when I was a college counselor I remember some Latino/a students being insulted when I recommended for them to take an ethnic studies or Latin American history courses. I vividly remember one student telling me, "We are in America now. Learning about Latin American history and culture is useless."

The denial of their cultural heritage is also promoted through the loss of Spanish fluency. To be clear, we are not saying that one has to speak Spanish to be a proud Latina/o. However, there is a wide body of research that points to the connection between Spanish fluency and ethnic identity (Hipolito-Delgado, 2007; Ontai-Grzebik & Raffaelli, 2004; Torres, 2003). Moreover, the inability to speak Spanish limits access to elders, cultural artifacts, and cultural performances which can often require Spanish fluency (Hipolito-Delgado & Diaz, 2013). SGP, a Latina graduate student in school counseling, describes her experience working with Latina/o parents who find Spanish to be a roadblock to their children's success:

> I have met many Latina/o parents who do not want to teach their children Spanish, believing their children will be more successful in education and in life if they speak English only. What these parents neglect are the cognitive and economic benefits of being bilingual. By denying their cultural heritage, these Latina/o parents accept the oppressive notion that their cultural heritage is, in some way, an obstacle to their children's success in the United States.

And when parents do encourage their children to learn Spanish, TIB added:

> I have Latina/o students that enroll in my Spanish classes because they claim they are forced to learn the language by their parents. Several of these students have asked me, "Why is it important to learn Spanish when we live in the United States, where English is the official language?" Throughout the school year, these students also often question the Latina/o cultural traditions and celebrations and sometimes regard them as being "dumb" and "weird."

Another manifestation of internalized oppression that results from devaluing Latina/o culture and attempting to assimilate is the acceptance of social and political positions, which are damaging to Latinas/os. By taking on conservative political positions, such as being anti-immigration, anti-affirmative action, and pro-English only, Latinas/os reaffirm oppressive dominant discourse. Additionally, when anti-immigrant and pro-English only positions are taken by Latinas/os, they accept the notion that people of their cultural heritage are impediments to U.S. progress and that assimilation is the key to success in the United States. TIB narrated:

> I often hear Latina/o students comment on how undocumented immigrants abuse U.S. social systems. They believe that undocumented immigrants come to this country to take away jobs meant for Americans and to live off welfare and food stamps. They say things like, "We work hard and pay taxes to pay for these people's medical bills and food stamps." Some students also believe that undocumented immigrants

are able to go to college because they get more financial aid compared to U.S. citizens. Others have also used the term "anchor babies" to describe illegal immigrants who come to the United States only to have their child be born here and to take advantage of the social systems.

SGP added:

> I have heard Latina/o students who are more assimilated express resentment toward other Latinas/os for not ascribing to American values. Less acculturated Latinas/os are often called derogatory names such as "paisa" or "ghetto." What is worse is that by affirming politically conservative positions, Latinas/os are damaging their own sociopolitical interests.

In addition to accepting inferiorizing, denigrating, and oppressive messages about Latinas/os that lead to within-group discrimination, internalized oppression in Latinas/os is also often manifested in the idealization of White skin color and other typical European physical features (Montalvo, 2004; Telzer & Vazquez Garcia, 2009). Since colonial times, ideals of beauty and physiognomy—the judgment of character through physical features—have favored Europeans (Fortes de Leff, 2002; Montalvo, 2004, 2009). This preference is reinforced by the fact that Latinas/os who are able to pass as White are rewarded with privileges and social mobility not afforded their darker skinned peers (Fergus, 2009). The preference for European features manifests in cosmetic practices and in discourse. In an attempt to access white privilege or to fit the European ideals of beauty, Latinas/os might turn to whitening creams, which espouse to lighten darker skin. Other practices such as avoiding the sun, the bleaching of hair, and the use of colored contact lenses might be used to attain more European features. CPH-D narrated:

> I had a Latina colleague whose mother frequently criticized her for being dark-skinned. My colleague internalized these negative messages and avoided being out in the sun whenever possible. She had a boyfriend who was an avid surfer. Whenever she went with him to the beach she would hide inside a mummy sleeping bag so she would not tan.

SGP added:

> I recall an instance in high school when I returned from vacation and had noticeably tanned. A classmate remarked how I had gotten so dark. I remember feeling ashamed and embarrassed and not really

understanding why. For the next couple of years, I made a conscious effort to stay out of the sun so that I could go back to being lighter skinned and more "white." It wasn't until I went to college, took Chicana/o studies courses, and joined cultural organizations that I realized the beauty of my culture. These experiences in college increased my self-confidence and helped me to accept my features, my skin color, and my ethnic identity.

Internalized oppression may also manifest through discourse, in that terms that reference people of darker skin tones (such as *Indio, Prieto,* and *Negro*) are considered derogatory (Montalvo, 2004). These terms associate dark skin color with ignorance, low moral character, and being members of the lower class (Montalvo, 2004). By accepting European notions of beauty and by degrading those with dark skin, Latinas/os accept oppressive notions of European superiority.

Lower Academic Achievement

Scholars are quick to blame Latina/o students for their lack of educational attainment (Valencia, 2002; Velez & Saenz, 2001). Unfortunately, many Latina/o youth internalize messages that they are not as skilled academically as their white peers and, in order to maintain their self-esteem, these students psychologically disassociate from academics (Schmader, Major, & Gramzow, 2001; Velez & Saenz, 2001). The consequence of this psychological disassociation for Latina/o students are lowered academic expectations, the belief that school is a "White thing," or the devaluing of education (Schmader et al., 2001; Velez & Saenz, 2001). Psychological disassociation results in Latina/o students placing less effort in or ascribing less importance to their academic achievement (Schmader et al., 2001), until they either dropout or are pushed out of school (Velez & Saenz, 2001). Some students will espouse messages that they are "not school material", that Latinas/os are not good at school, or that school is meant for White people. SGP, who has 10 years of experience working with Latina/o youth, stated:

> Many Latina/o 9th graders think that school is "not for them" and that they are not capable of going to college, simply because they are Latina/o. Many times these youth lack Latina/o role models who have successfully navigated the educational pipeline. Instead, what they most often see are other Latinas/os dropping out of school. Academically successful Latinas/os are so rare that many Latina/o students are usually shocked to learn that I—a Latina just like them—attended their high school and am now seeking a graduate degree.

MENTAL AND BEHAVIORAL HEALTH IMPLICATIONS OF INTERNALIZED OPPRESSION

The internalization of oppression can potentially have various mental and behavioral health implications for Latinas/os. Unfortunately, there is a void in the literature regarding the psychological health implications of internalized oppression among this group. However, through our practice with Latinas/os, we have encountered mental and behavioral health consequences related to assimilation and idealization of whiteness. We combine our personal experiences with findings of relevant literature on other groups to make the argument that internalized oppression has several negative effects on Latina/o mental and behavioral health.

Assimilation

There are several mental and behavioral health consequences of internalized oppression for Latinas/os. Some of these consequences include ethnic self-hatred, loss of ethnic identity, and feelings of exclusion. Hipolito-Delgado (2010) found a direct relationship between U.S. cultural identity and internalized racism. Based on this finding, he argued that there is a direct relationship between assimilation and ethnic self-hatred. Ethnic self-hatred can lead to embarrassment about one's family, particularly those who are less acculturated, and toward Latina/o cultural values, arts, music, and food. As TIB stated:

> There had been many occasions during parent-teacher conferences where I witnessed Latina/o students who are embarrassed of their parents. Many times these students expressed being embarrassed because their parents could not speak any English or because they could not speak English properly. I had several students comment on how embarrassed they felt when their parents asked questions or made comments during the meetings. One student in particular told me, "I do not understand why my parents would question my teachers. They are not even educated and do not speak English. They should not be giving opinions when they do not understand what happens in the schools here in the United States." On another occasion, a student told me that he did not accompany his parents to the parent-teacher conferences because his parents dressed differently. This student was ashamed that his parents were not Americanized enough in their dress and behaviors.

At its most extreme, ethnic self-hatred can lead to rage, which can be directed at family members or other Latinas/os. Please see Delgado-Romero (1999) for examples of this and the consequences of extreme ethnic self-hatred. Ethnic self-hatred is believed to have negative consequences for self-concept, self-esteem, and adversely impact familial relations. In communities of African descent, internalized racism is positively related to depressive symptoms (Taylor, Henderson, & Jackson, 1991) and stress (Tull, Sheu, Butler, & Cornelious, 2005).

In his model of Chicana/o ethnic identity development, Ruiz (1990) argues that the internalization of discriminatory messages leads to the development of ethnic self-hatred, which in turn leads to the abandonment of ethnic identity. This notion is supported by the research of Cokley (2002), who found a relationship between the internalization of negative racial stereotypes and the early stages of racial identity development in Black college students. Ethnic identity is a crucial construct in understanding the mental and behavioral health of Latinas/os. In Latinas/os, ethnic identity is positively associated with self-esteem (Umaña-Taylor, 2004), coping and optimism (Roberts et al., 1999), and academic achievement (Altschul, Oyserman, & Bybee, 2006; Zarate, Bhimji, & Reese, 2005). As such, the loss of ethnic identity should be of concern among Latinas/os, as it is likely to have negative consequences for their mental health and academic achievement. Further, research with other ethnic minority communities indicates that ethnic identity serves as a protective buffer between perceived racism and self-esteem (Cassidy, O'Conner, Howe, & Warden, 2004; Mossakowski, 2003). Research examining if ethnic identity serves as a protective factor for Latinas/os has not been conducted, but, given the shared experience of minority communities in the United States, there is reason to believe that such a relationship among Latinas/os might also exist.

Loss of ethnic identity may also lead to loss of peer support groups and feelings of exclusion, which may negatively affect mental health and well-being. In the United States, ethnicity is a dominant identity, one that is readily used to organize and group people (Robinson-Wood, 2009). This is particularly true in the K-16 educational contexts where students either self-select or are encouraged, both subtly and overtly, to associate with peers of their same ethnicity (Tatum, 1997). Latina/o students who reject their ethnicity are often shunned by their Latina/o peers. Those students who reject their ethnicity are referred to as "sell outs" and are accused of trying to act white. CPH-D shared:

> As an undergraduate I was involved with Chicana/o student organizations. Occasionally, Chicana/o or Latina/o students who were not knowledgeable about their cultural heritage or who seemed "white washed" would try to join these student groups. These new students were typically ignored by current members and purposely excluded from group functions. These students were never explicitly told that they could not join, but were made to feel unwelcome so that they would opt out.

For Latina/o students who are able to "pass" into other ethnic circles, these feelings of rejection might be diminished by the social support they receive from non-Latina/o peers. However, for Latina/o students who are unable to pass or are rejected by other ethnic circles, the feelings of isolation and rejection are heightened. Berry (1997) hypothesized that those who experience rejection by both their heritage and the dominant cultures experience marginalization, and are likely to experience intense social isolation and depression.

Idealization of Whiteness

When European-American ideals of beauty are internalized, there are negative socio-economic, physical, and mental health implications for Latinas/os. Although some Latinas/os are able to pass as white and might be less likely to experience stress related to conforming to European American ideals of beauty, many more Latinas/os are unable to pass and consequently experience negative psychological reactions. Researchers have identified that for Latinas/os darker skin color is associated with diminished educational outcomes, lower socio-economic status, lower self-esteem, and negative body image (Telzer & Vasquez Garcia, 2009). This is consistent with research on communities of African descent where internalized racism is positively related to waist circumference (Butler, Tull, Chambers, & Taylor, 2002; Chambers et al., 2004). In our experience, we have noted that Latinas/os who accept European American ideals of beauty often have low self-esteem and negative body image. As SGP shared:

> When I was younger, I often hated my physical features because they were not what American culture deemed as beautiful. Growing up I collected Barbie dolls that had colored eyes and "perfect" female proportions. I often compared myself to Barbie. Unfortunately, I did not have colored eyes or straight hair and my body proportions were not like Barbie or the White women I saw on television. This led me to have poor self-esteem throughout middle and high school.

Latinas/os who endorse European American ideals are more likely to have distorted body image and increased rates of depression (Xie et al., 2010). To fit the European American ideal of beauty, many Latinas/os undergo plastic surgery. A recent trend in the United States and Latin America is to buy plastic surgery as a gift for young Latinas' *quinceñera* (Chajin, 2010). Having a distorted body image also contributes to unhealthy eating and dieting practices (Xie et al., 2010), which may lead to the development of eating disorders. Once thought of as a "White phenomenon," eating disorders are on the rise in the Latina/o community (Gordon, Castro,

Sitnikov, & Holm-Denoma, 2010; Granillo, Jones-Rodriguez, & Carvajal, 2005; Reyes-Rodriguez et al., 2010; Xie et al., 2010). The mental and behavioral consequences of eating disorders are well-documented in the counseling and psychology literature. For Latinas/os, eating disorders are related to low self-esteem, negative affectivity, depression, and substance abuse (Granillo et al., 2005; Reyes-Rodriguez et al., 2010). Mental health practitioners are called to consider how eating disorders among Latinas/os might be a result of internalized oppression.

CLINICAL AND COMMUNITY PROGRAMS FOR INTERNALIZED OPPRESSION

Considering the systemic oppression experienced by Latinas/os, the dominant contemporary American discourse that promotes ethnic self-hatred, and the troubling mental health implications of internalized oppression for this group, it is crucial to have in place programs that promote and encourage positive attitudes toward Latina/o culture. Promoting a positive ethnic identity in Latinas/os is a crucial component to resisting internalized oppression.

Montalvo (2004) argued that many Latinas/os have a preference for European features and bias against dark skin. Montalvo (2009) and Organista (2009) encouraged clinicians to ask Latina/o clients how skin color privilege or bias has impacted their life. Organista (2009) suggests that therapists display empathy toward, normalize experiences with, educate about the roots of, and challenge the skin color bias or privilege. Montalvo (2009) made the following recommendations to aid therapists in dealing with skin color privilege and bias in Latina/o clients: (1) train therapists in conducting critical incident interviews; (2) reduce implicit bias in therapists; and (3) conduct empirical research on skin color bias. The development of ethnic identity is particularly crucial in combating the negative self-perception associated with the idealization of whiteness (Telzer & Vazquez Garcia, 2009). By increasing ethnic identification and connections to their cultural groups, therapists can help Latina/o clients obtain social and psychological support that serves as a buffer against Eurocentric ideals of beauty (Telzer & Vazquez Garcia, 2009). The American School Counseling Association suggests incorporating cultural events, classroom guidance presentations, psychoeducational groups, and clubs at schools that highlight Latina/o culture (Villalba, Akos, Keeter, & Ames, 2007). TIB provided the following narrative on how she tries to promote the ethnic identity of her Latina/o students:

> As a Spanish teacher, I continuously incorporate cultural and historical activities in class to educate Latina/o students about their community

and to give students the opportunity to connect and understand their culture. Latina/o music, movies, literature, and poems are all included in the class curriculum. I also often share with students my personal stories and experiences as a Latina in the United States to encourage students to celebrate their own heritages. These stories, which highlight our culture, ethnic identity, and academic achievement, help students challenge popular discourse and promote a positive Latina/o ethnic identity. I try to set myself up as a role model, to show students that I do not have to forget about my heritage in order to become successful.

In *Hijas Americanas: Beauty, Body Image and Growing Up Latina*, Molinary (2007) stated that Latinas often struggle to bring together the realities of two identities: their cultural values and the values of mainstream American society. This is especially true when it relates to beauty and body image, making Latinas vulnerable to eating disorders, weight gain, body image dissatisfaction, and low self-esteem. TIB developed and implemented a Gardening Group program for Latinas who attended high school in a predominantly White community. The goals of the program included promoting positive self-esteem and the feelings of love and belonging. Reality therapy, art therapy, and gardening were incorporated along with cultural and body image presentations into the 8-week program. Reality-therapy was incorporated because it highly emphasizes peer support and collaboration, values that are culturally relevant to Latinas/os (Hipolito-Delgado & Diaz, 2013), as well as self-direction. Thus, the program attempted to build a positive self-esteem among the participants and allowing them to openly share and learn about their experiences as Latinas/os. Art therapy and gardening were incorporated to allow the students to communicate their experiences and thoughts through their own personalized viewpoints. The tangible activities allowed the students to process, build, and reshape views of their self-image and ethnic identity. The students challenged dominant discourse and created individualized points of view of their self and body. TIB stated:

> The activities incorporated in the program allowed the students to build a positive self-esteem and body image. At the beginning of the program, the majority of the girls were hesitant to speak and all reported feeling different from their White classmates. A lot of them used words like "fat," "different," "out of place," and "too curvy" to describe themselves in the prequestionnaire. Since the activities allowed the students to make connections with their culture, heritage, and with each other, the students began building a positive self-esteem through mutual collaboration and understanding of their personal stories. In the closing activity, students described themselves using words such as "strong," "proud," "beautiful," "wise," "confident," and "powerful Latina."

Promoting academic self-efficacy and career awareness in Latinas/os requires incorporating a variety of positive activities where students can be actively involved in the process of making academic and career decisions. This is especially important because Latinas/os tend to have lower expectations of their academic and career abilities, a consequence of internalized oppression. In a study carried out by Gushue, Clarke, Pantzer, and Scanlan (2006), Latina/o students who were presented with career exploration activities in high school felt more confident in the career decision-making process and had a better understanding of their goals, interests, and abilities. According to the Theory of Possible Selves, Latinas'/os' lower aspirations are mainly due to the imbalance of their possible selves (Yowell, 2002). Their expected-selves (what they could become) far outweighs their hoped-for selves (what they would like to become). The expected-self is mainly influenced by society and is more likely to affect the adaptation of behaviors and thoughts. Gushue et al. (2006) explained that since Latinas/os recognize and internalize the various obstacles in society, such as racism and discrimination, they have less motivation to be involved in career exploration and fail to understand the connection between education and the world of work. Therefore, Latina/o "vocational inclinations can only become career interests. . . [when they] believe they can perform the tasks required in a given occupation and do not perceive overwhelming obstacles to their success" (Gushue et al., 2006, p. 308).

Consistent with Gushue et al.'s (2006) recommendations, TIB developed and implemented a program at a continuation high school where students gained awareness, knowledge, confidence, and experience with the academic and career decision process. Most importantly, the program challenged the students' attitudes and perceptions about their hoped-for selves. The purpose of this program was to educate students about the role of education and the world of work, to increase the students' level of confidence in their academic and career abilities, and to inform students about their educational options. The program included various components such as career interest assessments, academic planning, occupation clusters and information, role-playing, development of a portfolio, and a presentation of life's goals and achievements. According to TIB:

> The majority of the students were unaware of their post-secondary and career options when they began the program. Additionally, all students had limited knowledge or confidence in their academic and career abilities. When asked about their hoped-for selves, all students responded with the answers like "janitor," "electrician," or "construction worker." Some students began writing careers such as "lawyer" or "doctor," but laughed and told me that they would never be able to accomplish those dreams. These self-perceptions are influenced

by internalized oppression. Nonetheless, it was astounding to see the students' progress through the program. Many students commented that the hands-on activities helped them gain confidence and believe in their abilities. The confidence and positive self-growth was obvious when the students presented their final portfolios and emotional exit-interview presentations. All of the students spoke about their struggles, but most importantly, about who they were and what they wanted to become.

Various mentoring programs exist in secondary and post-secondary institutions to help Latinas/os navigate the education system. Nationwide programs, such as Big Brothers Big Sisters' Hispanic Mentoring Program, work hand in hand with schools to provide Latina/o students with role models and guidance. Mentoring programs typically focus on educating Latinas/os about their culture, educational opportunities, and career awareness. However, mentoring programs can also help Latinas/os with their psychosocial needs. According to Bordes and Arredondo (2005), Latino college students who are part of mentoring programs also transition more positively into their college lives.

FUTURE RESEARCH AND SERVICE DIRECTIONS

From this chapter it is evident that Latinas/os suffer mental, behavioral, academic, and sociopolitical consequences from the internalization of the oppression. Equally evident is the dearth of research on internalized oppression as experienced by Latinas/os. Research is needed to identify the conditions that lead Latinas/os to internalize oppression, as well as research on the consequences of internalized oppression and the efficacy of interventions that attempt to prevent or address internalized oppression. Identifying the conditions that lead to the internalization of oppression among Latinas/os is a crucial first step for research. Not only will such research identify the underlying etiology of internalized oppression among Latinas/os, it would also aid theorists and practitioners in developing interventions that might block or eradicate the internalization of oppression.

Research is also needed on the mental, behavioral, academic, and sociopolitical consequences of internalized oppression among Latinas/os. The outcomes of such research would help establish the importance of this line of inquiry, inspiring increased awareness of internalized oppression as experienced by Latinas/os. This increased awareness might aid practitioners to recognize the effects that internalized oppression may have on their clients, inspire other researchers to further investigate this line of inquiry, and force policy makers to recognize the systemic inequities that contribute to the oppression of Latinas/os. Until researchers are able to concretely document the repercussions of internalized oppression for Latinas/os, the mental health fields and society as a whole can feel justified in ignoring this topic.

Once the previous lines of research begin to yield results, earnest effort can be made to develop interventions to prevent and address the internalization of oppression among Latinas/os. In addition to developing interventions, practitioners and researchers must also document the efficacy of said interventions. A mistake the mental health professions have made for too long is not empirically demonstrating the outcomes of our work. By developing interventions and properly assessing their outcomes, practitioners can continue to refine interventions and better serve communities.

CONCLUSION

Internalized oppression in Latinas/os has received limited attention in the counseling and psychology literature. As such, a void exists in understanding the manifestations and behavioral and mental health implications of internalized oppression. We hope that this chapter is a step toward filling this void. In addition to inspiring trainees and practitioners to consider the topic of internalized oppression in Latinas/os, we hope this chapter inspires researchers to pursue empirical inquiry on internalized oppression in Latinas/os. Lastly, we hope that this chapter inspires the reader to consider how historical oppression and current systemic oppression negatively impacts Latinas/os. The internalization of oppression in Latinas/os is a product of centuries of discrimination and oppression. Until we as a mental health profession recognize and address sociopolitical inequities and systemic oppression, we will continue to see clients who experience, and suffer from the consequences of, internalized oppression.

REFERENCES

Acuña, R. (2000). *Occupied America: A history of Chicanos* (4th ed.). Melo Park, CA: Longman.

Alaniz, Y., & Cornish, M. (2008). *Viva la raza: A history of Chicano identity & resistance.* Seattle, WA: Red Letter Press.

Altschul, I., Oyserman, D., & Bybee, D. (2006). Racial-ethnic Identity in mid-adolescence: Content and change as predictors of academic achievement. *Child Development, 77,* 1155–1169. doi:10.1111/j.1467-8624.2006.00926.x

Berry, J. W. (1997). Immigration, acculturation, and adaptation. *Applied Psychology: An International Review, 46,* 5–68.

Bordes, V., & Arredondo, P. (2005). Mentoring and 1st-year latina/o college students. *Journal of Hispanic Higher Education, 4,* 114–133.

Butler, C., Tull, E. S., Chambers, E. C., & Taylor, J. (2002). Internalized racism, body fat distribution and abnormal fasting glucose among African-Caribbean women in Dominica, West Indies. *Journal of National Medical Association, 94,* 143–148.

Cassidy, C., O'Conner, R. C., Howe, C., & Warden, D. (2004). Perceived discrimination and psychological distress: The role of personal and ethnic self-esteem. *Journal of Counseling Psychology, 51,* 329–339.

Chajin, F. (2010, April 20). Quinceañeras get breast implants. Retrieved from http://news.terra.com/quinceaneras-get-breast-implants,c478dbcf458a7310 VgnCLD200000bbcceb0aRCRD.html

Chambers, E. C., Tull, E. S., Fraser, H. S., Mutuhu, N. R., Sobers, N., & Niles, E. (2004). The relationship of internalized racism to body fat distribution and insulin resistance among African adolescent youth. *Journal of the National Medical Association, 96,* 1594–1598.

Chapman, C., Laird, J., Ifill, N., and KewalRamani, A. (2011). *Trends in High School Dropout and Completion Rates in the United States: 1972–2009* (NCES 2012–006). U.S. Department of Education. Washington, DC: National Center for Education Statistics. Retrieved from http://nces.ed.gov/pubsearch.

Chasteen, J. C. (2006). *Born in blood & fire: A concise history of Latin America* (2nd ed.). New York, NY: W. W. Norton & Company.

Chincilla, N. S., & Hamilton, N. (2004). Central American immigrants: Diverse populations, changing communities. In D. G. Gutiérrez (Ed.), *The Columbia history of Latinos in the United States since 1960* (pp. 187–228). Chichester, NY: Columbia University Press.

Cokley, K. O. (2002). Testing Cross's revised racial identity model: An examination of the relationship between racial identity and internalized racialism. *Journal of Counseling Psychology, 49,* 476–483.

Delgado-Romero, E. A. (1999). The face of racism. *Journal of Counseling & Development, 77,* 23–25. doi:10.1002/j.1556-6676.1999.tb02408.x

DeNavas-Walt, C., Proctor, B. D., & Smith, J. C. (2011). *Income, poverty, and health insurance coverage in the United States: 2010.* Washington DC: United States Census Bureau. Retrieved from http://www.census.gov/prod/2011pubs/ p60-239.pdf

Ennis, S. R., & Albert, N. G. (2011). *The Hispanic population: 2010.* Washington D.C.: United States Census Bureau. Retrieved from http://www.census .gov/prod/cen2010/briefs/c2010br-04.pdf.

Federal Bureau of Justice. (2012). *Quick facts about bureau of prisons.* Retrieved from http://www.bop.gov/about/facts.jsp

Fergus, E. (2009). Understanding Latino students' schooling experiences: The relevance of skin color among Mexican and Puerto Rican high school students. *Teachers College Record, 111,* 339–375.

Fortes de Leff, J. (2002). Racism in Mexico: Cultural roots and clinical interventions. *Family Process, 41*, 619–623.

García, M. C. (2004). Exiles, immigrants, and transnationals: The Cuban communities of the United States. In D. G. Gutiérrez (Ed.), *The Columbia history of Latinos in the United States since 1960* (pp. 146–186). Chichester, NY: Columbia University Press.

Gordon, K. H., Castro, Y., Sitnikov, L., & Holm-Denoma, J. M. (2010). Cultural body shape ideals and eating disorder symptoms among White, Latina, and Black college women. *Cultural Diversity and Ethnic Minority Psychology, 16*, 135–143. doi:10.1037/a0018671

Granillo, R., Jones-Rodriguez, G., & Carvajal, S. C. (2005). Prevalence of eating disorders in Latina adolescents: Associations with substance use and other correlate. *Journal of Adolescent Health, 36*, 214–220.

Gushue, G. V., Clarke, C. P., Pantzer, K. M., & Scanlan, K. R. L. (2006). Self-efficacy,perceptions of barriers, vocational identity, and the career exploration behavior of Latino/a high school students. *The Career Development Quarterly, 54*, 307–317.

Gutierrez, D. G. (2004). Demography and the Shifting boundaries of "Community": Reflections on "U.S. Latinos" and the Evolution of Latino Studies. In D. G. Gutiérrez (Ed.), *The Columbia history of Latinos in the United States since 1960* (pp. 1–42). Chichester, NY: Columbia Press.

Gutierrez, R. A. (1998). Hispanic diaspora and Chicano identity in the United States. *The South Atlantic Quarterly, 1/2*, 203–215.

Hipolito-Delgado, C. P. (2007). Internalized racism and ethnic identity in Chicana/o and Latina/o college students. Doctoral dissertation, Available from ProQuest Dissertations and Theses database. (UMI No. AAT 3277390).

Hipolito-Delgado, C. P. (2010). Exploring the etiology of ethnic self-hatred: Internalized racism in Chicana/o and Latina/o college students. *Journal of College Student Development, 51*, 319–331.

Hipolito-Delgado, C. P., & Diaz, J. M. (2013). A conceptual approach to counseling with Latina/o culture in mind. In C. C. Lee (Ed.), *Multicultural counseling: New approaches to diversity* (4th ed., pp. 67–86). Alexandria, VA: American Counseling Association.

Hipolito-Delgado, C. P., & Lee, C. C. (2007). Empowerment theory for the professional school counselor: A manifesto for what really matters. *Professional School Counseling, 10*, 327–332.

Huynh, V. W. (2012). Ethnic microaggressions and the depressive and somatic symptoms of Latino and Asian American adolescents. *Journal of Youth and Adolescence, 41*, 831–846.

Kochhar, R., Fry, R., & Taylor, P. (2011). *Hispanic household wealth fell by 66% from 2005 to 2009*. Washington, D.C.: Pew Hispanic Center. Retrieved from http://www.pewhispanic.org/2011/07/26/the-toll-of-the-great-recession/

Levitt, P. (2004). Transnational ties and incorporation: The case of dominicans in the United States. In D. G. Gutiérrez (Ed.), *The Columbia history of Latinos in the United States since 1960* (pp. 229–256). Chichester, NY: Columbia University Press.

Lipsitz, G. (1998). *The possessive investment in Whiteness: How White people profit from identity politics.* Philadelphia, PA: Temple University Press.

Loewen, J.W. (1995). *Lies my teacher told me: Everything your American history textbook got wrong.* New York: The New Press.

Lopez, M. H., & Light, M. (2009). *A Rising Share: Hispanics and Federal Crime.* Washington, DC: Pew Hispanic Center. Retrieved from http://www.pewhispanic.org/2009/02/18/a-rising-share-hispanics-and-federal-crime/

Lopez, M. H., & Velasco, G. (2011). *The toll of the great recession childhood poverty among Hispanics sets record, leads nation.* Washington, DC: Pew Hispanic Center. Retrieved from http://www.pewhispanic.org/2011/09/28/childhood-poverty-among-hispanics-sets-record-leads-nation/

Mauer, M., & King, R. S. (2007). *Uneven Justice: states rates of incarceration by race and ethnicity.* Retrieved from http://www.prisonterminal.comwww.prisonterminal.com/documents/rd_stateratesofincbyraceandethnicity.pdf

Molinary, R. (2007). *Hijas Americanas: Beauty, body image and growing up latina.* Emeryville, CA: Seal Press.

Montalvo, F. F. (2004). Surviving Race: Skin Color and the Socialization and Acculturation of Latinas. *Journal of Ethnic & Cultural Diversity in Social Work: Innovation in Theory, Research & Practice, 13,* 25–43.

Montalvo, F. F. (2009). Ethnoracial gap in clinical practice with Latinos. *Clinical Social Work Journal, 37,* 277–286.

Mossakowski, K. N. (2003). Coping with perceived discrimination: Does ethnic identity protect mental health? *Journal of Health and Social Behavior, 44,* 318–331.

Motel, S., & Pattern, E. (2012a). *Hispanics of Salvadorian origin in the United States, 2010.* Washington, DC: Pew Hispanic Center. Retrieved from http://www.pewhispanic.org/2012/06/27/hispanics-of-salvadoran-origin-in-the-united-states-2010/

Motel, S., & Pattern, E. (2012b). *The 10 largest Hispanic origin groups: Characteristics, rankings, top counties.* Washington, DC: Pew Hispanic Center. Retrieved from http://www.pewhispanic.org/files/2012/06/The-10-Largest-Hispanic-Origin-Groups.pdf

Ontai-Grzebik, L. L., & Raffaelli, M. (2004). Individual and social influences on ethnic identity among Latino young adults. *Journal of Adolescent Research, 19,* 559–575.

Organista, K. C. (2009). Latino clinical perspectives on Montalvo's ethnoracial gap in clinical practice with Latinos. *Clinical Social Work Journal, 37,* 287–293.

Passel, D., Cohn, D., & Gonzalez-Barrera, A. (2012). *Net migration from Mexico Falls to Zero—and perhaps less.* Washington, D.C.: Pew Hispanic Center. Retrieved September 20, 2012, from http://www.pewhispanic.org/2012/04/23/net-migration-from-mexico-falls-to-zero-and-perhaps-less/.

Potts, R. G. (2003). Emancipatory education versus school-based prevention in African American communities. *American Journal of Community Psychology, 31,* 173–183.

Reyes-Rodriguez, M. L., Franko, D. L., Matos-Lamout, A., Bulik, C. M., Von Holle, A., Camara-Fuentes, L. R., . . . Suarez-Torres, A. (2010). Eating disorder symptomatology: Prevalence among Latino College freshmen students. *Journal of Clinical Psychology, 66*, 666–679. doi:10.1002/jclp.20684

Roberts, R. E., Phinney, J. S., Masses, L. C., Chen, Y. R., Roberts, C. R., & Romero, A. (1999). The structure of ethnic identity of young adolescents from diverse ethnocultural groups. *Journal of Early Adolescence, 19*, 301–322.

Robinson-Wood, T. L. (2009). Extending cultural understanding beyond race and ethnicity. In C. C. Lee, D. A. Burnhill, A. L. Butler, C. P. Hipolito-Delgado, M. Humphrey, O. Muñoz, & H. J. Shin (Eds.), *Elements of culture in counseling* (pp. 31–41). Columbus, OH: Pearson.

Rothstein, R. (2004). *Class and school: Using social, economic and educational reform to close the black-white achievement gap.* Washington, DC: Economic Policy Institute.

Ruiz, A. S. (1990). Ethnic identity: Crisis and resolution. *Journal of Multicultural Counseling and Development, 18*, 29–40.

Santiago-Valles, K. A., & Jiménez-Muñoz, G. M. (2004). Social polarization and colonized labor: Puerto Ricans in the United States, 1945-2000. In D. G. Gutiérrez (Ed.), *The Columbia history of Latinos in the United States since 1960* (pp. 87–145). Chichester, NY: Columbia University Press.

Schmader, T., Major, B., & Gramzow, R. H. (2001). Coping with ethnic stereotypes in academic domain: Perceived injustice and psychological disengagement. *Journal of Social Issues, 57*, 93–111.

Spring, J. (2007). *Deculturalization and the struggle for equality: A brief history of the education of dominated cultures in the United States.* San Francisco, CA: McGraw Hill Higher Education.

Takaki, R. (1993). *A different mirror: A history of multicultural America.* New York, NY: Back Bay Books.

Tatum, B. D. (1997). *Why are the Black kids sitting together in the cafeteria? And other conversations about race.* New York, NY: Basic Books.

Taylor, J., Henderson, D., & Jackson, B. B. (1991). A holistic model for understanding and predicting depressive symptoms in African American women. *Journal of Counseling Psychology, 19*, 306–320.

Taylor, P., Lopez, H. M., Velasco, G., & Motel, S. (2012). *Hispanics say they have the worst of a bad economy.* Washington, DC: Pew Hispanic Center. Retrieved from http://www.pewhispanic.org/2012/01/26/hispanics-say-they-have-the-worst-of-a-bad-economy/

Telzer, E. H., & Vasquez Garcia, H. A. (2009). Skin color and self-perceptions of immigrant and U.S.-born Latinas: The moderating role of racial socialization and ethnic identity. *Hispanic Journal of Behavioral Sciences, 31*, 357–374.

Thorton, J. (1998). *Africa and Africans in the making of the Atlantic world, 1400–1800* (2nd ed.). New York, NY: Cambridge University Press.

Torres, V. (2003). Influences on ethnic identity development of Latino college students in the first two years of college. *Journal of College Student Development, 44*, 532–547.

Tull, E. S., Sheu, Y. T., Butler, C., & Corenlious, K. (2005). Relationships between perceived stress, coping behavior and cortisol secretion in women with high and low levels of internalized racism. *Journal of the National Medical Association, 97,* 206–212.

Umaña-Taylor, A. J. (2004). Ethnic identity and self-esteem: Examining the role of social context. *Journal of Adolescence, 27,* 139–146.

U.S. Bureau of Labor Statistics. (2011). Labor force characteristics, by race and ethnicity, 2011. Retrieved from http://stats.bls.gov/cps/cpsrace2011.pdf

U.S. Department of Education, National Center for Education Statistics. (2012a). *The condition of education 2012* (NCES 2012-045). Retrieved from http://nces.ed.gov/pubs2012/2012045.pdf

U.S. Department of Education, National Center for Education Statistics. (2012b). *The condition of education 2012* (NCES 2012-045). Retrieved from http://nces.ed.gov/fastfacts/display.asp?id=16

Valencia, R. (2002). *Chicano school failure and success: Past, present, and future* (2nd ed.). London: Routledge.

Velez, W., & Saenz, R. (2001). Toward a comprehensive model of the school leaving process among Latinos. *School Psychology Quarterly, 14,* 445–467.

Villalba, J. A., Akos, P., Keeter, K., & Ames, A. (2007). Promoting Latino student achievement and development through the ASCA national model. *Professional School Counseling, 10,* 464–474.

Xie, B., Unger, J. B., Gallaher, P., Johnson, C. A., Wu, Q., & Chou, C. P. (2010). Overweight, body image, and depression in Asian and Hispanic adolescents. *American Journal of Health Behavior, 34,* 476–488. doi: 10.5993/AJHB.34.4.9

Yowell, C. M. (2002). Dreams of the future: The pursuit of education and career possible selves among ninth grade Latino youth. *Applied Developmental Science, 6,* 62–72.

Zarate, M. E., Bhimji, F., & Reese, L. (2005). Ethnic identity and academic achievement among Latina/o Adolescents. *Journal of Latinos and Education, 4,* 95–114.

Zinn, H. (2003). *A people's history of the United States.* New York, NY: Perennial Classics.

Internalized Racial Oppression in the African American Community

Tamba-Kuii M. Bailey, Wendi S. Williams,
and Brian Favors

Individual and systemic racial oppression faced by African Americans have been a mainstay in the history of the United States since its formation. It has been argued that in order to maintain this system of racial oppression, it is necessary to have a psychological element that is self-perpetuating and internalized by the oppressed group (Bailey, Chung, Williams, Singh, & Terrell, 2011; Wilson, 1993). Bailey and colleagues described internalized racial oppression (IRO) among African Americans as a process where individuals:

> internalize and accept the dominant White culture's oppressive actions and beliefs toward Black people (e.g., negative stereotypes, discrimination, hatred, falsification of historical facts, racist doctrines, White supremacist ideology), while at the same time rejecting the African worldview and cultural motifs. (p. 481)

Once racial oppression is accepted and internalized, the need to enforce this system of oppression by the White majority is eliminated because the oppressed group will impose the oppression upon themselves (Bailey et al., 2011; Poupart, 2003; Woodson, 1990). Literature on IRO has indicated that it is a cumulative experience that spans across generations (Brave Heart, 1998; Speight, 2007) and is the most psychologically damaging component of racial oppression (Speight, 2007). Acknowledging these factors,

Speight (2007) asserted that any analysis of the psychological effects of racism is incomplete without considering how it is internalized. As a means of discussing African Americans' experience of IRO, we examine the demographic profile of African Americans, their experiences of historical and contemporary forms of racial oppression, the common manifestations of IRO among this group, the mental and behavioral health implications of IRO, and clinical and community interventions for addressing IRO. In addition to reviewing the published literature in these areas, we also offer some real life examples of the ways in which African Americans have experienced and have IRO. These examples are from individuals who have participated in programs developed by the Sankofa Community Empowerment, Inc. (Sankofa Community Empowerment [SCE], 2012), as relayed by the third author (BF), who is the co-founder and director of SCE.

DEMOGRAPHIC PROFILE OF AFRICAN AMERICANS

In this chapter we use the term African American, in line with the U.S. Census Bureau (2011) definition, to represent individuals " . . . having origins in any of the Black racial groups of Africa" (p. 3). African Americans can trace their family lineage and ancestral origins to Africa and throughout the diaspora. As a group, African Americans constitute approximately 13% (39 million) of the U.S. population. The mean income for African Americans is approximately $32,000 per household, with 27.6% of the African American population living at or below the poverty level (U.S. Census Bureau, 2011). The unemployment rate among African Americans is 13.4%, which is the highest among all racial groups in the United States. (U.S. Department of Labor, 2012). In terms of educational attainment, approximately 57% of African Americans have a high school diploma or an equivalent diploma, and 25% of the population has associate's or bachelor's degrees. The current social status and experiences of African Americans are linked to a history of enslavement, oppression and marginalization, and its continuance through laws and policies set to perpetuate societal inequities. Thus, these demographic descriptors are reflective of that history and representative of how African Americans have attempted to survive in the United States.

HISTORICAL OPPRESSION

In this section we discuss historical experiences of racial oppression experienced by African Americans. We outline the experience of slavery, black codes, and Jim Crow/legal segregation. These events shaped the power relationship between African Americans and Whites at individual and institutional levels. It was this imbalanced power relationship that led to African Americans' experiences of racial oppression in the United States.

Slavery

Starting in 1619, African Americans first began to experience racial oppression in the United States as indentured servants. However, the position of African Americans quickly changed to that of enslaved individuals as a result of this highly profitable system of free labor (Clarke, 1991). Clarke estimated between 20 and 30 million Africans were captured and sold into slavery for the United States. The system of chattel slavery has been described as the most diabolical form of mental and physical torture experienced by any one group (Clarke, 1991). In this system, African Americans had no legal rights; they could not own property, make contracts, legally marry, or constitute a family of any form (Du Bois, 1998). This absolute power by the plantation owners led to great oppression and cruelty of African Americans beyond any conception. During slavery, African Americans experienced degradation, starvation, whipping and beating, lynching, rape, separation from family members, and the absolute negation of human rights at the hands of the White majority (Du Bois, 1998; Elkins, 1976).

In addition to this extreme physical torture, African Americans were made to suffer great psychological abuse during the experience of slavery. This treatment of Africans was used to reduce their status to that of objects and remove all sense of perceived humanity and equality in their interactions with the White majority (Asante & Mattson, 1998). It was a systematic process of psychological dehumanization of Africans that espoused and enforced feelings of inferiority in the African and superiority in White Americans (Du Bois, 1998). It was this system of chattel slavery that initiated the cruelest forms of racial oppression experienced by African Americans.

Black Codes

When the system of slavery ended in 1863, a new system of racial oppression was constructed and legalized across the south by 1865 (Du Bois, 1998). Du Bois indicated that this new legalized system of oppression, called Black Codes, consisted of infamous pieces of legislation designed to maintain the components of slavery in everything but name. These laws forced African Americans to work under similar conditions experienced during slavery and held in place a system of racial oppression. One example of a Black code, in South Carolina, was a law that stated employers were to be referred to as "masters" and African American employees were referred to as "servants." These "masters" were given the right to whip "servants" under the age of 18 years old as a means of disciplining any actions that were perceived by the "masters" as being unruly behaviors. Another law, this one in Louisiana, stated that employees (African Americans) were given only 10 days at the beginning of the year to find a job and sign a 1-year labor contract. Once the employees entered into these contracts, they could not quit or stop work until the contract was fulfilled. Otherwise, the employee would face punishment and loss of wages. In Mississippi, there was a law that allowed anyone to apprehend and return, by force, any employee who quit the services of his or her employer prior to expiration of a work contract. These types of Black code laws continued the oppression experienced by African Americans that began during slavery.

Segregation and Jim Crow Racism

It was the 1896 Supreme Court decision in the *Plessy v. Ferguson* case that institutionalized segregation in the United States through the simple doctrine of "separate but equal" (Tussman, 1963). This decision led to 58 years of legalized segregation in the United States. During this period of history, African Americans experienced segregation laws covering transportation and the use of public facilities; state laws that led to disenfranchisement provisions of African Americans; and segregated housing and unfair practices (Bell, 1980). These sanctioned actions continued the experiences of oppression, degradation, marginalization, and negation of human rights for African Americans.

CONTEMPORARY OPPRESSION

The 1954 Supreme Court's decision in the *Brown v. Board of Education* case and the 1964 Civil Rights Act marked the end of legal segregation and sanctioned racial oppression in the United States (Klarman, 2004). While legalized racial oppression and discrimination were no longer accepted in the United States, racial discrimination remained a barrier to African Americans' full economic, political, and social participation in various institutions within the country (Higginbotham & Andersen, 2006). Literature on racial oppression has documented the evolution of contemporary manifestations of racial oppression, which has gone from being blatant, overt, and systemically sanctioned (laws and accepted practices) to being more covert and subtly ingrained into the fabric of U.S. society (Henry & Sears, 2002; Sears, 1988; Sue et al., 2007). In this section we discuss symbolic racism, aversive racism, color-blind racism, and racial microaggressions as more contemporary forms of racial oppression experienced by African Americans as well some of the physical and mental health consequences of said oppression.

Symbolic Racism

Symbolic racism, initially defined by Kinder and Sears (1981), is believed to have emerged after the implementation of civil rights legislation in the United States (Sears & Henry, 2003). Kinder and Sears (1981) described symbolic racism as a form of resistance to the postdesegregation racial status quo that was based on negative affect toward African Americans and conservative moral feelings that African Americans violate traditional American values, work ethic, obedience, and discipline. This form of racial oppression has been described as "symbolic" as a means of recognizing the way African Americans are targeted as an abstract collective and not directed toward any one individual African American (Henry & Sears, 2002). Further, symbolic racism is also grounded in abstract moral values as opposed to concrete personal experiences or events (Henry & Sears, 2002). The literature on symbolic racism has characterized this form of racial oppression into four specific components: (1) a denial of continued racial discrimination—the belief that African Americans no longer face as much prejudice in today's society; (2) a belief that African Americans' failure to progress is a result of their unwillingness to work hard enough; (3) "excessive demands"—the belief that African Americans are demanding too much; and (4) "undeserved advantage"—the belief that African Americans have received more than they deserve (Henry & Sears, 2002; Kinder and Sears, 1981; Sears & Henry, 2003; Sears, Van Laar, Carrillo, & Kosterman, 1997).

Research suggests that symbolic racism plays a role in policy and candidate support (Henry & Sears, 2002; Tarman & Sears, 2005; Weigel & Howes, 1985). Similarly, Henry and Sears (2002) found that symbolic racism was predictive of conservative political predispositions among White individuals; an approach identified as the "Southern Strategy," in which political parties play on the fears of Whites to garner political support (Alexander, 2010). These types of beliefs, to a certain degree, support and uphold policies that do not address racial inequities. We view the continued questioning of President Obama's place of birth and his religious affiliation from Tea Party members and other conservatives as an example of symbolic racism in our society today.

Aversive Racism

Another form of racial oppression experienced by African Americans, similar to symbolic racism, is aversive racism. Aversive racism is rooted in the belief of fair and just treatment for all individuals, but supports the unconscious harboring of negative and uneasy feelings toward African Americans, which may lead to the avoidance of interracial interactions (Gaertner & Dovidio, 2005). Dovidio and Gaertner suggested that aversive racism is a form of racial discrimination that is more likely to manifest itself in situations where a negative response may be justified without a threat to the egalitarian self-image. Conversely, when a negative response cannot be justified by nonracial rationalization, White individuals may behave without regard to an African American individual's race or in a manner that favors an African American individual. This behavior is based on the belief that a negative response toward an African American without any nonracial rationale would be a threat to an egalitarian self-image. Because of the egalitarian self-image and often unconscious biases associated with aversive racism, the actions of White individuals who engage in aversive racism may appear more variable and inconsistent (Gaertner & Dovidio, 2005).

Additionally, Gartner and Dovidio hypothesized that aversive racism has contributed to patterns of subtle discrimination in hiring practices, admission processes, and criminal court cases and sentencing of African Americans. Based on the potential outcomes of the aversive racism framework, while it may be variable and inconsistent, it is easy to see that this form of racial oppression can have dire consequences for many African Americans. Rooted in the belief of fairness and justice, aversive racism can contribute to any resistance against any programs, policies, or actions perceived to benefit African Americans over White individuals (Murrell, Dietz-Uhler, Dovidio, Gaertner, & Drout, 1994). Some modern-day examples of ascribing to attitudes of perceived fairness and justice, and acting in a manner that supports in-group favoritism, may be seen in several Supreme Court cases (see *Gratz et al. v. Bollinger et al.* and *Grutter v. Bollinger*) that have challenged affirmative action policies.

Color-Blind Racism

Like symbolic and aversive racism, color-blind racism is believed to have emerged in the late 1960 (Bonilla-Silva, 2006). Color-blind racism presents attitudes that reflect a denial, distortion, or minimization of race and racism (Neville, Spanierman, & Doan, 2006). Bonilla-Silva (2006) viewed color-blind racism as central to the maintenance of White privilege. Through this dominant racially based framework, individuals, groups, and systems may consciously or unconsciously use color-blind racism as a means of justifying the racial status quo or explaining away racial inequities in the United States (Neville et al., 2006).

Color-blind racism was hypothesized to consist of four central themes: abstract liberalism, naturalization, cultural racism, and minimization of racism (Bonilla-Silva, 2006). These themes further articulate the nature of color-blind racism and its impact on African Americans. It seems that many people have engaged in color-blind racism by asserting that the United States is experiencing a post-racial period of existence with the election of Barack Obama as the first African American President of the United States (Haney López, 2011), while negating the continued incidents of racism and discrimination that African Americans experience on a daily basis along the with social, economic, and political inequities faced by African Americans.

Racial Microaggressions

Another form of contemporary racial oppression experienced by African Americans has been that of racial microaggressions. Racial microaggressions, initially conceptualized by Pierce's (1969) description of daily racist experiences, are defined as subtle and often automatic, nonverbal exchanges meant to "put down" African Americans (Pierce, Carew, Pierce-Gonzalez, & Wills, 1978). Building on this initial conceptualization of racial microaggressions, Sue et al. (2007) defined racial microaggressions as "brief and commonplace daily verbal, behavioral, environmental indignities, whether intentional or unintentional, that communicate hostile, derogatory, or negative racial slights and insults to the target person or group" (Sue et al., 2007, p. 273). Sue and his team identified three forms of racial microaggressions: microassault, microinsult, and microinvalidations, which are delivered through verbal, behavioral, and environmental means (Sue, 2010).

Microassaults are explicit racial derogations identified usually as verbal or nonverbal attacks meant to harm the intended victim by name-calling, avoidant behavior, or intentional discriminatory actions (Sue et al., 2007). For African Americans, microassaults may occur in the form of being called "nigger" or other racially derogatory terms, being refused services, or an outward display of deliberate discrimination based on race (Sue, 2010). Microinsults are described as actions or communications meant to convey rudeness and insensitivity, which demean a person based on racial heritage (Sue et al., 2007). Examples of microinsults are assumptions of being intellectually inferior or lacking common sense, being treated as second-class citizens, a belief that all African Americans are potential criminals or prone to violent behaviors, and assumptions of inferior status and credentials (Sue et al., 2008). Microinvalidations are characterized as communications or other environmental cues that exclude, negate, or nullify the psychological thoughts, experiences, feelings, or experiential reality of people of Color (Sue, 2010).

BF recalled some discussions during a support group conducted by SCE that are good examples of racial microaggressions typically experienced by African American professionals:

> While discussing their experiences working in a corporate environment, several individuals reported experiences where coworkers would frequently make statements reflecting many of the negative stereotypes of the intellectual abilities of African Americans. Also, group members reported being mistaken as support staff or low-level personnel by their colleagues, being nicknamed stereotypical monikers like "G money" for someone named "Greg," or receiving less desirable work assignments. These experiences typify microinsults and microinvalidations that many African Americans experience on a daily basis.

Impact of Racism on African Americans

There is a significant amount of literature outlining the effects of racial oppression on African Americans (Akbar, 1996; Bulhan, 1985; Clarke, 1991; Clark & Clark, 1947; Fanon, 1963; Peters, 2004; Rollock & Gordon, 2000). Researchers have found that racial oppression, especially perceived racism, negatively affects areas of mental health such as psychological distress (Landrine & Klonoff, 1996), self-esteem (Fischer & Shaw, 1999), and well-being (Pierre & Mahalik, 2005; Tran, Wright, & Chatters, 1991). Similarly, Paradies (2006), in a meta-analysis of 138 quantitative studies on self-reported experiences of racial oppression and health, found a consistent association between experiences of racial oppression and negative mental health outcomes (e.g., psychological/emotional distress, depressive symptoms, obsessive-compulsive symptoms, anxiety, and negative effects). However, it is the internalization of racism that may arguably be the most damaging psychological injury due to racism (Speight, 2007).

MANIFESTATIONS OF INTERNALIZED OPPRESSION

Scholars have characterized IRO as a response to experiences of racism (Alleyne, 2005) and slavery (post-traumatic slave syndrome [PTSS]; Degruy Leary, 2005), which shape African Americans' tendency to absorb racist notions about their racial group and lead to negative psychological and behavioral manifestations among them. It has also been asserted that oppressed individuals may come to believe that they are inferior to the oppressors as a part of the internalization process (David, 2009). IRO among African Americans has taken on a multitude of forms, and these vary depending on the social and cultural context in which individuals find themselves. Bailey et al. (2011), in the development of a measure of IRO among African Americans, identified the following four attitudinal and behavioral manifestations of IRO: (1) belief in a biased representation of history; (2) alteration of one's physical appearance; (3) internalization of negative stereotypes about African Americans; and (4) changing one's hair texture and style to fit a more European aesthetic. Some examples of IRO are reflected in the experiences shared by a former gang member during an SCE support group, as recalled by BF:

> As a part of a support group, "Sean" (pseudonym), an African American adolescent, reported that when he was involved in the gang he would frequently steal from African Americans, but he would never steal from any White individuals. When Sean further explored his actions in the support group, he realized that at that time he valued White individuals' lives over the lives of the African Americans that he encountered. Sean stated that he despised African Americans and saw them as "less important" than White individuals. These beliefs and actions by Sean may be connected to his internalization of negative stereotypes and a belief that African Americans are inferior to White individuals.

As another example of one of the IRO manifestations found by Bailey et al. (2011), BF recalled a discussion in one of the Sister Circle meetings at SCE:

> During one meeting several African American women discussed why they purchase hair-straightening products, hair weaves, and color contacts. They reported using these produces to "escape" from the way they looked, which they viewed as unattractive and inferior to a White standard of beauty.

Joy Degruy Leary's (2005) seminal work outlining the contemporary effects of enslavement on the life experiences of African Americans reintroduced and contextualized the work of African American psychologists. These psychologists have presented the deleterious effects of inculcation in White hegemonic culture on the development of internalized racist notions of Blackness among African American individuals and consequences for mental health and well-being (Akbar, 1996; Azibo, 1997). Racial identity theorists have examined the statuses and dimensions of racial identification and there are implications for internalization of negative racial notions. IRO attitudes are representative of less developed racial identity statuses (Cross, 1991; Helms, 1990), as well as negative affective and evaluative judgment of one's race based on personal experiences and perceptions of non-Black persons (Sellers, Smith, Shelton, Roweley, & Chavous, 1998).

These manifestations of IRO are shaped by the context and intersection of other salient identities (e.g., gender, disability, sexuality, etc.) among African Americans. Although empirical studies of these manifestations is scarce, the existing research considers the work/career lives of African Americans, experiences in relationships and marriage, and ways IRO is influenced by one's experience of his or her gender. Indeed, the characteristics of IRO are a complex composition of affective, behavioral, and cognitive distortions of one's attitudes about his or her race and other social group membership. Aymer's (2010) clinical case study work with a 35-year-old African American man, Edward, is an example of this complexity.

> Edward characterized himself as a "light-skinned, educated" Black man and felt that he did not "fit the stereotypical image of a potential criminal or thug" assigned to African American men. Additionally, Edward differentiated himself from other African American men, perceiving them as "stupid" and being brought to anger when stereotyped and followed by security guards when he entered most stores. Aymer (2010) described Edward being filled with "indignation, bewilderment, and outrage" due to being subjected to racial profiling. As a result of these attitudes, Edward described feelings of guilt, anxiety, shame, and denial. Further complicating these feelings was his frustration that while he felt isolated, he was ultimately an African American man and could not escape the linked fate he shared with these same men from whom he sought to distinguish himself. Aymer's therapeutic counseling with the client centered on working through his narcissistic need to be deemed "special," which was due to his skin color, education, higher SES, and ways of life that, within predominant White settings, made him feel different and better than other African Americans; particularly from other African American men. Franklin (2004) suggests that African American men, like Edward, seek opportunities to feel special in an effort to offset a sense of invisibility and vulnerability experienced by them in American society (Franklin, 2004). For Edward, to be special might mean potential avoidance of dangers associated with being an African American man, and also had the unintended consequence of leaving him to feel alienated from other African Americans. This sentiment is exemplified in the fact that though he described "relatively good relationships with his African American coworkers," he preferred to socialize with his White colleagues whom he would see "occasionally for drinks."

Notions of maleness, blackness, age, and class intersect to produce manifestations of IRO that are different across various cohort groups. For example, what it means to be male and powerful in American society impacts the identity of African American men and boys differently than White men. Wester, Vogel, Wei, and McLain (2006) found that African American men who sought to align their notion of manhood with mainstream notions of manhood (which include patriarchal domination and sexist legitimization of power over women and children) were more likely to endorse IRO ideas and higher levels of psychological distress. IRO has been associated with destructive behaviors associated with hypermasculinity typically descriptive of Western manhood. Bryant (2011) found that Black male youths (ages 14–19) recruited from varying contexts (e.g., a public school, African-centered charter school, juvenile detention school, and youth on parole/probation) had a higher propensity for violent behavior when they endorsed IRO attitudes. Self-destructive behaviors in the form of violence (toward self and others), disengaged goal orientation, alcohol abuse, sexual promiscuity, and other behaviors that compromise physical health may all be viewed within the context of low internalized self-regard/worth predicated on a societal view that one's racial group is less valued.

IRO also manifests among African American women and girls in ways shaped by their specific standpoints as members of multiple oppressed groups (i.e., gender and race), especially when additional salient identities, such as sexual orientation, low SES, and education serve to further marginalize their identification and placement in social hierarchies. Drawing on Lipsky's (1977) seminal work on internalized oppression, Gainor (1992) addressed the consequences of IRO exemplified in African American women's relationships with one another. Though the relationships between African American women have been lauded for being safe and supportive, and thus fostering strong bonds of sisterhood, Gainor pointed out that destructive relational dynamics characterized as manifestations of IRO have impeded the effectiveness of group counseling among them. Conflicts related to physicality (namely skin complexion, hair texture, and body size and shape), along with judgments about what exemplifies appropriate sexual behavior and expressions of affection, have been noted and related to competition (among heterosexual African American women) for romantic relationships with African American men. Gainor noted that a type of competitiveness regarding "Who has it worse?" based on some of the aspects described above interfered with women's ability to take advantage of their common experiences for support in therapeutic contexts.

IRO has also been demonstrated to have potential negative impact on familial relationships and health within African American families. In an early study exploring the effect of IRO on marital satisfaction among heterosexual married couples, Taylor (1990) found that partners with higher

IRO scores reported lower marital satisfaction (Taylor, 1990). Relative to the effect of IRO on relationships with children, Nuru-Jeter et al. (2009) explored the effect of race and racism on expectant African American mothers and potential birth outcomes. They found these mothers harbored concerns about their own IRO attitudes, relative to their children and aspects of rearing them, as well as the potential for their children to absorb IRO attitudes and the negative effect this could have for their development and well-being. Issues of physicality associated with colorism (preference for children with light over dark skin complexions and consequent dynamics), as well as other approximations to Anglo features (facial features—shape of nose and lips, hair texture, etc.) have shaped dynamics in African American families and transmission of IRO attitudes across generations (Boyd-Franklin, 1991; Parmer, Arnold, Natt, & Janson, 2004). Parmer et al. (2004) found that among African American families, negative correlates (Anglo features) of physical attractiveness continue to be representative of IRO attitudes. Further, as IRO attitudes engender feelings of shame, embarrassment, and anxiety due to the fact affected people have such low regard for themselves and their racial group, it causes the phenomenon to manifest implicitly, resulting in family secrets and other damaging dynamics that perpetuate their continued effect and transmission (Boyd-Franklin, 1991; Parmer et al., 2004).

While many of these dynamics are initiated and transmitted within families and across generations, they are endorsed and reinforced among African American individuals in the wider community and even the workplace. In a study exploring the effect of IRO in the workplace, Alleyne (2005) suggests that African American employees bring this IRO "baggage" to the workplace, resulting in processes that work against them as employees. She stated, African American employees manage "outdated constructs" like being reminded to "know your place" in the contemporary workforce, which interferes with their ability to be fully creative, productive, and adequately compensated for their labor. Alleyne suggested their "internal oppressor" is constantly at work by undermining their personal authority and manifests itself as low self-esteem, self-hate, and disowning ones' own group. Alleyne further suggested that this internal oppressor creates a complex set of defensive behaviors such as narcissistic injury, projective identification, and personal unresolved difficulties with power and domination.

MENTAL AND BEHAVIORAL HEALTH IMPLICATIONS OF INTERNALIZED OPPRESSION

Psychologists have theorized about the deleterious effects of race and racism on the lives of African Americans for decades (Akbar, 1996;

Azibo, 1997; Wilson, 1993). Historically, African American psychologists have identified the failure of an African American person to: (1) recognize himself or herself as an African; (2) prioritize Africans interests, survival, and proactive development; (3) respect and perpetuate all things that are African and; (4) support a standard of conduct that neutralizes people and things that are anti-African, as exemplars of having a false African consciousness as a result of racism (Azibo, 1997). More recently, psychologists have described the effects of race and racism on the lives of African American individuals as race-related stress and have begun to contextualize these effects under the guise of psychological injury (Carter, 2007). In line with Robert Carter's (2007) seminal work on race-related stress, scholars have conducted studies examining the psychological and emotional injury of mostly external experiences of racism (i.e., instances of institutional and personally mediated racism) linked to public health concerns (Jones, 2000) as well as mental health concerns among African American individuals (Franklin-Jackson & Carter, 2007; Jones, Cross, & DeFour, 2007). Carter (2007) suggested that theorists, such as Bulhan (1985), have indicated that racial psychological injury may result from the internalization of racism and consequent negative attitudes and treatment of oneself and one's group. However, at the time of his work, little research existed to support specific mental and behavioral health consequences of IRO (Speight, 2007).

As a means of further legitimizing the veracity of IRO effects, scholars have studied the physical effects of internalized race-related stress (Chambers et al., 2004; Peters, 2004; Tull, Sheu, Butler, & Cornelius, 2005), with later work exploring the impact of IRO on psychological distress and threats to well-being. Furthermore, coinciding with the development of theoretical conceptualizations of intersectionality with other marginalized identities, IRO has been examined alongside internalized heterosexism (homophobia; Szymanski & Gupta, 2009) and internalized sexism (Szymanski & Stewart, 2010) among women, and considered in light of gender role conflicts among men (Wester et al., 2006).

The physical and mental health consequences relative to IRO among African Americans are conceptualized as consequences of the stress and affective responses (e.g., shame, guilt, anxiety, and resentment) one feels for having self-blamed or self-hated themselves for their racial characteristics, racial group membership, or feelings about other members of their racial group. Researchers examining the effects of stress responses on the physical health of African American individuals have found negative implications for a Caribbean population (Chambers et al., 2004; Tull et al., 2005), with findings linking IRO attitudes to dysfunctional coping, abdominal obesity, and glucose intolerance complicit in the development of Type 2 diabetes (Liebman, 2010). Further, drawing connections between IRO and physical/mental health in a U.S.-based sample, Peters (2004) found a relationship between experiences of racism and hypertension among 162 urban African American individuals. This relationship was moderated by age such that adults 40 and above reported more distress, higher blood pressure levels, and a tendency to suppress anger. Interestingly, in this study, the highest blood pressure levels were found among the oldest participants who were likely to categorize their experiences as "perceived" rather than "actual" racism, suggesting the possibility that they may not categorize a racist experience as such, and therefore may be at risk for the event. The findings of the above studies underscore the complex relationship of suppressed feelings and emotional experiences relative to exposure to the effects of race and racism, and perhaps draw attention to the mind-body connection linking the environmental experiences of racism to internalized processing, which results in the psychological and physical health injury among African Americans

Developing savvy for the myriad ways IRO manifests in the lives of African American individuals has led to empirical studies of the mental health impact of intersecting, multiple oppressed identities on African American men and women and lesbian, gay, bisexual, and transgender persons. Szymanski and Stewart (2010) explored racism and sexism correlates for African American women's psychological distress and found that while racist and sexist experiences were related to more psychological distress, and that perceived racist experiences correlated with sexist events, IRO, and internalized sexism were not. They suggested that the lack of relation between IRO and psychological distress might be indicative of IRO serving as a protective agent, which may serve to minimize psychological distress for African American women. However, an alternate interpretation may be that the women in this study have internalized the "strong Black woman" self-image that when imposed may serve to disallow Black women to experience or express vulnerability or distress and minimize or deny their stressors (Harrington, Crowther, & Shipherd, 2010). Relative to the experiences of African American men, Wester et al. (2006) explored IRO and its impact on gender role conflict and found that African American men who endorsed IRO attitudes suffered more psychological distress in their attempts to navigate traditional male gender roles. Wester et al. (2006) concluded that the assimilation of an external racial and gender self-image was unhealthy, and thus led to psychological distress, a similar finding to those for African American women (Parks, Carter, & Gushue, 1996).

In another study examining the relationship between IRO and internalized homophobia among African American men and women, Szymanski and Gupta (2009) found that internalized racism and internalized homophobia predicted lower self-esteem and higher psychological distress. Homophobia is largely an issue because it challenges patriarchy and traditional notions of manhood and masculinity. In their conclusion,

Szymanski and Gupta (2009) highlighted the challenges to African American lesbian/gay/bisexual/transgender/questioning (LGBTQ) men and women in their racial/ethnic community. Characterized for its sexually conservative politics and adherence to the politics of respectability (see Higginbotham, 1993), the African American community in general has not extended support for its members who are LGBTQ, placing them at increased risk for the joint negative effects of intersecting and internalized racism and homophobia.

CLINICAL AND COMMUNITY PROGRAMS FOR INTERNALIZED OPPRESSION

As the behavioral and mental health consequences of IRO manifest across the lives of African Americans in various ways and multiple contexts, intervention programs seeking to ameliorate these concerns are best executed at the individual and group levels in clinical and community settings. While conceptualization of the effect of IRO on mental health concerns among African Americans has been explored for some time (Taylor, Henderson, & Jackson, 1991), development of intervention programs to assist persons grappling with these specific concerns are relatively new in their development. A review of the literature relative to clinically and community-based programming addressing IRO concerns among African Americans is presented in this section. This discussion is followed by an exploration of current community and educational programs not likely described in the psychological literature, yet provide an "on-the-ground" view of the work various organizations and community groups engage to address IRO at a grass roots level. We will end by identifying several community-based programs and discussing distinct components of each program that have been expressly developed in addressing IRO as experienced by African Americans.

Clinical Approaches

Psychotherapists have realized the extent to which race-based traumatic experiences impact the life functioning and mental health of African Americans. Group and individual-based interventions have been designed to address the development of mental illness among African Americans. Bryant-Davis and Ocampo (2006) described a thematic approach to treating racist-incident-based trauma, in which IRO is conceptualized as the shame and self-blame characteristically experienced by trauma victims. In their work, they highlighted the importance of counselor competence for multicultural-based trauma work to effectively offset the client's tendency to take responsibility for the cognitive and emotional effects of racism. The use of narrative or narrative-influenced methodologies has also been identified for treating issues of IRO among African Americans. Semmler and Williams (2000) describe the application of narrative therapy to a client case in which IRO figures prominently. In working with a 32-year-old African American woman client, they describe the effectiveness of narrative therapeutic techniques such as: (1) deconstructing the influence of dominant cultural narratives on the client's understanding of herself and her life; (2) externalizing the problem; (3) re-authoring the story; and (4) providing a context for a new, preferred life narrative. These techniques were shown to be effective in shifting the client's view, empowering her to redefine her experiences in ways wherein she does not internalize the responsibility of oppressive notions about who she is. Similar results can be found through the use of reflective-writing. Kaufka (2009) describes the effectiveness of reflective writing, a creative treatment modality that borrows from narrative therapy and composition studies, with the potential for similar emancipatory processes as narrative work. She describes reflective writing as being expressive, multivoiced, and engendering multiple perspectives that empowers individuals to interrogate their experiences and re-author them.

Other creative approaches to addressing IRO have been endorsed by psychotherapists and educators. Frame, Williams, and Green (1999) acknowledged the importance of incorporating aspects of the spiritual and communal traditions of African-centered cultures to address IRO in psychotherapeutic interventions with African American women. Additionally, Harper (2006) and Haney López (2011) discussed the effectiveness of group-based interventions in educational context. Harper (2006) described the role of peer support groups among high achieving African American male college students supporting leadership and achievement as a means to combat the "acting White" mantra espoused as an explanation for achievement gaps. Further, Haney López (2011) described the "Tubman Theater Project," a culturally relevant drama program for middle and high school students that enacts the students' writings of their life experiences as a means of confronting racism, classism, and unexamined IRO attitudes. While these programs have dealt IRO as a by-product of some of their work, we will explore those programs designed with the primary focus of addressing IRO.

Community Approaches

An example of a community-based program that attempts to address IRO is the SCE, which is a nonprofit organization operating in Brooklyn,

New York, and Philadelphia, Pennsylvania. SCE works to confront the various manifestations of IRO within urban youth, college students, and community members using after-school programs, community workshops, art education, and Rites of Passage programs (SCE, 2012). Since its inception, SCE has successfully assisted thousands of participants in confronting and healing from IRO. The SCE utilizes the Nguzo Saba, which are the principles of Kwanzaa (Karenga, 2008), as foundational knowledge that is infused in all group lesson plans, activities, and workshops (SCE, 2012). Additionally, the SCE incorporates a variety of African-centered rituals in its programs, which are intended to introduce participants to traditional African practices and healing methods. The Nguzo Saba and rituals are important components used in addressing IRO, as these practices provide a sense of community and belonging while reinforcing African traditions and values.

SCE's workshops bring together various individuals within the African American community to support one another while discussing critical issues that impact the broader group (SCE, 2012). These sessions, called Sankofa Circles, provide therapeutic and supportive experiences that enable participants to confront the alienation, fear, and distrust caused by IRO. These experiences empower participants to recognize their common struggles while learning about the root causes behind the problems they share. Unlike many programs, these sessions are specifically geared toward participants of African descent and are intentionally designed to serve as a support group, educational forum, and community mobilization mechanism. An example of a session topic that reflects SCE's attempt to address IRO is a discussion on colorism (see Williams, 1996, for further explanation of colorism), which focuses on the skin complexion and the multiple meanings ascribed to complexion within the African American community.

An example of the ways in which participants utilize and benefit from the programs in SCE can be found in the story of "Michael" (pseudonym), as shared by BF:

> Michael, an adolescent African American, was a battle rapper who used his rap lyrics to degrade other rap artists and promote negativity in his raps. Michael, like many other beginning participants at SCE, entered the program naïve to African culture, pessimistic about the possibilities of changing his community, and reluctant to accept the idea that he suffered from IRO. While going through the program, Michael began to realize how the SCE program provided a safe space for him to share and reflect on his experiences and learn ways to heal and start to develop a healthier racial identity. In the program, Michael learned how his experiences of racism and other forms of racial oppression had contributed to his internalization of racial

oppression. After going through classes, workshops, and the Sankofa circle, Michael was able to connect his current condition to events in the past and learn to develop a healthier racial identity.

Another community-based program with a mission to address IRO is The People's Institute for Survival and Beyond. Based in New Orleans, Louisiana, this group is an international collective of antiracist, multicultural community organizers, and educators dedicated to building an effective movement for social transformation (The People's Institute for Survival and Beyond, 2012). This organization believes that African Americans, White individuals, and other people of Color have experienced trauma related to IRO. They contend that African Americans have internalized negative perceptions of themselves as a result of racial oppression, while White individuals have experienced a false sense of superiority as a result of the internalization of White supremacist ideologies. It is based on this notion that the People's Institute for Survival and Beyond has developed interventions that are inclusive of all people, regardless of race, with an understanding that diverse groups of people can have healthy relationships with one another after examining the ways in which they have internalized racism.

Finally, the Spirit of a Woman (SOW) Leadership Development Institute in Brooklyn, New York, which was founded in 2002, provides Rites of Passage programs that are specifically designed to ameliorate characteristics of IRO that are typically faced by adolescent African American girls (Spirit of a Woman Leadership Development Institute, 2012). The SOW employs a holistic healing approach to combating IRO through discussion groups, experiential and participatory learning, leadership development, team-building, conflict resolution, and goal-oriented activities. These experiences have been developed to address depression, anger, and low self-esteem, which the organization attributes, in large part, to IRO. These community-based programs have developed and implemented various interventions to address IRO in youth, adults, in homogenous and heterogeneous groups, and across geographical locations to grapple with the ways racism has impacted the health of all citizens of the United States.

FUTURE RESEARCH AND SERVICE DIRECTIONS

Few of the issues facing African American communities exist in isolation. They are inter-related and usually find their root in slavery, colonization, and the many cycles that these traumatic conditions have produced (Degruy Leary, 2005). It is essential that service providers develop a greater understanding of the ways in which IRO manifests in various mental and behavioral health-related issues that are common in

African American communities. The high levels of gang involvement, domestic and sexual violence, drug and alcohol abuse, and other self-destructive behaviors that are prevalent in the African American community are symptoms of IRO that are often neglected or misunderstood by service providers. As a result, many individuals and organizations are ill-equipped to prepare participants or clients with the tools they need to transcend their oppression.

There is a need for more research that explores the various instruments that measure IRO and its many manifestations. The Internalized Racial Oppression Scale (IROS) developed by Bailey et al. (2011) and the Nadanolitization Scale (NAD) developed by Taylor and Grundy (1996) have initiated this development. Research with appropriate measures has the potential to provide empirical data about the relationships between IRO and educational, mental, and physical health, and well-being as well as provide a solid framework that can be used to understand the dynamics of the IRO construct. Beyond informing the psychological literature, this research could be empowering to clinical and community programs that work with African American populations, while providing useful outcome measures for their work. As most programs currently pay very little attention to the relationship between IRO and mental or physical health patterns, this research holds great potential to validate their work.

Educational institutions and community-based programs could also benefit from this research. Since African Americans are less likely than other groups to seek out therapy and counseling for mental health issues (U.S. Office of the Surgeon General, U.S. Center for Mental Health Services, & U.S. National Institute of Mental Health, 2001), programs that confront IRO can be offered in public institutions like schools, churches, and community centers. These education-based interventions, which have demonstrated potential for effectiveness in minimizing the effect of oppressive socio-political context on the development of IRO (Cort et al., 2009), can offer African Americans access to institutional mechanisms designed to support and empower them as they work to develop a healthy sense of self-esteem and cultural pride. This access can in turn prepare African Americans to navigate and counter the societal forces that promote IRO.

Schools and community organizations must create culturally responsive programs that employ curricula that empower participants to confront IRO. Groundbreaking research surrounding the relationship between positive racial identity and academic achievement of African Americans has influenced major philanthropic organizations like the Heinz Foundation to fund culturally relevant approaches to educating African Americans (Stone Haley & Noblit, 2009). In their review, Stone Haley and Noblit found results from several studies that suggest African American students performed best in settings that built on their culture and promoted positive racial identity development. In the same way, research surrounding racial identity, mental health, and physical health may also play a role in the allocation of resources toward service providers who work with African Americans through clinical and community organizations.

Professional development workshops that train staff and service providers to better understand and deconstruct IRO must also be implemented. This is critical because service providers who fail to develop a solid understanding of IRO will not be able to confront it as it manifests within their own programs, which has the potential to undermining their effectiveness. Whether it is in the transmission of internalized racial superiority from White service providers through Eurocentric values and history, or internalized racial inferiority from Black service providers who have learned to assimilate, all contribute to the negative racial identity development of African Americans, which makes them even more vulnerable to increased mental and physical health risks. For example, an African American educator that has assimilated to the dominant White cultural ethos as a means to achieve success may in his/her work with at-risk youth rely on this coping strategy and encourage students to assimilate to the dominant culture. However, they typically do so without recognizing the potential risks associated with this type of adaptations.

Organizations and institutions that successfully implement programs and services that address IRO must be supported and promoted. As a result of being under-resourced, many programs like these often fail to carry out their mission. Additionally, because many of these programs are underfunded and understaffed, their overall impact cannot be assessed, evaluated, nor researched for effectiveness. Conversely, institutions that demonstrate high rates of cultural incompetence are also not appropriately evaluated, and thus, their lack of effectiveness and potentially their role in perpetuating their African American participants' IRO goes unchecked.

Finally, it is impossible to ignore the political issues surrounding the creation and sustainability of institutions that address IRO. The downsizing and elimination of Black studies and African/African American studies departments in the nation's universities, the promotion of a "post-racial" ideological movement that challenges the necessity for Historically Black Colleges and University, and the lack of African-centered programs and curriculum in schools makes it increasingly difficult to gain momentum to address IRO in a comprehensive way. Additionally, Arizona governor Jan Brewer's 2010 approval and signing of a bill to ban ethnic studies because she believed that these programs "promote resentment" among minorities provides an example of the political challenges that hinder the development of these programs. Because African American healing requires a re-education process that examines slavery, colonization, and existing racial oppression, there are always a variety of powerful forces that will work against this, fearing the idea of oppressed minorities becoming liberated from IRO and acting on their power. As was the case during slavery, African American IRO enables powerful elites to maintain power and privilege that many do not wish to share, leaving little incentive to support the development of mechanisms that can heal African Americans. Thus, the transformation from internalizing negative attitudes and behaviors about oneself to excavating these ideas and embracing the actual image of oneself is at the heart of intrapersonal liberation required for the health and development of African American people.

REFERENCES

Akbar, N. (1996). *Breaking the chains of psychological slavery.* Tallahassee, FL: Mind Productions.

Alexander, M. (2010). *The new Jim crow.* New York, NY: The New Press.

Alleyne, A. (2005). Invisible injuries and silent witnesses: The shadow of racial oppression in workplace contexts. *Psychodynamic Practice, 11*(3), 283–299.

Asante, M. K., & Mattson, M. T. (1998). *The African-American atlas: Black history and culture-An illustrated reference* (2nd ed.). New York, NY: Macmillan.

Aymer, S. (2010). The case of Edward: Exploration of intraracial dynamics and internalized oppression in the context of clinical practice. *Families in Society: The Journal of Contemporary Human Services, 91*(3), 287–292. doi:10.160611044-38944007

Azibo, D. A. (1997). *African psychology: In historical perspective and related commentary.* Trenton, NJ: Africa World Press.

Bailey, T.-K. M., Chung, Y. B., Williams, W. S., Singh, A. A., & Terrell, H. K. (2011). Development and validation of the Internalized Racial Oppression Scale for Black individuals. *Journal of Counseling Psychology, 58*, 481–593. doi:10.1037/a0023585

Bell, D. (1980). Dialectics of school desegregation. *Alabama Law Review, 32*, 281–297.

Bonilla-Silva, E. (2006). *Racism without racist: Color-blind racism and the persistence of racial inequality in the United States.* Lanham, MD: Rowman and Littlefield.

Boyd-Franklin, N. (1991). Recurrent themes in the treatment of African American women in group psychotherapy. *Women & Therapy, 11*(2), 25–40. doi:10.1300/J015V11N02_04

Brave Heart, M. Y. H. (1998). The return to the sacred path: Healing the historical trauma and historical unresolved grief response among the Lakota through a psychological group intervention. *Smith College Studies in Social Work, 68*, 287–305.

Bryant, W. W. (2011). Internalized racism's association with African American male youth's propensity for violence. *Journal of Black Studies, 42*(4), 690–707. doi:10.1177/0021934710393243

Bryant-Davis, T., & Ocampo, C. (2006). A therapeutic approach to the treatment of racist-incident-based trauma. Journal *of Emotional Abuse, 6*, 1–22. doi: 10.1300/J135v06n04_01

Bulhan, H. A. (1985). *Frantz Fanon and the psychology of oppression.* New York, NY: Plenum Press.

Carter, R. T. (2007). Racism and psychological and emotional injury: Recognizing and assessing race-based traumatic stress. *The Counseling Psychologist, 35*, 1–93.

Chambers, E. C., Tull, E. S., Fraser, H. S., Mutunhu, N. R., Sobers, N., & Niles, E. (2004). The relationship of internalized racism to body fat distribution and insulin resistance among African adolescent youth. *Journal of the National Medical Association, 96*(12), 1594–1598.

Clark, K. B., & Clark, M. P. (1947). Racial identification and preference in Negro children. In T. N. Newcomb, & E. L. Hartley (Eds.), *Readings in social psychology* (pp. 169–178). New York, NY: Henry Holt.

Clarke, J. H. (1991). *Notes for an African world revolution: Africans at the cross-roads.* Trenton, NJ: Africa World Press.

Cort, M. A., Tull, E. S., Gwebu, K., Dlamini, P., Pinkney, E., Gramby, E., . . . Gwebu, E. T. (2009). Education and internalized racism in socio-political context: Zimbabwe and Swaziland. *The Social Science Journal, 46*, 644–655. doi:10.1016/j.soscij.2009.08.001

Cross, W. E., Jr. (1991). *Shades of Black: Diversity in African-American identity.* Philadelphia, PA: Temple University Press.

David, E. J. R. (2009). Internalized oppression, psychopathology, and cognitive behavioral therapy among historically oppressed groups. *Journal of Psychological Practice, 15*, 71–103.

Degruy Leary, J. (2005). *Post traumatic slave syndrome: America's legacy of enduring injury and healing.* Milwaukie, OR: Uptone Press.

Du Bois, W. E. B. (1998). *Black reconstruction in America: 1860–1880.* New York, NY: The Free Press.

Elkins, S. M. (1976). *Slavery: A problem in American institutional and intellectual life.* Chicago, IL: University of Chicago Press.

Fanon, F. (1963). *The wretched of the Earth.* New York, NY: Grove Press.

Fischer, A. R., & Shaw, C. M. (1999). African Americans' mental health and perceptions of racist discrimination: The moderating effects of racial socialization experiences and self-esteem. *Journal of Counseling Psychology, 46*, 395–407. doi: 10.1037/0022-0167.46.3.395

Frame, M. W., Williams, C. B., & Green, E. L. (1999). Balm in Gilead: Spiritual dimensions in counseling African American women. *Journal of Multicultural Counseling and Development, 27*, 182–192. doi:10.1002/j.2161-1912.1999.tb00334.x

Franklin, A. J. (2004). *From brotherhood to manhood: How Black men rescue their relationships and dreams from the invisibility syndrome.* New York, NY: Wiley.

Franklin-Jackson, D., & Carter, R. (2007). The relationships between race-related stress, racial identity and mental health for Black Americans. *Journal of Black Psychology, 33*(5), 5–26.

Gaertner, S. L., & Dovidio, J. F. (2005). Understanding and addressing contemporary racism: From aversive racism to the common in group identity model. *Journal of social issues, 61,* 615–639.

Gainor, K. A. (1992). Internalized oppression as barrier to effective group work with Black women. *The Journal for Specialists in Group Work, 17*(4), 235–242.

Haney López, I. F. (2011). Is the "posted" in host-racial the "blind" in colorblind? *Cardozo Law Review, 32,* 807–831. Retrieved from http://www.heinonline.org.ezproxy.library.und.edu/HOL/Print?handle=hein.journals/cdozo32&div=26&collection=journals&set_as_cursor=4&men_tab=srchresults

Harper, S. R. (2006). Peer support for African American male college achievement: Beyond internalized racism and the burden of "acting white." *The Journal of Men's Studies, 14*(3), 337–358.

Harrington, E. F., Crowther, J. H., & Shipherd, J. C. (2010). Trauma, binge eating, and the "strong Black woman." *Journal of Consulting and Clinical Psychology, 78,* 469–479. doi:10.1037/a0019174

Helms, J. E. (1990). *Black and White racial identity: Theory, research, and practice.* Westport, CN: Praeger Publishers.

Henry, P. J., & Sears, D. O. (2002). The symbolic racism 2000 scale. *Political Psychology, 23,* 253–283. Retrieved from http://www.jstor.org.ezproxy.gsu.edu/stable/pdfplus/3792290.pdf?acceptTC=true

Higginbotham, E. (1993). Sociology and the multicultural curriculum: The challenges of the 1990's and beyond. *Race, Sex and Class, 1,* 13–24.

Higginbotham, E., & Andersen, M. L. (2006). *Race and ethnicity in society: The changing landscape.* Belmont, CA: ThomsonWadsworth.

Jones, C. P. (2000). Levels of racism: A theoretic framework and gardener's tale. *American Journal of Public Health, 90*(8), 1212–1215.

Jones, H. L., Cross, W. E., & DeFour, D. C. (2007). Race-related stress, racial identity attitudes and mental health among Black women. *Journal of Black Psychology, 33,* 208–231.

Karenga, M. (2008). *Kwanzaa: A celebration of family, community, and culture* (2nd ed.). Los Angeles: University of Sankore Press.

Kaufka, B. (2009). The shadow within: Internalized racism and reflective writing. *Reflective Practice, 10*(2), 137–148. doi:10.1080/14623940902786115.

Kinder, D. R., & Sears, D. O. (1981). Prejudice and politics: Symbolic racism versus racial threats to the good life. *Journal of Personality and Social Psychology, 40,* 414–431. Retrieved from web.ebscohost.com.ezproxy.gsu.edu/ehost/pdfviewer/pdfviewer?vid=3&hid=14&sid=15d851c3-a97f-4e61-a401-e1cbd2471182%40sessionmgr15

Klarman, M. J. (2004). *From Jim Crow to civil rights: The Supreme Court and the struggle for racial equality.* New York, NY: Oxford University press.

Landrine, H., & Klonoff, E. A. (1996). The schedule of racist events: A measure of racial discrimination and a study of its negative physical and mental health consequences. *Journal of Black Psychology, 22,* 144–168.

Liebman, T. (2010). The role of cortisol and abdominal obesity in the epidemic of type 2 diabetes. *Undergraduate Research Journal for the Human Sciences, 9.* Retrieved from http://www.kon.org/urc/v9/liebman.html

Lipsky, S. (1977). Internalized oppression. *Black Reemergence, 2,* 5–10.

Murrell, A. J., Dietz-Uhler, B. L., Dovidio, J. F., Gaertner, S. L., & Drout, C. (1994). Aversiveracism and resistance to affirmative action: perceptions of justice are not necessarily colorblind. *Basic and applied Social Psychology, 15,* 71–86.

Neville, H., Spanierman, L., & Doan, B.-T. (2006). Exploring the association between color blind racial ideology and multicultural counseling competencies. *Cultural Diversity and Ethnic Minority Psychology, 12,* 275–290. doi:10.1037/1099-9809.12.2.275

Nuru-Jeter, A., Dominguez, T. P., Hammond, W. P., Leu, J., Skaff, M., Egerter, S., . . . Braveman, P. (2009). It's the skin you're in: African American women talk about their experiences of racism. An exploratory study to develop measures of racism for birth outcome studies. *Maternal Child Health Journal, 13,* 29–39. doi:10.1007/510995-008-0357-x

Paradies, Y. (2006). A systematic review of empirical research on self-reported racism and health. *International Journal of Epidemiology, 35,* 888–901.

Parks, E. E., Carter, R. G., & Gushue, G. V. (1996). At the crossroads: Racial and womanist identity development in Black and White women. *Journal of Counseling and Development, 74,* 624–631.

Parmer, T., Arnold, M. S., Natt, T., & Janson, C. (2004). Physical attractiveness as a process of internalized oppression and multigenerational transmission in African American families. *The Family Journal, 12,* 230–242. doi:10.1177/1066480704264931

Peters, R. (2004). Racism & hypertension among African Americans, *Western Journal of Nursing Research, 26*(6), 652–631.

Pierce, C. M. (1969). Is bigotry the basis of the medical problems of the ghetto? In J. C. Norman (Ed.), *Medicine in the Ghetto*. New York, NY: Appleton-Century-Crofts.

Pierce, C. M., Carew, J. V., Pierce-Gonzalez, D., & Wills, D. (1978). An Experiment in Racism: TV commercials. In C. M. Pierce (Ed.), *Television and education* (pp. 62–88). Beverly Hills, CA: Sage.

Pierre, M. R., & Mahalik, J. R. (2005). Examining African self-consciousness and Black racial identity as predictors of Black men's psychological well-being. *Cultural Diversity and Mental Health, 11,* 28–40.

Poupart, L. (2003). The familiar face of genocide: Internalized oppression among American Indians. *Hypatia, 18*(2), 86–100.

Rollock, D., & Gordon, E. W. (2000). Racism and mental health into the 21st century: Perspectives and parameters. *American Journal of Orthopsychiatry, 70*(1), 5–13.

Sankofa Community Empowerment (2012). Who is SCE? Retrieved from http://sankofaempowerment.org/

Sears, D. O. (1988). Symbolic racism. In P. A. Katz & D. A. Taylor (Eds.), *Eliminating racism: Profiles in controversy* (pp. 53–84). New York, NY: Plenum Press.

Sears, D. O., & Henry, P. J. (2003). The origins of symbolic racism. *Journal of Personality and Social psychology, 85,* 259–275. doi:10.1037/0022-3514.85.2.259

Sears, D. O., Van Laar, C., Carrillo, M., & Kosterman, R. (1997). Is it really racism? The origins of White Americans opposition to race targeted policies. *Public Opinion Quarterly, 61*, 16–53. Retrieved from http://web. ebscohost.com/ehost/pdfviewer/pdfviewer?vid=3&hid=110&sid=4271 24e7-3f13-4834-8937-9cd4a2bdf74a%40sessionmgr110

Sellers, R. M., Smith, M., Shelton, J. N., Roweley, S. J., & Chavous, T. M. (1998). Multidimensional model of racial Identity: A reconceptualization of African American racial identity. *Personality and Social Psychology Review, 2*, 18–39. Retrieved from http://web.ebscohost.com.ezproxy.gsu. edu/ehost/pdfviewer/pdfviewer?vid=3&sid=eed97f13-d954-497b-925c-f360e94b3545%40sessionmgr112&hid=125

Semmler, P. L., & Williams, C. B. (2000). Narrative therapy: a storied context for multicultural counseling. *Journal of Multicultural Counseling and Development, 28*, 51–62. doi:10.1002/j.2161-1912.2000.tb00227.x

Speight, S. L. (2007). Internalized racism: One more piece of the puzzle. *The Counseling Psychologist, 35*, 126–134. doi:10.1177/0011000006295119

Spirit of a Woman Leadership Development Institute (2012). Retrieved from http://www.sowleadership.com/index.html

Stone Haley, M., & Noblit, G. W. (2009). Cultural responsiveness, racial identity, and academic success: A review of the literature. Retrieved from http://www.heinz.org/UserFiles/Library/Culture-Report_FINAL.pdf

Sue, D. W. (2010). *Microaggressions in everyday life: Race, gender, and sexual orientation.* Hoboken, NJ: John Wiley and Sons.

Sue, D. W., Capodilupo, C. M., Torino, G. C., Bucceri, J. M., Holder, A. M. B., Nadal, K. L., & Esquilin, M. (2007). Racial microaggressions in everyday life: Implications for clinical practice. *American Psychologist, 62*, 271–286. doi:10.1037/0003066X.62.4.271

Sue, D. W., Nadal, K. L., Capodilupo, C. M., Lin, A. I., Torino, G. C., & Rivera, P. I. (2008). Racial microaggressions against Black Americans: Implications for counseling. *Journal of Counseling & Development, 86*, 330–338. Retrieved from http://web.ebscohost.com.ezproxy.library.und .edu/ehost/pdfviewer/pdfviewer?vid=4&hid=104&sid=dccac8cf -1c09-475d-8b44-d99896dd9218%40sessionmgr114

Szymanski, D. M., & Gupta, A. (2009). Examining the relationship between multiple internalized oppressions and African American lesbian, gay, bisexual and questioning persons' self-esteem and psychological distress. *Journal of Counseling Psychology, 56*(1), 110–118. doi:10.1037/a00112981

Szymanski, D. M., & Stewart, D. N. (2010). Racism and sexism as correlates of African American women's psychological distress. *Sex Roles, 63*, 226–238.

Tarman, C., & Sears, D. O. (2005). The conceptualization and measurement of symbolic racism. *The Journal of Politics, 67*, 731–761. doi: 10.1111/j.1468-2508 .2005.00337.x

Taylor, J. (1990). Relationship between internalized racism and marital satisfaction. *The Journal of Black Psychology, 16*(2), 45–53.

Taylor, J., & Grundy, C. (1996). Measuring black internalization of white stereotypes about blacks: The Nadanolitization Scale. In R. L. Jones (Ed.), *Handbook of tests and measurements for black populations* (pp. 217–221). Hampton, VA: Cobb and Henry.

Taylor, J., Henderson, D., & Jackson, B. B. (1991). A holistic model for understanding and predicting depressive symptoms in African-American women. *Journal of Community Psychology, 19*, 306–320. Retrieved from http://web.ebscohost.com.ezproxy.gsu.edu/ehost/pdfviewer/pdfviewer? vid=3&sid=a6ccb107-d73a-4e53-ad54-8afe94689575%40sessionmgr114& hid=19

The People's Institute for Survival and Beyond (2012). *Our principles*. Retrieved from http://www.pisab.org/our-principles

Tran, T. V., Wright, R., & Chatters, L. (1991). Health, stress, psychological resources, and subjective well-being among older Blacks. *Psychology and Aging, 6*, 100–108.

Tull, E. S., Sheu, Y., Butler, C., & Cornelius, K. (2005). Relationships between perceived stress, coping behavior and cortisol secretion in women with high and low levels of internalized racism. *Journal of the National Medical Association, 97*(2), 206–212.

Tussman, J. (1963). *The Supreme Court racial discrimination*. New York, NY: Oxford University Press.

U. S. Census Bureau (2011). Overview of Race and Hispanic Origin: 2010. Retrieved from http://www.census.gov/prod/cen2010/briefs/c2010br -02.pdf

U.S. Department of Labor, Bureau of Labor Statistics (2012). Economic News Release: Employment status of the civilian population by race, sex, and age. Retrieved from http://www.bls.gov/news.release/empsit.t02.htm

U.S. Office of the Surgeon General, U.S. Center for Mental Health Services, & U.S. National Institute of Mental Health (2001). *Mental health: Culture, race, and ethnicity: A supplement to Mental health: A report of the Surgeon General*. Rockville, MD: Substance Abuse and Mental Health Services Administration (US). Retrieved from http://www.ncbi.nlm.nih.gov/ books/NBK44243/

Weigel, R. H., & Howes, P. W. (1985). Conceptions of racial prejudice: symbolic racism reconsidered. *Journal of Social Issues, 41*, 117–138.

Wester, S. R., Vogel, D. L., Wei, M., & McLain, R. (2006). African American men, gender, role conflict and psychological distress: The role of racial identity. *Journal of Counseling and Development, 84*, 419–429.

Williams, A. L. (1996). Skin color in psychotherapy. In P. Foster, M. Moskowitz, & R. A. Javier (Eds.), *Reaching across boundaries of culture and class: Widening the scope of psychotherapy* (pp. 211–224). Northvale, NJ: Josh Aronson, Inc.

Wilson, A. (1993). *The falsification of African consciousness*. New York, NY: Afrikan World InfoSystems.

Woodson, C. G. (1990). *The miseducation of the Negro*. Nashville, TN: Winston-Derek.

Asian Americans and Internalized Oppression: Do We Deserve This?

James B. Millan and Alvin N. Alvarez

The little fourth-grade boy always wondered why Mrs. Rugen treated him differently. When they were playing dodge ball, if he was a little too enthusiastic (as little boys often are), she would yank his arm harshly and scold him. If he was too loud when they were playing tetherball, she would blow the whistle and yell at him for making too much noise. For some reason she hated him. And one morning, as he overheard Mrs. Rugen talking with another teacher, he figured out why. Later, as an adult, he would remember that one comment in that conversation "shot out at me a like a bullet. She referred to me as 'that little Jap boy.' I felt shock, pain, rage, and shame all the time . . . I had the queasy feeling that her calling me 'Jap' had something to do with our having been in camp. And camp . . . was something like jail . . . where people who had done bad things were sent. I had a gnawing sense of guilt about our time in camp. I could not fully understand it but perhaps we had it coming to us to be punished. Maybe we deserved to be called this painful word—Jap." (Takei, 1994)

As you read this story, take a moment to think about how familiar this scene is to you or perhaps your friends or family members? Have there been times when someone—a neighbor, a teacher, a peer, a complete stranger, or a coach—treated you differently or called you a racial slur? More importantly, have there been times when you have questioned why this has happened and perhaps even questioned—as this little boy did—if this was something you deserved? A nagging questioning and uncertainty not only about being harassed, but a questioning, uncertainty, and perhaps even shame about yourself. Indeed, imagine a lifetime of this treatment and the accompanying questioning and uncertainty. If any of this rings true—for you, your friends, and your family—then perhaps you have experienced some aspects of internalized oppression—a process by which individuals come to believe and accept the dominant group's stereotypical portrayals of the inferiority of one's group and the superiority of the dominant group (David, 2011; Freire, 1973). In the case of this little Japanese American boy named George Takei, who later grew up to play the character of Mr. Sulu on *Star Trek* and was one of the first prominent Asian American actors on television, racial discrimination was a part of the fabric of growing up in the United States. Indeed, the 1942 incarceration of the Takei family at Tule Lake along with 120,000 other Japanese Americans in internment camps across the continental United States without due process or evidence of wrongdoing is arguably one of the most striking instances of institutional racism against Asian Americans (Ancheta, 1998; Chan, 1991). Now, despite the fact that this story occurred 70 years ago, the experience of racism continues to be a factor in the lives of Asian Americans (Alvarez, 2009; Alvarez & Shin, 2013; Chan, 1991; Gee, Ro, Shariff-Marco, & Chae, 2009). As a result, the question of how Asian Americans respond to racism and its impact on how they regard and value themselves and their communities also continues to be a critical issue for mental health scholars and practitioners alike.

To place Mr. Takei's and perhaps some of your, your friends', and your family's experience in a broader context, this chapter will examine the experience of internalized oppression within the Asian American community. The chapter opens with a demographic overview that clarifies the breadth and diversity of the individuals that comprise the Asian American community. In order to provide a context for the roots of Asian Americans' experiences with internalized oppression, the chapter then examines the experiences of discrimination—both historical and contemporary—that have targeted Asian Americans. This section will then be followed by an overview of the common manifestations of internalized oppression that have been theoretically proposed and the mental health and behavioral implications that have been found in the empirical literature. Lastly, the chapter concludes with an introduction to the theoretical and applied literature that addresses the critical issue of how to challenge the internalization of one's oppression. In other words, how does one begin to challenge and shift how George (and others like him) perceives himself and the oppression that targets both himself and his community?

DEMOGRAPHICS

To better understand where George, the individual—as the son of first-generation immigrants who came to this country at the turn of the century—fits within the breadth of the Asian American community, it may be helpful to review the demographic characteristics of this diverse community. Asian Americans are the fastest growing racial group in the past decade, a rate that was four times faster than that of the total U.S. population (Hoefell, Rastogi, Kim, & Shahid, 2012). According to the 2010 Census (Hoefell et al., 2012), Asian Americans—alone and in combination with other racial groups—grew by 45% during 2000 to 2010, from 11.8 million to 17.3 million. Asians make up 5.6% of the American population—with the largest Asian ethnic groups consisting of the Chinese (4.0 million), followed by Filipinos (3.4 million) and Indians (3.2 million). While Asian Americans as a community have been traditionally identified with East Asian ethnic groups (e.g., Chinese, Japanese, Koreans), the fastest growing ethnic groups between 2000 and 2010—Bhutanese (9,000%), Nepalese (532%), and Burmese (499%)—all point to a changing demographic landscape among Asian Americans. Although admittedly these ethnic groups are still numerically small, the fastest growing groups among the major Asian ethnic groups—Asian Indian (68%), Filipino (44%), and Vietnamese (42%)—continue to point to an evolution of who will constitute the Asian American community (Hoefell et al., 2012). Geographically, nearly half of Asian Americas reside in the West (46%), with the rest living in the South (22%), Northeast (20%), and Midwest (12%). The most concentrated Asian populations are in California (5.6 million), New York (1.6 million), Texas (1.1 million), New Jersey (0.8 million), and Hawaii (0.8 million; Hoefell et al., 2012). In short, the composition and geographic distribution of Asian America has and continues to evolve.

Approximately 60% of Asians in America were born outside the United States—the highest proportion of any racial groups—and 57% are U.S. citizens (Asian American Center for Advancing Justice [AACAJ], 2011). Vietnamese have naturalization rates of 73% and Taiwanese, Filipino, Cambodian, Laotian, and Chinese Americans have similarly high rates of naturalization of about 60% or more—rates that far exceed the 43% naturalization rate for foreign-born U.S. residents overall (AACAJ, 2011). The level of education, employment, and earned income vary across Asian American groups. While there is a high level of educational attainment for Asian Americans overall (i.e., 86% have completed high school and 49% have a bachelors' degree or higher), the aggregation of this educational data has obscured critical ethnic group differences (Lee, Wong, & Alvarez, 2009). For instance, although Taiwanese, Indonesians, Japanese, Sri Lankans, Koreans, and Filipinos have the highest rates of high school completion, at about 90%, it is equally important to note that Hmong, Cambodian, and Laotian have the lowest rates at around 60%

(AACAJ, 2011). Indeed, the college completion rates for these last three groups—between 12% and 14%—point to critical educational disparities that are often overshadowed by aggregate data.

These educational disparities continue to be mirrored in employment, occupational, and income disparities. For instance, although Asian Americans as a whole have the lowest unemployment rates in comparison to other racial groups, Hmong, Cambodian, and Laotian Americans have unemployment rates of around 10%, which is comparable to that of Latinos and African Americans (AACAJ, 2011). Filipinos, Indian, and Japanese Americans tend to work in management and professional fields, while Bangladeshi, Cambodian, and Hmong Americans work mostly in transportation and production related jobs (AACAJ, 2011). The per capita income for Asian Americans between 2007 and 2009 was about $28,000, which was below non-Hispanic Whites, but above other racial groups; however, Hmong and Cambodian Americans had the lowest per capita income ($10,000–$15,000) and the highest rates (18%–20%) of poverty among all ethnic groups (AACAJ, 2011). Yet even among Asian Americans who have obtained high-skilled professional and managerial positions, scholars have pointed to income-to-education disparities that indicate that Asian Americans may earn less than White Americans despite comparable educational credentials. For instance, Kim and Sakamoto (2010) found that native-born Asian American men with college degrees earned 8% less than native-born non-Hispanic White men with similar educational, demographic, family, and geographic characteristics. Thus, contrary to the "model minority" myth (Lee et al., 2009), not all Asian Americans are academically and financially successful. Indeed, many Asian American ethnic groups struggle to get an education and live below the poverty line.

Parallel to these educational and employment risks, Asian Americans have also been found to be at risk for health disparities. For instance, Asian Americans have the highest risk for hepatitis and stomach and liver cancer among all ethnic groups (AACAJ, 2011). Indian Americans are among the groups most at risk for diabetes. In terms of mental health, posttraumatic stress disorder and depression are common in Cambodian and Vietnamese American refugees (AACAJ, 2011). Moreover, suicide is also prevalent among Asian Americans, with 15% of high school students endorsing suicidal ideation and women over 65 having the highest rates of suicide (AACAJ, 2011). Despite the fact that Asian Americans are prone to these health risks, they are among the least likely to seek health services. Approximately 4% of Asian Americans between 2004 and 2006 have not seen a health care provider in over 5 years, a rate that is twice that of non-Hispanic Whites (AACAJ, 2011). Likewise, these help-seeking behaviors are further exacerbated by the elevated rates of medically uninsured among certain Asian American ethnic groups. For instance, compared to the 15%

of the U.S. population as a whole who have no medical insurance, 20% or more of Cambodian, Korean, Bangladeshi, and Pakistani communities are medically uninsured (AACAJ, 2011). Consequently, as this chapter reviews the historical and contemporary experiences of Asian Americans, it is critical to remain cognizant of the within-group diversity of this community.

HISTORICAL OPPRESSION

Despite these notable within-group differences in demographics, education, incomes, and health, Asian Americans—across the different ethnic groups—have had strikingly similar experiences of racism and oppression before and after arriving in America. European countries from the 1500s up to the mid-1950s have colonized parts of Asia: Great Britain had colonies in India and Singapore from 1824 to 1957; France governed Vietnam and Indochina from 1859 to 1954; and the Philippines was ruled by Spain from 1511 to 1898 and by the United States from 1898 to 1945 (Nadal, 2009). Regardless of the colonial power or the time period, European colonizers consistently instilled notions of European superiority throughout Asia while degrading indigenous cultures (Nadal, 2009)—thus internalized oppression for certain Asian ethnic groups began with the experience of colonialism. As a continuation of these colonial experiences, Asians who immigrated to the United States were also looked down upon, considered of lower status, and were thus discriminated against, exploited, and, at worst, violently attacked and murdered (Chan, 1991). In effect, Asian Americans—along with other oppressed groups—were the targets of racism—"the transformation of race prejudice and/or ethnocentrism through the exercise of power against a racial group defined as inferior, by individuals and institutions with the intentional and unintentional support of the entire culture" (Jones, 1997, p. 172). According to Jones, racism can be classified as cultural, institutional, and individual. Cultural racism occurs when the values, norms, and beliefs of a group encourage and instill a sense of superiority over another racial group, often leading to the oppression of racial groups deemed inferior (Jones, 1997). In effect, cultural racism is the underlying belief system that legitimizes and fuels both institutional and individual forms of racism. Building upon these assumptions of inferiority by Euro-Americans, Asians were also oppressed through institutional racism—the use of legislation, policies, and laws based on a racial ideology to restrict the rights of a group (Jones, 1997). Likewise, given that Asians had few institutional rights or protections from the law, they were also the targets of individual racism, whereby an individual, believing in his or her sense of racial superiority, acts out against an individual or group who is regarded as inferior (Jones, 1997).

The belief widely embraced by Euro-Americans at the time—circa 1500 to 1960s—was that nonwhites were "inferior," a racist ideology that often led to the degradation of Asians. The Chinese, the first to arrive in America in large numbers, were viewed as "beasts," "heathens," and "addicts" (Chan, 1991). Filipinos were referred to as "little brown monkeys" (David, 2011) and Asian Indians were called "ragheads," a derogatory term that was based on the turbans Asian Indians wore (Chan, 1991). The dehumanization of Asians served to justify the discriminatory practices—both institutional and individual—imposed on them by the dominant White group. If Asians were "less human," then they were not entitled to the same rights given to Whites. The perception that Asians were inferior and that their lives were of lesser value (i.e., cultural racism) was the rationalization used to justify the oppression and violence that was inflicted upon them.

Fueled by cultural racism, Asian Americans also experienced institutional racism that affected them economically and limited their social mobility. No matter what jobs they held, Asians were financially exploited through laws and regulations that targeted them specifically. For instance, the Foreign Miner's Tax of 1850 was enforced only on Chinese miners and multiple states passed legislation to prevent Chinese, Japanese, Korean, and Asian Indian immigrant farmers from leasing or working any land (Ancheta, 1998; Chan, 1991). Laws were also created to prevent Asians from being naturalized, and anti-immigration laws like the Page Law of 1875 (which was used to target Chinese immigrants although it was ostensibly designed to bar prostitution), the Chinese Exclusion Act of 1882 (the first immigration law to target a specific ethnic group), the Gentlemen's Agreement of 1907, and the Tydings-McDuffie Act of 1934 limited the number of Chinese, Japanese, and Filipinos, respectively, emigrating to America (Ancheta, 1998; Chan, 1991). Asians were also segregated in schools and prevented from marrying Whites through antimiscegenation laws (Chan, 1991).

Parallel to institutional racism and discrimination, Asians also encountered individual and group violence—often with the tacit support of institutional systems. Chan (1991) describes how Chinese coal miners were harassed and even murdered by tax collectors, and how Filipinos were attacked by mobs of Euro Americans in racial riots. The violence that Asians encountered was oftentimes the result of workers looking for someone to blame for their financial hardships. For instance in 1885, Chinese coal miners were killed by a mob of White coal miners angry about low wages. In 1921, Japanese farm workers were threatened, rounded up, and forced to leave town by local White farmers. Further, in 1930, angry mobs of White "hunting parties" in Watsonville scoured the town in search of Filipino laborers (Chan, 1991). Indeed, scholars have argued that this systemic, race-based violence against Asian Americans provided the precedent for the most blatant and systemic instance of institutional racism against Asian Americans—when 120,000 Japanese Americans in 1942 were forced to sell their homes and possessions, separated from their families, and forcibly incarcerated in internment camps during World War II without due process or evidence of crimes (Ancheta, 1998). In short, Asians were a historically easy scapegoat with few rights and little protection against institutional laws and individual worldviews that regarded them as less than human. Consequently, it is clear that Asians have had longstanding historical experiences with racism and oppression—whether through colonialism or immigration—experiences that in turn may lead to the questioning and devaluing of oneself that characterizes internalized oppression.

CONTEMPORARY OPPRESSION

Although conditions for Asians greatly improved in the later half of the 20th century, racism continues to be a familiar and contemporary experience for Asians—whether it be in the form of cultural, institutional, or individual racism. In spite of the fact that the image of Asians is seemingly more positive than in the past, cultural racism continues to fuel stereotypes about Asian Americans and distorts how they are perceived by the dominant White majority as well as other communities of color. Among the most prevalent of these stereotypes, the myth of the "model minority" was first used in the 1960s by sociologist Petersen (1966) to allude to the relative success of Asians in America. By the 1980s, reports based on data from the U.S. Census Bureau were used to tout the fact that Japanese and Chinese were ahead of Whites in regards to higher education, white-collar jobs occupied, and earned income (Chan, 1991). However, Asian American scholars (Lee et al., 2009; Suzuki, 1977) argued that the data from the U.S. Census Bureau was misleading, as all Asians were combined into one group, and within-group differences in education, income, and occupational status were not accounted for (Yoo, Burrola, & Steger, 2010)—thereby obscuring critical inequities in certain Asian ethnic groups. Moreover, social and cultural factors such as the influx of well-educated Asian immigrants or the size of Asian families and the number of members that contribute to family income were also ignored (Yoo et al., 2010). For instance, over 60% of adult Indian and Taiwanese immigrants arrive in the United States with college degrees, whereas only 5% of Cambodian and Laotian adult immigrants arrive with a college degree (Kao & Thompson, 2003). Thus, as Kao and Thompson (2003) have argued, it is important to recognize not only that educational disparities exist among Asian Americans but that the educational achievements of this community are often a reflection of selective immigration practices and hard work in one's country of origin, rather than postimmigration educational and financial attainment. This nuance is particularly important since the image of the model minority initially emerged within the context of the turmoil of the Civil Rights movement and comparing the success of Asians in America with the economic and educational failures of African Americans, Latinos, and Native Americans was used as a racial wedge (Lee et al., 2009). The misreading of the U.S. Census Bureau data and overgeneralization of findings resulted in the misleading stereotype that all Asians are faring well in America—they are educated, earning good income, and free of social problems. In effect, the critical economic, educational, and health needs of certain Asian ethnic groups were overlooked.

In addition to the model minority stereotype, Asian Americans also encounter gender stereotypes. Asian women are portrayed in the media as exotic and sexual objects, often associated with notions of prostitution, obedience, and powerlessness (Iijima Hall, 2009), creating a culture of sexism and oppression around Asian women. For instance, Filipina women are perceived as subservient, sexually submissive, and good housekeepers who are idolized as the perfect housewife by American men, a stereotype that perpetuates the mail-order bride industry in the Philippines (Felipe, 2010). On the contrary, Asian men are negatively portrayed in the media, usually as villains or workers with thick accents, and often characterized as submissive and asexual (Iwamoto & Liu, 2009). The demasculinization of Asian men in America instills a message that Asian men cannot be the "prince in shinning armor," as Asian men are short, nerdy, asexual, and not fit to be a strong male partner; a message that has been internalized by some Asian women who may reject Asian men and prefer to date only White men (Iwamoto & Liu, 2009).

Tuan (1998) has also argued that Asian Americans have been and continue to be perceived through the stereotype of the perpetual foreigner—the persistent belief that despite generations in the United States, Asian Americans continue to be perceived as being unassimilable and not fitting in with the image of what constitutes an "American." Given their phenotypic differences, Tuan observed that Whiteness "is equated with being American; Asianness is not" (p. 139). Indeed, this perception of being a perpetual foreigner has fueled both historical and contemporary expressions of racial discrimination ranging from institutional to individual and daily racism. For instance, despite the fact that 62% of the Japanese Americans who were incarcerated in internment camps during World War II were American citizens, they were stripped of their constitutional and legal rights to due process because they were perceived as being disloyal and the "enemy race" (Chan, 1991). Likewise, in what is arguably one of the most significant incidents of contemporary racism against Asian Americans, the murder of Vincent Chin by disgruntled autoworkers in

Detroit, Michigan, in 1982 was fueled largely by a recession in which the Japanese auto industry—and by extension Japanese, Japanese Americans, and Asian Americans more broadly—were regarded as economic threats (Chan, 1991). Strikingly, Mr. Chin was actually a Chinese American draftsman and his connection to the Japan auto industry was virtually nonexistent. Indeed, on a daily level, the contemporary experiences of Asian Americans who are questioned about their language abilities, their place of birth, and their length of residence in the America are all rooted in assumptions of this community as being perpetual foreigners.

Parallel to cultural racism and these stereotypes, Asian Americans continue to face racism institutionally—especially in terms of barriers in the education system and in the world of work. Despite the common perception that Asian Americans have "taken over" higher education in the United States, the increase in enrollment for Asian Americans in colleges from 1987 to 2004 has actually been no different from that of African Americans and Latinos (National Commission on Asian American and Pacific Islander Research in Education, 2008). Nevertheless, Asian Americans have been targeted by discriminatory educational practices such as being held to higher standards for admission than that of other ethnic groups, and being excluded from affirmative action policies, all of which have prevented higher rates of enrollment in prominent, elite colleges (National Commission on Asian American and Pacific Islander Research in Education, 2008). In addition, Asian Americans have also encountered institutional discrimination in the workplace, preventing them from securing higher management positions—a phenomenon termed the "glass ceiling" (U.S. Equal Employment Opportunity Commission [USEEOC], 2011). In the work environment, Asians are often stereotyped as being foreign, antisocial, and unassertive, and therefore may be unfairly perceived to lack the communication, interpersonal, and leadership skills required for top-level positions (USEEOC, 2011). In addition, glass ceiling effects as well as longer times to promotion can also be found in lower incomes for Asian American employees, despite similar degree qualifications (Woo, 2000). To highlight the prevalence of this phenomenon, it is striking to note that Asian Americans report being the target of discrimination at a rate higher than any other racial or ethnic group (Gallup, 2005). Lastly, Asian Americans have also been targeted by linguistic discrimination, from English-only initiatives to language and accent discrimination (Ancheta, 1998). For instance, in the largest language discrimination suit in U.S. history, the Equal Employment Opportunity Commission filed and settled a lawsuit against the Delano Regional Medical Center in California on behalf of 70 Filipinos who were targeted for harassment, ridicule, and threats of dismissal for speaking Tagalog and other Filipino dialects, even when speakers of other languages were not targeted. Indeed, this group was specifically targeted to the point where surveillance equipment was installed and supervisors and colleagues were encouraged to act as vigilantes and report incidences of language violations (Equal Employment Opportunity Commission, 2011).

The most powerful evidence of the persistence of individual racism against Asian Americans is reflected in the racial violence that continues to plague these communities. In the 2002 Audit of Violence Against Asian Pacific Americans, the National Asian Pacific American Legal Consortium (2003) reported that from 1995 to 2002 Asian Americans were victims of racially motivated crimes throughout the United States. The incidences reported in the audit reflect anti-Asian sentiments that have historically incited violence against Asians, particularly that Asians are foreigners who are taking jobs and do not belong in the United States. For instance, the audit describes how a Chinese family was attacked by a man who blamed the Chinese for "taking our money." In another incident, a Korean woman was approached by a White male and asked if she was Korean and was then told, "Go back to where you came from." Other cases in the audit reflect post-9/11 anti-Arab and anti-Muslim fervor. In several incidents, men of East Asian decent were attacked and called a "Taliban" or "terrorists." For instance, in Oak Creek, Wisconsin, a man with membership in neo-Nazi organizations attacked and killed a group of Sikh-Americans at their temple (Hennessey-Fiske, 2012). Although the 9/11 attacks have created new pretexts to attack Asian Americans, what has remained relatively the same is the ways in which institutions often downplay these racially motivated hate crimes.

As with other Asian Americans, contemporary racism has also affected the lives of the authors of this chapter. For instance, the first author of the chapter (James) writes about his early experiences as a new immigrant:

> I immigrated to America from the Philippines as a child, and even at such an early age I would encounter racism, an experience that left me feeling confused, different, and unwanted. Growing up in Southern California I went to grade school with only a handful of Asians, and some Latinos and African Americans; the rest of the school was predominately White. Like most kids, I was aware of racial differences, but not concerned nor did I think much about it. One day, while on the playground, out of nowhere a White classmate called me "gook" and told me to "go home to where I came from." I can still recall the shock and confusion I felt, and the uncertainty of how to react. That definitely would not be the last time I experienced racism—too many other incidents to recall—but that afternoon on the playground I vividly remember the hot afternoon, the grassy playground, the boy's face, his name, the confusion, and how unwanted I felt, for it was the first time that I became conscious of being Filipino/Asian, being foreign, and the consequences of being racially different.

More recently, racism against Asians has been more public as Asians and Asian Americans gain greater recognition in the entertainment world, particularly in sports. Manny Pacquiao, a Filipino boxer who has gained prominence in the boxing world, was a target of a racial rant from boxer Floyd Mayweather, who called Pacquiao "yellow" (referring to race) and repeatedly associated Pacquiao with various rice dishes (Floyd Mayweather, 2010). The emergence of Chinese American NBA player Jeremy Lin also created a stir in the media when a writer from ESPN, a well-known sports media outlet, used the headline "Chink in the Armor" for an article on Jeremy Lin, while other writers used phrases like "deceptively quick" or "quicker than he looks" (Greenberg, 2012). The ways in which these racist remarks were blatantly committed, lacking discretion or forethought of how they may be received by Asians, and the lack of backlash from the public, reflects how ingrained anti-Asian sentiments are in American culture. Indeed, a national poll by the Committee of 100 (2009)—a Chinese American advocacy group—found that 45% of Americans believed that Asian Americans were more loyal to their country of origin (although close to 60% are U.S. citizens) and that they were "unassimilable"—precisely the belief system underlying the perpetual foreigner stereotype. Consequently, given the persistent patterns of racial discrimination and oppression that Asian Americans have faced, it is not surprising that Asian Americans may also internalize this oppression and question how they perceive themselves and their racial group—much in the same way that George Takei did as a little boy nearly 70 years ago.

COMMON MANIFESTATIONS OF INTERNALIZED OPPRESSION

Despite the clear evidence of both historical and contemporary racism against Asian Americans, the psychological literature about their experiences of being the target of oppression has only recently emerged (Alvarez & Shin, 2013; Gee et al., 2009). Of particular importance for this chapter is the question of how overt acts of racism, such as those listed in the prior section, become psychologically internalized to affect the manner in which Asian Americans regard themselves or in terms of George's experience, how does one reach the point where you wonder, "maybe we deserved to be" treated this way? Consequently, the following section reviews theoretical models and concepts within the psychological literature that address how internalized oppression may manifest itself in Asian Americans.

Given Asian Americans' historical experiences with longstanding colonialism, it is critical to examine colonial mentality—a form of internalized oppression that can manifest among Asian Americans. Studies on colonial mentality among Asians have focused mainly on Filipinos, due to the Philippines's long history of being colonized by both the United

States and Spain; however, it is important to note that, conceptually, the experience of colonial mentality may be applicable to other Asian ethnic groups and future research will be needed to examine this proposition. David and Okazaki (2006) theorized that Filipinos exhibited multiple aspects of colonial mentality that include: (a) denigration of Filipino self—feelings of shame, guilt, or self-hatred about being Filipino; (b) devaluation of Filipino culture including physical characteristics; (c) discrimination against Filipinos who are regarded as less "American"; and (d) a tolerance for the oppression of Filipinos both historical and contemporary. The denigration of oneself and one's culture reflects an internalization of the dominant group's messages of Filipinos as being inferior and White Americans as being superior in areas ranging from physical appearance, cultural values, language, material goods, and so forth. Likewise, discriminating against Filipinos who are perceived as less "American" may also be an interpersonal manifestation of distancing oneself from other Filipinos who epitomize what may be regarded as inferior Filipino characteristics (e.g., speech, clothes, values) as well as an attempt to conform to more White American values and norms. Lastly, in what Rimonte (1997) refers to as colonial debt, Filipinos may come to accept and perhaps regard as normative the discrimination that is perpetrated upon them—in effect, Filipinos come to identify with and tacitly accept the behaviors of their oppressors. In one of their early studies, David and Okazaki (2006) found that 30% of Filipino Americans exhibited some characteristic of colonial mentality. Filipinos with colonial mentality unconsciously and automatically associate anything Filipino with inferiority and automatically accept anything American as being superior (David & Okazaki, 2010).

Aspects of colonial mentality, particularly discrimination against less Americanized Asians, are also evident among other Asian groups (Nadal, 2009). The process of "intraethnic othering," whereby an individual singles out and discriminates against other individuals of the same ethnic group who are less assimilated to American culture, is a means by which Asian Americans deflect and create distance from the stigma created by Asian stereotypes of inferiority as well as a way to gain acceptance from White acquaintances (Pyke & Dang, 2003). Those who are considered less American—Asian immigrants, Asians who speak their native language and speak with an accent, or Asians who uphold cultural practices—are looked down upon, treated with disdain, and segregated. For example, Pyke and Dang (2003) describe how Hannah, a 19-year-old Vietnamese student at a predominately White college, distances herself from other Vietnamese by denigrating Vietnamese culture and rejecting her Vietnamese identity in order to legitimize her "Americaness." She says:

> My last name is Vietnamese and that's it . . . None of my friends are Vietnamese . . . in high school all the Vietnamese people were like FOBs

[fresh off the boat] . . . They all speak Vietnamese, the way they dress . . . I didn't want to be Vietnamese because all of the Vietnamese people I saw, I'm just kind of like, "I'm not you, so I don't want to be associated with you. And if that's all that you are, and that's what everybody thinks Vietnamese is, then I'm really not Vietnamese because I'm just so not like you." (p. 165)

In addition to a colonial mentality, Asian Americans may also exhibit internalized oppression by their internalization of Asian American stereotypes such as the model minority myth—the belief that Asians are more successful than other minority groups and that this success is due only to work ethic. Unlike colonial mentality, the problems associated with internalizing a seemingly "positive stereotype" may not be readily apparent at first glance. However, various scholars have argued that internalizing the model minority myth may be associated with greater pressures to succeed, higher psychological distress, elevated sense of shame in failing to realize social and family expectations, and inhibitions from seeking help (Lee et al., 2009; Yoo et al., 2010). Yoo et al. argued that there are two key dimensions of this internalization: (a) the Model Minority Myth of Achievement Orientation—the idea that Asians are more successful than other racial groups and that they are an exemplar for other groups; and (b) the Model Minority Myth of Unrestricted Mobility—the notion that the success of Asian Americans is associated with a lack of racial barriers. Indeed, Yoo et al. (2010) found that a common belief held by Asian American college students is that Asians are more successful than other ethnic groups because Asians work harder, are more driven, and do not experience institutional barriers. Expanding upon Yoo et al.'s work, Shen, Wang, and Swanson (2011) argued that the internalization of Asian American stereotypes goes beyond the model minority stereotype and that this internalization potentially involves both positive and negative stereotypes. In short, Shen et al. argued that that there is a need for a more comprehensive examination of the full range of stereotypes that Asian Americans potentially internalize. Specifically, Shen et al. proposed a model that examines Asian Americans' internalization of: (a) exceptional academic success; (b) excelling in math and science; (c) success in high prestige careers; (d) being poor in English; (e) being loyal to one's family; (f) being deferential to authority; and (g) lacking in emotional expression. Although the scale that was constructed from this model only assessed four out of the seven stereotypes, the central contribution of Shen et al.'s work is the impetus to consider the possibility that Asian Americans may internalize a wide variety of stereotypes, in addition to the model minority myth. Nevertheless, the work of Yoo et al. (2010) as well as Shen and her colleagues underscores the need to recognize the adverse impact of stereotype internalization.

In line with the argument that stereotype internalization is critical to examine, the manner in which Asian Americans potentially internalize White standards of beauty—from skin tone to body image to eye shape—is also worthy of examination, particularly since this has not been examined by scholars of stereotype internalization (Shen et al., 2011; Yoo et al., 2010). While lighter skin has been valued historically among Asians, as it symbolized a higher social class, the colonization of Asia by Europeans further strengthened and instilled the association between lighter skin and social power as well as beauty (Kawamura & Rice, 2009). Aside from being considered more beautiful, having lighter skin also afforded people with special privileges and advantages. For instance, lighter skinned Asians are more sought after by the entertainment industry and are paid higher wages (Nadal, 2009). Likewise, Kawamura and Rice (2009) observed that Asian Americans' body image (i.e., thoughts, attitudes and belief about one's physical appearance) has also shifted as people internalize Western standards of beauty. For instance, both men and women experience higher levels of body dissatisfaction as women feel pressured to be smaller and thinner and men feel pressured to be larger and more muscular. In addition to body image, some Asians prefer and consider double eyelids, more common to Europeans, to be more attractive than the single eyelids that are characteristic of Asians (Kawamura & Rice, 2009). Thus, having double eyelids is a means for Asians to appear less Asian (Munzer, 2011) and reflects not only a dimension of internalized oppression but also the "medicalization" of racism in which Asian features are considered abnormalities that need to be corrected (Kawamura & Rice, 2009).

As the first author of the chapter writes, the experience of internalized oppression—much like the experience of racial discrimination—is also a personal and poignant experience that was strikingly underscored in a recent trip to the Philippines:

> During the final edits of this chapter (ironically) I went on vacation to the Philippines, and while writing was the last thing on my mind I could not help but think about the issues presented here—racism, oppression, colonialism, colonial mentality—each a shadow in the daily experiences of Filipinos. While spending time with a friend and his wife, he commented on how he had told his wife that a friend from the "States" was coming to visit, at which point she assumed that I was White, but was soon disappointed to learn that I was Filipino. Half jokingly I replied that I was sorry to disappoint, and that I was just as dark as them. Despite making light of the situation I could not help reflect on the assumed, unquestioned superiority of "Whiteness" and the implied inferiority of being Filipino that transpired. On another occasion, I was with a group and someone commented on how much more beautiful their cousin was now that she was lighter, and how she must have used

some kind of cream to lighten her skin. They further commented on how common it was to use lightening cream in the Philippines. What struck me most was not the use of creams or equating beauty to lighter skin, but rather the matter of fact way people spoke of these issues—a tone that simply highlights just how ingrained and normative internalized oppression can become.

Perhaps the most insidious manifestation of internalized oppression for Asian Americans—as well as any other person of color—can be found in belief systems that deny or minimize the existence of racial oppression. Since the 1970s, scholars have proposed various models of racial identity (Helms, 1990) in order to describe the qualitative differences in how people of color identify with their racial group and the dominant White community, as well as their understanding and perceptions of racism. While various models have proposed a range of different developmental stages of identity (Cokley, 2007; Helms, 1995), one of the consistent themes across all models of racial identity is the description of a stage in which individuals reject their racial group, conform to dominant White values and norms, and deny the significance of racism. Indeed, in the first model to address Asian Americans specifically, Sue and Sue (1971) described the Marginal Person as a Chinese American who identifies exclusively with White culture and denigrates Asian culture. Likewise, Helms (1995) describes a developmental schema she calls Conformity—a belief system in which individuals deny or minimize the existence of racism and the racial aspects of themselves while identifying with the dominant White majority. Neville and her colleagues have elaborated upon this concept by developing a model of color-blind racial attitudes—the denial of racial dynamics and racism (Neville, Lilly, Duran, Lee, & Browne, 2000). Neville et al. theorized that a color-blind racial worldview consisted of a denial or minimal awareness of the following: (a) Racial Privilege—the racial privileges of the White majority; (b) Institutional Discrimination—the existence of systemic racism; and (c) Blatant Racism—the pervasiveness of overt racism. While Neville et al. argued that color blindness can be present in any racial group, she also argued that the presence of color-blind racial attitudes in people of color is most likely a function of internalized oppression (Thompson & Neville, 1999). Thus, of all the manifestations of internalized oppression, an argument can be made that a color-blind worldview is perhaps the most insidious and damaging manifestation—because rather than focusing on Asian Americans' beliefs about themselves or their racial group as various scholars have argued (David & Okazaki, 2006; Shen et al., 2011; Yoo et al., 2010), color blindness convinces Asian Americans to deny the very existence of the oppression of which they are the target. Indeed, a color-blind worldview may provide the foundation upon which Asian Americans denigrate themselves and their community.

MENTAL HEALTH AND BEHAVIORAL MANIFESTATIONS

Despite being a newly emerging area of scholarship, the negative consequences of racism on the psychological and physical well-being of Asian Americans is well documented. The experience of racial discrimination—particularly racial microaggressions—against Asian Americans has been linked to suicide, psychological distress, substance abuse, depression, lower self-esteem, as well as physical conditions like cardiovascular disease, respiratory problems, cholesterol levels, and diabetic symptoms (Alvarez & Shin, 2013; Gee et al., 2009). Although internalized oppression is directly related to being the target of racism, the direct effects of internalized oppression on health have received less empirical attention. Nevertheless, the limited number of empirical studies on colonial mentality and the model minority myth suggest that internalized feelings of inferiority and Asian stereotypes have an adverse impact on the psychological, interpersonal, and physical well-being of Asian Americans. For instance, in terms of psychological impact, David and Okazaki (2006) found that Filipino Americans who exhibited at least one form of colonial mentality had lower self-esteem than Filipino Americans with no indication of colonial mentality. Moreover, the authors found that Filipino Americans with colonial mentality had significantly higher depression scores that those without colonial mentality. In a follow-up study, David (2008) found that colonial mentality better accounted for the depressive symptoms experienced by Filipino Americans, having a more significant and direct effect on depression than other factors such as ethnic identity, personal and collective self-esteem, or enculturation; in effect, these findings suggest that internalized oppression—relative to other psychological constructs—may be a powerful influence on Asian Americans' psychological well-being. Although the findings on colonial mentality and self-esteem and depression are based on Filipino Americans, extrapolating from these findings suggests that Asian Americans who have experienced racism and internalized oppression have the potential to experience similar negative psychological consequences.

Consistent with the findings on colonial mentality, the internalization of the model minority myth has also been correlated with higher psychological distress, somatic symptoms, and lower ethnic pride among Asian Americans (Yoo et al., 2010). In a study of Asian American students, Yoo et al. found that the internalization of the model minority myth was positively correlated to the belief that the success of Asians was due to fair treatment and lack of racial barriers. Likewise, Shen et al. found that lower self-esteem was associated with internalization of Asian American stereotypes such as poor English fluency and being emotionally reserved. In addition, Asian Americans' satisfaction with their quality of life—particularly in terms of their psychological, physical, and social well-being—decreased as they internalized Asian American stereotypes (Shen et al., 2011). In another study of Asian Americans adults, Gupta, Szymanski, and Leong (2011) found similar results, namely that Asian Americans who subscribe to positive Asian stereotypes (such as that Asians are generally intelligent) experienced higher levels of psychological distress. A central feature of the model minority myth is that Asian Americans are smart, hard working, successful, and for individuals who ascribe to these positive stereotypes but who do not meet these standards, increased distress may be experienced as they face unrealistic or unattainable educational or financial expectations (Gupta et al., 2011; Yoo et al., 2010).

In addition, internalized oppression may also have interpersonal consequences through ethnic and racial distancing. For instance, Asian Americans use the derogatory term "FOB"—fresh off the boat—to affirm their Americanized identity and distance themselves from those perceived as "too Asian" (Pyke & Dang, 2003). The term FOB has been documented in multiple Asian ethnic groups—among Filipinos, Koreans, and Vietnamese (David, 2011; Pyke & Dang, 2003). In Pyke and Dang (2003), a Vietnamese American describes how he avoided and treated his immigrant cousin coldly, saying, "When I'd see him, I just looked at him, made eye contact in an unfriendly way . . . I did that because he's a FOB and I don't associate with Vietnamese even though I'm Vietnamese" (p. 165). Likewise, David (2011) discusses Filipino Americans' negative attitudes towards Filipinos who do not speak English or speak with Filipino accents—individuals who are regarded as "second-rate citizens." Indeed, the considerable pressure to distance oneself from other FOBs can be illustrated in this Korean American's comments as he talks about ridiculing another Korean who could not speak English, stating "I just stood there and laughed with my friend . . . Inside it made me mad . . . but I was Americanized so that I didn't want to seem like I was a FOB too" (p. 164). Nadal (2009) writes that the stigma and shame around being Filipino can be so powerful that this has led Filipino American actors to deny their Filipino identity, and claim other ethnicities such as Hispanic, Spanish, or Hawaiian. Similarly, Cheryan and Monin (2005) found that when Asian American students were not recognized as being "American" and were seen as "foreigners," they were more likely to respond to this treatment through a process they described as identity assertion, that is, the attempt to prove that one belongs to the dominant in-group—in this case, White Americans—by demonstrating cultural knowledge and practices of that group. Thus, internalized oppression has the potential to influence Asian Americans' fundamental sense of their racial and ethnic identities—the sense of who they are and, more importantly, who they do not want to be.

The internalization of White standards of beauty has also resulted in body image problems among Asian American men and women. Lau,

Lum, Chronister, and Forrest (2006) found that Asian American women who internalized American images of beauty through the media reported higher rates of body dissatisfaction than those who did not internalize the images. The dissatisfaction experienced by Asian American women can be so great that it often leads them to change their physical characteristics in order to appear more White. For instance, whiter skin is so highly sought after that Asians go to great lengths to maintain or obtain lighter skin. Asians will often wear protective gear to prevent dark skin, and Asians from Hong Kong, Malaysia, South Korea, Taiwan, and the Philippines report using creams to lighten their skin (Kawamura & Rice, 2009). Chinese, Japanese, and Asian Indians also report greater dissatisfaction with their facial features, especially in regards to their eyes; indeed, double eyelid surgery is the most requested procedure among Asian Americans, and among Asians in China, Taiwan, Japan, and South Korea (Kawamura & Rice, 2009). Moreover, Japanese exchange students have been shown to develop unhealthy eating patterns common to eating disorders while residing in America (Harris & Kuba, 1997).

Lastly, the research on color-blind racial attitudes and racial identity development suggests that internalized oppression may influence Asian Americans' racial attitudes and their perceptions of racism. For instance, Neville et al. (2000) found that individuals who endorsed color-blind racial attitudes were more likely to also endorse greater racial prejudice and gender intolerance. Neville argued that endorsing such color-blind attitudes reflects a belief in a distorted perspective on race and race relations that in turn may actually perpetuate systems of oppression. Deepening our understanding of the linkage between color-blind attitudes and racial identity, Chen, LePhuoc, Guzman, Rude, and Dodd (2006) found that an early stage of Asian American racial identity development—namely the Conformity schema—was associated with color-blind racial attitudes that minimized or denied the existence of White racial privilege, institutional racism, and blatant racism. Interestingly, Chen and her colleagues also found that this color-blind racial worldview was also related to lower levels of stress related to racism—in effect, this suggests that naiveté about racism and oppression may offer advantages for Asian Americans by shielding them from the stress associated with exposure to and acknowledgement of the harsh realities of racism. Indeed, as participants in Chen et al.'s study became more aware of racism and race-relations, they also exhibited higher levels of race-related stress. While few would argue that coming to an awareness of racism is a pain-free process, it is also important to point out that there may be psychological costs associated with maintaining the denial associated with color-blind racial worldview. For instance, Alvarez and Juang (2010) reported that using avoidance and denial as a means of coping with racism was associated with higher levels of psychological distress and lower levels of self-esteem. In other words, despite the intuitive appeal of trying to disregard racism, denying a chronic and pervasive phenomenon such as racial oppression may be psychologically taxing and challenging to maintain in the long term.

CLINICAL AND COMMUNITY PROGRAMS

Given the insidious nature of internalized oppression and, more importantly, the adverse impact it can have on the lives of Asian Americans, a critical question for mental health professionals revolves around the treatment of internalized oppression. In other words, how can Asian Americans come to an awareness of the racial messages they are beginning to internalize, recognize this as problematic, and ultimately undo the manner in which they have been racially socialized? In short, how can Asian Americans heal what Osajima (1993) refers to as the "hidden injuries of race" and what Duran, Firehammer, and Gonzalez (2008) refer to as "cultural soul wounds"? While the scope of this chapter does not permit a review of all the literature that addresses this question, it is our hope that the chapter can provide an introduction to this topic that can be a catalyst for readers to continue their exploration.

To better understand programs designed to address internalized oppression, an understanding of their theoretical foundations is vital. While various theoretical models such as empowerment theory (Cattaneo & Chapman, 2010), racial identity theory (Helms, 1990), colonial mentality theory (David, 2011; Fanon, 1963), and sociopolitical development theory (Moane, 2010; Watts, Williams, & Jagers, 2003) have all grappled with the process of healing from these "hidden injuries of race," a common thread in this healing process is Freire's (1973) idea of critical consciousness or conscientization. According to Freire, critical consciousness involves the process of deconstructing the root causes of social inequity and coming to an awareness of the oppression that is present in the lives of marginalized people. Without this consciousness, oppressed people perpetuate the cycle of oppression. Freire (1973) wrote that, "as long as the oppressed remain unaware of the causes of their conditions, they fatalistically 'accept' their exploitation" (p. 64). Elaborating upon the concept of conscientization, Watts, Diemer, and Voight (2011) argued that there are three core dimensions of critical consciousness: (a) critical reflection; (b) political efficacy; and (c) critical action. According to Watts et al., critical reflection is the analysis of social inequities and its structural and historical foundations in institutional policies and practices. In other words, critical reflection is a deconstruction of the institutional and cultural systems (e.g., educational, political, health, economic, and so forth) that maintain cycles of oppression. As individuals critically reflect upon their oppressed conditions, Freire theorized that individuals would also be compelled to act upon and change those conditions—a component of critical consciousness referred to as critical action. Specifically, Watts et al. define critical action as individual or collective actions designed to address social disparities and systemic policies and practices that are oppressive. Thus, it is important to note that critical consciousness theory is not simply about one's awareness but also one's actions in addressing social justice. As critical reflection spurs an individual to take critical action, taking critical action can also deepen that individual's understanding of oppression; in short, both action and reflection have a reciprocal effect on one another that fosters the development of critical consciousness. Lastly, Watts et al. argued that the relationship between critical reflection and action is influenced by political efficacy—a person's belief that individual and collective actions can be socially and institutionally transformative. In other words, the key link between reflection and action is the belief that one's actions *can* have an impact on oppressive systems; presumably, people are more likely to act when they believe in themselves as agents of change.

Particularly since Freire was as much—if not more so—a practitioner as he was a theorist, it may be helpful to describe a number of programs designed to address the internalized oppression among Asian Americans. For instance, Titiangco-Cubales and Sacramento (2009) describe a community-based curricular intervention called Pinayist pedagogy designed to empower Filipina American women (i.e., Pinays) through "an individual and communal process of decolonization, humanization, self-determination, and relationship building, ultimately moving toward liberation" (p. 180). Targeting predominantly Filipino American students, Pinayist workshops focus on three key goals that are consistent with Freire's cycle of praxis. First, participants are encouraged to identify and reflect upon the problems facing Pinays—from sexism, sex trafficking, and domestic violence to depression, eating disorders, and suicide. Second, participants then examine and analyze these issues in greater depth using empirical data to establish linkages between the historical and contemporary experiences of Pinays as well as the experiences of Pinays both locally and globally. Lastly, the participants create action plans that outline how both individuals and communities can take action to effect change in their personal lives, their local communities, and at a national and global level. Although beyond the scope of these workshops, participants are also encouraged to implement these action plans and to evaluate their outcomes. As a result, participants are encouraged to resist the oppression that they face as individuals and as communities by making a commitment to ongoing personal and social transformations (i.e., critical action). As one high school student commented on her experiences in these workshops, "It challenged me to love myself and to see beyond my internalized perceptions of what the world thinks of me" (p. 181).

Similar to Pinayist pedagogy, David (2011) describes a decolonization program also rooted in Freire's work that he calls the Filipino American Decolonization Experience (FADE). A unique aspect of the FADE program is the intentional incorporation of clinical interventions and techniques (e.g., psychoeducation, journals) derived from cognitive behavioral theory—a strategy designed to facilitate the integration of the decolonization process into the repertoire of mental health professionals working with Filipino American clients. In the initial sessions, FADE participants begin the consciousness-raising process by gaining a better understanding of themselves and how their personal experiences are interconnected with the collective experiences of Filipinos as a community—both historically and currently. Through lectures and group dialogues, participants undergo an awakening—often a painful one—to collective histories and oppression that many never realized existed. As one participant remarked, "I never realized how much the Filipinos were subjected to the cruelty and unfairness by other countries. It angered me. . ." (p. 204). As they immerse themselves in this awakening, participants begin an intensive and critical process of questioning their experiences, their family and friends' experiences, and what they have been taught and not taught about the experiences of Filipinos. To facilitate their understanding of how this history influences them currently, FADE participants undergo an assessment of their colonial mentality, learn about colonial mentality's impact on psychological well-being, and complete ongoing logs that track their observations of their mental health, oppression, and colonial mentality. As a result, participants begin to develop the ability to critically analyze and recognize the: (a) Historical-Contemporary Connections—the linkage between historical experiences and the present; (b) Within-Group Connections—the linkage between personal experiences and that of other Filipinos; (c) Intergroup Connections—the commonalities in the experiences of oppressed groups; and (d) Mental Health Connections—the transgenerational impact of history on mental health. In addition, FADE becomes a catalyst for taking critical action against oppression and for continuing the process of undoing and reclaiming their understanding of themselves as Filipino Americans.

Using research as the tool for critical consciousness, Suyemoto, Kim, Tanabe, Tawa, and Day (2009) developed a "student-as-researcher" course that attempts to connect the lived experiences of Asian American students with the scholarship of Asian American Studies. As students become engaged in research projects on Asian American issues, they contribute not only to the body of literature in the field but also to their own personal transformation as Asian Americans. In particular, Suyemoto et al. and her students (both undergraduate and graduate) designed a qualitative study called the Asian American Needs Assessment project to investigate the underserved educational and psychological needs of Asian American college students. A qualitative methodology was chosen in order to immerse student researchers into an engaged dialogue with participants that could also serve as a powerful catalyst for personal reflection and transformation. The research team met on a regular basis to discuss and present their findings in the literature and to design the interview protocol. Both group meetings and individual meetings with the team were designed as an opportunity for developing trusting relationships as well as a space for critical reflection and analysis of the literature on Asian Americans and its congruence with the team's personal experiences. Through a collaborative process, the research team developed a semistructured interview protocol in which students were primarily responsible for interviewing faculty, staff, and student participants about the experiences of Asian American college students. The student researchers kept a journal and were required to write a paper about their reflections of the impact of the project on themselves, their understanding of scholarship, and its impact on the university community. As a result of this process, student researchers were able to "integrate their own experiences with their growing understanding of the experiences of other Asian Americans, within a shared history, in the context of current realities of social inequality, and in relation to existing social structures of race, culture, and education" (p. 52). Moreover, the process of conducting research that was personally meaningful empowered students to recognize research as a transformative tool that could challenge and illuminate institutional oppression. As one student poignantly observed, "I believe that research is one powerful way to make our collective voice a stronger one" (p. 52).

FUTURE RESEARCH AND SERVICE DIRECTIONS

Just as scholars have only recently begun to examine Asian Americans' experiences with racism, the theoretical and empirical literature on internalized oppression among Asian Americans is only just emerging. Nevertheless, the future of this area of research is clearly promising both as an area of scholarship and as a foundation for applied interventions. In terms of theoretical foundations, the concepts of colonial mentality (David, 2011), stereotype internalization (Shen et al., 2011; Yoo et al., 2010), and color-blind racial attitudes (Neville et al., 2000) all provide groundbreaking models that should be catalysts for further scholarship on internalized oppression among Asian Americans. Indeed, the potential for growth in this field is particularly promising given that these scholars have each developed psychometrically rigorous instruments to measure their respective constructs. However, in terms of theoretical advancement, it will be equally important for scholars to disentangle the similarities and differences between the concepts of internalized oppression, colonial mentality, and stereotype internalization. As it currently stands, there is no global theory of internalized oppression specific for Asian Americans in general and it is unclear if the specificity of existing theoretical frameworks (e.g., the focus on the experience of Filipino Americans in colonial mentality) obscures aspects of internalized oppression for Asian Americans as a whole. For instance, is a model of colonial mentality based primarily on Filipino Americans applicable to the experiences of other Asian ethnic groups who were also colonized, or perhaps even Asian ethnic groups who were not colonized? Likewise, given the focus of Yoo et al.'s work on a single Asian American stereotype (i.e., model minority) and that Shen et al.'s instrument only captures a portion of the stereotypes she proposed, what theoretical and measurement advancements are needed to capture the internalization of other stereotypes? In short, are there other forms of internalized oppression that are in need of investigation? Given the diversity within the Asian American community, it stands to reason that theoretical diversity will also be needed to investigate the full breadth of the experience of internalized oppression.

With an expansion of theoretical foundations, it stands to reason that the literature on internalized oppression would also experience an expansion in the breadth, depth, and sophistication of the research questions under investigation. For instance, the scholars would be better able to explore the issue of within-group differences—both demographic (i.e., ethnicity, gender, socioeconomic status) and psychological (i.e., racial and ethnic identity, acculturation, self-esteem)—as they relate to internalized oppression. As with the literature on racism and Asian Americans, the literature on internalized oppression has focused largely on psychological outcomes. However, future research may also be needed to examine the impact of internalized oppression on physical health (e.g., cardiovascular fitness, diabetes, obesity) and behavioral health (e.g., smoking, alcoholism, suicide, help-seeking) as well as domain-specific investigations of internalized oppression (e.g., career advancement, academic achievement, marital, and relationship satisfaction). Lastly, given that internalized oppression appears to be consistently related to adverse outcomes, a central question for scholars will involve the identification of the factors that mitigate these outcomes. In other words, what are the potential moderators and mediators of the experience of internalized oppression (e.g., racial socialization, collective or personal self-esteem) and what are the mechanisms or pathways underlying these relationships? For practitioners working with Asian Americans who are coping with the adverse outcomes of internalized oppression, an understanding of the factors that buffer such outcomes will be essential.

Given the transformational and praxis goals of critical consciousness theory (Freire, 1973; Watts et al., 2011), it is clear that advancements in the scholarship on internalized oppression must also be complemented by advancements in the applied literature in this area. While various critical consciousness programs have been reviewed in the current chapter, it is important to note that these programs focus on only one segment of the Asian American community—namely, high school and college students. Subsequently, it is not clear how one fosters critical consciousness in younger Asian Americans or adult and/or elderly groups of Asian Americans. In a similar vein, with the exception of Tintiangco-Cubales and Sacramento's (2009) Pinayist pedagogy, the programs appear to focus largely on racial and cultural dimensions of oppression. However, given the multiple identities that shape the complexity of Asian Americans' lives and the intersectionality of those identities, it may be helpful to examine how consciousness-raising programs address and integrate racial oppression with other reference group identities (e.g., sexual orientation, socioeconomic status, religion, age) that may be sources of oppression as well as privilege. In effect, future work may be needed to refine how such consciousness-raising programs respond to the diversity within the Asian American community.

Although many programs all point to critical action as a long-term objective of the consciousness-raising process, it is less clear what is needed to translate critical reflection into critical action. In other words, what are the conditions and best practices associated with helping individuals to resist oppression and take action against social inequities? Particularly, in light of the fact that participants presumably "complete" these consciousness-raising programs at some point and leave the support of their peers and facilitators, it would be vital to identify those practices that sustain Asian Americans' commitment to social justice over the long term. As another sustainability strategy, it is important to assist Asian Americans in finding allies in other communities of color and recognize that coalitions may be an effective means of reaffirming support, broadening networks, and amplifying the political strength of a numerically small community. David (2011) has observed that as critical reflection emerges, individuals develop an awareness of the shared experiences of oppression across different groups. Consequently, it would be vital for individuals to obtain a better understanding of the fundamentals of coalition building—from outreach to finding common agendas to power sharing. In order to realize the long-term and systemic changes to which these consciousness raising programs aspire, it will be critical to help participants find a way to sustain the passion and commitment to continue resisting oppression once they complete the program.

In a similar vein, it will also be important to instill this commitment to undoing internalized oppression in the next generation of educators. While much of the applied literature on internalized oppression has focused on students and clients, it will also be critical to develop programs and curricula designed to educate future trainers of consciousness-raising programs. Given the clear challenges of facilitating such a program, it would be important to provide trainers with the resources—readings, films, lesson plans, exercises, and so forth—needed to be a transformative educator. Indeed, it is clear that one way to propagate one's commitment to social justice would be to share the collective wisdom and experience of one generation of facilitators with future trainers. As the historical experiences of individuals such as George Takei clearly indicate, the racial oppression targeting Asian Americans is both chronic and pervasive—all of which underscores the need not only to provide transformative education but also to train transformative educators.

REFERENCES

Alvarez, A. N. (2009). Racism: "It isn't fair." In N. Tewari & A. Alvarez (Eds.), *Asian American psychology: Current perspectives* (pp. 399–419). New York, NY: Psychology Press.

Alvarez, A. N., & Juang, L. P. (2010). Filipino Americans and racism: A multiple mediation model of coping. *Journal of Counseling Psychology, 57*(2), 167–178. doi:10.1037/a0019091

Alvarez, A. N., & Shin, J. (2013). Racism, mental health and health consequences. In G. Yoo, M. Le, & A. Oda (Eds.), *Handbook of Asian American health* (pp. 155–172). New York, NY: Springer.

Ancheta, A. N. (1998). *Race, rights and the Asian American experience.* New Brunswick, NJ: Rutgers University Press.

Asian American Center for Advancing Justice. (2011). *A community of contrasts: Asian Americans in the United States 2011.* Washington, D.C.: Author.

Cattaneo, L., & Chapman, A. R. (2010). The process of empowerment: A model for use in research and practice. *American Psychologist, 65*(7), 646–659. doi:10.1037/a0018854

Chan, S. (1991). *Asian Americans: An interpretive history.* Massachusetts, MA: Twayne Publishers.

Chen, G. A., LePhuoc, P., Guzmán, M. R., Rude, S. S., & Dodd, B. G. (2006). Exploring Asian American racial identity. *Cultural Diversity and Ethnic Minority Psychology, 12*(3), 461–476. doi:10.1037/1099-9809.12.3.461

Cheryan, S., & Monin, B. (2005). "Where are you really from?": Asian Americans and identity denial. *Journal of Personality and Social Psychology, 89*(5), 717–730. doi:10.1037/0022-3514.89.5.717

Cokley, K. (2007). Critical issues in the measurement of ethnic and racial identity: A referendum on the state of the field. *Journal of Counseling Psychology, 54*(3), 224–234. doi:10.1037/0022-0167.54.3.224

Committee of 100. (2009). *Still the other: Public attitudes towards Chinese and Asian Americans.* New York, NY: Author.

David, E. J. R. (2008). A colonial mentality model of depression for Filipino Americans. *Cultural Diversity and Ethnic Minority Psychology, 14*(2), 118–127. doi:10.1037/1099-9809.14.2.118

David, E. J. R. (2011). *Filipino-/American postcolonial psychology: Oppression, colonial mentality, and decolonization.* Bloomington, IN: AuthorHouse.

David, E. J. R., & Okazaki, S. (2006). The colonial mentality scale (CMS) for Filipino Americans: Scale construction and psychological implications. *Journal of Counseling Psychology, 53*(2), 241–252. doi:10.1037/0022-0167.53.2.241

David, E. J. R., & Okazaki, S. (2010). Activation and automaticity of colonial mentality. *Journal of Applied Social Psychology, 40*(4), 850–887. doi:10.1111/j.1559-1816.2010.00601.x

Duran, E., Firehammer, J., & Gonzalez, J. (2008). Liberation psychology as the path toward healing cultural soul wounds. *Journal of Counseling & Development, 86*(3), 288–295. doi:10.1002/j.1556-6678.2008.tb00511.x

Fanon, F. (1963). *The wretched of the earth.* Boston, MA: Grove Press.

Felipe, L. C. S. (2010). *Relationship of colonial mentality with Filipina American experiences of racism and sexism* (Doctoral dissertation, California School of Profession Psychology). ProQuest Dissertations and Theses.

Floyd Mayweather's racist rant caught on tape. (2010, September 2). *Huffington post.* Retrieved from http://www.huffingtonpost.com/2010/09/02/floyd-mayweather-racist-rant_n_703731.html

Freire, P. (1973). *Pedagogy of the oppressed.* London: Penguin Books.

Gallup. (2005). *Employee Discrimination in the Workplace.* Washington, D.C.: Author.

Gee, G. C., Ro, A., Shariff-Marco, S., & Chae, D. (2009). Racial discrimination and health among Asian Americans: Evidence, assessment, and directions for future research. *Epidemiologic Reviews, 31*, 130–151. doi:10.1093/epirev/mxp009

Greenberg, C. (2012, February 18). ESPN racist Jeremy Lin headline: Network apologizes for insensitive headline for Knicks loss. *Huffington Post.* Retrieved from http://www.huffingtonpost.com/2012/02/18/espn-racist-jeremy-lin-headline-mobile-apology_n_1286277.html

Gupta, A., Szymanski, D. M., & Leong, F. T. L. (2011). The "model minority myth": Internalized racialism of positive stereotypes as correlates of psychological distress, and attitudes toward help-seeking. *Asian American Journal of Psychology, 2*(2), 101–114. doi:10.1037/a0024183

Harris, D. J., & Kuba, S. A. (1997). Ethnocultural identity and eating disorders in women of color. *Professional Psychology: Research and Practice, 28*(4), 341–347.

Helms, J. E. (1990). *Black and White racial identity: Theory, research, and practice.* New York, NY, England: Greenwood Press.

Helms, J. E. (1995). An update on Helms' White and People of Color racial identity models. In J. G. Ponterotto, J. M. Casas, L. A. Suzuki, & C. M. Alexander (Eds.), *Handbook of multicultural counseling* (pp. 181–198). Thousand Oaks, CA: Sage.

Hennessey-Fiske (2012, August 6). Sikh temple shooting: Wisconsin gunman had a record. *Los Angeles Times.* Retrieved from http://articles.latimes.com/2012/aug/06/nation/la-na-milwaukee-sikh-shootings-20120807

Hoeffel, E. M., Rastogi, S., Kim, M. O., & Shahid, H. (2012). *The Asian population: 2010 census briefs: C2010BR-11.* Washington, D.C.: U.S. Department of Commerce.

Iijima Hall, C. C. (2009). Asian American women. In N. Tewari & A. Alvarez (Eds.), *Asian American psychology: Current perspectives* (pp. 153–172). New York, NY: Psychology Press.

Iwamoto, D. K., & Liu, W. M. (2009). Asian American men and Asianized attribution. In N. Tewari & A. Alvarez (Eds.), *Asian American psychology: Current perspectives* (pp. 153–172). New York, NY: Psychology Press.

Jones, J. M. (1997). *Prejudice and racism* (2nd ed.). New York, NY: McGraw Hill.

Kao, G., & Thompson, J. S. (2003). Racial and ethnic stratification in educational achievement and attainment. *Annual Review of Sociology, 29*, 417–442. doi:10.1146/annurev.soc.29.010202.100019

Kawamura, K., & Rice, T. (2009). Body image among Asian Americans. In N. Tewari & A. Alvarez (Eds.), *Asian American psychology: Current perspectives* (pp. 539–559). New York, NY: Psychology Press.

Kim, C. H., & Sakamoto, A. (2010). Have Asian American men achieved labor market parity with White American men? *American Sociological Review, 75*(6), 934–957.

Lau, A. M., Lum, S. K., Chronister, K. M., & Forrest, L. (2006). Asian American college women's body image: A pilot study. *Cultural Diversity and Ethnic Minority Psychology, 12*(2), 259–274. doi:10.1037/1099-9809.12.2.259

Lee, S. J., Wong, N., & Alvarez, A. N. (2009). The model minority and perpetual foreigner: Stereotypes of Asian Americans. In N. Tewari & A. N. Alvarez's (Eds.), *Asian American psychology: Current perspectives* (pp. 69–84). New York, NY: Psychology Press.

Moane, G. (2010). Sociopolitical development and political activism: Synergies between feminist and liberation psychology. *Psychology of Women Quarterly, 34*(4), 521–529. doi:10.1111/j.1471-6402.2010.01601.x

Munzer, S. R. (2011). Cosmetic surgery, racial identity, and aesthetics. *Configurations, 19*, 243–286.

Nadal, K. L. (2009). Colonialism: Societal and psychological impacts on Asian Americans and Pacific Islanders. In N. Tewari & A. Alvarez (Eds.), *Asian American psychology: Current perspectives* (pp. 153–172). New York, NY: Psychology Press.

National Asian Pacific American Legal Consortium. (2003). *Remembering: A ten year retrospective*. Washington, D. C.: Author.

National Commission on Asian American and Pacific Islander Research in Education. (2008). *Asian Americans and Pacific Islanders: Facts, not fiction: Setting the record straight*. New York, NY: College Board.

Neville, H. A., Lilly, R. L., Duran, G., Lee, R. M., & Browne, L. (2000). Construction and initial validation of the Color-Blind Racial Attitudes Scale (CoBRAS). *Journal of Counseling Psychology, 47*(1), 59–70. doi:10.1037/0022-0167.47.1.59

Osajima, K. (1993). The hidden injuries of race. In L. A. Revilla, G. M. Nomura, S. Wong, & S. Hune (Eds.), *Bearing dreams, shaping visions* (pp. 81–91). Pullman, Washington: Washington State University Press.

Petersen, W. (1966, January 9). Success story, Japanese American style. *New York Times Magazine*, VI–20.

Pyke, K., & Dang, T. (2003). "FOB" and "Whitewashed": Identity and internalized racism among second generation Asian Americans. *Qualitative Sociology, 26*(3), 147–172.

Rimonte, R. (1997). Colonialism's legacy: The inferiorizing of the Filipino. In M. P. P. Root (Ed.), *Filipino Americans: Transformation and identity* (pp. 39–61). Thousand Oaks, CA: Sage.

Shen, F. C., Wang, Y., & Swanson, J. L. (2011). Development and initial validation of the Internalization of Asian American Stereotypes Scale. *Cultural Diversity and Ethnic Minority Psychology, 17*(3), 283–294. doi:10.1037/a0024727

Sue, S., & Sue, D. W. (1971). Chinese American personality and mental health. *Ameriasia Journal, 1,* 36–49.

Suyemoto, K. L., Kim, G. S., Tanabe, M., Tawa, J., & Day, S. C. (2009). Challenging the model minority myth: Engaging Asian American students in research on Asian American college student experiences. *New Directions for Institutional Research,* (142), 41–55.

Suzuki, B. H. (1977). Education and the socialization of Asian Americans: A revisionist analysis of the 'Model Minority' Thesis. *Amerasia Journal, 2,* 23–51.

Takei, G. (1994). *To the stars: The autobiography of George Takei,* Star Trek's *Mr. Sulu.* New York, NY: Simon & Schuster.

Thompson, C. E., & Neville, H. A. (1999). Racism, mental health, and mental health practice. *Counseling Psychologist, 27,* 155–223.

Tintiangco-Cubales, A., & Sacramento, J. (2009). Practicing pinayist pedagogy. *Amerasia Journal, 35*(1), 179–187.

Tuan, M. (1998). *Forever foreigners or honorary Whites? The Asian ethnic experience today.* New Brunswick, NJ: Rutgers University Press.

U.S. Equal Employment Opportunity Commission. (2011). *Asian American and Pacific Islander work group report to the chair of the equal employment opportunity commission.* Retrieved from the EEOC Web site via GPO Access: http://www.eeoc.gov/federal/reports/aapi.html

Watts, R. J., Diemer, M. A., & Voight, A. M. (2011). Critical consciousness: Current status and future directions. *New Directions for Child and Adolescent Development, 134,* 43–57.

Watts, R. J., Williams, N., & Jagers, R. J. (2003). Sociopolitical development. *American Journal of Community Psychology, 31*(1–2), 185–194. doi:10.1023/A:1023091024140

Woo, D. (2000). *Glass ceilings and Asian Americans: The new face of workplace barriers.* Walnut Creek, CA: AltaMira Press.

Yoo, H., Burrola, K. S., & Steger, M. F. (2010). A preliminary report on a new measure: Internalization of the Model Minority Myth Measure (IM-4) and its psychological correlates among Asian American college students. *Journal of Counseling Psychology, 57*(1), 114–127. doi:10.1037/a0017871

Girls, Women, and Internalized Sexism

Steve Bearman and Marielle Amrhein

Notice how it comes up when I start writing this chapter. I am a woman. I have worked with hundreds of women and girls around the world. I have a masters degree from a prestigious university. I am articulate and intelligent. And still as I write my part for this chapter, some part of me is already judging, comparing, and deferring to the primary author who is a man. I struggle with feeling ashamed for even having this feeling. The feeling did not come from something he said. In contrast, he has shown he values, trusts, and wants my input, ideas, and experiences for this chapter. Yet still I worry that I am not going to be good enough or sound intelligent enough to be a co-contributor.

—Marielle

I can't tell you how many people have asked me why, as a man, I care so much about internalized sexism. My life is populated by women who have been hurt by sexism. I've felt helpless when I witness them unable to see their own power, or locked in self-criticism about their looks, or putting each other down to try to feel better about themselves, or sacrificing their own needs and desires for those of men. Even after decades of work on myself as a man in a sexist society, I still struggle to be an ally to women in overcoming the effects of sexism, to do more good than I do harm. As an outsider, I strive to see things clearly that can be invisible to someone who's grown up internalizing sexism.

I want to help make the invisible visible, so that Marielle and all the women in my life can come to fully believe in themselves, be allies for one another, and work together to create a world without sexism.

—Steve

When we asked some of the women in our community to share their experiences of internalized sexism with us, here are a few of the responses we received. There are more throughout the chapter.

I used to flirt a lot. This group of women in my community started ostracizing me. I found out, after the fact, that they were assuming I was having sex with all the men I flirted with. I wasn't, but they didn't ask. I still feel very hurt. I've only just now realized that that's why I stopped flirting.

During a visit, my mother-in-law said to me that the house needed a deep cleaning. Before her comments, I was content with how clean my floors were, but afterwards I was upset and confused. I didn't really know what my own thoughts were on the subject. All I could think of was what my mother-in-law thought was appropriate. After some tears and feeling betrayed by my mother-in-law, I came to see things more clearly. She thinks clean floors are more important than I do.

I was on the boys soccer team in middle school and one of the boys said to me, "Hey, you're good." I quickly replied, "Yeah—for a girl!" In retrospect, I think he was just acknowledging that I was good. I was the one who devalued my skill by comparing myself with boys.

Sexism occurs on three levels. To overcome sexism, we need to understand all of them.

1. Institutionalized sexism occurs when sexism is woven into political, social, and economic institutions. Laws that limit women's rights, or media that portrays women primarily as sex objects, are examples of institutionalized sexism.
2. Interpersonal sexism occurs on a more individual scale within interpersonal interactions. Someone expressing a stereotype that portrays women as inferior, and therefore deserving of fewer rights than men, or sexual harassment wherein a man nonconsensually treats a woman as a sex object, are examples of interpersonal sexism.
3. Internalized sexism, often left out of the discussion, is acted out within or between women, even when no men are present. A woman believing herself to be inferior, and undeserving of equal rights, or women treating other women or girls as if their worth is based on their sexual attractiveness, are examples of internalized sexism.

self or woman to woman [handwritten margin note]

As can be seen by looking at the cases of unequal rights and of sexual objectification, these three levels are interrelated. Eliminating sexism, therefore, requires change on all three levels. To dismantle the system of sexism, internalized sexism must be identified and uprooted. This chapter provides some ways to do this. First, however, let us make sure we understand the full range of what sexism is.

WHAT WE USUALLY THINK SEXISM IS

Women and girls make up more than half of the world's population. Though the cultural communities they inhabit vary dramatically, sexism nonetheless is built into every community's cultural norms and practices, its moral code, its notions of common sense, and often into its laws as well. The term "sexism" is meant to illuminate not merely the ways in which females are treated differently across the world, but specifically the ways females are mistreated and disadvantaged by the difference.

Historically, sexism has taken a number of overt and undeniable forms, most of them instances of institutionalized sexism (Eitzen, Baca Zinn, & Smith, 2012). For example, laws in many countries limit women's rights to vote, attend school, or occupy certain professions; define the ownership and control of girls and women by men, including wives by their husbands; legitimize sexual coercion and violence; and limit reproductive rights. Trafficking of girls and women for use as sex slaves remains rampant in many communities. Rape, sexual assault, and domestic violence traumatize girls and women, make family and community life unsafe, and limit women's freedom of movement through public spaces. Discrimination prevents women from holding certain jobs, and in other communities makes it more difficult for women to secure positions. When they do manage to secure them, women systematically make less money than men, even with equivalent education and experience. Sexual harassment, on the job and elsewhere, hinders women's success and adds daily stress to their lives. Leadership positions in business and in government are disproportionately occupied by men.

In industrialized countries where the women's rights movement has dramatically improved circumstances for women, some of the forms of old-fashioned sexism on the above list are, thankfully, obsolete. Cultural evolution occurs unevenly, however (Beck & Cowan, 1996), such that all forms of sexism that have ever existed persist to this day in some communities.

THE REST OF WHAT SEXISM IS

Even in places where feminism and the women's rights movement have been successful, sexism persists, not only in overt forms, but also in mundane daily expressions, many of which are instances of interpersonal sexism.

Some of these expressions of sexism are subtle enough to have little effect one instance at a time. Given both their ubiquitous and repetitive nature, however, even the most subtle aspects of sexism have cumulative effects. As an example, imagine yourself in the following scenario, and then answer the question at the end. This is a thought experiment that both women and men can use to try to grasp some of the cumulative effects of everyday sexism.

You will grow up in a world that will teach you to doubt your own capabilities, to lower your expectations of yourself, and to channel your interests toward domesticity, away from many respected professions. This logic will be reinforced by the relative absence of role models that share your gender in those professions, in powerful positions, and in the history you will learn. You will be treated as if you need to be protected and taken care of, but you will paradoxically be expected to be a caretaker for others, particularly people of the other gender, sacrificing your own needs for theirs. You will be criticized or ostracized for being too assertive, visible, or outspoken, but what is "too much" will always be a guessing game. Your opinions will often be discounted and invalidated, especially if you show emotions. If you become a leader, you will be disliked if you are assertive but liked if you are nurturing. You will be taught and shown that your worth is dependent upon your looks, your weight, and your body shape. No matter how you look, you will learn to criticize yourself, and you will be expected to spend considerable time and money modifying your physical appearance. You will be treated as a sexual being, even when you are engaged in activities fully unrelated to sexuality, and required to manage unwanted sexual attention and physical contact from people of the other gender. In many of the places you go, you will need to be vigilant against the possibility of sexual violence. Rather than identifying and pursuing your own desires, you will be encouraged to be passive in sex, dating, and relationships. If you get married, you will lose your name. In conversations and in writing that you read, pronouns and other language constructs will leave out people of your gender, considering people of the other gender to be normal people. Should you complain about these experiences, and about the stress and hardship you undergo as a result, many people will deny that anything is really happening. Many of these influences will be subtle, but they will usually go unquestioned or unnoticed, and they will happen every day, everywhere you go, for years without end. Over time, what effect will all of these influences have on you?

If overt, old-fashioned expressions of sexism stand out in the foreground of discussions about sexism, the kinds of everyday, mundane expressions of sexism in the scenario above form the background of girls' and women's lives (Klonoff & Landrine, 1995; Matteson & Moradi, 2005). Researchers have referred to aspects of this background as subtle sexism (Swim, Mallett, & Stangor, 2004), benevolent sexism (Glick & Fiske, 1996), modern sexism (Benokraitis & Feagin, 1995), everyday sexism (Swim, Hyers, Cohen, & Ferguson, 2001; The Everyday Sexism Project, 2012), and gender microaggressions (Capodilupo et al., 2010; Sue, 2010; The Microaggressions Project, 2010).

The things that we experience on a daily basis come to influence what we believe, how we behave, and who we are. When sexism is a part of day-to-day life, it gets into a person, shapes her beliefs, alters how she conducts her relationships, and how she moves through the world. Because sexism takes many forms, so does the internalization of sexism. Internalized sexism may lead girls and women to invalidate their own and one another's experiences, to put each other down in the ways they have been put down, to believe that the way their bodies look represents something essential about who they really are, to lose their sense of separate self, deferring instead to the needs and agendas of others, to compete with one another for the limited resources it seems are available to them, to believe that their options are constrained to those appropriate to the female role, and to fail to recognize their own power and as a result act powerlessly in a range of important domains. On an individual level, internalized sexism may have secondary effects, potentially contributing to depression, low self-esteem, body shame, eating disorders, chronic stress, diminished academic and job performance, and more (Frost, 2011; Syzmanski, Moffitt, & Carr, 2011), though any such list of negative psychological outcomes will only scratch the surface of the ways in which internalized sexism can limit women's lives.

So sexism, in both overt and subtle forms, gets internalized over time. Before we can delve deeper into some of the ways in which internalized sexism is practiced by women, and what to do about it, we must first explain some of the mechanisms of internalization.

HOW IS SEXISM INTERNALIZED?

We are born with a biological sex, but we are not born with a gender. We have to learn how to perform our genders (Butler, 1990; West & Zimmerman, 1987). Luckily, as cultural beings, we are built to imitate. Much of what we learn, we learn by doing what the people around us are doing, particularly people older than us. Gender roles are self-sustaining in part because they are passed down through the power of imitation from parents to children, from older siblings and peers to younger ones (Hill & Lynch, 1983). However, modeling and imitation are only part of the story. In order to get young people to fit within gender roles that cut them off from essential aspects of their humanity, we have to condition them as well. This is called *gender role conditioning.*

There is an exercise in understanding gender role conditioning that Steve, one of the authors of this chapter, has facilitated with dozens of diverse groups of women and men. He first asks the women to brainstorm a list of all the ways they learned growing up that they were supposed to be as females: qualities they were supposed to embody, things they were supposed to do. These may be things they learned from their family members, peers, teachers, religious institutions, or the media. He next asks them to make a list of ways they learned they were NOT supposed to be. Then the men brainstorm two such lists, and the results look something like a much longer version of Figure 8.1.

One feature of these lists is that they tend to divide all kinds of desirable human qualities, denying some to one gender and enforcing them on the other. Note how the quality of being sensitive is on the supposed-to list for females and the not-supposed-to list for males. Strong, on the other hand, is on the not-supposed-to list for females and the supposed-to list for males. All humans are born with the capacity to become sensitive and to become strong, and both these capacities are desirable ones, each providing personal and relational benefits. If many such qualities are desirable for human beings regardless of biological sex, how do we convince young people to abandon half of the desirable human qualities in support of their gender role? That is where the next set of questions comes in.

"What happened to you when you didn't act in the ways you were supposed to act? What happened when you acted in the ways you weren't supposed to act? What about when you did what you were supposed to and not what you weren't?" The answers to these questions spell out the nature of gender role conditioning. Behaving outside the role can lead to exclusion, ostracization, withholding of love, violence, threats of violence,

Female: supposed to (be)	Female: NOT supposed to (be)	Male: supposed to (be)	Male: NOT supposed to (be)
Thin	Strong	Successful	Show fear
Agreeable	Loud	Protect women	Quiet
Caretaker	Ugly	Fight	Cry
Shave legs	Ambitious	Strong	Need help
Like boys	TOO sexual	Self-reliant	Sensitive
Sensitive	Needy	Like sports	Wear pink
Helpful	Powerful	Get laid	Lazy
Sexual	Have bodily functions	Noble	Affectionate with other men

FIGURE 8.1   Examples of gender role expectations for women and men.

humiliation, loss, and other forms of punishment. Acting within the role can lead to acceptance, approval, admiration, connection, inclusion, freedom from violence, and other forms of reward. Such punishments and rewards are not always dramatic. Most of the time, they are subtle, everyday responses to behavior that fits within or fails to fit within the gender roles: a disapproving glance, encouraging words, subtle shaming, being invited to join a group, name-calling. The subtlety of these punishments and rewards is made up for by their persistence, repetition, and wide acceptance as ways of behaving. We are conditioned, over time, by learning to seek the rewards and avoid the punishments, to act out the gender role assigned to us.

Unfortunately, sexism is built into gender roles. Even though the gender role system is dehumanizing for both females and males, robbing each group of valuable human qualities, the two resulting roles are complementary in a way that disadvantages females. The roles encourage men to dominate and women to submit to domination, women to give away their power and men to take it from them. Taking on the female role means internalizing sexism.

There are three important things to note about female gender role conditioning:

1. *Conditioning into the female role is both direct and subtle.* Conditioning includes both clear, memorable, dramatic instances of reward and punishment, and many more mundane, subtle, repetitive instances that have a cumulative effect over time.

2. *Conditioning into the female role is ongoing, even now.* Childhood, adolescence in particular, is a formative period for adopting the attitudes and behaviors that make up the female role (Eccles, Templeton, Barber, & Stone, 2003; Hill & Lynch, 1983). Still, even into adulthood, women continue to live in a gendered world, one that attempts to condition them every day to constrain their ways of being human to the ones assigned to women. Society still offers a steady stream of approval and disapproval depending on how we behave, and continues to bombard us with images, models, and expectations of what it means to be female. Even if we have done the work needed to uncover our own gender role conditioning and shake it loose, we still must find a way to contend with society's ceaseless attempts to condition us today.

3. *Conditioning into the female role is perpetuated by both men and women.* Although some aspects of sexism are perpetrated primarily by men upon women, gender role conditioning is also enforced upon females by other females. Females have a special role to play in the socialization of other females into gender roles, and in making sure that, once indoctrinated, females do not stray too far from the female role.

Sexism gets into the psyches and informs the behaviors of individual women, and it plays out in interactions between women. This is why understanding internalized sexism is crucial to eliminating sexism. Just like men, women need to learn to stop being perpetrators of sexism if they are to become effective allies against oppression.

DOES INTERNALIZED SEXISM PROTECT AGAINST EXTERNAL SEXISM?

Why do females actively work to keep other females within sexist roles? Ironically, women may be trying to protect girls and other women from the sexism in the world by encouraging them to internalize sexism within themselves. To make sense of this seeming paradox, let us take a look at the case of objectification. Objectification is a feature of sexism that remains relatively untouched even in communities where other aspects of sexism have been thwarted by the women's liberation movement (Wolf, 1991). The media, bombarding us with images of women, teaches us to see women as bodies and faces, and as objects of sexual desire. Men's gazes create environments in which women are looked at and evaluated based on their appearance as part of everyday life. Objectification, at the most basic level, is the process by which we confuse what a person looks like with who they are (Bulik, 2012). When a woman is thought of as a whole person, we recognize her complexity and multidimensionality, the richness of her inner experience. Reducing a woman to an *object* means that we only view her from the outside, believing that we know who she really is based on how she looks, and assessing her worth by how well she matches the cultural standards of beauty and desirability that we have learned.

Women and girls are hurt by objectification, and yet women and girls objectify themselves and one another all the time. Consider:

- The older female relative who, each time she sees you, greets you by looking you up and down and commenting on whether you have gained or lost weight
- The teenager who says to her friend, "You can't go to school with your hair like that"
- The group of women criticizing a mutual acquaintance, stating, "If she doesn't want to be treated like that by men, then why does she dress so slutty?"

Why would women hurt each other by perpetuating objectification? Paradoxically, women may be hurting each other in an effort to protect one another from sexism. There are at least three different kinds of ways a woman may be objectified: (1) she can receive *validating objectification*, being affirmed, complimented, and rewarded for her appearance;

(2) she can receive *derogatory objectification*, being criticized, insulted, or punished for her appearance; and (3) in the absence of validating or derogatory objectification, a woman may encounter *social invisibility*, along with the implicit exclusion that comes from not being seen. If forced to choose between these options offered up by sexism, most of us would probably choose validating objectification. If women help other women become validated for their looks, their bodies, and their sexualities, they protect their fellow women from the worse fates of derogation and invisibility.

Internalized sexism often has this quality. Women enforce gender role conditioning on one another in an attempt, deliberate or otherwise, to create a protective buffer against the effects of sexism. Rather than intending to oppress one another, women may be working to improve one another's prospects. Yet training each other to accept and participate in sexism, in order to keep from being hurt in worse ways, can only ever be a partial answer. Though their motivations are often to be caring and supportive, when women play the part of enforcing gender role conditioning upon girls and other women, they are occupying an essential supporting role in keeping the overall system of sexism intact.

Internalized oppression can be hard to see. Because we live inside of it, it can be like an invisible gas with no odor. Unless we can add some kind of stink to the gas, we will not be able to tell whether it is accumulating in the room, about to suffocate us, or to explode. We need to understand the ways in which internalized sexism is practiced from day to day, so that we can see what damage it may be doing to us. Once we understand all the practices of internalized sexism, the ways of behaving and relating that keep sexism alive within and between women, we can consider better alternatives, ways of acting outside the oppression that more than superficially protect against oppression's worst effects.

Below, we explore six different kinds of practices of internalized sexism, and in the next section suggest alternative practices for each. The six kinds of practices are:

1. Powerlessness—whereby women believe themselves to be more limited and less capable than they actually are
2. Objectification—whereby women come to think of themselves as bodies seen from the outside
3. Loss of self—whereby women fail to recognize, or sacrifice, their own needs and desires
4. Invalidation—whereby women discount their own feelings and thoughts, specifically when they don't match male standards
5. Derogation—whereby women use criticism as a form of gender role policing
6. Competition between women—whereby other women take the blame for the limited resources and hardships imposed by sexism

Keep in mind that while these practices tend to be universal to the experience of women, they can take dramatically different forms in different cultural contexts, spanning the range from overt to subtle. Women may experience relative freedom from some types of internalized sexism while still being susceptible to others. For example, a woman may occupy a high leadership position in a male-dominated profession, having overcome an internalized sense of her limitations, yet still compare her body with media images of women every time she looks in the mirror due to self-objectification. Even "liberated" women, who have had enough resource to step out of some, or even most, of the gender role conditioning, may benefit from an inventory of how internalized sexism still operates within them. For them, the ongoing effects of internalized sexism may be harder to identify and feel more shameful to acknowledge. The effects could be experienced as a discomfort in the roles she occupies, an internal sense of emptiness or aloneness, restlessness, or a persistent anxiety or tension. She might harbor silent resentment at doing housework, while convincing herself that she is choosing to do it because she wants to. She might find herself justifying the nontraditional role she is assuming, celebrating her victory in the struggle for gender equality by occupying a leadership position formerly occupied by only men, but then perpetuating the subtly sexist ways men have acted in that role. As universal as these practices tend to be, they vary across cultural communities and between individual women.

THE PRACTICES OF INTERNALIZED SEXISM

Internalized Powerlessness

What do you believe you can't do? What do you consider to be your limitations? What would you like to see change about the world, but assume there's nothing you can do about it? These questions about your limitations are also questions about how powerful you consider yourself to be. We define power as the ability to influence yourself, others, and the world around you, to make the world more how you wish it to be. Internalized sexism can lead women to believe that they are less powerful, and more limited, than they actually are. While it is true that everyone has their limits, it is also true that oppression robs groups of people of some of their power. Can you tell the difference between your actual limits, and the limits you have come to believe are yours due to the effects of sexism?

Sexism disproportionately distributes power between women and men. Women lose access to resources, status, economic advantage, self-determination, and safety, while men benefit from the gain of resources that women have lost. Internalized sexism helps keep the unequal balance of power in place by insuring that girls and women feel relatively powerless and therefore act relatively powerlessly (Freire, 1970; Jackins, 1997).

A learned sense of powerlessness (Peterson, Maier, & Seligman, 1993) may be the most damaging aspect of internalized sexism, leading girls and women to limit themselves and one another, to believe themselves confined to behaviors that fit within the female role, to act passively in some contexts, and to believe that these limitations are natural or permanent.

> Back when I was a nurse, I was telling a friend that I was always taught I could do anything I wanted to, that women could do the same things as men. She immediately said to me, "Oh yeah? Then how come you're a nurse instead of a doctor?" I was shocked. I realized at that moment that it had never occurred to me, not for a single moment in all my preparations for a career in medicine, and then in all my years in the field, that I could be a doctor. Not that there's anything wrong with being a nurse. I had simply never perceived that I had the choice.

Because of the history of sexism, girls are provided with few female role models in some fields. For instance, girls may not see women in the sciences serving as models of what is possible for them when they grow up. This lack may come to seem natural, leading some women to imagine that men are just better scientists than women (Huang, 2013). As a result, they may expect girls to have low mathematical and scientific abilities, may even question the overall intelligence of girls, leading them to discourage girls from developing these capacities (Eccles, Barber, Jozefowicz, Malenchuk, & Vida, 1999; Jacobs, Davis-Kean, Bleeker, Eccles, & Malanchuk, 2005). When a girl has internalized low expectations or received outright discouragement, she may come to declare that she is "just no good at math and science." The belief that girls will not make good scientists leads to a lack of support for girls to pursue science, which leads to fewer female scientists, which leads back to the belief that girls will not make good scientists. Internalized sexism helps to perpetuate the cycle, to pass limiting beliefs from one generation to the next.

Socially established gender roles limit women's options in two ways: by *discouraging* women from participating in careers and activities prescribed for men (like in the science example); and by *encouraging* them to fill their lives with activities prescribed for women. At the same time as women's options are constrained, their resources are commandeered by the demands of the female role: the need to look, speak, and act "like a woman." There is only so much a person can do within any given time frame. If you have been trained to occupy yourself fulfilling all the expectations of femalehood such as managing your appearance, attending to other people's needs, fixating on dating, maintaining certain kinds of social bonds, consuming media designed for women, and so on, there is only so much time and energy left. Internalizing the expectation that your time should be taken up with female-specific activities means less time available for the vast range of options we humans have available to us.

Internalized powerlessness can take the form of learned passivity, helplessness, and submission. We all begin life with less power than we have now. Young people, due to their limited size and strength, inexperience, lack of information, and dependence upon adults for survival, have limited power to determine their own fates, and are inherently vulnerable to victimization. Sexism compounds this risk for girls. Fighting back against someone who is hurting you or trying to control you is not always an option; in many circumstances, resisting can lead to being hurt even worse. If fighting back or speaking out makes things worse, remaining passive, silent, paralyzed, or submissive can be a helpful self-preservation strategy. Later on, despite having grown up, having more information and experience, and more resources, women may continue to occupy the victim role, feeling as powerless as they did earlier on in life and acting relatively powerlessly as a result: silenced and immobilized by their own internalized oppressors. In a situation where a woman could otherwise use her voice to stop something from happening, say no, get herself out of undesirable circumstances, or recruit help, she may instead default to passivity. Passivity can feel less risky and more congruent with the learned female role. Acting on one's own behalf, or on behalf of other women, may actually be the safer option, but this requires overcoming internalized powerlessness that can develop over time due to sexism. Learned helplessness can far outlast circumstances of actual victimization (Peterson et al., 1993).

Internalized powerlessness, whether in the form of learned helplessness or perceived limitations, may seem to be natural, as if it is an essential part of being female. Internalized sexism, after all, is not just happening to one woman at a time. If we look at the women in our communities, we are likely to encounter role models that have also come to believe themselves to be more limited than they actually are. Each new generation is able to improve the overall landscape of sexism, but because previous generations grew up in a more sexist world, older generations will tend to model internalized sexism for younger ones. Furthermore, because other forms of oppression besides sexism lead people in target groups to feel powerless, it may not be possible to sort out the sense of powerlessness that comes from internalized sexism from that which comes from internalized racism, internalized young people's oppression, or other forms of internalized oppression. When these oppressions intersect in women who also belong to other oppressed groups, the work of reclaiming power becomes even more essential.

Reclaiming Power

It is possible to reclaim both a sense of one's own power (to act powerfully on one's own behalf) and on behalf of the changes you see the world needs. Power imbalance between genders, and feelings of powerlessness in women, is recognized worldwide as an issue demanding attention socially, economically, politically, and legally. One of the United Nations Millennium Development Goals is to "promote gender equality and empower women" (UN Department of Public Information, 2010), a goal indicated as necessary for the health of our world. As a result, there are many organizations worldwide that address this goal through programs for "girl's leadership," "empowering women," and "gender equality." One of the authors, Marielle, has worked with a number of these organizations in many parts of the world. She has found that successful programs generally follow a model with three main components:

1. Girls and women are at the center of participation, and of efforts to take action, creating a platform for women's voices to be heard.
2. The focus is not just on outer change, but on self-reflection and personal growth, guiding women to understand their inner worlds, their beliefs, and their emotions.
3. Programs that explicitly follow a liberation framework include explicit consciousness-raising about systems of oppression, specifically sexism and internalized sexism.

Involvement in these kinds of programs helps women and girls develop a sense of self, develop confidence, think for themselves, and make contributions to their community. The result is that women reclaim their own power. With an internalized sense of power, women are able make choices about what they want for themselves, including the pursuit of highly challenging goals.

One reason that women coming together, not only to learn about oppression, but to understand their inner emotional landscapes, is necessary to reclaim power has to do with the relationship between anger and power. Identifying and expressing *anger* is often a key to reclaiming power. An internalized sense of powerlessness silences and paralyzes women. Anger begins the process of mobilizing power by getting energy moving and transmuting silence into sound. This is only the first stage, however, as raw, righteous indignation can sometimes manifest as noise and fury without any real impact. A second stage in the process of reclaiming power involves learning to direct anger toward the source of injustice, to use anger in a goal-directed way to raise consciousness, speak truth to power, and interrupt sexism. Goal-directed anger is far more likely to affect change than raw, undirected anger, but anger in any form can only take us so far. A third stage is necessary in order for women to become creative leaders, one that transcends anger in favor of the many other tools and resources also needed to take on the complex and entrenched forces of oppression. Anger may still be used skillfully as one strategy to organize people and foster change. In the beginning, anger helps mobilize the power that has been suppressed by internalized oppression. In the end, remaining stuck at the anger stage of the reclaiming process hinders the development of women's creative power. Women can help other women both to access their anger, and then eventually to surpass it, rather that remain limited by it.

Internalized Objectification

What does it mean for a woman to become an object? It begins when people believe her physical appearance to be a true representation of who she is. Confusing a person with her looks requires a blindness to that which cannot be so easily seen, a failure to imagine what her inner world might be like: her rich, moment-to-moment lived experience of being a person. To the objectifier, she stops being a person, experiencing the world and making choices based on complex motivations, and instead becomes an object, to be evaluated and enjoyed, disparaged, or ignored according to the viewer.

Being objectified by others is only part of the process of objectification. After a long enough immersion in social environments where they and other women are objectified, women start to internalize the objectifier, to adopt the stance of an outside observer in understanding their own bodies. They begin to self-objectify (Fredrickson & Roberts, 1997; Fredrickson, Roberts, Noll, Quinn, & Twenge, 1998; Hebl, King, & Lin, 2004). The social importance of physical appearance begins to outweigh the personal importance of inner felt-sense experience, and a kind of disembodiment results. Instead of feeling their bodies from the inside, and inhabiting them from within, women imagine how their bodies are seen from the outside, and evaluate them from without (de Beauvoir, 1961; Tolman & Porche, 2000). One result of this change in viewpoint is that women can conflate their self-image with their body-image (Bulik, 2012). Even if a woman has come to hold very negative beliefs about her own body, in the absence of self-objectification, she might still be able to have a very high sense of self-worth, because self-image and body-image would not seem to be one and the same. Research on self-objectification in women has demonstrated that self-objectification can reduce overall well-being, and that it contributes to depression, eating disorders, and cosmetic surgery (Breines, Crocker, & Garcia, 2008; Fredrickson et al., 1998; Muehlenkamp & Saris-Baglama, 2002; Szymanski & Henning, 2007). Self-objectification, though it allows women to play the social game of managing their appearances to meet the demands of a sexist society, does so at great cost.

As previously introduced, there are three social consequences of objectification: *validating objectification* (affirms women for their appearances);

derogating objectification (criticizes women based on appearance); and *social invisibility* (women being overlooked if they do not match social appearance standards). Of the three, validating objectification seems to provide the most social benefit, but it comes with its own costs. Even when women put considerable effort into making themselves appealing to observers, they still may not enjoy being looked at. This is the "validation as violation" phenomenon. Attracting attention may mean attracting unwanted attention, but even when the attention is wanted, it still may not produce the positive feelings that are expected. Being reduced to one's appearance can feel like a violation of one's basic nature. It can lead to simultaneous desires to be looked at and not to be looked at, such that nothing feels quite right. If we add the disembodiment that comes from self-objectification, then reinforcing a woman's sense that her body exists to be seen, rather than experienced from within, helps to further internalize her self-objectification.

A specific danger of self-objectification is self-sexualization, when self-worth is conflated with sexual desirability, even in contexts when sexuality is irrelevant. If a woman comes to see herself as a sex object in contexts that have nothing to do with sex, she is self-sexualizing. Even for someone who enjoys being sexual in sexual contexts, the sense of oneself as existing simply as an object of sexual desire can start to pervade everything. For instance, a woman may be monogamous, in a satisfying relationship, and not interested in bringing her sexuality into any other arena in her life besides her partnership. Nonetheless, she may feel the need to think of herself in terms of sexual attractiveness and desirability across social contexts. If self-worth has become tied up in self-objectification, and if the kind of object that is being objectified is a sexual one, then self-worth gets tied into sexualization (Gill, 2003; Halliwell, Malson, & Tischner, 2011). This is a precursor to many women losing a sense of their own sexual interests and desires, a topic we expand upon in the section on loss of self below.

Both objectification and self-objectification for women intersect with other forms of oppression. Agism, the social invalidation and dehumanization of people above a certain age, intersects with sexism to lower women's sense of self-worth as their appearances drift ever further from the social ideal of youthfulness. The "beauty" industry instructs women to maintain a youthful appearance as they age, a goal that becomes increasingly impossible to attain. For women who manage to resist the imperative to look younger than they are, a great freedom sometimes becomes available. For the first time in many women's lives, they may find themselves free of the internalized expectation that they need to try to match any standard at all. Giving up on playing the impossible game can mean finding other ways to sense one's self-worth and other foundations for being a woman in the world.

Racism is another form of oppression that intersects with sexism to create external standards for women to compare themselves against. The concept of objectification has classically been associated with body size and shape, and with standards of sexual attractiveness. For women of color, however, self-objectification may have as much to do with ethnic characteristics, such as skin color and hair type, as it has to do with body size or general looks. Consider, as an example, the international phenomenon of skin lightening creams. In parts of the world where racism leads people to value lighter shades of skin over darker ones, especially in countries with a history of colonization by European empires, skin lightening creams and pills (which are often toxic; Ladizinski, Mistry, & Kundu, 2011) may feature centrally in the appearance modification industry. Advertising for these products plays on people who self-objectify with an eye for ethnicity and an internalized preference for Whiteness. Another example of internalized racism coloring self-objectification is in the internalized preference for straight hair among communities such as African Americans, where most people's hair is naturally kinky. A tremendous amount of time, energy, and money goes into hair relaxing, straightening, and extending products and procedures for African American women. In addition to being a significant resource drain, this particular focus on appearance modification also contributes directly to the disembodying effects of self-objectification, as many African American women cite, as a reason for not exercising, the concerns that sweating and vigorous activity will ruin their hair (Hall et al., 2013).

Unconditional Beauty

What is everything you think should be different about your body and your appearance? Participants at Steve's workshops on healing body shame start out by exchanging their answers to that question with several strangers. Self-objectification, it turns out, is reinforced by a near-universal sense of shame we learn to hold about our bodies. Before we can get so many women to pour their resources into modifying their appearances, we have to get them to feel bad about their unmodified appearance. The purpose of this initial exercise is to normalize the shame and self-judgment that so many of us carry, to expose it so we can all start where we are. The journey workshop participants take is toward the goal of fully loving and accepting their bodies exactly as they already are. First, however, it helps to see the ways we have learned to divide our bodies and faces into a collection of parts, compare those parts against other people's parts, or against external standards imposed on us, and then to allow our internalized critics to tell us what is wrong with us every time we look in the mirror.

How do we get from derogating self-objectification to unconditional self-acceptance? A first step that is key involves women reclaiming power in the face of the sexist lies they have internalized about their bodies. The internalized critic needs to be interrupted each time it tries to repeat the lies it has received from the outside. One way to do this is to face the inner critic directly, mustering one's full force of will and fiercely declaring, "I refuse to believe the lies anymore!" Using her full strength of will to talk back to the inner critic can allow a woman to simultaneously resist self-objectification while at the same time reclaiming her power to determine her own destiny. As an alternative, the interruption can be gentle and compassionate, "Hey now, critic. We don't talk to people like that around here. Thank you for trying, once again, to protect me from sexism by criticizing my appearance, but I'm afraid your efforts are misguided and I need to remind you that my body is already just right." The full force of will, often accompanied by anger, can be a first step toward reclaiming power. Finding compassion and care, while firmly interrupting internalized sexism, may be the next.

Coming to understand the concept of unconditional beauty continues the journey toward deep self-acceptance. Once the self-objectifying internalized critic has been effectively interrupted, something outside of the conditioning needs to take its place. A classic feminist approach to the problem of objectification, much propagated through women's studies classes at universities, is to take the focus off appearance entirely, instead training people to appreciate girls and women for anything and everything about them besides their looks: their intelligence, personalities, accomplishments and contributions, and relationships. While this approach compensates for objectification's incredible over-emphasis on appearance, it may fail to compensate for the history of shaming and self-shaming that accompanies self-objectification. That is where unconditional beauty comes in.

Learning to see unconditional beauty means learning to appreciate the unique physical beauty of each person, not simply their "inner beauty," but their bodies and faces as well. What is the difference between validating objectification and unconditional appreciation? The first is evaluative ("You have such pretty eyes," "Wow—you've really lost some weight—you look great!"), offering conditional, positive reinforcement about appearance while leaving the recipient of the validation wondering what will happen when they no longer meet the conditions ("So my eyes are pretty, but what about the rest of me?", "I look great to you now, but what did you think about me before, and what will you think if I gain weight?"). In contrast, appreciation of unconditional beauty is nonevaluative ("I really enjoy looking into your eyes," "Your body is just right—nothing needs to change."). This concept is subtle, as the intention is to really see someone and acknowledge her genuine beauty, without making any comparisons between her and anyone else, between her present self with her past or future selves, or between parts of her body, instead seeing her body as a unified whole. Appreciating beauty in a way that does not require someone to meet any conditions is a missing link in antiobjectification efforts. It replaces sexism with a kind of much-needed acknowledgement of how beautiful human beings are before any standards of conditional beauty have ever been imposed upon them.

Part of the rationale for the healing body shame workshop is to help individuals to heal, to free themselves from conditioning, and to discover for themselves the truth. Part of the rationale is to teach participants, women in particular, to do this for one another. If self-objectification can be transmitted from one woman to another, the de-shaming, deconditioning alternatives of interrupting self-derogation, and replacing it with unconditional appreciation can also be passed on. Preferred practices can also circulate through communities, displacing the old practices of internalized sexism.

A second outcome of anti-objectification efforts is re-embodiment. Many organizations provide opportunities for girls to have a more varied experience of their bodies, so that they relate to it from the inside out, as a source of power, strength, health, and as the vehicle that carries them through life. Through wilderness trips, sports, construction, or dance, girls can push the limits of what their bodies are capable of doing, challenging their conditioning and fueling self-confidence. Some organizations emphasize somatic and emotional awareness education, helping girls better know themselves by developing inner awareness of how their life experiences are sensed in their bodies. Others focus on healthy eating as a pretext for teaching a nuanced understanding of physiology and wellness. Girls and women who participate in these programs experience their physical power and deepen their bodily inner awareness. The result is an experience of embodiment that does not depend at all on visual appearance, allowing participants to delight in their bodies for what they are, not how they look.

Loss of Self

Sexism teaches girls to be subservient to men in relationships, families, and other social groups. As sexism is internalized, girls learn to relinquish their own needs and desires in favor of men's needs, and the needs of others that women are expected to serve and take care of. Marielle interviewed women and girls in communities of South Delhi as part of a leadership development and education program. Here is an excerpt from an interview between a 17-year-old girl, Meena, and her mother, Asha.

Meena: I want to keep going to school to be a doctor.
Asha: You can't do that. We won't find a husband for you if you do that.
Meena: Well then, I'll be a beautician.
Asha: If you do that, how will you cook?
Meena: I'm not going to obey you, mom. I'll wait until I'm married, and do what my husband wants then.

Asha matter-of-factly directs Meena to sacrifice her dreams, even much-diminished ones, for the needs of a hypothetical husband. It is unfathomable that Meena could live without a husband and equally as unrealistic that she could have a husband and still pursue her desires. Men come first, and a woman's value and place in the world is determined by her marriageability. Asha, having internalized this message, is passing it on to her daughter as a way to protect her in a society where a woman's status is largely determined by marriage and by how well she takes care of her husband. Meena quickly takes on the expectation, downgrades her aspirations in service to her husband, and then reminds Asha that her future husband, a man, will have higher status than her mother, a woman.

Some level of prioritizing others' needs is of real value in families and communities, but sexism demands that women go further, denying their dreams, desires, and aspirations in order to fully occupy the self-sacrificing role of caretaker. Meena and Asha, like women around the world, have internalized the belief that cooking, cleaning, and raising children is central to the female role they have been cast to play. No matter how great the personal cost, Meena is expected by her mother to reduce herself from a teenager with personal aspirations, into a woman who will do whatever her husband wants her to.

How do we know whether our desires are truly our own? When women put their needs and desires aside for long enough, their ability to sense what they want and need may atrophy, if it even had a chance to develop in the first place. What begins as compliance with the demand to prioritize men and others over themselves becomes a gradual loss of self, an inability to identify their desires, or to tell the difference between what they want for themselves and what others want for them. For those of us who have kept our internal sense of desire intact, it is easy to take for granted how much our day-to-day motivations are determined by what we want. When the internal sense of wanting is weak or lacking, motivation has to come from some other source. That source is likely to be the desires of others, including men who were conditioned to prioritize their needs and desires over those of women.

Sexuality is a particular area in which women are expected to meet the needs of men. When asked her motivations for choosing a sexual partner or engaging in a sexual activity, a woman in touch with her own desires might simply say that she was pursuing what she wanted. If a woman or a girl has never discovered her own desires, however, and instead learned that the purpose of her sexuality is to please men, secure male partnership, gain status, or avoid conflict, her desire may be left out entirely (Fine, 1998). The empty space may be filled in by training to fulfill others' desires instead (Sanchez, Crocker, & Boike, 2005). This training may encourage her to have sex when she does not want to, before she is ready to, with someone who is not her choice, or to please men without expecting to be pleased herself. She may also learn not to ask for what she wants (particularly if she doesn't even know what she would want to ask for), to dress in sexually revealing ways, sexually engage with other women solely for the benefit of men (Thompson, 2010), maintain modesty or composure during sex, or fake enjoyment or orgasm. The culture of sexual violence and sexual abuse that accompanies sexism reinforces this training.

Prioritizing Self

To counteract the conditioning to self-sacrifice, women can prioritize their needs and desires. First, it can be helpful to examine the balance between fulfilling one's own desires and those of others. Second, in service of the personal fulfillment side of that balance, some women may need to learn, or re-learn, how to sense what their own needs and desires are. Third, when women disrupt or resist the social order by putting themselves first, they need allies to help them withstand the repercussions.

How do we find the right balance between fulfilling our desires and taking care of others? Consider these questions. First, ask what you want most in life, what brings you enjoyment, makes your life meaningful, nourishes, and fulfills you. Next, ask what your responsibilities are, what your social roles require of you, who needs you, and what you have chosen or agreed to give to them. Both questions are important, but which seems to be more important? How much more important? Are both questions equally easy for you to answer, or is one set of answers fuzzy while the other is clear? How much do the answers to the two questions overlap? Is there a difference between what you want for yourself and what is expected of you? The goal is not to suggest what the right balance is between self-care and caretaking for others. Rather, it is to help determine whether our thinking, and our lives, are organized strongly around one of these objectives and not the other (Neff & Harter, 2002). Both are always needed. Even if we choose to make caretaking our primary objective, some amount of self-care is required in order to do so. There is a good reason airlines tell us to put on our own oxygen mask first.

If we do not have a clear answer to the question of what we want for ourselves, we may need to learn, or re-learn, what our own needs are and how to sense them. Women, of course, have the same full complement of human needs that men do: needs for rest and nourishment and safety, for belonging and connection and understanding, for autonomy, meaning, self-expression, and many others (Rosenberg, 2003). When learning to prioritize our own needs, we can inventory each need and register which specific needs are being met and which ones are not. In order to tell, we need to be able to sense, even on a somatic level, that a need has not been met. Until we learn to sense the need, learning how to meet the need will be more difficult. Desires are the same way. They are sensed, in part, as impulses in the body. Developing a sense of sexual agency, for instance, the ability to genuinely know one's own desires in the sexual realm, and to act on them to determine one's own sexual destiny, requires that desire is sensed from the inside. The sex-positive movement, with women's sexual empowerment at its center, has offered up numerous approaches over the years for women to cultivate this internal sense (Dodson, 1974; Queen, 1996).

When it comes to sexism, the personal is political (Hanisch, 1970), so when women prioritize their desires, they may find themselves needing to reorganize a social order that puts them last.

> When I moved from America to Yemen to live with my husband's family, I was invited for a luncheon at my in-law's house. I was forced to wait in the kitchen with the other women until the men finished eating with their hands from the communal plates on the living room floor. After the men left, the other women and I were indicated to eat from the men's leftovers which by then had been strewn all over the place. I was mortified and felt so diminished. I wasn't about to pick at the bits of meat that remained on a chicken leg bone or gather granules of rice that had fallen on the carpet to make a mouthful from. I didn't eat. My mother-in-law was angry with me and complained that I acted as if I was better than the other women. From then on she always saved a separate plate of food just for me before serving the men. That would have been nice, except every time she served it to me, she also served me a stern, disapproving look.

In this excerpt, a woman traversing cultural communities disrupts the mealtime arrangement of "men first, women second" that the women in her new family help to maintain. When she resists, her mother-in-law uses guilt, a common tool of social conditioning, to try to pressure her into compliance with the existing social order. Rather than get upset that the daughter-in-law wants her status to be equal to that of men, she frames her accusation in terms of competition between women. If the other women are complying and she is not, she must consider herself superior to them. Despite her disapproval, the mother-in-law ultimately supports the daughter-in-law to prioritize herself, and her needs.

There is always a cost to disrupting the social order. In this case, the cost is to the relationship between daughter-in-law and mother-in-law.

Imagine, however, if the mother-in-law were to act on her behalf, or on behalf of all the women in the family, to question the entire arrangement of men being served first. The social cost to her would potentially be far greater. Such changes are difficult to make alone, without allies. Women can become allies to one another in this project. Remember that internalized sexism occurs on two levels. It is not just internal to individuals. It is internal to communities of women as well. When women support other women to identify their own needs, and then stand with them as they take on the consequences, internalized sexism is thwarted on both levels.

Internalized Invalidation

Decisions shape our fates, both on a large scale (e.g., governments and institutions) and on a small scale (e.g., families and dyadic relationships). Maintaining oppressive power means holding a disproportionate amount of control over decision-making. In much the same way that sexism conditions women to sacrifice their own needs and desires to fulfill those of men, it also conditions women to give over decision-making power to men. To make this maneuver possible, internalized sexism encourages women to systematically invalidate themselves and other women.

Sexism invalidates women's thoughts, opinions, beliefs, values, feelings, preferences, and choices in favor of men's. As women internalize this invalidation of their experiences, they learn to silence their voices, mistrust their own judgments, and yield their thinking to that of men and other women (Brown & Gilligan, 1993; Jack, 1991; Jack & Dill, 1992). If a woman does not speak because she believes she has nothing worth saying, no one would be interested, she does not have the right to take up space in a conversation, or that men and others who speak more confidently must be right, internalized invalidation has silenced her. If a woman lets someone else make decisions for her, trusts other people's judgments more than her own, and gives over her authority to men and others who assert superiority, internalized invalidation has caused her to abdicate her self-determination.

Ways of being that are relegated to females by gender role conditioning are devalued by the society. For instance, sexism encourages us to value rationality over feelings, justice over caring, factual knowledge over self-knowledge, independence over relatedness, assertiveness over inclusion, and accomplishment over presence. Men's oppression plays an important role in disparaging the values and qualities that are considered "feminine." Because the human qualities that are assigned to women are the same human qualities that are denied men, these disavowed parts of men's humanity become the invalidated parts of women's humanity. This is one reason why the entire gender role system has to be dismantled at once. Women and men are dehumanized in complementary ways, and both result in a tendency to invalidate women's opinions and decisions when they are based on these devalued traits.

Invalidation occurs in a number of forms that are not immediately obvious. Women may minimize their own or each other's concerns, invalidating them with responses like, "It's no big deal," "You'll get over it," or "Stop being so sensitive." Reassuring, though often well-intentioned, is a related way to minimize. Consider the difference between a reassuring response like, "You'll be fine. It's going to be okay," to one that directly acknowledges a woman's feelings or concerns such as, "That really wasn't okay. I'm sorry it happened. I imagine that must hurt." The reassurance may be meant to provide comfort or support, but it fails to validate the experience of the woman expressing the concern.

Women who have been working on behalf of their own liberation from internalized sexism may invalidate other women who appear to remain imprisoned by female gender role conditioning. Take the example of the college woman who decides to stop shaving her legs and who then dismisses women who continue to shave as having made a less valid decision. By choosing not to follow a traditional standard of beauty, she is empowering herself and thwarting internalized objectification. However, in the process, she may be perpetuating internalized sexism by invalidating other women's choices.

Validating Women's Ways

There are multiple valid ways of navigating the world. Differences between cultural communities, for instance, produce many different ways to make sense of the world and operate within it. When human experience is divided by gender role conditioning into two different sets of permissible ways of being, we end up with men's ways and women's ways as well. Both are variations on the human imperative to find our way in a complex world, but because women's ways have been invalidated by sexism, women may need to put special effort into reclaiming women's ways in order to overcome internalized invalidation. Two examinations of socialized gender differences highlight the importance of valuing women's ways: one about women's conversational styles, the other about women's moral development.

First, women and men learn to use conversation for different social purposes (Tannen, 1990). We always interpret *what people say* through our understanding of *why we think they're saying it*. A woman may make a suggestion or share a complaint to create rapport, seek empathy, or open a negotiation, whereas a man making a similar suggestion or sharing a similar complaint may be doing it to establish status, solicit advice, or assert independence. If women and men can learn to understand these differences, we can be more attuned listeners, no longer assuming people of the other gender mean what we would mean if we said the same thing. More importantly, however, for thwarting internalized sexism, women can learn to validate the social motivations behind their conversational styles. Rather than believe, as sexism might wish them to, that they don't make any sense, should be more rational, or direct, or assertive, women can speak to the importance of making a different kind of sense, one that values emotions, interdependence, or social harmony.

Another example of validating women's ways comes from understanding how we develop a sense of morality. The predominant theory of how we become ethical (Kohlberg, 1981) assumes that our relationship to justice determines how we learn to make ethical decisions. We begin by wishing to avoid getting in trouble, come to respect the importance of rules and laws, and eventually come to recognize that more universal ethical principles should guide us, whether or not they are reflected in a given rule system. This justice-based story of human development, however, may be male-centric, and an alternative story can be told by studying the moral development of women (Gilligan, 1982). This alternative narrative suggests that our relationship to care and caring determines how we come to make ethical decisions. We begin oriented toward self-interest, learn that care for others requires self-sacrifice, eventually temper that self-sacrifice by including ourselves in who we care for, and eventually extend our concept of caring beyond those who are personally meaningful to us, comprehending our universal interconnectedness. If we believe acting ethically requires an orientation to justice, then women who make moral decisions based on caring will believe their motivations to be inferior or less developed. If, instead, women's and men's ways are understood to form a more complete whole, then caring becomes an indispensable component of true ethical behavior.

Valuing women's ways on a cultural level is key to validating women, but there remains the question of how to validate women's experiences on a more personal level. Is it possible to validate a woman's thoughts, beliefs, opinions, feelings, and choices, without assuming she is always right, or always acting in optimal ways? Fortunately, validation does not require that we agree with anyone, or share anyone's preferences and opinions. Instead, we need to recognize their importance and meaning to the woman who holds them, which is the source of real empathy. If we fully understood why a woman felt and acted as she does, we could respect her intelligence and validate her desires even if we engaged in a conversation about how our perspective differs dramatically from hers.

Encouraging women to trust their own thinking is integral to overcoming internalized sexism. Even if your thinking is flawed or undeveloped, it is still ultimately all you have. If you choose to trust someone else's thinking, it is you making that choice based on your best thinking about theirs. Either you give over your authority to someone else, letting them do your thinking and make your decisions for you, as sexism might steer you to do, or you trust your own thinking.

Internalized Derogation

Overt forms of sexism often include insults and put-downs, derogatory terms that refer specifically to women. Some of these criticisms are designed to make women feel "less than," as when the phrase "like a girl" means "not as good," when "woman" is used as a demeaning title in place of someone's name, or when terms like "bimbo" suggest that women are unintelligent. Many derogatory terms, however, target women who behave outside the bounds of the female role. If a woman acts in ways that are not in accordance with gender role conditioning, a carefully aimed insult can be the form of punishment needed to adequately discourage the behavior. Like other aspects of sexism, derogation can be internalized, used by women to criticize themselves and one another in the ongoing process of gender role conditioning (Gilbert, Clarke, Hempel, Miles, & Irons, 2004; Thompson & Zuroff, 2004).

There are two categories of derogatory terms that function as gender role policing—pushing women back behind the borders, should they wander into territory outside the female role. The first category is gender-specific insults such as "bitch," a term used to refer to women who are vocal or outspoken, assertive or unyielding, directive, or self-prioritizing. These characteristics defy a gender role that requires women to be quiet or silent, passive or submissive, compliant, and self-sacrificing. Several slurs punish women for being embodied, sensual, sexually self-expressed, or pursuing what brings them physical pleasure on their own terms: words like "slut," "whore," "hussy," "harlot," "skank," "easy," and "promiscuous." On the other side of the spectrum, terms like "frigid," "prude," and "tease" coerce women to be more sexual than they wish to be. The range of insults on both ends of the spectrum serves to regulate women's sexual expression, to encourage submission to the needs and desires of men who claim dominion over a woman's sexuality.

Another category of derogatory terms used to condition women are mental health-related insults. Consider this exchange between two college friends from a study done by Steve and colleagues (Bearman, Korobov, & Thorne, 2009):

Angie: Do you know what happened? Okay listen to this. My mom sent me a card today in the mail. . . no, this actually happened, and it has like a little Chinese proverb on it, saying like, you know, like birds sometimes they can't fly, and they don't let things get them down, but if they make a nest, you know, out of those problems: it was something like that. And then, so she writes in the card, she's like, "Dearest Angie, I know that you've been having problems, blah blah blah, and you sent me this card, and nah nah nah," and then she signs it with my name, saying "Love, Angie," and I was like, are you on crack, mom? I'm like, thanks for the, the card, but it was like, okay.

Beth: Your mom's funny.

Angie: My mom's a little whack.

Angie's mother is making an attempt at offering support, but apparently not in a way that her daughter prefers. The result: her mental state is criticized, first by the question, "I was like, are you on crack, mom?" and then by the declaration, "My mom's a little whack." The frequent depiction of women as crazy and irrational occurs because men's ways are considered "normal" in a sexist society, making women's ways "abnormal" in comparison, invalidating emotional expression in particular.

Sexism would have us believe that women are crazy. In the study that the example above comes from, one out of every four instances of internalized derogation consisted of critiques of a woman's mental health. Women were labeled as "weird," "strange," "abnormal," "crazy," "insane," "psycho," "obsessed," "OCD," "anal," and "paranoid." Other terms such as "hysterical" were not used by the group of women in the study, but have long histories in the pathologizing of women's experiences, including the disproportionate incarceration of women in asylums and mental hospitals. Mental health slurs such as these carry along with them a real threat. If women deviate from a standard of normality determined by sexism, they risk exposing themselves to the stigma associated with mental illness.

Interrupting Derogation

Because we have all been conditioned to be agents of oppression, we have all learned to use insults and put-downs to make others feel bad. Though this is a habit, it is not a necessary feature of life. To be an ally to women, we can make the decision never again to malign other women. This may not be an easy decision to stick by. Choosing to interrupt our inner critics is a helpful first step. Once we have that down, we can learn to respond effectively to other people's not-so-inner critics.

Start by recognizing any ways we have internalized sexist criticisms. We all have inner critics. We need them to help us evaluate whether or not we are matching up to the images of ourselves we wish to live up to. Unfortunately, this natural evaluative process gets co-opted by internalized sexism in a couple ways that need correcting. First, if the image we wish to match is an image fed to us by gender role conditioning, it needs to be questioned, deconstructed, and replaced with a better image of our choosing. Second, if our inner critic has gone beyond simple self-evaluation (to help us achieve desirable objectives), and instead it keeps us down and makes us feel terrible about ourselves, it needs to be schooled. If our inner critic is acting as an agent of internalized sexism, we can interrupt it the same way we would interrupt someone else saying sexist things to someone we care about. Being an ally to ourselves by refusing to perpetuate sexism in our own minds is the place to begin. This is challenging and easy to forget to do, but replacing oppressive habits with conscious practices is well worth putting the work in for.

To be an ally to other women, we can interrupt derogation whenever we come across it. The key to interrupting oppression is to say something, anything. If we are not practiced at interrupting oppression, we will probably do it clumsily. We may not be very effective, and we may wind up with the insults directed at us instead. This is okay. Consider simple interventions like, "Hey. That thing you just said. Not cool," or "Ouch. It hurts to hear you talk about another woman that way." One strategy is to avoid low-status forms of intervention such as moralizing, in favor of high-status forms like jokes or storytelling (Guerin, 2003). Imagine, for instance, interrupting a sexist joke by saying, "This woman walks into a bar and tells a sexist joke—no one laughs!" Another strategy is to aim for compassion. If certain men or women are passing on sexism through language, quite possibly in unaware ways, we can assume they are doing so because of some unhealed hurt they are trying to work out, or an unmet need they do not know how to meet. Imagine a response like, "It sounds like you're really angry about that, like there's something you really need that you're not getting." We can offer that kind of compassion when we remember that we are all in this together. Treat everyone as if, given the chance, they would prefer to be an ally to women in overcoming sexism, and we can always find a way to appeal to the person's humanity beneath the sexist language, to recruit them as an ally by finding a way to be theirs.

Competition Between Women

Like all forms of oppression, sexism inequitably divides up resources. Men benefit, leaving women with less money, fewer high-status positions, less decision-making power, less ability to leverage historical advantage, less social assumption of competence, and so on. The lack of resources available to women means that women may need to work harder to achieve the same objectives as men. It means that additional stresses occur in the daily lives of women. Women lacking needed resources and incurring daily stresses as a result do not necessarily blame the problem on sexism. Instead, they may end up blaming other women who are competing with them in order to meet their needs (Chesler, 2001; Cowan, Neighbors, DeLaMoreaux, & Behnke, 1998).

Competition within an oppressed group is one of the fundamental manifestations of internalized oppression. How does this within-group competition occur, and how can we correct it?

Internalized sexism divides women, a division that keeps sexism in place by preventing women from acting in a unified way to dismantle sexism in all its forms. When things are hard for us, or when we do not have enough, we tend to look around us to see how much other people have, and whether they have it harder or easier than us. This social comparison helps us know what we should expect, what we should accept, and what we should strive for. When we cast our gaze to make these comparisons, however, it is easiest to compare ourselves to people who are similar to us, rather than people who have considerable privilege relative to us (Crosby, 1976; Walker & Smith, 2002). Women are more likely to compare themselves to other women than to men. As a result, when women are dissatisfied with their lot, they are most likely to resent and compete with other women.

Competition between women is often for ostensibly limited social resources, such as favored social positions, desired partners, respect, support, and valuable social ties (Eckert, 1990; Guendouzi, 2001). In communities of girls and women, such competition may take the forms of social aggression: malicious gossip, social exclusion, zero-sum comparisons (for someone to win someone has to lose), and women putting one another down or maneuvering each other into lower-status positions to make themselves look or feel better (Goodwin, 2002; Underwood, 2003; Wiseman, 2002).

> I had been best of friends with Ellen since eighth grade. She was my confidant and closer to me than anyone else. My junior year, I started dating this boy who I really liked. I knew she thought he was cute, but I didn't know that she had a crush on him. Within weeks, Ellen started being mean to me. She started making up stories about me, calling me a slut, telling people intimate details of my sex life that I had shared only with her. She got all our friends on her side and they would shun me when I walked by. She even told a fake story to our teacher about me and I got kicked out of a project I was a leader for. I was so confused and hurt. I felt she was trying to ruin my life, and I didn't understand why. I thought she should be happy that I was in love.

This example from Jennifer, a student at a New York high school where Marielle ran a girls' empowerment program, was not an unusual story. One girl "wins" a social resource that another wants. A "friend break-up" results, leading to very real forms of social aggression that fracture a community of friends. Without solidarity, in which women learn to support each other when their needs are not being met, internalized sexism can lead girls and women to take out their anger on one another.

Building Solidarity

The practice of developing solidarity is the antidote to internalized sexism's practice of constructing women as competitors. Solidarity implies that sexism affects all women. If women can recognize the ways their sister women have been limited and impacted by sexism, they can come together and develop collective ways to overcome those effects. The practice of competing with other women stems from a model that it is not possible for everyone to get their needs met; solidarity requires a belief that everyone can. We do not have to sacrifice being successful (or happy) in order for others to be successful. Developing solidarity requires an acknowledgement of the damage caused by practices of internalized sexism, followed by a commitment to mutual understanding and collaboration among women, to ultimately serve the larger project of women's liberation and empowerment.

Let us look at the example of Ellen and Jennifer through the lens of solidarity. What if they knew in advance how destructive and painful their competition and "friend break-up" was going to be? What if Ellen refused to insult or slander Jennifer and instead was able to express her hurt so they could listen to each other and find a mutually supportive solution? Chances are, this would have brought them closer as friends, circumvented the competition, and led to growth for them as individuals. For any of this to be possible, however, they would have to have learned these alternative practices.

Women's groups can help women build solidarity with one another. Through sharing personal narratives, women can come to more deeply understand how they have been hurt by sexism, and how they have come to internalize it and act it out on one another. Women's groups are often venues for learning, healing, support, empowerment, and collaboration. They help women to: learn about being allies for other women; identify places where they tend to criticize, undermine, or insult other women; examine their unaware uses of power in the form of social aggression; and learn about what kinds of support other women need to overcome internalized sexism. As a truly democratic structure, they can be formed by any group of women anywhere.

SUMMARY AND CONCLUSION: HOW TO BE AN ALLY TO GIRLS AND WOMEN

It is now clear that internalized sexism is composed of diverse practices. Bringing together these practices under the banner of internalized sexism helps girls and women to identify the ways in which sexism gets in. Internalized sexism leads women to believe themselves and other women to be more limited than they are; feel powerless and act powerlessly; conflate self-worth and body-image; become disembodied as they encourage other women to be preoccupied with their looks; sacrifice their own needs and desires while teaching other women to do the same; invalidate their own and other women's thoughts, values, and choices; insult and criticize themselves and other women as a way of policing the gender role; and compete with other women, often through the use of social aggression.

All of these practices perpetuate sexism, and they do so even when no men are present. The purpose of identifying the practices of internalized sexism is not to blame women for sexism. Rather, it is to recognize how women unwittingly play an active role in keeping sexism alive, a role that can change once it has been exposed. Like sexism, internalized sexism is an ongoing relational process, produced and reproduced within the networks of social interactions that make up our day-to-day existence. Understanding how internalized sexism makes the rounds makes it possible to replace all of these conditioned ways of behaving with deliberate, conscious practices that work to counteract internalized sexism. Understanding is the beginning of becoming an ally to girls and women.

Oppression excludes no one. Learning to be an ally against oppression is a task for all people everywhere to take on (Bishop, 2002). When it comes to sexism, it is important to remember that gender role conditioning, sexism, internalized sexism, and men's oppression all form an integrated system (Bearman, 2000; hooks, 2004), a system in which we are all caught. Luckily, we can all become one another's allies in dismantling it. Once we have come to understand some of the practices of internalized sexism, we might consider replacing them with some of these ways to be an ally:

- Hold high standards for women. Hold out that there are no limits to what women are capable of, no limits to their intelligence, no limits to how powerful they can become.
- Support women to find and express their anger about sexism, but don't let them get stuck in anger.
- Encourage women to become leaders. Sometimes this will mean yielding leadership to them or mentoring them in leadership.
- Help women inhabit, rather than objectify, their own bodies. Support them in learning to cultivate their felt sense experience, use their physical power, and develop physical abilities.
- Be wary of objectifying evaluations of women. Instead learn to appreciate unconditional beauty.
- Help women identify their needs and desires, which means learning to sense what they want from the inside. Support them to discover who they want to be as sexual beings on their own terms.

- Don't stand for women settling, especially for the sake of men. Expect them to prioritize themselves, which will sometimes mean putting themselves first, other women second, and men third. Even if the eventual goal is to find the right balance between self-care and care for others, sometimes tipping the scale the other way first helps to create balance.
- Validate women's ways, watching out for male-centric values and preferences, and encourage women to do the same for themselves.
- Take women's feelings and concerns seriously. Even if you disagree with them, find a way to validate their experiences by offering empathy.
- Encourage women to trust their own thinking, and to find and share their voices.
- Model not criticizing, disparaging, or invalidating women.
- Interrupt the derogation of women when you see it, even if it is women derogating one another.
- Don't stand for women competing with each other. Help redirect the impulse toward the real problem: sexism. Support women to collaborate with one another instead.
- Model how to be an ally to women. Remind others, and yourself, that we're all in this together.

Helping girls and women get free from the effects of internalized sexism is key to creating a world without sexism. Whether you are female, male, or any other gendered or genderless flavor of human being, you can learn to become an excellent ally to women and girls. Every time any one of us chooses to be an ally, all of us benefit.

REFERENCES

Bearman, S. (2000). Why men are so obsessed with sex. In K. Kay, J. Nagle, & B. Gould (Eds.), *Male lust: Pleasure, power, and transformation* (pp. 215–222). New York, NY: Harrington Park Press.

Bearman, S., Korobov, N., & Thorne, A. (2009). The Fabric of Internalized Sexism. *Journal of Integrated Social Sciences, 1*, 10–47.

Beck, D. E., & Cowan, C. C. (1996). *Spiral dynamics: Mastering values, leadership, and change.* Malden, MA: Blackwell Publishing.

Benokraitis, N. V., & Feagin, J. R. (1995). *Modern sexism: Blatant, subtle, and covert discrimination* (2nd ed.). Englewood Cliffs, NJ: Prentice Hall.

Bishop, A. (2002). *Becoming an ally: Breaking the cycle of oppression in people* (2nd ed.). London: Zed Books.

Breines, J. G., Crocker, J., & Garcia, J. A. (2008). Self-objectification and well-being in women's daily lives. *Personality and Social Psychology Bulletin, 34*, 583–598.

Brown, L. M., & Gilligan, C. (1993). Meeting at the crossroads: Women's psychology and girls' development. *Feminism & Psychology, 3*, 11–35.

Bulik, C. M. (2012). *The woman in the mirror: How to stop confusing what you look like with who you are.* London: Bloomsbury.

Butler, J. (1990). *Gender trouble: Feminism and the subversion of identity.* New York, NY: Routledge.

Capodilupo, C. M., Nadal, K. L., Corman, L., Hamit, S., Lyons, O. B., & Weinberg, A. (2010). The manifestation of gender microaggressions. In D. W. Sue (Ed.), *Microaggressions and marginalized groups in society: Race, gender, sexual orientation, class, international and religious manifestations* (pp. 193–216). Hoboken, NJ: John Wiley & Sons.

Chesler, P. (2001). *Woman's inhumanity to woman.* New York, NY: Thunder's Mouth Press/Nation Books.

Cowan, G., Neighbors, C., DeLaMoreaux, J., & Behnke, C. (1998). Women's hostility toward women. *Psychology of Women Quarterly, 22*, 267–284.

Crosby, F. (1976). A model of egoistical relative deprivation. *Psychological review, 83*, 85–113.

de Beauvoir, S. (1961). *The second sex.* New York, NY: Bantam Books.

Dodson, B. (1974). *Sex for one: The joy of selfloving.* New York, NY: Three Rivers Press.

Eccles, J., Barber, B., Jozefowicz, D., Malenchuk, O., & Vida, M. (1999). Self-evaluations of competence, task values, and self-esteem. In N. G. Johnson & M. C. Roberts (Eds.), *Beyond appearance: A new look at adolescent girls* (pp. 53–83). Washington, DC: American Psychological Association.

Eccles, J., Templeton, J., Barber, B., & Stone, M. (2003). Adolescence and emerging adulthood: The critical passage ways to adulthood. In M. H. Bornstein & L. Davidson (Eds.), *Well-being: Positive development across the life course* (pp. 383–406). Mahwah, NJ: Lawrence Erlbaum Associates.

Eckert, P. (1990). Cooperative competition in adolescent "girl talk." *Discourse Processes, 13*, 91–122.

Eitzen, D. S., Baca Zinn, M., & Smith, K. E. (2012). *Social problems* (12th ed.). Boston, MA: Pearson Higher Education.

Fine, M. (1988). Sexuality, schooling, and adolescent females: The missing discourse of desire. *Harvard Educational Review, 58*, 29–53.

Fredrickson, B. L., & Roberts, T. (1997). Objectification theory: Toward understanding women's lived experiences and mental health risks. *Psychology of Women Quarterly, 21*, 173–206.

Fredrickson, B. L., Roberts, T., Noll, S. M., Quinn, D. M., & Twenge, J. M. (1998). That swimsuit becomes you: Sex differences in self-objectification, restrained eating, and math performance. *Journal of Personality and Social Psychology, 75*, 269–284.

Freire, P. (1970). *Pedagogy of the oppressed.* New York, NY: Continuum.

Frost, D. M. (2011). Social stigma and its consequences for the socially stigmatized. *Social and Personality Psychology Compass, 5*, 824–839.

Gilbert, P., Clarke, M., Hempel, S., Miles, J. N. V., & Irons, C. (2004). Criticizing and reassuring oneself: An exploration of forms, styles and reasons in female students. *British Journal of Clinical Psychology, 43*, 31–50.

Gill, R. (2003). From sexual objectification to sexual subjectification: The resexualisation of women's bodies in the media. *Feminist Media Studies, 3*, 100–108.

Gilligan, C. (1982). *In a different voice: Psychological theory and women's development.* Cambridge, MA: Harvard University Press.

Glick, P., & Fiske, S. T. (1996). The ambivalent sexism inventory: Differentiating hostile and benevolent sexism. *Journal of Personality and Social Psychology, 70*, 491–512.

Goodwin, M. H. (2002). Building power asymmetries in girls' interaction. *Discourse & Society, 13*, 715–730.

Guendouzi, J. (2001). 'You'll think we're always bitching': The functions of cooperativity and competition in women's gossip. *Discourse Studies, 3*, 29–51.

Guerin, B. (2003). Combating prejudice and racism: New interventions from a functional analysis of racist language. *Journal of Community and Applied Social Psychology, 13*, 29–45.

Hall, R. R., Francis, S., Whitt-Glover, M., Loftin-Bell, K., Swett, K., & McMichael, A. J. (2013). Hair care practices as a barrier to physical activity in African American women. *JAMA Dermatology, 149*, 310–314.

Halliwell, E., Malson, H., & Tischner, I. (2011). Are contemporary media images which seem to display women as sexually empowered actually harmful to women? *Psychology of Women Quarterly, 35*, 38–45.

Hanisch, C. (1970). The personal is political. In S. Firestone & A. Koedt (Eds.), *Notes from the Second Year: Women's Liberation.* New York, NY: Radical Feminists.

Hebl, M. R., King, E. B., & Lin, J. (2004). The swimsuit becomes us all: Ethnicity, gender, and vulnerability to self-objectification. *Personality and Social Psychology Bulletin, 30*, 1322–1331.

Hill, J. P., & Lynch, M. E. (1983). The intensification of gender-related role expectations during early adolescence. In J. Brooks-Gunn & A. C. Petersen (Eds.), *Girls at puberty: Biological and psychosocial perspectives* (pp. 201–228). New York, NY: Plenum Press.

hooks, b. (2004). *The will to change: Men, masculinity, and love.* New York, NY: Washington Square.

Huang, C. (2013). Gender differences in academic self-efficacy: A meta-analysis. *European Journal of Psychology of Education, 28*, 1–35.

Jack, D. C. (1991). *Silencing the self: Women and depression.* Cambridge, MA: Harvard University.

Jack, D. C., & Dill, D. (1992). The Silencing the Self Scale: Schemas of intimacy associated with depression in women. *Psychology of Women Quarterly, 16*, 97–106.

Jackins, H. (1997). *The list.* Seattle, WA: Rational Island Publishers.

Jacobs, J. E., Davis-Kean, P., Bleeker, M., Eccles, J. S., & Malanchuk, O. (2005). "I can, but I don't want to": The impact of parents, interests, and activities on gender differences in math. In A. M. Gallagher & J. C. Kaufman (Eds.), *Gender differences in mathematics: An integrative psychological approach* (pp. 246–263). New York, NY: Cambridge University.

Klonoff, E. A., & Landrine, H. (1995). The schedule of sexist events: A measure of lifetime and recent sexist discrimination in women's lives. *Psychology of Women Quarterly, 19,* 439–472.

Kohlberg, L. (1981). *Essays on moral development, Vol. I: The Philosophy of moral development.* San Francisco, CA: Harper & Row.

Ladizinski, B., Mistry, N., & Kundu, R. V. (2011). Widespread use of toxic skin lightening compounds: Medical and psychosocial aspects. *Dermatologic Clinics, 29,* 111–123.

Matteson, A. V., & Moradi, B. (2005). Examining the structure of the schedule of sexist events: Replication and extension. *Psychology of Women Quarterly, 29,* 47–57.

Muehlenkamp, J. J., & Saris-Baglama, R. N. (2002). Self-objectification and its psychological outcomes for college women. *Psychology of Women Quarterly, 26,* 371–379.

Neff, K. D., & Harter, S. (2002). The authenticity of conflict resolutions among adult couples: Does women's other-oriented behavior reflect their true selves? *Sex Roles, 47,* 403–417.

Peterson, C., Maier, S. F., & Seligman, M. E. P. (1993). *Learned helplessness: A theory for the age of personal control.* New York, NY: Oxford University.

Queen, C. (1996). *Real live nude girl: Chronicles of sex-positive culture.* Pittsburgh, PA: Cleis Press.

Rosenberg, M. B. (2003). *Nonviolent communication: A language of life.* Encinitas, CA: PuddleDancer.

Sanchez, D. T., Crocker, J., & Boike, K. R. (2005). Doing gender in the bedroom: Investing in gender norms and the sexual experience. *Personality and Social Psychology Bulletin, 31,* 1445–1455.

Sue, D. W. (2010). *Microaggressions in everyday life: Race, gender, and sexual orientation.* Hoboken, NJ: John Wiley & Sons.

Swim, J. K., Hyers, L. L., Cohen, L. L., & Ferguson, M. J. (2001). Everyday sexism: Evidence for its incidence, nature, and psychological impact from three daily diary studies. *Journal of Social Issues, 57,* 31–53.

Swim, J. K., Mallett, R., & Stangor, C. (2004). Understanding subtle sexism: Detection and use of sexist language. *Sex Roles, 51,* 117–128.

Szymanski, D. M., & Henning, S. L. (2007). The role of self-objectification in women's depression: A test of self-objectification theory. *Sex Roles, 56,* 45–53.

Szymanski, D. M., Moffitt, L. B., & Carr, E. R. (2011). Sexual objectification of women: Advances to theory and research. *The Counseling Psychologist, 39,* 6–38.

Tannen, D. (1990). *You just don't understand: Women and men in conversation.* New York, NY: Ballantine Books.

The Everyday Sexism Project. (2012). Retreived from http://www .everydaysexism.com

The Microaggressions Project. (2010). Retreived from http://www .microaggressions.com

Thompson, E. M. (2010). *Young women's same-sex experiences under the "male gaze": Listening for both objectification and sexual agency* (Doctoral dissertation). Retrieved from ProQuest Information & Learning. (AAI3367757)

Thompson, R., & Zuroff, D. C. (2004). The levels of self-criticism scale: Comparative self-criticism and internalized self-criticism. *Personality & Individual Differences, 36,* 419–430.

Tolman, D. L., & Porche, M. V. (2000). The adolescent femininity ideology scale: Development and validation of a new measure for girls. *Psychology of Women Quarterly, 24,* 365–376.

UN Department of Public Information. (2010). Promote gender equality and empower women. *United Nations Millennium Development Goals.* Retrieved from http://www.un.org/millenniumgoals/pdf/MDG_FS_3_EN.pdf

Underwood, M. (2003). *Social aggression among girls.* New York, NY: Guilford Press.

Walker, I., & Smith, H. J. (2002). Fifty years of relative deprivation research. In I. Walker & H. J. Smith (Eds.), *Relative deprivation: Specification, development, and integration* (pp. 1–9). New York, NY: Cambridge University.

West, C., & Zimmerman, D. H. (1987). Doing gender. *Gender & Society, 1,* 125–151.

Wiseman, R. (2002). *Queen bees and wannabes: Helping your daughter survive cliques, gossip, boyfriends, and other realities of adolescence.* New York, NY: Piatkus Books.

Wolf, N. (1991). *The beauty myth.* New York, NY: William Morrow and Company.

9

Internalized Oppression and the Lesbian, Gay, Bisexual, and Transgender Community

Kevin L. Nadal and RJ Mendoza

Over the past 30 years, there have been many significant events in the United States that may indicate an increase in the civil rights of lesbian, gay, bisexual, and transgender (LGBT) people (see Nadal, 2013, for a review). For example, in 2004, Massachusetts became the first state to legalize same-sex marriage, allowing LGBT couples in the state to get married and receive the same benefits and rights as their heterosexual counterparts. In 2009, President Barack Obama signed the Matthew Shepard and James Byrd Jr. Hate Crimes Bill, which added sexual orientation and gender identity to the list of protected classes in federal hate crime legislation. In 2011, President Obama also repealed "Don't Ask, Don't Tell," which formerly prohibited openly gay men and lesbian women from serving in any branches of the military. In June 2013, the Supreme Court of the United States ruled that the Defense of Marriage Act was unconstitutional, allowing same-sex marriages to be recognized on the federal level. And by August of 2013, Washington, DC, and 13 states recognized same-sex marriage; these included Massachusetts, Connecticut, Iowa, Vermont, New Hampshire, New York, Washington, Maine, Maryland, California, Delaware, Rhode Island, and Minnesota.

Despite these strides toward equality for LGBT people, it is evident that LGBT individuals are still victimized by discrimination and prejudice due to their sexual orientation or gender identity. Systemic and institutionalized discrimination as represented by various policies and laws, as well as continued discrimination on the interpersonal level, are still salient parts of the LGBT experience on a daily basis. For instance, the Federal Bureau of Investigation (FBI) reported that there were 1,470 hate crime offenses motivated by sexual orientation in 2010 in the United States, which consisted of about 19% of the total number of hate crime cases (FBI, 2011). It has also been reported that only 21 out of 50 U.S. states outlaw discrimination based on sexual orientation and only 15 states outlaw discrimination based on gender identity (Levitt et al., 2009). Furthermore, same-sex couples are denied 1,138 benefits, rights, and protections, all of which negatively affect their social security, taxes, employee benefits, and medical care (Levitt et al., 2009). Finally, while Title VII of the Civil Rights Act (1964) prohibits workplace discrimination based on sex, race, color, religion, and national origin, it does not directly cover sexual orientation or gender identity (Berkley & Watt, 2006).

On interpersonal levels, LGBT people experience an array of discrimination that may have a negative impact on their mental health and development. For example, the 2009 National School Climate Survey found that nearly 9 out of 10 LGBT students experienced harassment at school and that nearly two-thirds felt unsafe because of their sexual orientation (Gay, Lesbian, & Straight Education Network, 2010). In the same report, it was revealed that nearly a third of LGBT students skipped at least one day of school in the past month, and that those who were harassed more regularly had lower grade point averages than those who were less harassed. LGBT adults also may experience discrimination because of their sexual orientation and gender identity. For instance, one study revealed that 20% of respondents experienced a personal or property crime because of their sexual orientation, about half encountered verbal harassment because of their sexual orientation, and a tenth reported having experienced employment or housing discrimination (Herek, 2009).

Given these negative experiences with discrimination, it is quite common for lesbian, gay, and bisexual (LGB) people to develop *internalized homophobia* and for transgender people to develop *internalized transphobia*. Internalized homophobia has been defined as a "gay person's direction of negative social attitudes toward the self" (Meyer & Dean, 1998, p. 161). Internalized homophobia has also been described as an LGB person's unconscious need or desire to be heterosexual, despite one's same-sex sexual and romantic attractions (Herek, 2004). Similarly, internalized transphobia can be defined as the negative societal attitudes and prejudices that are learned and adopted by transgender people (Hendricks & Testa, 2012).

Indeed, because societal messages of heterosexism are so strong, it may be difficult for LGB people to combat negative stereotypes and feelings they have developed about themselves. Some research has found that internalized homophobia is related to an array of negative outcomes, including mental health issues, physical health disparities, and difficulties with romantic relationships (Frost & Meyer, 2009; Herek, Cogan, Gillis, & Glunt, 1998; Meyer & Dean, 1998; Rowen & Malcolm, 2002;

Szymanski, Kashubeck-West, & Meyer, 2008). To this end, the purpose of this chapter is to highlight the internalized oppression that may be experienced by LGBT people, particularly the internalized homophobia of LGB people and the internalized transphobia of transgender people. First, we highlight the LGBT community's historical and contemporary experiences with oppression, in order to emphasize the negative messages that LGBT people may receive from society, their families, and their peers. Next, we describe some of the common manifestations of inter-nalized oppression for LGBT people, including the ways that internal-ized oppression may influence mental health and relationships. Finally, we describe implications for research and clinical practice. Throughout the chapter, the second author (RJ Mendoza), a self-identified gay man and active member in the LGBT community, shares some of his own experiences with internalized homophobia in order to demonstrate how internalized oppression can manifest in everyday life.

DEMOGRAPHIC PROFILE

In order to learn more about this population, it may first be important to know how many LGBT people there are in the United States. However, it is difficult to report what percentage of the population is LGBT-identified for a number of reasons. First, the U.S. Census does not ask questions about sexual orientation or gender identity, making it difficult to estimate the number of LGBT people in the same way that the census can report race or gender. Second, because many LGBT people may have various levels of identity, some people may not identify as LGBT, even though their behaviors may indicate otherwise. For example, while some people may engage in same-sex sexual behaviors, they may identify as heterosexual, they may deny their homosexual or bisexual identities, or both. However, there are some studies that may provide some insight in to the number of people who identify as LGBT in the United States. One of the earliest studies on sexual orientation by Alfred Kinsey suggested that 1 in 10 men were likely "exclusively homosexual" (Kinsey, Pomeroy, & Martin, 1948). However, some have critiqued that these studies are biased because participants were selected from convenience samples and not from randomized samples (Maslow & Sakoda, 1952). Thus, many have argued that this statistic proposed by Kinsey may be an overesti-mate. More recently, a report by the Williams Institute at the University of California at Los Angeles estimates the LGBT population based on a comprehensive review of several studies and found the following:

1. Approximately 3.5% of adults in the United States identify as lesbian, gay, or bisexual and an estimated 0.3% of adults are transgender,

implying that there are approximately 9 million LGBT Americans, a figure roughly equivalent to the population of New Jersey.
2. Approximately 19 million Americans (8.2%) report that they have engaged in same-sex sexual behavior and nearly 25.6 million Americans (11%) acknowledge at least some same-sex sexual attraction (Gates, 2011).

These numbers match a recent study focusing on youth in San Francisco and found that 3.8% of middle school students identify as lesbian, gay, or bisexual, while 1.3% of middle school students identify as transgender (Shields et al., 2012).

Furthermore, it is necessary to recognize that certain areas in the United States may have larger percentages of LGBT-identified individuals. For instance, San Francisco had the largest percentage of LGBT-identified people (94,000, or 15.4% of the total population); similarly, New York City had the largest population of LGBT-identified people, with 272,000 individuals or 6.5% of the population (Gates, 2006). Thus, perhaps the aforementioned "1 in 10" statistic proposed by Kinsey and colleagues (1948) may be more accurate for metropolitan areas.

DEFINITIONS

Before describing how internalized oppression may negatively affect LGBT people, it is necessary to initially provide various definitions involving this community, as well as a basic overview of its demographics. First, it is necessary to note the difference between sexual orientation and gender identity. Sexual orientation is an individual's sense of personal and social identity based on one's sexual attractions, behaviors expressing those sexual attractions, and membership in a community of others who share them (Nadal, 2010a). For instance, people who identify as gay, lesbian, or bisexual may develop these identities not only because of their same-sex attractions and behaviors but also because they belong to a community of people who share similar experiences. On the other hand, gender identity is an individual's personal sense of identification as male, female, neither, or both (Nadal, 2010a). It is important to note that an individual's gender identity is independent of one's sexual orientation. For instance, a gay man may identify as gay (i.e., he is sexually and romantically attracted to other men), but his gender identity may be gender-conforming (i.e., he identifies as a man and is comfortable and happy with his gender). Meanwhile, a transgender female-to-male (FTM) may identify as a man (gender identity); however, because he is attracted to women, he would consider himself to be heterosexual (sexual orientation).

It is also important to note the difference between heterosexism and homophobia. Homophobia is the term generally used to describe negative attitudes toward gay, lesbian, bisexual, and queer individuals. A psychologist named George Weinberg (1972) is said to have first coined the term, when he defined homophobia as "the dread of being in close quarters with homosexuals" (p. 4). One limitation to the term "homophobia" is that it is defined as a "phobia," meaning that it is an irrational fear of, aversion to, or discrimination against homosexuality (Nadal, Rivera, & Corpus, 2010). In contemporary society, many people may have prejudice toward LGBT people, but may not necessarily have an unreasonable fear of them. Thus, some scholars have advocated that the term "heterosexism" may be more appropriate to describe the types of bias people may have, as heterosexism can be defined as particularly the attitudes, biases, and discrimination in favor of opposite-sex sexuality and relationships. Similarly, the term "genderism" has been used to depict the prejudiced attitudes and biases that people have toward transgender people. Perhaps this term might be more suitable since "transphobia" implies an irrational fear toward transgender people. Given this, while we will use the terms "internalized homophobia" and "internalized transphobia" throughout the chapter, we recognize that "internalized heterosexism" and "internalized genderism" may be more appropriate terms to describe the negative feelings that some LGBT people may have about themselves.

Finally, it is important to have an understanding of gender roles and the psychological distress that may be experienced as a result of these roles. The phrase "gender roles" refers to the behaviors, expectations, and values defined by society as masculine and feminine (Nadal, 2010b). Individuals may learn various messages about gender roles from their families, school systems, communities, and the media—particularly about how a person should act, speak, or dress based on birth sex. While gender role expectations may affect the entire population in various ways, they may significantly impact LGBT people in much different ways than heterosexual or cisgender people. Specifically, because LGBT people are taught they should act in ways that match their birth sex, they may have difficulty in exploring or accepting their sexual orientation or gender identity. For instance, if a young boy is interested in playing with dolls or wearing pink clothes, he may be punished for doing so; as a result, he may have difficulty exploring his sexual orientation or may learn that acting femininely is bad. Similarly, if the male child identifies as a girl and wishes to wear dresses or explore his gender identity, he may be scolded or chastised. As a result, the child may feel shame, stigma, or self-hate, and may learn that being transgender is unacceptable, unnatural, or something that is morally wrong.

EXPERIENCES OF HISTORICAL AND CONTEMPORARY OPPRESSION FOR LGBT PEOPLE

Although many history books may not include the experience of LGBT people throughout the history of the world, the existence of LGBT people has been documented as early as the 25th century BCE (see Nadal, 2013 for a review). In Ancient Rome and Ancient Greece, historical figures like Alexander the Great and Julius Caesar have been recorded as being bisexual or being involved in same-sex relationships. Even in the Old Testament of the Bible there are several individuals whom historians have interpreted as being involved in same-sex sexual and romantic relationships. For example, in the story of Ruth and Naomi, a well-known bible passage involves Ruth writing to Naomi: "Where you go, I will go; where you lodge, I will lodge." Similarly, David (who is known for slaying Goliath) is also said to have been in a relationship with a man named Jonathan. While the nature of their relationship is not explicitly defined, the language that is used to discuss the relationship between David and Jonathan is parallel to the language that is used to describe heterosexual couples in the bible.

Despite this rich history of LGBT people throughout the history of the world, homosexuality became criminalized in the 1800s (see Nadal, 2013 for a review). In the United States and in Europe, many gay men and transgender women were arrested or convicted of sodomy, which was defined as a sexual act usually involving anal or other copulation, historically involving two men, or a man and an animal. Sodomy was illegal in every state during this time, which in essence meant that any two gay men that had sexual relations (even if consensual and in the privacy for their homes) could be arrested and charged with a crime. It was not until 1961 that Illinois became the first state to remove sodomy from its criminal code, and it wasn't until 2003 that the U.S. Supreme Court ruled that sodomy laws were unconstitutional. In addition to sodomy laws that targeted LGBT people, anti-LGBT sentiment began to develop in the middle of the century. In fact, in 1953, President Dwight Eisenhower issued an executive order dismissing all homosexuals from federal employment—which included both civilian and military positions.

In terms of mental health, the *Diagnostic and Statistical Manual of Mental Disorders* (*DSM*) first listed homosexuality as a "sociopathic personality disturbance" (American Psychiatric Association, 1952). As a result, many mental health practitioners, particularly psychiatrists and psychologists, attempted to "cure" homosexual people of their "disorder" through an array of ineffective methods including electroshock therapy, lobotomy, hormone and drug treatments, and even castration (Institute of Medicine, 2011). In 1973, homosexuality was removed from the *DSM*, signifying that a nonheterosexual sexual orientation would no longer be viewed as psychologically abnormal and that any treatment attempting to "cure" homosexuality would be viewed as unethical, harmful, and ineffective

(Chernin & Johnson, 2003). Meanwhile, gender identity disorder and "adult transsexualism" are still listed as sexual paraphilias in the *DSM*, suggesting that transgender persons are still considered abnormal, pathological, or in need of mental health treatment (Nadal, Skolnik, & Wong, 2012).

Anti-LGBT sentiments increased even more in the 1980s, when the HIV/AIDS virus was first discovered in major metropolitan areas like New York and San Francisco. Because the disease was found mostly in gay men, it was initially labeled as the "Gay Disease" (Nadal, 2013). This eventually led to a national antigay sentiment, particularly from religious groups who proclaimed messages like "God hates fags" or "AIDS kills fags." Although thousands of gay men were dying from the disease for years, President Ronald Regan ignored the epidemic, which many believed represented the government's lack of care for LGBT people.

Finally, hate crimes against LGBT people have been quite common throughout the history of the United States. While many LGBT people have been documented as being victimized, assaulted, and murdered for their sexual orientation and gender identity, hate crimes tended to go under-reported for a number of reasons. First, when LGBT people are victims of hate crimes, they may have difficulty reporting such instances to law enforcement because of shame, stigma, or fear of retribution. For instance, if a bisexual man is assaulted because of his sexual orientation, and he is not "out of the closet," he may not report the crime because he may feel embarrassed or ashamed, because he does not feel comfortable admitting to his identity, or both. Furthermore, LGBT people have reported that mistreatment from police officers may also lead to an unwillingness to report crimes. Hate crimes against LGBT people became more publicized in the media when Matthew Shepard, a gay White male, was killed in Laramie, Wyoming, in 1999. Ten years later, President Obama signed the aforementioned Hate Crimes Prevention Act, which made committing a hate crime against LGBT people a federal crime.

In recent years, many authors have described how discrimination toward LGBT people has become less direct and much more subtle than more overt and blatant discrimination; these forms of subtler discrimination are sometimes known as *microaggressions*. Microaggressions are brief and commonplace daily verbal, behavioral, or environmental indignities, whether intentional or unintentional, which communicate hostile, derogatory, or negative slights and insults toward members of oppressed groups (Nadal, 2013). While a majority of the literature on microaggressions focuses on race, some studies on sexual orientation microaggressions (e.g., Nadal, Issa et al., 2011; Nadal, Wong et al., 2011) and gender identity microaggressions (e.g., Nadal et al., 2012) have found that microaggressions do exist along these axes as well and that these subtle forms of discrimination negatively impact the lives of LGBT people. Nadal and colleagues (2010) proposed a theoretical taxonomy on sexual orientation and transgender microaggressions, citing several categories of microaggressions that may target LGBT persons. First, the *use of heterosexist and transphobic terminology* occurs when people use derogatory heterosexist language toward LGBT persons (e.g., saying words like "faggot," "dyke," "tranny," or using terms like "That's so gay" to describe something that is bad or undesirable). Second, *endorsement of heteronormative or gender binary culture/behaviors* transpires when an LGB person is expected to act or be heterosexual or when a transgender person is expected to conform to her or his birth sex. For instance, a heterosexual person telling a gay individual not to "act gay in public" or a parent forcing her or his child to dress according to her or his birth sex would be examples of endorsing heteronormative values. Third, *assumption of universal LGBT experience* occurs when heterosexual people assume that all LGBT persons are the same (e.g., assuming all gay men to be fashionable or stereotyping all transgender women to be sex workers). Fourth, *exoticization microaggressions* take place when LGBT people are dehumanized or treated as objects (e.g., when someone is referred to as a "token gay friend"). Fifth, *discomfort/disapproval of LGBT experience* occurs when LGBT people are treated with disrespect and criticism. For example, a stranger may stare at an affectionate lesbian couple with disgust or a heterosexual person tells an LGBT individual that she or he is "going to hell." Sixth, *denial of the reality of heterosexism* transpires when people deny that heterosexism and homophobia exist (e.g., a coworker telling a gay friend that he's being paranoid by thinking someone is discriminating against him). Seventh, *assumptions of sexual pathology/abnormality* come about when heterosexual people oversexualize LGBT persons and consider them sexual deviants. For example, many people may assume that all gay men have HIV/AIDS and are child molesters. Finally, *denial of individual heterosexism* occurs when heterosexual people deny their own heterosexist and transgender biases and prejudice (e.g., someone saying: "I am not homophobic, I have a gay friend!").

When LGBT individuals experience discrimination, overt or covert, it is possible for them to develop internalized oppression. For instance, when an LGBT person experiences a microaggression, she or he may unconsciously believe that the message that is communicated is accurate or correct. In the following paragraphs, RJ describes how microaggressions may have influenced his internalized oppression.

> When I was in my twenties, I remember having a conversation with a friend about being gay. She asked me if being gay was a choice. I stated clearly that being gay was not something that I chose. I didn't decide to be part of a community that was hated, rejected, and vilified. I did not want to choose an identity that made it hard to feel good about myself, because I was consistently ridiculed and mocked, and even occasionally threatened. I've narrowly avoided being gay-bashed by a group of men, and gotten into physical altercations with men who called me a "faggot"; how could I choose this life?

Occasionally, it is still hard to feel good about myself as a gay man. There are times in social situations where I am made to feel as the "token gay guy" and apparently have to field and answer questions about everything that is gay. When people tell me that they always knew I was gay, that they want me to be their "gay best friend," or even when they introduce me as their "gay friend," I get upset. I wonder if they would proudly introduce someone else as their "Arab friend" or their "disabled friend" or if they would ever confidently say to someone "I always knew you were autistic/schizophrenic/diabetic/etc." When I voice these concerns, I'm often told to "get over it" or that I'm being "overly sensitive." Sometimes, experiences like these make me not want to say anything at all. Other times, I start to feel resentful that heterosexuals and cisgender people don't ever have to experience the same things that LGBT people do.

Another microaggression that stands out for me is a time when I went out to a nightclub with some friends. Like many people in their early adulthood, I consumed enough alcohol to make me lose my inhibitions. I danced like no one was watching, I talked excessively to anyone who was interested, and I laughed uncontrollably whenever I was entertained. At the end of the night, my friend said to me, "You should tone it down! People were looking at you. And if you act that way around this crowd, I don't know if I can bring you around them again." At first, I thought that maybe I was over the top. I would never fit in with this crowd if I acted like a fool. But before I could finish that thought, I caught myself. She was basically telling me that I was "too much" because I was being too flamboyant, too loud, and too open about my gayness. It was not the fact that I was dancing, talking, and laughing; it was that I was dancing, talking, and laughing "like a gay person." Everyone else was having a good time. I was not the only person who was drinking or losing my inhibitions. But I was the only gay person, and I was definitely the only person who challenged gender role behaviors and expectations.

It was at this point that I realized that I could never change who I was and that I did not want to. I spent a good portion of my adolescent years trying to assimilate to the norms, and I tried vehemently to change myself and "fit in" with the heterosexual standard. It only made me feel worse when I didn't succeed, and I wasn't going to go through that again. So I promised myself that I would not. Nowadays, if anyone would ever tell me to "tone it down" or to try to act more masculine, I would probably challenge her or his homophobia and continue the "controversial" behavior. However, I am fully aware that if I was not comfortable with who I am, I probably wouldn't fight back and I would likely internalize that something was wrong with me.

COMMON MANIFESTATIONS OF INTERNALIZED HOMOPHOBIA AND TRANSPHOBIA

In order to fully understand internalized homophobia and transphobia, it is necessary to examine the literature and the ways that the construct has been previously measured. The Internalized Homophobia Scale (Martin & Dean, 1987) is one of the earliest and most commonly used internalized homophobia scales; a sample item included: "If someone offered me the chance to be completely heterosexual, I would accept the chance." An individual who answers this item affirmatively is someone who is not completely happy with her or his sexual orientation. While some individuals may believe that they accept their sexual orientations, LGBT people who secretly desire to be heterosexual would be considered to possess internalized homophobia.

Some measures on internalized homophobia yield several dimensions, highlighting the myriad ways that internalized oppression may exist. The Internalized Homophobia Scale (Ross & Rosser, 1996) consists of four factors that highlight the types of internalized homophobia that is experienced by their sample of gay men. These factors include: (1) Public identification as gay, (2) Perception of stigma associated with being gay, (3) Social comfort with gay men, and (4) Moral and religious acceptability of being gay. Thus, internalized homophobia may not only consist of how one feels about her or his sexual orientation and how "out" one is publicly, but also includes how one feels about being around other LGBT people and about how one deals with the religious and moral lessons that have been taught about sexual orientation.

A similar scale was developed for lesbians—the Lesbian Internalized Homophobia Scale—which consists of five subscales: (1) Connection with the lesbian community, (2) Public identification as a lesbian, (3) Personal feelings about being a lesbian, (4) Moral and religious attitudes, and (5) Attitudes toward other lesbians (Szymanski & Chung, 2001). Similar to the aforementioned scales, internalized homophobia for women may manifest in how one publicly identifies and how one copes with moral and religious messages. However, the scale differs in measuring one's connection with the lesbian community and one's attitudes about other lesbians separately. Simply stated, one can have internalized homophobia in that she has negative attitudes about other lesbians, she is disconnected from the lesbian community, or both.

A recent scale, the Multifactor Internalized Homophobia Inventory, which focused on LGBT people in Italy, described eight factors that contribute to one's internalized homophobia. These include: (1) Fear of coming out, (2) Regret about being homosexual, (3) Moral condemnation, (4) Gay-lesbian parenting, (5) Integration in the homosexual community, (6) Counter-prejudicial attitudes, (7) Homosexual marriage, and

(8) Adherence to stereotypes (Flebus & Montano, 2012). This scale differs in that it includes feelings about LGBT parenting and same-sex marriage. An individual with internalized homophobia may view same-sex marriage as being immoral or inferior to heterosexual marriage, while also viewing LGBT parents as being unable to nurture or raise children as well as their heterosexual counterparts.

Finally, Hatzenbuehler and colleagues (2009) conducted a study with LGB participants to measure antigay attitudes that are either explicit (i.e., participants self-report their internalized homophobic beliefs) or implicit (i.e., participants took the Implicit Attitudes Test to measure their inherent or unconscious biases about LGB people). While a majority of the participants did not self-report explicit antigay attitudes, one-third of the sample did self-report moderate-to-high levels of explicit internalized homophobia. Additionally, results indicated that negative implicit self-stigmatization predicted psychological distress, while explicit self-stigmatization did not. In other words, whether someone possessed internalized homophobia was a determinant of mental health, while conscious feelings about homophobia were not. Furthermore, LGB participants who scored higher in implicit antigay attitudes were also more likely to use rumination and suppression as coping strategies, suggesting that individuals with internalized homophobia may also use ineffective coping strategies, which may further exacerbate negative feelings about themselves and their identities.

While all of these aforementioned studies help to understand how internalized homophobia may manifest in LGBT people's lives, it is crucial to reiterate that these measures focus explicitly on sexual orientation and not on gender identity. While it is likely that transgender and gender nonconforming people may experience similar dimensions of internalized transphobia, there is a need for more research to support the claim that these scales are applicable and parallel. Perhaps transgender people with internalized transphobia may have similar experiences in that they may wish that they were not transgender; they may not be comfortable in affirming their transgender identity openly; or they may not feel connected to other transgender people. However, there may also be an array of nuances that distinguish transgender experiences from other LGB people.

INTERNALIZED OPPRESSION AND THE COMING OUT PROCESS

One of the major findings regarding internalized homophobia is that it appears that LGBT people may have difficulty in developing healthy sexual identities, particularly with coming out of the closet. For example, some studies (Mayfield, 2001; Rowen & Malcolm, 2002) have found that internalized homophobia is negatively related to healthy gay identity development. In other words, the more internalized homophobia a person maintains, the less likely she or he would be happy with her or his sexual orientation. In fact, when individuals possess greater amounts of internalized homophobia, it may be difficult for them to come out of the closet, even postponing their ability to come to terms with themselves. In the following narrative, RJ describes the difficult process of coming out of the closet due to internalized homophobia.

For years, it seemed everyone around me (my sister, my mother, my father, and close friends) knew that I was in fact, gay. However, I was in denial about it. I knew I was gay for a long time—perhaps from when I was 7 or 8 years old. Rumors went around about me behind my back— particularly in my mother's workplace and among family and family friends. There was also a cultural component to it—my father emigrated to the United States from the Philippines, and although we lived in New York City, we were in a small pocket of Filipino immigrants. Because Filipinos tended to view being gay as being immoral or unnatural, I hid it as best as I could.

There were so many jokes and negative messages that were made about gays or "baklas" (the Filipino word that translates to gay, transgender male-to-female, or "faggot"). Hearing these jokes or homophobic language contributed heavily to my denial. I did not want to be made fun of or become the target of hurtful jokes. I did not want to prove everyone right. In fact, because everyone had assumed or made comments that I was gay, I wanted to fight against their assumption and prove that I was heterosexual. So, I began to shift myself in an inauthentic way. I, too, made jokes about other gay people, in an attempt to take any negative attention away from me, and I even changed my hair and clothes all in an attempt to fit in.

My turning point was in high school. I was able to attend a high school that was somewhat far away from my neighborhood. In many ways, I was happy because I was able to escape from the assumptions that people may have had about me in my neighborhood. At this school, there was one openly gay male student. He was flamboyant, he was quite feminine in his presentation and behaviors, and he walked with his head held high. Though he seemed to be somewhat confident, others made fun of him or gossiped about him being gay. So in order to fit in (and to divert any attention away from me), I would give him unfriendly looks, and I would join in the whispers about him. In retrospect, I wasn't proud of this at all. In fact, while all of this was happening, I was silently apologizing to him (and to myself) for treating him the way I was treated. I knew I was gay, and I hated myself for it. But I especially hated myself for the way I treated him.

In reviewing RJ's narrative, there are several themes that emerge. First, he describes the idea of self-hate, which he attributes primarily to his sexual orientation. Because he grew up in an environment where being gay was viewed negatively, he attempted to hide this part of himself as much as he could. He changed his own appearance or behaviors in order to "pass" and to avoid being the victim of discrimination. He even admits to mistreating an openly gay classmate, in order to divert attention away from himself, an example of within-group discrimination that is a common expression of internalized oppression. Because an individual is unhappy, disgusted, or disappointed with one of their identities or some other aspect of themselves, it can be common to project self-hatred onto others. Both researchers and clinicians have supported the phenomenon that people who are homophobic may secretly be gay or may subsconsciously possess homosexual desires. For instance, one study found that participants who identify as heterosexual but who may have unconscious same-sex attractions or desires (i.e., they scored higher on a same-sex Implicit Association Test) may possess stronger antigay biases than those who do not have unconscious same-sex attractions or desires (Weinstein et al., 2012). Perhaps people who may identify as heterosexual but who harbor same-sex feelings may feel threatened by LGBT people who are comfortable and "out." Perhaps these individuals have internalized so much self-hatred about themselves that they develop intense negative feelings about LGBT people (and sometimes participate in bullying or other homophobic behaviors) in order to cope.

RJ continues to describe how his coming out process was influenced by the negative messages about being gay that he received from his own family, messages that led to him developing internalized homophobia:

> During my high school years, I had a crush on another male student. He was tall, dark, and handsome, and he had a well-defined physique. The only problem was that he was heterosexual. I wrote a letter to him where I proclaimed my love for him, which I never had any intention of letting him or anyone else see. However, I accidentally left the letter in my journal on our kitchen table, and my mother took liberty to read it (obviously without my permission). When I came home that day, she accused me of being gay, in a hurtful and nonsupportive way. My sister found out about the situation, and she also expressed her disgust and disdain. Meanwhile, my father was silent throughout all of the yelling. While all of this was happening, I stayed silent too. I did not have any intentions of coming out—at that time or potentially ever. I wasn't going to go through the agony of being gossiped about, being made fun of, or having anyone make any assumptions about me. I did not want to admit to something, simply because I was caught or being forced to. I also did not want to fight back against something I was not ready for. If everyone around me thought

that being gay was so bad, how was I supposed to defend myself against it, especially if I felt the same way? So I just let my mom and sister make their comments, and I decided to ignore it as best as I could.

When I did finally come out, it was because of several reasons. I had entered my first same-sex relationship and my boyfriend had broken up with me unexpectedly. I was crushed. I found myself withdrawing from every aspect of my life. I was angry. I was depressed. I tried to isolate myself. I tried to keep it all to myself, but I was also tired of pretending to be something I wasn't. One day, I was crying on the living room couch, and my father demanded to know why. Without hesitation and without thinking about the potential consequences, I blurted: "I'm crying because my boyfriend broke up with me!" He replied "Oh . . . So you *are* gay. I'm sorry he broke up with you." He ended up sharing with me how he was disappointed that I couldn't tell him about who I was. I was just happy to know that he still loved me and accepted me. If only I knew about his support long ago, I may have had an easier time coming to terms with being gay.

Through RJ's narrative, it is clear that loved ones (e.g., parents, siblings, and other family members) may have a huge influence on one's coming out process, as well as in her or his development of internalized oppression. Sometimes LGBT individuals may hear negative messages from family members, which may contribute to feelings of self-hatred and negate an LGBT person's ability to come to terms with her or his identity. However, as demonstrated through RJ's recollection of his father's reaction, it is evident that positive messages can be helpful in assisting an individual develop a healthy sexual identity. Perhaps if his mother and sister were more supportive of his sexual orientation, or at least were more aware of how their words were hurtful, he could have felt more comfortable in disclosing his identity to them. Perhaps if his father were more vocal about his acceptance of his son's sexuality, RJ would have felt more able to come out to him at an earlier time. Thus, in order for family members and other loved ones to help to decrease internalized homophobia among LGBT people, it is not only necessary to create a safe environment that is free of homophobia, but it may also be necessary to vocalize or express one's support and acceptance.

Besides one's immediate family members, LGBT people may also develop internalized homophobia from messages that they learn from their extended families, communities, school environments, and religions. For instance, RJ describes how his extended family, religion, and the inter-actions between them, influenced his coming out process:

When I was around 23 years old, I relocated from New York to Hawai'i for 5 years, and I temporarily stayed with an aunt and uncle who were part of a religion that believes that homosexuality is a sin. At the time, I was in a serious relationship with another man. However, because I was living with them, because I wanted to appease them, and because I did believe in a higher power, I started to actively attend the same church as them. One day, when I was having tea with my aunt, she asked me if I thought my boyfriend was "the one." I told her that I had dated a few men in my life and that I was feeling good about him. While she appeared to listen to me, the conversation eventually went awry when she suggested that I "walk away from this lifestyle of homosexuality that has been cursed on me." I started to question my reality. My desire to nurture my relationship with God became a tangled web of contradictions and justifications. I wanted to believe that there was a place in Heaven for my boyfriend and me, but I questioned whether it was really going to happen. Every so often, my aunt and uncle would drop hints about how dangerous being gay was— particularly how I wouldn't get into Heaven and how I could potentially get AIDS and die. My first reaction was to be angry and infuriated by their seemingly uncompassionate views. However, my second instinct was to entertain their thoughts. I began to wonder if they were right.

By questioning my gayness and my relationship, I began to make concessions. Perhaps if my boyfriend and I both started going to this church, then God would be okay with us being together. Perhaps if I tithed my earnings and gave an additional 10% of my paycheck to the church, God would forgive me. Perhaps if I preached to other gay folks that monogamy was the norm and that promiscuity was evil, then it would be okay. As I started to give money to the church, I noticed that I was becoming more financially strained. Because of my desire to preach to others, I started to lose friendships with people who didn't agree with me. Worst of all, I started to get into constant fights with my then-boyfriend who, despite his own internalized homophobia, refused to go to church with me. I begged and pleaded with him. "God may not have wanted this, but if we are going to Church and if we are doing good things he will make an exception. . . . This is our redemption!" He still refused.

Eventually, I realized that my attempts to reconcile my spiritual and religious values with my same-sex relationship were futile. But one moment eventually changed my views about the church completely. One time when I asked my aunt to sit and pray with me for a friend who was diagnosed with a positive HIV status, she refused to do so. She lectured about the consequences of this "generational curse" for gays. She again preached that I could walk away from this "lifestyle" if I fully accepted God into my heart. I couldn't deal with this ignorance and hatred. There was no way that I could reconcile something that I knew was so natural to me and was part of who I was, and I refused to have anyone tell me that there was something wrong with me. So two days after that conversation, I moved out of my aunt's home, and I decided to never take part in any religion or any group who did not accept me for who I am.

DETRIMENTAL INFLUENCES OF INTERNALIZED HOMOPHOBIA AND TRANSPHOBIA ON MENTAL HEALTH

Over the past 20 years, there has been a breadth of literature in psychology and education describing the types and effects of discrimination experienced by LGBT people. For instance, research involving sexual/antigay harassment and prejudice (e.g., Burn, Kadlec, & Rexer, 2005; Herek, 2000), sexual stigma (e.g., Herek, 2007), modern homonegativity (e.g., Morrison & Morrison, 2002), modern heterosexism (e.g., Walls, 2008), and transphobia (e.g., Hill & Willoughby, 2005) have all pointed to the detrimental impacts of discrimination on the psychological experiences of LGBT persons. Some studies have suggested that LGBT individuals experience higher levels psychological distress and social stress or "minority stress" because of their sexual orientation or gender identity (Meyer, 1995, 2003). One study found a high prevalence of reported suicide attempts in an urban and rural sample of LGBT youth, with 42% of the urban sample and 32% of the rural sample attempting suicide at least once (Waldo, Hesson-McInnis, & D'Augelli, 1998). Another study reported that LGBT youth scored significantly higher on a scale of depressive symptomatology than their heterosexual counterparts (Almeida, Johnson, Corliss, Molnar, & Azrael, 2009). In a review of several empirical studies, Meyer (2003) found that gay and lesbian individuals were 2.5 times more likely to have a mental health problem in their lifetime compared to their heterosexual counterparts.

Also over the past 20 years, there has been an abundance of empirical literature that has described the many ways that internalized homophobia negatively affects the lives of LGB people. Some authors have described how internalized homophobia is necessary to overcome in order for LGB people to develop healthy self-esteems and optimal mental health (Fingerhut, Peplau, & Ghavami, 2005; Mayfield, 2001; Rowen & Malcolm, 2002). Moreover, previous literature has described how internalized homophobia may be very difficult to overcome, even for LGB individuals who have come out of the closet and proclaim a strong LGB identity (Gonsiorek, 1988). Finally, while there is a limited amount of literature on internalized transphobia, it is hypothesized that similar processes would occur. In fact, previous authors have cited that transgender and gender nonconforming people may develop low self-esteem as a result of the negative transphobic messages that are pervasive in society (Hendricks & Testa, 2012).

Szymanski et al. (2008) provide a comprehensive overview of the various studies involving internalized homophobia, focusing on an array of variables that have been found to be related to or influenced by internalized homophobia. For instance, previous studies have found that internalized homophobia is related to various aspects of mental, psychosocial, and physical health. Some studies have found that LGB people with higher levels of homophobia may have lower self-esteem (e.g., Herek et al., 1998; Peterson & Gerrity, 2006; Rowen & Malcolm, 2002). Other studies have reported that internalized homophobia can predict depression (Herek et al., 1998; Szymanski, Chung, & Balsam, 2001). One study found that internalized homophobia is a predictor of suicidal ideation among LGB people (D'Augelli, Grossman, Hershberger, & O'Connell, 2001). Finally, as aforementioned, implicit internalized homophobia has been found to predict psychological distress (Hatzenbuehler, Dovidio, Nolen-Hoeksema, & Phills, 2009).

Internalized homophobia has also been found to negatively affect behavioral health (see Szymanski et al., 2008, for a review). For instance, LGB people with higher levels of internalized homophobia were also likely to abuse alcohol and other drugs (DiPlacido, 1998), and internalized homophobia has also been found to influence body image issues and body dissatisfaction, particularly for gay men (Kimmel & Mahlalik, 2005). Earlier studies have supported a significant relationship between internalized homophobia and risky sexual behaviors (see Williamson, 2000, for a review). One of the main arguments for this correlation is that LGB people with internalized homophobia may also have low self-esteem, which in turn may lead to risky sexual behaviors. Perhaps LGB people internalize an array of negative stereotypes that they may have learned, particularly stereotypes related to HIV/AIDS. Perhaps LGB people believe that they are not worthy of healthy romantic relationships and thus engage in risky sexual behaviors as a slow suicidal process. RJ's narrative illustrates how internalized homophobia can affect every aspect of a person's mental health, particularly one's self-esteem and mental health, as well as one's unhealthy or risky behaviors.

When I was 18, I made the decision to have sexual intercourse with another man for the first time. I met him on the Internet, and he was probably well into his forties. I still didn't want people to know about my sexuality and I was convinced that I would never find a guy that was my age that would like me. I didn't find the man attractive, and I often wonder, to this day, why I chose that man to give away my virginity. I had only met this man casually, but I allowed him to penetrate me without a condom. It did not last very long and I didn't let him penetrate me very deeply. He ejaculated on my leg. I immediately ran to the bathroom, got dressed, and ran out. I assumed that I was HIV-positive from that moment on, but I refused to get myself tested.

When I officially came out, I started openly dating men and having sexual encounters, and I still refused to find out my HIV status. My biggest fear was finding out that I was HIV-positive, and that everyone else would find out. The stigma of HIV and AIDS haunted me, and I especially worried about my mother. In the 1980s and 1990s, she lost a number of friends to AIDS-related complications. When I first started having sex, I started to think, "It's bad enough I'm gay. I don't want her to know I have AIDS." Part of me thought that being gay automatically meant that I would get HIV/AIDS and die early. Part of me thought that I would never live a life of happiness and that I would never get to live the "fairytale" that heterosexual people could.

So, throughout my late teens and early twenties, I had multiple partners, sometimes under the influence of alcohol and other substances. I figured I was probably HIV-positive anyway, so it wouldn't have mattered. If I ever could find the courage to get tested (and officially find out my destiny), I thought to plan an elaborate suicide that would look like an accident because I didn't want to be one of those gay men who died of AIDS. I was depressed. I felt hopeless. I felt worthless. I continued to make a lot of bad decisions (with drugs, with alcohol, and with anonymous sex) in order to cope with it all.

Eventually, at the request and moral support of a friend, I finally accessed an HIV test when I was 22 years old. The counselor was helpful and comforting, and he allowed me to express my negative and irrational internalized thoughts while we waited for the results. When I learned that I was in fact HIV-negative, I cried hysterically. I was relieved that I wasn't going to be one of those gay guys who died of AIDS. There was a period of time after that in which I didn't get tested, but I still put myself at risk. I had encounters with men who I knew were HIV-positive, as well as with some whose status I simply didn't know. Although I tried to take precautions, the thought of HIV/AIDS still haunted me in the back of my mind. When I mustered up the courage again to get tested, I was attending an evangelical Christian church and struggling with my gay identity. Unlike the first time I got tested in New York, this test used a different method than my previous one and I had to wait a week for the results as opposed to thirty minutes. For several days, I found myself again assuming that I was already HIV-positive, and thinking, "This is what I get for being gay." Fortunately, the test came back negative, and every HIV test since then has been negative too.

While I have since been in a monogamous relationship and do not engage in any risky behavior, I still get a little anxious when I am tested for HIV. Because of the long stigma associated with gay men and HIV, I feel like I'll always have that thought in the back of my head that because I am gay, I will get AIDS and die. And while I know logically that there is no way this will happen if I make wise decisions and avoid engaging in any risky behavior, this thought still seems to linger. I suppose this shows how pervasive these negative thoughts may be. Because these harmful, homophobic negative messages have been engrained in me ever since I was a little kid, perhaps they may be harder to erase. Until then, the best I can do is to combat these internalized biases with healthy messages and images about LGBT people, while surrounding myself with support systems and role models who teach me that being gay can lead to a life full of happiness.

It is evident that RJ learned that being gay was negative and that it could potentially lead to him contracting HIV/AIDS. Because he was raised in an environment (and an era) where being a gay man was consistently equated with having HIV/AIDS, he thought he was destined to become HIV-positive and not have the same opportunities that heterosexuals might. As a result, he even engaged in behaviors (which he regrets in retrospect) that put himself at risk for HIV. RJ's experience demonstrates that hearing consistent negatives stereotypes and messages are particularly harmful. Sometimes, such stereotypes may lead to self-fulfilling prophecies, which occur when "perceivers' false beliefs about targets initiate a sequence of events that ultimately cause targets to exhibit expectancy-consistent behaviors, thereby causing perceivers' initially false beliefs to become true" (Madon, Willard, Guyll, & Scherr, 2011, p. 578). Perhaps if he did not learn these negative messages about gay men, he would not have assumed that he was destined to a life of HIV/AIDS; as a result, he may have developed a healthier self-esteem during his formative years and avoided putting his life at risk.

THE IMPACT OF INTERNALIZED HOMOPHOBIA AND TRANSPHOBIA ON RELATIONSHIPS

There has been a growing amount of literature that has focused on the negative impact of internalized homophobia on relationships—family relationships, friendships, and romantic relationships with partners. For instance, some studies have found that coming out to one's family members, particularly one's parents, can be a very stressful experience, which often leads to altered (and sometimes irreparable) parent–child relationships (Saltzburg, 2004). RJ describes how his internalized homophobia may impact his present-day relationships:

> Sometimes I wonder how my internalized homophobia may still affect me today. Well, one thing that I realize is that I am unwilling to introduce my current boyfriend to a majority of my extended family. From an outsider's perspective, it may seem to be quite strange, given that he shares the same ethnic and cultural background as them, and because he is someone whom they would probably like, admire, or get along with. However, I am not going to give anyone anything to talk about. Because of my family's religious upbringings and beliefs, I assume they would see our relationship as wrong, sinful, or bad. I imagine that any conversations about my relationship would only cause discomfort

among the family, and would likely even cause pain, anger, or distress in my parents' lives. So, I let them believe what they want.

Perhaps I'm unconsciously agreeing with them, in that I am not publicly announcing who I am and the man whom I love. But perhaps I am also saving myself significant psychological distress by avoiding conflicting, judgmental, or hurtful conversations that may lead to arguments, strife, and pain.

In retrospect, I believe the biggest sadness with all of this is that I wish I could tell my grandparents about my boyfriend. I wish they could sit down at dinner with us, and that they could tell us the story of how they met, how life was in the Philippines, and what it was like for them to immigrate to the Philippines. I wish that they could tell us how they were happy for us, potentially even pressuring us to have children and give them great-children (as I know they've done for my heterosexual sister and cousins).

In some ways, I think my grandparents know that I am gay. Rumors about me have circulated around the family, and I know that many jokes have been made at my expense. But if I don't acknowledge my sexuality officially, then it would not be a reality for them. If I do not come out to them, I do not get to disappoint them by living a life that is very likely against their values and beliefs. While I don't think I am hiding anything and pretending to be something I am not (i.e., I do not date women or tell them that I am interested in women), I am just not acknowledging that I am gay. Perhaps some of it is in fact internalized homophobia, but perhaps some of it is just the reality of my world.

In terms of internalized oppression's impact on romantic relationships, Ossana (2000) describes the many ways that internalized homophobia can be detrimental to same-sex romantic relationships and ways to address internalized homophobia in same-sex couples' therapy. In the review by Szymanski et al. (2008), it was found that many studies confirmed that internalized homophobia predicted relationship dissatisfaction, poorer relationship quality, and sometimes issues in commitment and sexual functioning. RJ's narrative below is an example of how internalized homophobia may affect romantic relationships.

I feel better about myself being gay when I am around other gay men, or in situations where LGBT sensitivity is taken seriously. Sometimes I just wish that people would stop suggesting that a heteronormative society is the ideal. When people do, either consciously or unconsciously, it makes me want to cut off ties with them. When I'm the only gay person in the room, or when I know that I have to hide my sexuality in certain settings, I start to become uncomfortable and withdraw. It is unfortunate to know that heterosexism can have such a negative effect on my relationships with others.

As I reflect on my life, I can also see how my internalized homophobia has affected my romantic relationships. In the past, I have often felt like my relationships with men weren't good enough, or at least weren't as good as heterosexual relationships. There were times when I thought that I couldn't raise children—not because I didn't think I would be a good parent, but because I thought that perhaps having an LGBT parent could somehow be damaging to a child. In fact, as much as I don't want to admit to it, I have internalized in many ways that a child *should* have a mother and a father.

Now that I am in a loving relationship with a man whom I love, it is amazing to know that I can finally see myself having a happy and healthy future as a gay man. I foresee marriage, children, and grandchildren. I see a home where it is natural to have two parents of the same gender, or where having gay grandparents is no big deal. It took me a while to get here, and I can definitely see how some people who are struggling with their identities may never ever imagine that this is possible. But it is.

IMPLICATIONS FOR RESEARCH, CLINICAL PRACTICE, AND SERVICE

Throughout the chapter we have provided a spectrum of ways that internalized oppression may manifest in LGBT people's lives, while also describing the many ways that internalized oppression may affect LGBT people's identity development, mental health, and relationships. We conclude this chapter by describing future research directions, as well as recommendations for clinical practice and service. Perhaps the most salient suggestion for research is to increase the amount of literature on internalized transphobia. As aforementioned, most of the studies involving internalized oppression in the LGBT community focus primarily on experiences of LGB people; while concepts and trends are hypothesized to be similar with transgender and gender nonconforming people, it is necessary for empirical research to emerge and to support theories about internalized transphobia. Furthermore, while there has been an increase in a number of variables that may be related to internalized homophobia (e.g., mental health, romantic relationships, substance abuse), it may be necessary to expand the research to look at protective factors (e.g., which variables may assist in protecting against internalized oppression) and risk factors (which variables may contribute to various physical and mental health disparities for individuals with internalized homophobia/transphobia). Finally, it may be necessary to further investigate subgroups within the LGBT community, particularly LGBT people of various racial and ethnic minority groups, as well as LGBT people with other intersectional identities (e.g., LGBT people with disabilities, LGBT people of religious minority groups). Perhaps individuals with multiple marginalized identities may suffer from significant psychological distress because of the negative messages that they may have learned about two or more of their identities. For instance, a lesbian woman of color with a disability may have to deal with internalized homophobia, as well as internalized sexism, internalized racism, and internalized ableism.

In terms of clinical practice and service, there are some ways that mental health practitioners can assist in addressing internalized oppression with their LGBT clients. First, it may be necessary for counselors and clinicians to directly ask their LGBT clients about the various messages that they may have learned about sexual orientation, gender identity, and gender roles. Inquiring directly about these belief systems might be necessary because clients may not even recognize the ways that internalized homophobia or transphobia negatively impact their lives. For instance, in RJ's narrative, he described how he believed that being gay meant that he would contract HIV/AIDS, or that there would be no way that he could have a healthy and happy relationship or family. He also described how he somehow believed that he was condemned or that he would not go to Heaven because he was gay. As a result, he shared how he became depressed, engaged in risky behaviors, and had difficulty in his romantic relationships because of this internalized oppression.

Thus, perhaps it is one role of the therapist to guide clients in unpacking and disputing any of their internalized oppression, particularly because the client may not even realize that his or her belief systems are problematic. Given the research that internalized homophobia may be both implicit and explicit, and that implicit internalized homophobia may have a more detrimental impact on mental health (Hatzenbuehler et al., 2009), psychotherapy could focus on what the client consciously reports, as well as what the client may have repressed. Furthermore, in working with LGBT clients of color, it may be important to unpack internalized racism as well. Given that research has also found that internalized racism is both covert and overt (David, 2010), culturally competent therapists can explore how internalized oppression negatively affects individuals with multiple identities.

Another recommendation for service is to create safe environments that advocate for LGBT people, which in turn may minimize LGBT people's internalized oppression. Creating an inclusive environment (i.e., one in which both heterosexual and LGBT lives are promoted) and immediately addressing discriminatory behavior (e.g., challenging homophobic language and educating people about microaggressions) are two simple ways that assist in minimizing homophobia, heterosexism, transphobia, and genderism. In creating such an environment, two outcomes may occur. First, heterosexual and gender-conforming people may learn to be more accepting of LGBT people, which may then prevent them from being discriminatory against LGBT people. Second, LGBT people may learn that being LGBT is a desirable, healthy identity, which in turn may help to combat the internalized homophobia and transphobia that would be learned in a prejudiced or biased environment.

While there are dozens of other methods that can assist in decreasing internalized oppression in LGBT people, it is clear that systems (e.g., government, media, schools) need to make changes to advocate for LGBT people. However, people on all levels can do their parts to decrease internalized oppression. Families need to create safe environments for their LGBT children, while promoting open-mindedness in their heterosexual and gender conforming children. Allies need to create communities in which discrimination is prohibited and inclusiveness is celebrated. Because we know that internalized homophobia and internalized transphobia have such negative influences on LGBT people's lives, it is necessary for everyone in society to do what we can to "make it better" for future generations.

REFERENCES

Almeida, J., Johnson, R. M., Corliss, H. L., Molnar, B. E., & Azrael, D. (2009). Emotional distress among LGBT youth: The influence of perceived discrimination based on sexual orientation. *Journal of Youth Adolescence, 38*, 1001–1014. doi:10.1007/s10964-009-9397-9

American Psychiatric Association. (1952). *Diagnostic and statistical manual of mental disorders*. Washington, DC: Author.

Berkley, R. A., & Watt, A. H. (2006). Impact of same-sex harassment and gender-role stereotypes on Title VII protection for gay, lesbian, and bisexual employees. *Employee Responsibilities & Rights Journal, 18*(1), 3–19.

Burn, S. M., Kadlec, K., & Rexer, R. (2005). Effects of subtle heterosexism on gays, lesbians, and bisexuals. *Journal of Homosexuality, 49*(2), 23–38.

Chernin, J. N., & Johnson, M. R. (2003). *Affirmative psychotherapy and counseling for lesbians and gay men*. Thousand Oaks, CA: Sage.

D'Augelli, A. R., Grossman, A. H., Hershberger, S. L., & O'Connell, T. S. (2001). Aspects of mental health among older lesbian, gay, and bisexual adults. *Aging & Mental Health, 5*(2), 149–158.

David, E. J. R. (2010). Testing the validity of the colonial mentality implicit association test and the interactive effects of covert and overt colonial mentality on Filipino American mental health. *Asian American Journal of Psychology, 1*(1), 31–45.

DiPlacido, J. (1998). Minority stress among lesbians, gay men, and bisexuals: A consequence of homophobia, heterosexism, and stigmatization. In G. M. Herek (Ed.), *Stigma and sexual orientation: Understanding prejudice against lesbians, gay men, and bisexuals* (pp. 138–159). Thousand Oaks, CA: Sage.

Federal Bureau of Investigation. (2011). *Uniform crime report, hate crime statistics, 2010*. Retrieved December 1, 2012, from http://www.fbi.gov/about-us/cjis/ucr/hate-crime/2010/narratives/hate-crime-2010-incidents-and-offenses.pdf

Fingerhut, A. W., Peplau, L. A., & Ghavami, N. (2005). A dual-identity framework for understanding lesbian experience. *Psychology of Women Quarterly, 29*, 129–139.

Flebus, G. B., & Montano, A. (2012). The multifactor internalized homophobia inventory. *Psychometrics, Methodology in Applied Psychology, 19*(3), 219–240.

Frost, D. M., & Meyer, I. H. (2009). Internalized homophobia and relationship quality among lesbians, gay men, and bisexuals. *Journal of Counseling Psychology, 56*(1), 97–109. doi:10.1037/a0012844. Special issue: Advances in Research with Sexual Minority People.

Gates, G. J. (2006). *Same-sex couples and the gay, lesbian, bisexual population: New estimates from the American Community Survey.* Los Angeles, CA: The Williams Institute on Sexual Orientation Law and Public Policy, UCLA School of Law.

Gates, G. J. (2011). *How many people are lesbian, gay, bisexual, and transgender?* University of California at Los Angeles: The Williams Institute. Retrieved from http://williamsinstitute.law.ucla.edu/wp-content/uploads/Gates-How-Many-People-LGBT-Apr-2011.pdf

Gay, Lesbian, & Straight Education Network. (2010). *The 2009 national school climate survey: The experiences of lesbian, gay, bisexual and transgender youth in our nation's schools.* New York, NY: GLSEN.

Gonsiorek, J. C. (1988). Mental health issues of gay and lesbian adolescents. *Journal of Adolescent Health Care, 9,* 114–122.

Hatzenbuehler, M. L., Dovidio, J. F., Nolen-Hoeksema, S., & Phills, C. E. (2009). An implicit measure of anti-gay attitudes: Prospective associations with emotion regulation strategies and psychological distress. *Journal of Experimental Social Psychology, 45*(6), 1316–1320.

Hendricks, M. L., & Testa, R. J. (2012). A Conceptual framework for clinical work with transgender and gender nonconforming clients: An Adaptation of the Minority Stress Model. *Professional Psychology: Research & Practice, 43*(5), 460–467.

Herek, G. M. (2000). The psychology of sexual prejudice. *Current Directions in Psychological Science, 9,* 19–22.

Herek, G. M. (2004). Beyond "homophobia": Thinking about sexual prejudice and stigma in the twenty-first century. *Sexuality Research & Social Policy, 1,* 6–24.

Herek, G. M. (2007). Confronting sexual stigma and prejudice: Theory and practice. *Journal of Social Issues, 63*(4), 905–925.

Herek, G. M. (2009). Hate crimes and stigma-related experiences among sexual minority adults in the United States: Prevalence estimates from a national probability sample. *Journal of Interpersonal Violence, 24*(1), 54–74.

Herek, G. M., Cogan, J. C., Gillis, J. R., & Glunt, E. K. (1998). Correlates of internalized homophobia in a community sample of lesbians and gay men. *Journal of the Gay and Lesbian Medical Association, 2,* 17–25.

Hill, D. B., & Willoughby, B. L. B. (2005). The development and validation of the genderism and transphobia scale. *Sex Roles, 53*(7/8), 531–544. doi:10.1007/s11199-005-7140-x

Institute of Medicine. (2011). *The health of lesbian, gay, bisexual, and transgender people: Building a foundation for better understanding.* Washington, DC: The National Academies Press.

Kimmel, S. B., & Mahlalik, J. R. (2005). Body image concerns of gay men: The roles of minority stress and conformity to masculine norms. *Journal of Consulting and Clinical Psychology, 73*, 1185–1190.

Kinsey, A. C., Pomeroy, W. B., & Martin, C. E. (1948). *Sexual behavior in the human male.* Philadelphia, PA: W. B. Saunders Company.

Levitt, H. M., Ovrebo, E., Anderson-Cleveland, M. B., Leone, C., Jeong, J. Y., Arm, J. R., . . . Horne, S. G. (2009). Balancing dangers: GLBT experience in a time of anti-GLBT legislation. *Journal of Counseling Psychology, 56*(1), 67–81.

Madon, S., Willard, J., Guyll, M., & Scherr, K. C. (2011). Self-fulfilling prophecies: Mechanisms, power, and links. *Social and Personality Compass, 8*, 578–590.

Martin, J., & Dean, L. (1987). *Ego-dystonic homosexuality scale.* Columbia University: School of Public Health.

Maslow, A. H., & Sakoda, J. (1952). Volunteer error in the Kinsey study. *Journal of Abnormal Psychology, 47*(2), 259–262.

Mayfield, W. (2001). The development of an internalized homonegativity inventory for gay men. *Journal of Homosexuality, 41*, 53–76.

Meyer, I. H. (1995). Minority stress and mental health in gay men. *Journal of Health and Social Behavior, 36*, 38–56. Retrieved from http://www.jstor.org/stable/2137286

Meyer, I. H. (2003). Prejudice, social stress, and mental health in lesbian, gay, and bisexual populations: Conceptual issues and research evidence. *Psychological Bulletin, 129*(5), 674–697. doi:10.1037/0033-2909.129.5.674

Meyer, I. H., & Dean, L. (1998). Internalized homophobia, intimacy, and sexual behavior among gay and bisexual men. In G. M. Herek (Ed.), *Stigma and sexual orientation: Understanding prejudice against lesbians, gay men, and bisexuals* (pp. 160–186). Thousand Oaks, CA: Sage.

Morrison, M. A., & Morrison, T. G. (2002). Development and validation of a scale measuring modern prejudice toward gay men and lesbian women. *Journal of Homosexuality, 43*(2), 15–37.

Nadal, K. L. (2010a). Sexual identity. In S. Goldstein & J. Naglieri (Eds.), *Encyclopedia of child behavior and development* (pp. 1344–1345). New York, NY: Springer.

Nadal, K. L. (2010b). Gender roles. In S. Goldstein & J. Naglieri (Eds.), *Encyclopedia of child behavior and development* (pp. 687–690). New York, NY: Springer.

Nadal, K. L. (2013). *That's so gay! Microaggressions and the lesbian, gay, bisexual, and transgender community.* Washington, DC: American Psychological Association.

Nadal, K. L., Issa, M., Leon, J., Meterko, V., Wideman, M., & Wong, Y. (2011). Sexual orientation microaggressions: "Death by a thousand cuts" for lesbian, gay, and bisexual youth. *Journal of LGBT Youth, 8*(3), 1–26.

Nadal, K. L., Rivera, D. P., & Corpus, M. J. H. (2010). Sexual orientation and transgender microaggressions in everyday life: Experiences of lesbians, gays, bisexuals, and transgender individuals. In D. W. Sue (Ed.), *Microaggressions and marginality: Manifestation, dynamics, and impact* (pp. 217–240). New York, NY: Wiley.

Nadal, K. L., Skolnik, A., & Wong, Y. (2012). Interpersonal and systemic micro-aggressions: Psychological impacts on transgender individuals and communities. *Journal of LGBT Issues in Counseling, 6*(1), 55–82.

Nadal, K. L., Wong, Y., Issa, M., Meterko, V., Leon, J., & Wideman, M. (2011). Sexual orientation microaggressions: Processes and coping mechanisms for lesbian, gay, and bisexual individuals. *Journal of LGBT Issues in Counseling, 5*(1), 21–46.

Ossana, S. M. (2000). Relationship and couples counseling. In R. M. Perez, K. A. DeBord, & J. J. Bieschke (Eds.), *Handbook of counseling and psychotherapy with lesbian, gay, and bisexual clients* (pp. 275–302). Washington, DC: American Psychological Association.

Peterson, T. L., & Gerrity, D. A. (2006). Internalized homophobia, lesbian identity development, and self-esteem in undergraduate women. *Journal of Homosexuality, 50,* 49–75.

Ross, M. W., & Rosser, B. R. S. (1996). Measurement and correlates of internalized homophobia: A factor analytic study. *Journal of Clinical Psychology, 52*(1), 15–21.

Rowen, C. J., & Malcolm, J. P. (2002). Correlates of internalized homo-phobia and homosexual identity formation in a sample of gay men. *Journal of Homosexuality, 43,* 77–92.

Saltzburg, S. (2004). Learning that an adolescent child is gay or lesbian: The parent experience. *Social Work, 49*(1), 109–118.

Shields, J. P., Cohen, R., Glassman, J. R., Whitaker, K., Franks, H., & Bertolini, I. (2012). Estimating population size and demographic characteristics of lesbian, gay, bisexual, and transgender youth in middle school. *Journal of Adolescent Health,* doi:10.1016/j.jadohealth.2012.06.016

Szymanski, D. M., & Chung, Y. B. (2001). The lesbian internalized homophobia scale: A rational/theoretical approach. *Journal of Homosexuality, 41*(2), 37–52.

Szymanski, D. M., Chung, Y. B., & Balsam, K. (2001). Psychosocial correlates of internalized homophobia in lesbians. *Measurement and Evaluation in Counseling and Development, 34,* 27–38.

Szymanski, D. M., Kashubeck-West, S., & Meyer, J. (2008). Internalized heterosexism: Measurement, psychosocial correlates, and research directions. *The Counseling Psychologist, 36*(4), 525–574.

Waldo, C. R., Hesson-McInnis, M. S., & D'Augelli, A. R. (1998). Antecedents and consequences of victimization of lesbian, gay, and bisexual young people: A structural model comparing rural university and urban samples. *American Journal of Community Psychology, 26*(2), 307–334. doi:10.1023/A:1022184704174

Walls, N. E. (2008). Toward a multidimensional understanding of heterosexism: The changing nature of prejudice. *Journal of Homosexuality, 55*(1), 1–51.

Weinberg, G. (1972). *Society and the healthy homosexual.* New York, NY: St. Martin's Press.

Weinstein, N., Ryan, W. S., DeHaan, C. R., Przybylski, A. K., Legate, N., & Ryan, R. M. (2012). Parental autonomy support and discrepancies between implicit and explicit sexual identities: Dynamics of self-acceptance and defense. *Journal of Personality and Social Psychology, 102*(4), 815–832.

Williamson. I. R. (2000). Internalized homophobia and health issues affecting lesbians and gay men. *Health Education Research, 15*(1), 97–107.

10

Disability and Internalized Oppression

Brian Watermeyer and Tristan Görgens

It may surprise some readers that disability appears in this book. To many, disability is not an issue associated with ideas such as discrimination or oppression, but a purely health-related concern. The truth, however, is that in the vast majority of disabled lives it is contextual factors such as discrimination and systemic exclusion that mediate social and economic destiny, not the nature of the body. In race it is not the skin that matters, but rather the meanings ascribed to that skin by ideology, and the consequent jaundiced ways in which society responds to its "inhabitant." So, too, in disability.

Over the past half-century, recognition of race, and more recently, gender, as axes of social injustice has gathered momentum in most parts of the world. The corresponding conversation regarding disability, by contrast, has hardly begun. While the international disability movement—in terms of one arguable date of departure—is now in its fourth decade, common-sense recognition of disability discrimination as a social ill to be corrected remains scarce. Structural, cultural, and interpersonal layers of disablism are woven into the very fabric of the social order, and remain invisible to most. In the influential words of Lennard J. Davis, "while we may acknowledge we are racist, we barely know we are ableist" (2002, p. 148).

For much of its life span, the discipline of disability studies, and the disability movement as a whole, has focused analysis on structural barriers to participation that keep disabled people at the margins.

This work is crucial, but it has become clear of late that more attention needs to be paid to the psychological nature of disablism, both in understanding what drives oppressive aversion to bodily difference, and what impressions are left on the emotional lives of individuals by prejudiced treatment. This chapter will aim to provide a broad, basic introduction to the social predicaments to which disabled people are subjected at the material, relational, and psychological levels, before offering some thoughts on conscientization and change. The first author (BW) is a disability studies researcher and a disabled person (severely sight impaired). The second author (TG) is a man living with quadriplegia, who provides the indented first person narratives to complement the chapter's research and theoretical material. We begin with a brief perspective on global disability prevalence.

THE WORLD'S DISABLED COMMUNITY

Definitions of disability are diverse and contested, and consequently estimates of prevalence vary (Coleridge, 1993). The fact that disability also occurs unevenly across contexts further complicates data description. The most comprehensive and sophisticated global data sets currently available are reflected in the World Report on Disability (WRD; World Health Organization [WHO], 2011). Data from the WHO's World Health Survey of 2002 to 2004 (used in the WRD) was drawn from 59 countries, and placed the average incidence of disability among adults (18 years and older) at 15.6% (WHO, 2011). This figure applies to adults described as experiencing "significant functional difficulties." The prevalence rate for adults with "very significant difficulties" was posted at 2.2%. In the context of familiar dilemmas to do with variation in research instruments for assessing disability, the WRD presents a combined worldwide population estimate of 720 million disabled people with "significant" functional difficulties, and a further 100 million with "severe" functional difficulties (WHO, 2011). Shakespeare and Officer (2011), in their review of the report, refer to "the world's one billion children and adults with disabilities" (p. 1491). Importantly, the international prevalence is set to expand significantly over coming decades, due to an aging population, a deteriorating natural environment, and the chronicity of war and violence (Albrecht & Verbrugge, 2000, in Braddock & Parish, 2001).

Perhaps surprisingly, evidence suggests that disability is more common in developed than developing contexts, although the majority of the world's disabled population reside in the developing world (Barnes & Mercer, 2005). Three sets of reasons contribute to this. First, life expectancy is higher in wealthier countries, leading to increased incidence of age-related disability. Second, greater access to health care and other social service supports means that persons suffering congenital impairment, illness, or accident in developed countries survive these experiences more often, swelling disabled numbers. In concert with this consideration is the fact that people are more likely to self-identify, or be *diagnosed*, as disabled in service-rich contexts. Lastly, in the developing world, less conspicuous impairments such as dyslexia or mild learning disability may go unnoticed, or be seen as not causing sufficient functional limitation to embody a disability (Barnes & Mercer, 2005; Coleridge, 1993; WHO, 2011).

As one approaches disability prevalence, it is apt to hold in mind that variations in functionality are inherent to the human condition. As we shall see, the ideology of statistically plotted normalcy, which has become fundamental to western conceptions of self and citizenship over the past century, has sustained heavy critique (Davis, 1995). At its heart, this strand of science charts the outline of an illusory boundary between normalcy and derangement, functioning to justify a host of social inequities to follow. Despite this prominent myth, the statistical reality is that the average person reaching 75 years of age will spend 13 years of life with functional limitation (Marks, 1999a). Thus, disability defines humanity, rather than diverging from it (Davis, 2002).

DISABLIST OPPRESSION: A BRIEF HISTORICAL PERSPECTIVE

World culture is replete with examples of how bodily difference is equated with personal shortcoming or moral laxity (Asch & Fine, 1988; Garland-Thomson, 1995; Morris, 1993). We carry deeply embedded prejudices based on the assumption that human worth is somehow reflected in somatic characteristics (Mitchell & Snyder, 1997). Physical attributes are by their nature compelling, potentially dominating our judgment during the important first moments of meeting. The body's materiality provides a *corporeal anchor*, which can lend an illusion of realness to fantasies about the other (Garland-Thomson, 1995). The universally powerful marker of skin color is a prime example of this (Frosh, 1989).

Cultural associations with impairment cement ideas of damage, rejection, frailty, and lack to the disabled figure (Marks, 1999a; Wendell, 1996). Simultaneously, modernity's technological striving for the bodily ideal identifies the *owner* of an *errant* body as not only undesirable, but morally negligent and irresponsible (Turner, 2001). We habitually receive observations regarding how closely our bodies mirror the cultural ideal as compliments, placing those with unconventional bodies in an invidious light.

Tropes of western capitalist culture position our health and vitality, our ability to work long hours and resist disease or aging, as admirable achievements, not the products of biological chance. However, such *compliments* have a very different ring when heard from within a disabled body (Wendell, 1997).

Denigrating social responses to bodily difference have a very long history (Stiker, 1982). Religious and artistic representations of the *marked* body dating from mediaeval times show clear associations with maleficence and shame. The English word "monster" is derived from the Latin *monstra*—translated literally as "a sign" (Garland-Thomson, 1997). According to Garland-Thomson, this etymology demonstrates how bodily difference, and in particular birth malformations, have historically appeared as sinister messages or punishments from the supernatural realm. The *Monster of Ravenna* (b. 1512) provides a documented account of how particular bodily impairments in infancy were interpreted as specific signals of divine anger poured out on a wayward humanity (Fiedler, 1978). These cultural associations may at first glance appear fanciful, but are argued to be products of deeply held aversions to physical difference that remain prevalent in current times (Marks, 1999a; Sinason, 1992; Watermeyer, 2006, 2013). Examination of the emotional struggles of parents trying to make sense of the birth of a congenitally disabled infant provides a picture of our shared cultural internalizations about the unusual body. Note, though, that these concerns must be seen in the context of the often inadequate social service support such parents receive (Ferguson, 2001).

Over the 19th and early 20th centuries, the cultural phenomenon of the freak show enjoyed its *golden age*, presenting audiences with formalized opportunities to participate in the demeaning of disabled people (Bogdan, 1988). According to Bogdan, the freak show functioned in the early United States as a mechanism for collective othering—building a new, self-idealizing nation based on the denigration of out-groups. Through the choreography of the show, racial, ethnic, and bodily contrasts were reified into the illusion of inherent human difference, serving to justify a world of structural inequalities to come (Garland-Thomson, 1997). Notwithstanding this evidence of oppression rooted in cultural representations, materialist historians of disability view the rise of industrialization in Europe as the pivotal moment in solidifying disability inequality (Finkelstein, 1980; Oliver, 1990). The materialist view, rooted in Marxist theory, regards exclusion from the world of work as the "most important factor in what happens to disabled people" (Oliver, 2001, p. 149). During industrialization, the sudden increase in need for labor fostered measurement and separation of individuals on the basis of functional ability, formalizing the marginal position of disabled people (Finkelstein, 1980). Later, these divisions were solidified into segregation through the bureaucratic assigning of labor status and the rise of institutionalization; the administrative category of "the disabled" had been born (Barnes, 1990).

Meanwhile, the rise of eugenics in the late 1800s began to propound an ideology of racial purification, which saw the elimination of *inferior* genetic stock as central to overcoming social problems such as poverty, crime, and mental illness (Trent, 1994). Davis (2002) implores that we never forget that it was physically and intellectually impaired persons who were first to be massacred in Nazi death camps. As many as 300,000 disabled people lost their lives, and unlike in the cases of other "racial undesirables," no prosecutions for these crimes were ever initiated (Marks, 1999b; Ravaud & Stiker, 2001). The growth of the eugenics movement occurred alongside the 20th century's burgeoning medicalization of disability, as unusual bodies increasingly attracted subduing controls characterized by Foucault (1979, p. 54) as the "racisms of the state." Eugenic principles and biological medicine combined in policies of enforced sterilization of, in particular, intellectually impaired persons that in some countries lasted well into the second half of the century (Pernick, 1997). Such policies, and the eugenic movement itself, were by no means intellectually or politically marginal; for many decades eugenic principles were championed by liberal voices in Europe and the United States (Hubbard, 1997). However, disabled and nondisabled alike were becoming ever more subject to an ideology of medical measurement that positioned all in some relation to a statistical normalcy (Fujiura & Rutkowski-Kmitta, 2001). The familiar notion of the *normal* emerged as late as the 19th century, facilitated by the development of modern statistics and the bell curve (Davis, 1995). Prior to this, ideas about human value rested on divine rather than corporeal standards, positioning human imperfection as a shared universal. However, as its divisive force took hold, *ableist* bias appeared not as a feature of a bigoted minority, but as the essence of enlightenment and of progress (Davis, 1995, 2002).

In the modern world, the continuing systemic exclusion suffered by disabled people rests on the institutional and cultural application of a *medical model* logic to disability inequality (Abberley, 1996; Barnes, 1990; Barnes & Mercer, 2005; Barnes, Oliver & Barton, 2002a, 2002b; Oliver, 1986). This label does not apply in any homogenizing way to medical science or its practitioners, but rather to a medicalizing view of society that places biological factors at center stage in making sense of social reality. It is fair to say that the core concern of Western medicine has been to identify and seek to correct structural or functional *defects* of the body (Engel, 1977; Kleinman, 1987). This has led, in health care as well as society at large, to a severe overemphasis on bodily factors in making sense of the marginal socioeconomic destiny of most disabled people. Correspondingly, little or no attention tends to be paid to the profound (and correctable) structural injustices that in fact are pivotal in most disabled lives (Swain, Finkelstein, French, & Oliver, 1993). In effect, what is a problem of discrimination becomes reduced to one of individual biological shortcomings, effectively blaming the victims of social injustice (Oliver, 1990, 1996). Disabled as well as nondisabled people are steeped in this logic, recapitulating the message that "the problem"—and cause of your marginality—is inside you. Some disability studies writers have labeled this approach a "personal tragedy theory" (Oliver, 1986), constructing disability as leading to an unavoidable, ideologically neutral inability to take part in the life of the community. In the words of Paul Abberley (1996), the medical model functions to "link together the experiences of an individual in a logic which attributes disadvantage to nature" (p. 62). Social factors implicated in keeping disabled people at the margins consequently remain unaddressed. As shared by TG, the pervasiveness of medical model thinking across society is demonstrated in the following:

> The "personal tragedy," medicalized focus on urgent rehabilitation of the "defective body" and the traditionalist discourses of disability as a form of divine or universal punishment can, in my experience, intersect in a powerful way. My most vivid experience of this, among many other examples, was during my rehabilitation period in hospital. As part of my rehab I would push around an open parking lot of a public library that was next to the hospital. This parking lot received a lot of foot traffic, primarily pedestrians walking from the railway station to the local CBD (Central Business District). I was ceaselessly amazed that people would take time out of their day, and actually break stride and approach me, to react in one way or another to my disability. The content of the reaction ran the full gamut—some paused to commend me on my bravery for being out in public, others needed to remark on how horrible it was that this happened to me. But a surprisingly large proportion, although still smaller than the previous two stock responses, needed to come over to explain that this was undoubtedly a sign of some moral or religious fault in my past, and that only by throwing myself on the mercy of God/Jesus could I become whole again. For someone whose identity as a "disabled person" was still raw and ill-defined, these moments filled me with a latent terror and foreboding about my new place in the world. All three reinforce the Otherness of the disabled body—an experience that endlessly deepens one's sense of alienation from society and oneself. These moments also exemplify my ongoing experience that a form of exoticism and vulnerability is associated with a visible disability, that somehow gives certain members of the public claim to your body and identity. Those who are willing to acknowledge your "tragedy" are compelled to react in some concrete way (whether it is to attempt to ameliorate the effects or blame you for its occurrence).

As we explain below, the urgency of this action indicates how intensely people need to psychically split off and dissociate the reality that we are reminded of by the sight of a physical impairment—the fragility of our bodies and lives, and ultimately our own mortality.

OPPRESSION IN THE AGE OF MODERNITY

The socioeconomic predicaments of the vast majority of disabled people around the globe remain dire. Even in the world's wealthy states, disabled people tend to be among the poorest of the poor (Barnes, Oliver, & Barton, 2002a). In the words of Schriner (2001), it is no exaggeration to declare that disabled people are "almost universally on the bottom rung of the socio-economic ladder" (p. 645). National rates of unemployment for disabled people regularly exceed 80%; correspondingly, average personal income typically falls into the lowest decile (Braddock & Parish, 2001). Most available figures apply to the developed world, but one may reasonably assume the position of disabled people in poorer contexts to be that much more precarious. Economic deprivation is maintained by a host of structural factors, beginning with stark inequality in access to education. According to one approximation, 2% of disabled children in the developing world receive a "meaningful" education (Flood, 2005); it is common for disabled children—especially girls—to be denied any education at all (UNESCO, 1995; UNESCAP, 2003 in Barnes & Mercer, 2005). The institutional gatekeeping of nonaccess to education may be used to effectively legitimate lifelong inequalities, through the attribution of low occupational status to failures in educational achievement (Harber & Davies, 1997 in Barton & Armstrong, 2001).

The history of disability is, in essence, a story of segregation, of isolation. The drive to create separation between disabled children and adults and their peers is evident everywhere, in forms ranging from elaborate policies of institutionalization to simple cultural distancing (Michalko, 2002; Stiker, 1982). At the heart of these phenomena is the persistent message that bodily or psychological difference disqualifies one from the ability or right to participate in the *mainstream* life of the community (Murphy, 1987). In poorer countries, simple economic deprivation cements this exclusion by denying access to crucial resources like transportation (Mutua, 2001) and basic assistive devices such as wheelchairs (Barnes & Mercer, 2005). Even in societies where disability-related social services are relatively plentiful, disabled people have typically been placed in life-worlds characterized by "a more pervasive form of segregation . . . than the most rigid policies of apartheid enacted by racist governments" (Drake, 2001; Hahn, 1997, p. 174).

The exclusion of disabled people from participation at all levels of community life is enacted via one quite simple reality—a social world prepared for the exclusive use of others. Built environments, administrative procedures, social service protocols, communications media, leisure amenities, technology for use in the home or workplace—these and every other trapping of social life are, almost without exception, constructed with only the needs of the nondisabled majority in mind. In Harlan Hahn's (2002) words, disabled citizens of both rich and poor countries face "formidable barriers to housing, transportation and freedom of movement, as well as exclusion or segregation in education and public accommodations" (p. 165). What is created in individual disabled lives is a sustained experience of unwelcome, through constant, even traumatic collision with resources that are only beneficial to others. The psychological impact of consistently confronting impossible barriers to participation must for many be substantial (Watermeyer, 2012a, 2013). Economic status undoubtedly mediates such experience to some degree, but as shown by TG below, does not define it.

> As a middle-class inhabitant of a developing world city, Cape Town in South Africa, I can never ignore the privilege of access that my economic position affords me. I am not forced to use public transport, or to rely on the state to provide me with health care or educational or economic opportunities. The physical, emotional, and social strain that depending on these often highly stretched, poorly resourced public services can involve is enough to completely disable any attempt to engage with opportunities in the public realm, or with mainstream society altogether. This stark inequity is underscored by the minister of finance's repeated utterance that the disability grant (which in 2012 is $130 a month) cannot be increased because it would heighten the incentive to "game the system." Imagine if your quality-of-life was determined by a politician or technocrat, based on the amount of bureaucratic hassle you represent. Worse, this technocrat publicly announces that your relegation to desperate poverty is an acceptable sacrifice in order to minimize the trouble you represent to the system.
>
> Yet in my own middle-class life I am reminded by constant, grinding experiences that this city wasn't built for me—sidewalks have no indentations, making it difficult to cross roads, the entrances to public and private buildings overwhelmingly have steps and narrow doorways that make them inaccessible, and so on. The striking thing is how habituated one becomes to living in a hostile environment. I recently travelled to São Paolo in Brazil—my first international experience since my impairment. I could not get over the feeling of moving around a city where both public and private spaces and buildings were mandated (and had actually complied) to be accessible to wheelchairs. This was a vivid reminder that the developing world can be made accessible and enabling. It is more often a matter of political will, rather than a question of whether there is the budget for it or not (the two cities are comparable on a number of economic indices).

Occupying a world in which resources taken for granted by others are either absent or unusable may create a chronic experience of alienation—of not belonging (Charlton, 1998). Material deprivation can present as a malignant confirmation of demeaning cultural ideas about what disabled life is like, or worth—tangible aspects of social treatment that inevitably carry personal and psychological resonances (Clegg, 2006; Watermeyer, 2013). As we have seen, the disabled identity carries emotive prejudices, associating its bearers with ideas of lack, frailty, shame, dependency, and rejection. According to the critical psychoanalytic view of disablist oppression (Marks, 1999a; Watermeyer, 2006, 2013), the devaluing of disabled people is in part motivated by unconscious, intrapsychic factors. In this line of argument, all humans have accumulated a range of largely unconscious existential conflicts to do with ability, acceptability, and worth, by virtue of having negotiated the struggles of development. One means of managing these disquieting emotional aspects is through projection onto a devalued out-group. The marginal, demeaned, and deprived position of a majority of the world's disabled people, as well as the perceived *fact* of impairment, makes this group available as a convincing target. Gill (2001) comments in this regard that it is "more difficult to dispute a distortion of fact than an outright fiction" (p. 366). In what has become a powerful, familiar phrase, disabled people in modern society function as "dustbins for disavowal" (Shakespeare, 1994)—an out-group culturally and materially prepared as symbolic containers for the "psychic dirt" of the balance of society. The capacity of disability to speak to anxiety-ridden, unconscious psychological aspects within the observer is attested to in the following passage:

> One of the first things that people want to know when they meet me is, "how did this happen?" The framing of the question depends on the individual—some ask with a sense of concern, others with an embarrassed air of curiosity, and still others with an interrogatory overtone. Initially I responded to it as a question triggered by curiosity, since disabled people remain so invisible that I am often one of the first that individuals have encountered one-on-one. But I later became familiar with a follow-up question that reveals the anxiety underpinning the conversation. "You see, I broke my neck diving into the ocean"—and this is where my response usually ends. The follow-up question inevitably revolves around the notion of blame. It could either be "Oh, so you jumped off a rock then?" or "Were you horsing around?" or "Oh, that was silly!" All are framed with the presumption that I am responsible for my injury; that this wouldn't happen to a "normal" person who was behaving "properly." But the sad reality is that it was the result of a freak accident. A sandbank had built up under the surface of the water far out to sea and I just happened to dive into that little patch of ocean. This impulse to blame the victim is triggered by the need to disavow the possibility of

this happening to "us"; to deny the reality that such a horrific event could happen to just anybody. We have a strong need to reject recognition of the fragility of our lives and bodies, and this is most easily accomplished by confirming that disabled people "deserved it" in some way.

Disabled selves are shaped through processes of lifelong socialization saturated with devaluing meanings, which work to prepare the individual for a marginal position in society (Watermeyer & Swartz, 2008). From the first moments of life, congenitally impaired children are almost certainly placed on a very different trajectory from their nondisabled contemporaries, involving radically different social responses at every level, from the family to the institution to the cultural world (Watermeyer, 2002a). Medicalizing logic is hegemonic at both institutional and colloquial levels, serving to create and justify deep divisions between the disabled child and her peers. Media representations either ignore the disabled community altogether, or mirror disabled lives as damaged or pathological (Hevey, 1992; Norden, 1994). Disability charity organizations, notwithstanding the essential services that they at times fulfill, reconstruct the idea that disabled people are unable to function as citizens, and thus may only survive in society through benevolence based on pity (Rioux, 2002). Within this discourse, participation is framed not as a human right for which governments are accountable, but as a charitable *add-on* that turns on the chance kindness of individuals. Dependence on kindness for essential access has the potential to corrode human relationship (Watermeyer & Swartz, 2008). Some relational consequences of living in an inaccessible society are illustrated by TG in the paragraphs that follow.

> This attitude is illustrated when I travel for business. When I book to stay in a hotel or go to a venue that I am not familiar with there is often an exaggerated process of checking the accessibility of the building and room. It is a hard-won lesson that able-bodied people live their lives blind to barriers to access, unless they consciously re-examine their environment with different eyes. On innumerable occasions I have been assured to the point of exasperation on the phone that a building is accessible, only to arrive and discover that there are one or two steps in front of the entrance or the lift. Then there is much apologizing and shaking of heads, and assuring of me that, "I just didn't ever see those before."
>
> But such "blindness" is often contrasted with exaggerated levels of "consideration" in other circumstances. I have been reprimanded on endless occasions for joining the queue when checking in at the airport. If a staff member notices me, he or she will invariably rush over and demand that I skip the queue, all the while scolding me for not doing this initially. While I don't have a strict rule about this kind of "special treatment," it is striking that it is most often applied in circumstances where it

is not strongly needed (such as skipping queues) while the inaccessibility of the everyday world is normalized. For example, the response, "Oh, we can just carry you up those stairs," ignoring the implications for my dignity or everyone's safety, is common. Also conspicuous is how annoyed people can be that I don't innately know about or claim the "special treatment" (when it's available), and how proud people are to be helping out someone "in my situation." There is nothing wrong with being proud about this impulse. But it does reinforce the experience that, as a disabled person, you are "lucky" to gain access to certain spaces or experiences. The implication is that under different circumstances you may well not be so lucky, and that you and your needs remain an anomaly that require "extra effort" for the rest of society to satisfy. The possible result is a toxic emotional cocktail, where one is grateful to individuals for making the effort to ensure you are included, but undercut by an awareness of not being welcome in the same way that everyone else is. Also present is guilt over the impact one's "special" needs have on others.

Social responses to the disabled figure take place against the backdrop of a modernist project of control, autonomy, and progress, to which *bodily frailty* appears as a nemesis (Hughes, 2002). Disability is a harbinger of all that modernity hopes to defeat; death, imperfection, fallibility, un-control. Narcissistic culture (Lasch, 1978) rejects these human realities in the most forceful terms, opting for reliance on surfaces, technologies, and self-aggrandisement as escape (Frosh, 1991). A world of controlling, corrective, distancing, demeaning and otherwise perverse social responses to the disabled community may be tracked back to the narcissistic psyche's drive to subdue its shames; ultimately, its losses.

Cultural and biomedical responses to disability combine in what is termed the imperative of *normalization*, demanding that disabled people pursue the closest approximation of normalcy with a tireless, even moral zeal (Foucault, 1976; Marks, 1999a). Although rehabilitation services are essential, these may at times play out at the level of ideology as a drive to uniformity, failing to question the aversion to differences that is at the heart of inequality (Rioux, 1994; Stiker, 1982; Turner, 2001). In disabled lives, medical professionals often bear a powerful, continuous influence, and yet evidence suggests that a majority of practitioners are at best skeptical regarding disabled people living fulfilling lives (Bach & Tilton, 1994; Shakespeare, Iezzoni, & Groce, 2009). Congenitally impaired children in the developed world may undergo early lives in which play is largely displaced by rehabilitation and therapy, embedding the obligation to "normalize" (French & Swain, 2001). An excessive, even punitive striving for greater levels of *independence* appears at times in rehabilitation programs with a traditional, biomedical basis (French, 1993). Unfortunately, little in the training of biomedical health professionals is likely to adequately illuminate the complex, socially engendered nature of disability struggle. In addition, since health professionals are primarily required to *cure*, the chronic *intractable* reality of disability may appear as an awkward, irredeemable intrusion on biomedicine's project (Asch & Fine, 1997; Sinason, 1992). Experiences of *medical socialization* may thus, over many years, sediment feelings of self-blame within disabled people, obscuring the influence of contextual factors on participation (Coleridge, 1993). Below, TG reflects on his own identity transition arising from adventitious impairment, and the imperatives toward normalization that consequently came into view.

> The experience of becoming disabled, as opposed to growing up with a disability, plunges you into a liminal space in which everything you knew about yourself and your body, your day-to-day life, your preferences and your dislikes, your relationships with both your closest friends and family members and mere acquaintances, and all of your hopes and aspirations for your future, need to be redefined. I was relatively lucky insofar as I was 20, in my second year at university, unmarried and had no kids, and had an incredibly supportive family who were willing to assist me in the journey. Most of the people I was in rehab with weren't so lucky—they were the primary breadwinners for their family, or had small children to raise, or were rejected by their families and their friends as an overwhelming burden that they couldn't or weren't willing to take on. Figuring out who you are and what you want from (your new) life in the context of those immediate and all-consuming burdens remains unimaginable to me.
>
> One of the biggest aspects of this remaking of "Who am I?" is making strategic choices about how you are going to invest your energy (something that is incredibly precious for the first few years after a spinal cord injury). One aspect of life that it becomes expressed in is the relative importance of independence and normality to you. Do you want to be able to do absolutely everything for yourself? Or are you willing to accept some kinds of support and not others? Or will you remain completely dependent on other people? This seems like a relatively elementary choice, right? You want to be as independent as possible, surely? But this choice is made against a background of contextual factors and the realities of your emotional state. For some people the only way they can recover emotionally and gain a sense of self is through an overwhelming investment of time, energy, and sometimes money in their independence—over time they will learn how to feed themselves, dress themselves, drive for themselves, and manage all the other aspects of their lives. But, depending on your injury, this may be a goal that you need to set aside a number of years to achieve.
>
> I decided to devote as much time and energy as was required to regain the levels of independence I needed to re-enter those aspects of

my life that I found most meaningful. My immediate goal was being able to go back to university and finish my degree. But this meant that after I had learnt how, I chose not to put on my shoes every morning—an ordeal that could take up to 20 minutes because of my level of impairment. I was content to ask somebody else to do this so that I could spend that time pursuing other goals that I thought were more important.

While the professions are steadily reforming themselves to become more client-centered, these kinds of choices remain an anathema to most rehab staff. Their raison d'être is addressing impairment and ensuring independence, and it is very difficult for many to hear and respect the idea that some forms of independence aren't worth the effort. It is a small point but one that makes a huge difference in the early days of rehab (and can have a lasting effect on the degree to which you are willing to draw upon professional expertise in the future).

A range of impairments present the need for personal assistance with the performance of daily tasks. These may be work-related (e.g., reading assistance for a sight-impaired person), or part of private life (such as washing and dressing assistance for a physically impaired person). Such helping relationships are typically complex and layered, involving dynamics of accommodation, gratitude, uncertainty about entitlement, and so forth (Watermeyer & Swartz, 2008). The predicament of putting others before oneself—of waiting, of accommodating—is familiar across all aspects of many disabled lives, by virtue of the need for help in managing an inaccessible world. As in charity discourse, what may be at work is an unspoken idea that disabled individuals, instead of having a right to the means of participation, should remain grateful for unreliable services provided through kindness, not citizenship rights. It is unfair and inappropriate to stereotype persons involved in disability-related altruistic work, but evidence suggests that motivations are often deeply personal and partially hidden (Watermeyer, 2013). There may, consequently, be confusion as to whose lifestyle choices are respected, with the voice of *rehabilitation* or *care* at times dominating the voice of the disabled experience (Kleinman, Das & Lock, 1997; Marks, 1999a). The complex, layered nature of helping relationships can be clearly seen in TG's narrative below.

As a quadriplegic I require full-time care to enable me to live a relatively normal and full life. I therefore employ two carers who work on a rotational basis, a week on and a week off, to take care of all of my needs. As I live in the developing world, the state offers no direct support for assistance to disabled people. Assistance thus represents a significant additional financial cost that I must cover as an individual. I am now married, after living with my parents on leaving hospital—I have always had a lot of support from people who love me. But a hard-won lesson has been to never be completely dependent on the people you love for your physical care (if this is a choice available to you). The grinding reality of dependency on others to help you perform basic everyday tasks, and the complicated emotional journey that is often part of navigating such a reality for both the person receiving the care and the carer, means that you don't want these tensions to become blended with the everyday emotional give-and-take of close or intimate relationships. Dependency means having to wait for people, having to correct them when they aren't doing a task to your liking, having to ask people to do things they would rather not, or delay or forego things in their own lives to take care of your needs. You don't want these kinds of frustrations intermingling with the everyday emotional life of important relationships.

Unfortunately, beyond being an employer, there are a range of other emotional demands that having carers places on your life. You become deeply affected by two other people, including what's happening with their families, because it affects whether they turn up on time, or their performance, or just their attitude. You have people who share your home and your most intimate spaces, and your most trivial and significant moments. In a developing context they are often people who are committed to caring, but this is mixed with desperate economic circumstances—they need the job even if they don't love it. This will complicate their relationship with you, the people in your life, and the tasks they have to perform. These relational complexities—in many contexts—are part of navigating a disabled identity.

Psychological accounts of disability have historically been dominated by an individual, decontextualized approach (Goodley & Lawthom, 2006). Such work has typically been styled after grief and bereavement theory, which sees the onset of disability as an experience of loss that must be *worked through* in order to arrive at a point of *acceptance* (Ferguson & Asch, 1989; Finkelstein & French, 1993). These ideas foster interventions based on the assumption that impairment leads to psychiatric problems (a "psychopathology of disability"), rather than foregrounding the pathogenic effects of social factors such as discrimination (a "psychology of disablism"; Linton, 1998). It is for this reason that the discipline of disability studies, as well as the international disability movement more broadly, has largely dissociated itself from psychological theorizing. The strongly materialist focus of *mainstream* disability studies has, however, been criticized by authors who believe that conceptualizing the psychological nature of life for impaired people in a disablist world is imperative (Crow, 1992; Hughes & Paterson, 1997; Morris, 1992; Thomas, 1999; Wendell, 1996).

INTERNALIZED OPPRESSION IN DISABLED LIVES

In the midst of lifelong socialization steeped in prejudice, disabled people struggle to see their oppression and their rights clearly (Biko, 1978; Charlton, 1998; Coleridge, 1993; Frosh, 1991). Unlike members of other minorities (e.g., ethnic), most disabled people grow up in families as a minority of one, without the empathy and validation granted by sharing an oppressed predicament with trusted others. The belief that one's inherent qualities make participation impossible or unreasonable encourages passive acquiescence in the face of inequality. Disabled people reared in such circumstances may express gratitude for what is, in fact, a profoundly marginal position based on identifiable injustice. Without at least the partial interpellation (that is, collusion) of disabled people, the appalling social destiny of most of the world's disabled minority would not be the stubborn, ubiquitous reality that it is (Watermeyer, 2012a).

In a world where one is consistently exposed to prejudiced assumptions about ability and competence, it makes sense to many disabled people to disguise their impairment. This may come in the form of "passing," where (for example) epilepsy or a sensory impairment is never mentioned in order to avoid a distancing, demeaning, or otherwise judgmental response (French, 1999; Thomas, 1999). At work here is the sedimented reality of a *medicalized culture*, in which repeated messaging disqualifies those with bodily difference from a legitimate claim to full citizenship. It is difficult to overstate the hegemony of the body ideal in western societies, with its concomitant denigration of any and all variations.

In the lives of persons with intellectual impairment, Sinason (1992) describes how the ongoing experience of a social world that expresses doubt and ascribed shame regarding ability may manifest in a "hibernatory" withdrawal from learning. In such individuals, the trauma of being viewed by all as incompetent renders it too emotionally dangerous to risk venturing into what Vygotsky (1978) termed the "zone of proximal development." This is the space of thought and action that is just beyond what one is confidently capable of, which must be entered for developmental shifts in ability. Due to being denied the emotional support and affirmation necessary for learning, intellectually impaired persons have been shown to manifest functional limitations that exceed identifiable organically based deficits (Sinason, 1992). What we see here is an amplified version of a difficulty faced by a vast range of disabled people—that is, the quandary of attempting to participate and function in social and occupational life in the face of substantial, even overwhelming expectations from the social world that one is not capable of doing so. For many, a withdrawal into passive acquiescence to these denigrating imputations is unavoidable, leading to lives of unrealized potential and damaged self-worth. With painful clarity, Micheline Mason expresses her own experience of internalized oppression as follows:

> Once oppression has been internalized, little force is needed to keep us submissive. We harbor inside ourselves the pain and the memories, the fears and the confusions, the negative self images and low expectations, turning them into weapons with which we re-injure ourselves every day of our lives. (as cited in Marks, 1999a, p.24)

Escaping the clutches of toxic social mirroring is the work of a painful confrontation with one's own history and consequent sense of self. Coleridge (1993) takes care to acknowledge how disabled people are very often drawn into playing a role in the chronicity of unequal relationships, stating that "discrimination and prejudice create the sense of being disabled that leads to further discrimination and prejudice" (p. 36). In order to grow, develop, and explore one's potential, all require expressions of faith from credible authority figures that one is both able and entitled to do so. Without these affirmations of potential one literally has "nothing to go on" in confronting the unknowns of a challenging world. Disabled people are more likely than others to be deprived of the healthy narcissistic resources that humans need for robust self-belief (Watermeyer, 2013). It is important to take care here to avoid stereotyping—we must not assume that disabled people lack self-belief. However, it is reasonable to suggest that disabled people are often called to attain self-belief despite the imputations of much of their social mirroring, rather than because of its support.

The pressure to attain the cultural ideal in terms of body shape and function is, according to one theoretical approach, demonstrated by the prominence in mass media of feats of "overcoming adversity" achieved by disabled people (Watermeyer & Swartz, 2008). Here, awareness of the powerful negative assumptions that disability elicits has led individuals to devote immense energy—even to the point of self-harm—to "stereotype-busting." Viewers' hearts are warmed by accounts of how, "despite their limitations" people have the courage to triumph over their *tragedy* by performing fantastic physical feats, such as climbing mountains or swimming straits. It is not the intention to pass any judgment on disabled people's lifestyle choices—on the contrary, the right to participation is at the core of an emancipatory view of disability. Instead, the aim is to direct attention at how this cultural phenomenon illuminates an everyday problem in disabled lives. This predicament involves being required to define oneself *in opposition* to a highly emotionally charged, negative cultural ascription. What we see in the imperative to show that one is "un-disabled" (Watermeyer, 2013) is a recognition that, unless one manages to *disprove* ascribed stereotypes, one is at risk of being defined by these completely. The result is an absurdly limited repertoire of identity possibilities available (at least in *mainstream* culture) to disabled lives, spanning the dichotomy between "invalid" and unreal, idealized hero(ine). Disabled people, in understandable fear of being stereotyped as dependent, damaged, or helpless, may grow into assuming public personas that repudiate any evidence of what may, in fact, be universally human fallibility. Constraints on what may be acknowledged publicly, and even to the self, lead one away from self-knowledge and self-acceptance, both of which are extremely important in the work of personal emancipation (Watermeyer, 2013). If one's energies are often devoted to demonstrating who one is *not*, this may render it more difficult to know who one *is*—an essential starting point in building an articulate, entitled, and secure voice of advocacy against discrimination.

What the foregoing suggests is that many disabled people occupy social spaces of relative invisibility, where authentic expression of experience and self comes with immense risk (Gill, 2001; Watermeyer, 2013; Watermeyer & Swartz, 2008). This ambivalence has translated into difficulty with developing the disabled minority into a unified, politically mobilized group campaigning for citizenship rights (Scotch, 1988). By far the majority of the world's disabled community would not identify themselves personally as disabled, let alone take the risk of a politicized "coming out" (Scotch, 1988). The disabled identity remains, for the most part, so devalued as to support such choices, leaving the community so dispersed as to make political conscientization very difficult

DISABILITY, OPPRESSION, AND MENTAL HEALTH

As explained above, part of life with a devalued ascribed identity is working to disprove imputed assumptions about who one is, rather than exploring—being—oneself (Watermeyer, 2009). What this presents is the risk of a "loss of self," as it is in authentic relating that movement toward greater psychological integration takes place (Rustin, 1996). The evocative nature of the disabled imago is such that the cultural atmosphere around disability is perpetually thick with cross-cutting imperatives, messages and assumptions about what disability is, what it does, what disabled people *need*, and so forth. The intense, often split debates within social services regarding theorizing and *intervening* in relation to disability bears testimony to this (Sinason, 1992). Consider, for example, these possible discursive forces at work in a congenitally impaired individual's life: the anxiety of well-meaning, distressed parents; the bewildering exile of segregated special schooling; the imperatives to normalize an early life of rehabilitation, therapy, and unspoken pathologization; the demand to gratefully acquiesce implicit in some disability social service institutions; the denigration and distancing of social responses from the schoolyard to the workplace; the physical and cultural unwelcome of a social world of inaccessible facilities and procedures; the list continues. In the face of this hum of judgments, expectations, and attributions, anyone would find it difficult to maintain a clear, grounded, and appropriately entitled awareness of self.

Elsewhere I draw on Frantz Fanon's (1952/1986, 1963/2004) classic work on race in constructing a picture of the psychological predicament of disabled people occupying a world in which the culturally condensed bodily ideal always comes with "nondisabled-ness" as part of the package (Watermeyer, 2012a, 2013). In these circumstances, things that might be aspired to in the life of a disabled child—a social group, a sports team, a comic book hero, film and fashion icons—all exist on the opposite end of a clearly delineated discursive boundary, separating disabled and damaged from nondisabled and ideal. Normal processes of identification with idealized figures thus place the disabled (and Black) child in a quandary, where aspiring to be like one's heroes involves an internal rejection of self (Davids, 1996). Film and media representations of disabled people are implicated here, through failing to mirror disabled people as normatively complex humans, muddling through life's struggles and possibilities. Instead, Hollywood consistently utilizes the disabled figure as a mechanism for delivering messages of morality, redemption, and the like, reinforcing the stereotype that *normal life* with impairment is out of the question.

Conceptualizing emotional trauma in disabled lives is politically thorny, due to the long history of *victim-blaming* pathologization of disabled people at the hands of psychology (Goodley & Lawthom, 2006; Linton, 1998). Disability studies has, understandably, been reluctant to devote resources to gathering epidemiological data on the mental health of the disabled minority, although this is beginning to change. One approach (Watermeyer, 2013) eschews any distinction between "disability struggle" and the broad trawl of human distress, rejecting traditional psychology's attempts at conceptualizing *disability issues* (Vash & Crewe, 2004). Instead, this model draws on critical psychoanalysis in making provision for the universality of unconscious existential conflicts—that is, psychological parts with the potential to attack the self. What *disablism* creates in the lives of impaired people is a world of perverse mirroring—a sustained assault on identity—which tends to selectively confirm and re-enliven these more troubled parts of self (Watermeyer, 2013). Disabled people are often denied the material and relational resources we all need to successfully shore up our healthy narcissism, in order to stave off fears regarding human fallibility to which all are constitutionally prone.

There is some evidence to suggest that mood and other psychiatric disorders are under-diagnosed among disabled people. Herr and Phil (1992), in reviewing cases of disabled people who had submitted requests to United States courts to be allowed assistance in suicide, note how psychiatric assessments of the individuals concerned routinely failed to diagnose mental disorders. It seems that these health practitioners—and likely many others—hold disability-related attitudes that view a suicidally depressed mood as *understandable* in the case of impairment, and thus not cause for treatment (Herr & Phil, 1992). In a study of medical records in cases of suicide, Conwell and Caine (1991) found that in excess of 90% of individuals ended their lives while suffering a diagnosable mental disorder. Severe depression is a life-threatening but treatable condition, implying an ethical obligation to provide psychotherapy and/or medication. Disability prejudice, it seems, has the power to disrupt this principle.

OVERCOMING INTERNALIZED OPPRESSION

The so-called "social model of disability" has proven to be a very useful political device in re-directing attention away from the body, and toward the complex of social factors implicated in disability inequality (Abberley, 1987; Barnes, 1990; Oliver, 1990; Swain et al., 1993). This model emerged in the United Kingdom in the 1970s, mobilizing the opposition to medical model thinking outlined in a previous section. Its key contribution was to make a conceptual distinction between "impairment," which came to denote presocial, biological differences in bodily structure or function, and "disability," which was defined as follows:

> The loss or limitation of opportunities that prevents people who have impairments from taking part in the normal life of the community on an equal level with others due to physical and social barriers. (Finkelstein & French, 1993, p. 27)

What this distinction achieved was a separation, in the minds of many disabled people, between inner uncertainties about ability (often engendered by socialization), and the reality of avoidable barriers to participation which contravene human rights. This, to some extent at least, allows for the *giving back* of accountability to an unjust society (Thomas, 1999). However, the social model's avoidance of the psychological realm, and its reliance on binary logic, has limited its potential for illuminating the personal nature of life in a disablist society (Watermeyer, 2013).

One strategy for overcoming the negative internalizations of a disablist world is the so-called "affirmative model" of disability (Swain & French, 2000, 2008). This approach seeks to re-claim and re-cast the disabled identity in a "nontragic" light, emphasizing lifestyle difference as positive and creative. Critics, however, maintain that it fails to fully get to the roots or impressions of denigration, instead colluding with prejudiced binaries by creating a forced counter-narrative (Watermeyer, 2012a, 2013). Perhaps more convincing is a radical strand of contemporary disability art and theater, which creates flux and discomfort in the observer through poking mischievous fun at disability-related identities, the brittle nature of the modernist bodily ideal, and much else (Conroy, 2008; Garland-Thomson, 2009).

As already noted, psychology as a discipline has largely failed to understand disability in a critical, contextual way. This holds, too, for the enterprise of psychotherapy (Asch & Rousso, 1985; Lenny, 1993). However, as has been shown in the development of feminist psychotherapy, this need not be so. In fact, depth-oriented, ideologically critical forms of psychotherapy have immense potential in showing how oppression has become internalized, and unlocking the trauma of discrimination that so often cements inequality (Olkin, 1999; Sinason, 1992; Watermeyer, 2002b, 2012b). Theoretical links between disability studies and critical psychoanalysis show great promise here.

Models of group-based conscientization, beginning with the work of Paolo Freire (1970), carry great potential for disability development (Peters, 1999; Watermeyer, 2012a). These methods, applied with the insights of critical psychoanalysis, bear the potential to combine deepening awareness of the often invisible mechanisms of exclusion with the growth of personal insight into internalized subordination. It is, of course, essential that such interventions be designed and delivered with the central involvement of disabled people. A growing number of voices from disability studies and the disability movement agree that political and personal emancipation must go hand in hand (Charlton, 1998; Coleridge, 1993; Thompson, 2003; Watermeyer, 2012a, 2013), echoing founding principles of the black consciousness movement (Biko, 1978; Davids, 1996; Fanon, 1952/1986, 1963/2004). Unfortunately, though, the historical materialist, social model position that has influenced much of the international disability movement has brought with it a failure to prioritize the emotional well-being of the disabled constituency. TG provides the following reflections on disablist oppression and the struggle for clear entitlement:

> The realization that alienation and exclusion from environments and opportunities stems from the way in which society treats difference, rather than the innate defectiveness of the disabled body, forms the

basis of conscientization. When I first returned to university, I felt very apologetic about requiring additional support in order to participate in class. Wherever possible I took on the additional burden rather than ask for consideration from staff. For example, I would approach fellow students (often strangers) after the first class to arrange to get copies of notes. Or I would do extra research to identify tutorial groups that meet in wheelchair-accessible venues (rather than simply requesting that an accessible venue be found). All of this was driven by a deep-seated fear that I would be further rejected once people recognized how my participation placed extra demands on others. It also manifested in my exaggerated need to manage other people's feelings, such as trying my best to make sure that my disability didn't make other people uncomfortable.

After about a year I began to recognize that asking the university to satisfy these "extra demands" was neither unfair nor disproportionate. Claiming your right to be a full and equal participant in the life of a public institution, even if this requires additional resources or considerations, is a basic part of being an equal citizen. Furthermore, by individualizing and personally trying to satisfy these needs I was weakening the claims of other current or future disabled people to such considerations. It is the difference between "this is how I am different from you, please don't hate me" and "this is who I am and this is what I need to be an equal participant in this relationship."

The theoretical ideas on political and psychological liberation described previously must be understood with an awareness that the majority of the world's population resides in developing contexts, where data regarding life circumstances is limited. Against the backdrop of unknown local variables to do with poverty, cultural representations, and prevalent hierarchy, the simplistic exporting of social model or human rights discourse is extremely problematic (Barnes & Mercer, 2005; Grech, 2009). For example, advocating for the creation of equity legislation is meaningless among communities possessing no resources for enforcement (Grech, 2009). Further, in environments of mass unemployment, the singling out of "disability exclusion" carries inherent contradictions, implying the need for a more broadly based, emancipatory politics of universal citizenship rights. The separatist identity politics that has often been central to the international disability movement must be questioned here, as it is accused of contributing to a splintered human rights agenda of competing minority needs, rather than investing in the notion of a caring society for all (Fraser, 1995; Shakespeare, 2006). The bewildering—or dazzling—diversity of impairment invests disability politics with unique potential for disrupting dominant scripts of identity, through showing up the instability of the essentialist notions of identity that modern society holds dear (Davis, 2002).

CONCLUSION

The world's disabled population remains dispersed, difficult to define and quantify, and largely unattached to civil rights politics. Silence regarding the often brutal injustice suffered by this community is maintained through immense levels of economic and social disempowerment, as well as an embedded human aversion to thinking about the universal reality of bodily fallibility. So embedded is the cultural idealization of bodily *normalcy* and vitality, that disability prejudice is not the premise of a bigoted few, but a pervasive, unspoken, and intrinsic social reality.

It has become clear to a growing number of writers in disability studies that psychological emancipation is a necessary part of political freedom, although the Marxist vanguard of social model politics has resisted this. It is very difficult, even politically dangerous, to speak about emotional aspects of oppression in the face of a culture all-too-ready to blame the victims of social injustice. This is a quandary that, no doubt, is echoed in other chapters of this book. However, for disabled people, the history of psycho-pathologization by biomedically oriented theorists means that to fail to articulate one's own struggle is to invite obliteration by an essentialist discourse. Now, therefore, is the time for disability scholars, activists, and community members to undertake a careful, yet decisive turn inward. Tracing the impressions of a harmful disablist ideology on subjectivity need not mean foregoing political struggle. On the contrary, to ignore how psychological life is shaped by disablist socialization is to elide essential aspects of oppression.

REFERENCES

Abberley, P. (1987). The concept of oppression and the development of a social theory of disability. *Disability, Handicap and Society, 2,* 5–19.

Abberley, P. (1996). Work, utopia and impairment. In L. Barton (Ed.), *Disability and society: Emerging issues and insights* (pp. 61–79). New York, NY: Addison Wesley Longman Ltd.

Asch, A., & Fine, M. (1988). Introduction: Beyond pedestals. In A. Asch & M. Fine (Eds.), *Women with disabilities: Essays in psychology, culture and politics* (pp. 1–38). Philadelphia, PA: Temple University Press.

Asch, A., & Fine, M. (1997). Nurturance, sexuality and women with disabilities: The example of women and literature. In L. Davis (Ed.), *The disability studies reader* (pp. 241–259). New York, NY: Routledge.

Asch, A., & Rousso, H. (1985). Therapists with disabilities: Theoretical and clinical issues. *Psychiatry, 48,* 1–12.

Bach, J. R., & Tilton, M. C. (1994). Life satisfaction and well-being measures in ventilator assisted individuals with traumatic tetraplegia. *Archives of Physical Medicine and Rehabilitation, 75,* 626–632.

Barnes, C. (1990). *"Cabbage syndrome": The social construction of dependence.* London: Falmer.

Barnes, C., & Mercer, G. (Eds.). (2005). *The social model of disability: Europe and the majority world.* Leeds: Disability Press.

Barnes, C., Oliver, M., & Barton, L. (2002a). Introduction. In C. Barnes, M. Oliver, & L. Barton (Eds.), *Disability studies today* (pp. 1–17). Cambridge: Polity Press.

Barnes, C., Oliver, M., & Barton, L. (2002b). Disability, the academy and the inclusive society. In C. Barnes, M. Oliver, & L. Barton (Eds.), *Disability studies today* (pp. 250–260). Cambridge: Polity Press.

Barton, L., & Armstrong, F. (2001). Disability, education, and inclusion: Cross-cultural issues and dilemmas. In G. Albrecht, K. Seelman, & M. Bury (Eds.), *Handbook of disability studies* (pp. 693–710). Thousand Oaks, CA: Sage Publications.

Biko, S. (1978). *I write what I like.* London: The Bowerdean Press.

Bogdan, R. (1988). *Freak show: Presenting human oddities for amusement and profit.* Chicago, IL: University of Chicago Press.

Braddock, D., & Parish, S. (2001). An institutional history of disability. In G. Albrecht, K. Seelman, & M. Bury (Eds.), *Handbook of disability studies* (pp. 11–68). Thousand Oaks, CA: Sage.

Charlton, J. (1998). *Nothing about us without us: Disability, oppression, and empowerment.* Berkeley, CA: University of California Press.

Clegg, J. (2006). Understanding intellectually disabled clients in clinical psychology. In D. Goodley, & R. Lawthom (Eds.), *Disability and psychology: Critical introductions and reflections* (pp. 123–140). Basingstoke: Palgrave Macmillan.

Coleridge, P. (1993). *Disability, liberation, and development.* Oxford: Oxfam.

Conroy, C. (2008). Active differences: Disability and identity beyond postmodernism. *Contemporary Theatre Review, 18,* 341–354.

Conwell, Y., & Caine, E. D. (1991). Rational suicide and the right to die: Reality and myth. *The New England Journal of Medicine, 325,* 1100–1101.

Crow, L. (1992). Renewing the social model of disability. *Coalition,* July, 5–9.

Davids, M. F. (1996). Frantz Fanon: The struggle for inner freedom. *Free Associations, 6,* 205–234.

Davis, L. J. (1995). *Enforcing normalcy: Disability, deafness, and the body.* New York, NY: Verso.

Davis, L. J. (2002). *Bending over backwards: Disability, dismodernism and other difficult positions.* New York, NY: New York University Press.

Drake, R. F. (2001). Welfare states and disabled people. In G. Albrecht, K. Seelman, & M. Bury (Eds.), *Handbook of disability studies* (pp. 412–429). Thousand Oaks, CA: Sage Publications.

Engel, G. (1977). The need for a new medical model. *Science, 196,* 129–136.

Fanon, F. (1986). *Black skin, white masks.* London: Pluto Press (Original work published 1952).

Fanon, F. (2004). *The wretched of the earth.* (R. Philcox, Trans.). New York, NY: Grove Press (Original work published 1963).

Ferguson, P. M. (2001). Mapping the family: Disability Studies and the exploration of parental response to disability. In G. Albrecht, K. Seelman, & M. Bury (Eds.), *Handbook of disability studies* (pp. 373–395). Thousand Oaks, CA: Sage Publications.

Ferguson, P., & Asch, A. (1989). Lessons from life: Personal and parental perspectives on school, childhood and disability. In D. Biklen, D. Ferguson, & A. Ford (Eds.), *Schooling and disability* (pp. 108–140). Chicago, IL: University of Chicago Press.

Fiedler, L. (1978). *Freaks: Myths and images of the secret self.* New York, NY: Simon and Schuster.

Finkelstein, V. (1980). *Attitudes and disabled people: Issues for discussion.* New York, NY: World Rehabilitation Fund.

Finkelstein, V., & French, S. (1993). Towards a psychology of disability. In J. Swain, V. Finkelstein, S. French, & M. Oliver (Eds.), *Disabling barriers—enabling environments* (pp. 26–33). London: Sage.

Flood, T. (2005). "Food" or "thought"? The social model and the majority world. In C. Barnes & G. Mercer (Eds.), *The social model of disability: Europe and the majority world* (pp. 180–192). Leeds: Disability Press.

Foucault, M. (1976). *Birth of the clinic: An archaeology of medical perception.* London: Vintage Books.

Foucault, M. (1979). *Discipline and punish: The birth of the prison* (A. Sheridan, Trans.). New York, NY: Vintage Books.

Fraser, N. (1995). From redistribution to recognition? Dilemmas of justice in a 'post-socialist' age. *New Left Review, 212,* 68–92.

Freire, P. (1970). *Pedagogy of the oppressed.* New York, NY: Continuum.

French, S. (1993). What's so great about independence? In J. Swain, V. Finkelstein, S. French, & M. Oliver (Eds.), *Disabling barriers—enabling environments* (pp. 44–48). London: Sage.

French, S. (1999). The wind gets in my way. In M. Corker, & S. French (Eds.), *Disability discourse* (pp. 21–27). Philadelphia, PA: Open University Press.

French, S., & Swain, J. (2001). The relationship between disabled people and health and welfare professionals. In G. Albrecht, K. Seelman, & M. Bury (Eds.), *Handbook of disability studies* (pp. 734–753). Thousand Oaks, CA: Sage.

Frosh, S. (1989). Psychoanalysis and racism. In B. Richards (Ed.), *Crises of the self: Further essays on psychoanalysis and politics* (pp. 229–244). London: Free Association Books.

Frosh, S. (1991). *Identity crisis: Modernity, psychoanalysis and the self.* London: MacMillan.

Fujiura, G.T., & Rutkowski-Kmitta, V. (2001). Counting disability. In G. Albrecht, K. Seelman, & M. Bury (Eds.), *Handbook of disability studies* (pp. 69–96). Thousand Oaks, CA: Sage.

Garland-Thomson, R. (1995). Ann Petry's Mrs. Hedges and the evil, one-eyed girl: A feminist exploration of the physically disabled female subject. *Women's Studies, 24,* 599–614.

Garland-Thomson, R. (1997). *Extraordinary bodies: Figuring physical disability in American culture and literature.* New York, NY: Columbia University Press.

Garland-Thomson, R. (2009). *Staring. How we look.* New York, NY: Oxford University Press.

Gill, C. J. (2001). Divided understandings: The social experience of disability. In G. Albrecht, K. Seelman, & M. Bury (Eds.), *Handbook of disability studies* (pp. 351–372). Thousand Oaks, CA: Sage.

Goodley, D., & Lawthom, R. (Eds.). (2006). *Disability and psychology: Critical introductions and reflections.* Basingstoke: Palgrave Macmillan.

Grech, S. (2009). Disability, poverty and development: Critical reflections on the majority world debate. *Disability & Society, 24,* 771–784.

Hahn, H. (1997). An agenda for citizens with disabilities: Pursuing identity and empowerment. *Journal of Vocational Rehabilitation, 9,* 31–37.

Hahn, H. (2002). Academic debates and political advocacy: The US disability movement. In C. Barnes, M. Oliver, & L. Barton (Eds.), *Disability Studies Today* (pp. 162–189). Cambridge: Polity Press.

Herr, S., & Phil, D. (1992). No place to go: Refusal of life-sustaining treatment by competent persons with physical disabilities. *Issues in Law and Medicine, 8,* 3–34.

Hevey, D. (1992). *The creatures time forgot: Photography and disability imagery.* London: Routledge.

Hubbard, R. (1997). Abortion and disability: Who should and who should not inhabit the world? In L. Davis (Ed.), *The disability studies reader* (pp. 187–200). New York, NY: Routledge.

Hughes, B. (2002). Bauman's strangers: Impairment and the invalidation of disabled people in modern and post-modern cultures. *Disability & Society, 17,* 571–584.

Hughes, B., & Paterson, K. (1997). The social model of disability and the disappearing body: Towards a sociology of impairment. *Disability & Society, 12,* 325–340.

Kleinman, A. (1987). Anthropology and psychiatry: The role of culture and cross-cultural research on illness. *British Journal of Psychiatry, 151,* 447–454.

Kleinman, A., Das, V., & Lock, M. (1997). *Social suffering.* Berkeley, CA: University of California Press.

Lasch, C. (1978). *The culture of narcissism: American life in an age of diminishing expectations.* New York, NY: W.W. Norton.

Lenny, J. (1993). Do disabled people need counselling? In J. Swain, V. Finkelstein, S. French, & M. Oliver (Eds.), *Disabling barriers—enabling environments* (pp. 233–240). London: Sage.

Linton, S. (1998). *Claiming disability: Knowledge and identity.* New York, NY: NY University Press.

Marks, D. (1999a). *Disability: Controversial debates and psychosocial perspectives.* London: Routledge.

Marks, D. (1999b). Dimensions of oppression: Theorising the embodied subject. *Disability & Society, 14,* 611–626.

Michalko, R. (2002). *The difference that disability makes.* Philadelphia, PA: Temple University Press.

Mitchell, D. T., & Snyder, S. L. (1997). Introduction: Disability studies and the double bind of representation. In D. T. Mitchell, & S. L. Snyder (Eds.), *The body and physical difference: Discourses of disability* (pp. 1–31). Detroit: University of Michigan Press.

Morris, J. (1992). Personal and political: A feminist perspective on researching physical disability. *Disability, Handicap and Society, 7,* 157–166.

Morris, J. (1993). Prejudice. In J. Swain, V. Finkelstein, S. French, & M. Oliver (Eds.), *Disabling barriers—enabling environments* (pp. 101–106). London: Sage.

Murphy, R. F. (1987). *The body silent.* New York, NY: Henry Holt and Company Inc.

Mutua, N. K. (2001). The semiotics of accessibility and the cultural construction of disability. In L. J. Rogers & B. B. Swadener (Eds.), *Semiotics and disability* (pp. 103–116). Albany, NY: State University of New York Press.

Norden, M. F. (1994). *The cinema of isolation: A history of physical disability in the movies.* New Brunswick: Rutgers University Press.

Oliver, M. (1986). Social policy and disability: Some theoretical issues. *Disability, Handicap and Society, 1,* 15–17.

Oliver, M. (1990). *The politics of disablement.* London: Macmillan.

Oliver, M. (1996). *Understanding disability: From theory to practice.* New York, NY: St. Martin's Press.

Oliver, M. (2001). Disability issues in the postmodern world. In L. Barton (Ed.), *Disability, politics, and the struggle for change* (pp. 149–159). London: David Fulton Publishers.

Olkin, R. (1999). *What psychotherapists should know about disability.* New York, NY: Guilford.

Pernick, M. S. (1997). Defining the defective: Eugenics, aesthetics and mass culture in early-twentieth century America. In D. T. Mitchell & S. L. Snyder (Eds.), *The body and physical difference: Discourses of disability* (pp. 89–110). Detroit: University of Michigan Press.

Peters, S. (1999). Transforming disability identity through critical literacy and the cultural politics of language. In M. Corker & S. French (Eds.), *Disability discourse* (pp. 103–113). Philadelphia, PA: Open University Press.

Ravaud, J. F., & Stiker, H. J. (2001). Inclusion/exclusion: An analysis of historical and cultural meanings. In G. Albrecht, K. Seelman, & M. Bury (Eds.), *Handbook of disability studies* (pp. 490–512). Thousand Oaks, CA: Sage.

Rioux, M. H. (1994). New research directions and paradigms: Disability is not measles. In M. Rioux & M. Bach (Eds.), *Disability is not measles: New research paradigms in disability* (pp. 1–8). Montreal, CA: Roeher Institute.

Rioux, M. H. (2002). Disability, citizenship and rights in a changing world. In C. Barnes, M. Oliver, & L. Barton (Eds.), *Disability studies today* (pp. 210–227). Cambridge: Polity Press.

Rustin, M. (1996). Attachment in context. In S. Kraemer & J. Roberts (Eds.), *The politics of attachment: Towards a secure society* (pp. 212–228). London: Free Association Books.

Schriner, K. (2001). A disability studies perspective on employment issues and policies for disabled people: an international view. In G. Albrecht, K. Seelman, & M. Bury (Eds.), *Handbook of disability studies* (pp. 642–662). Thousand Oaks, CA: Sage.

Scotch, R. (1988). Disability as the basis for a social movement: Advocacy and the politics of definition. *Journal of Social Issues, 44,* 159–172.

Shakespeare, T. (1994). Cultural representation of disabled people: Dustbins for disavowal? *Disability & Society, 9,* 283–299.

Shakespeare, T. (2006). *Disability rights and wrongs.* New York, NY: Routledge.

Shakespeare, T., & Officer, A. (2011). Editorial. *Disability and Rehabilitation, 33,* 1491–1492.

Shakespeare, T., Iezzoni, L. I., & Groce, N. E. (2009). The art of medicine: Disability and the training of health professionals. *The Lancet, 374,* 1815–1816.

Sinason, V. (1992). *Mental handicap and the human condition: New approaches from the Tavistock.* London: Free Association Books.

Stiker, H. J. (1982). *A history of disability.* (W. Sayers, Trans.). Ann Arbor, MI: University of Michigan Press.

Swain, J., Finkelstein, V., French, S., & Oliver, M. (Eds.), (1993). *Disabling barriers—enabling environments.* London: Sage.

Swain, J., & French, S. (2000). Towards an affirmation model of disability. *Disability & Society, 15,* 569–582.

Swain, J., & French, S. (2008). Affirming identity. In J. Swain & S. French (Eds.), *Disability on equal terms* (pp. 65–78). London: Sage.

Thomas, C. (1999). *Female forms: Experiencing and understanding disability.* Philadelphia, PA: Open University Press.

Thompson, N. (2003). *Promoting equality: Challenging discrimination and oppression* (2nd ed.). New York, NY: Palgrave Macmillan.

Trent, J. W. (1994). *Inventing the feeble mind: A history of mental retardation in the United States.* Berkeley, CA: University of California Press.

Turner, B. S. (2001). Disability and the sociology of the body. In G. Albrecht, K. Seelman, & M. Bury (Eds.), *Handbook of disability studies* (pp. 252–266). Thousand Oaks, CA: Sage.

Vash, C., & Crewe, N. M. (2004). *Psychology of disability: Second edition.* New York, NY: Springer

Vygotsky, L. (1978). *Mind and society.* Cambridge: Harvard University Press.

Watermeyer, B. (2002a). Blindness, attachment and self: Psychoanalysis and ideology. *Free Associations, 49,* 335–352.

Watermeyer, B. (2002b). Disability and psychotherapy: In ideologically charged relationship in community mental health service provision. In L. Swartz, K. Gibson, & T. Gelman (Eds.), *Reflective practice* (pp. 85–98). Pretoria: HSRC Press.

Watermeyer, B. (2006). Disability and psychoanalysis. In B. Watermeyer, L. Swartz, M. Schneider, T. Lorenzo, & M. Priestley (Eds.), *Disability and social change: A South African agenda* (pp. 31–43). Pretoria: HSRC Press.

Watermeyer, B. (2009). Claiming loss in disability. *Disability & Society, 24,* 91–102.

Watermeyer, B. (2012a). Is it possible to create a politically engaged, contextual psychology of disability? *Disability & Society, 27,* 161–174.

Watermeyer, B. (2012b). Disability and countertransference in group psychotherapy: Connecting social oppression with the clinical frame. *International Journal of Group Psychotherapy, 62,* 393–417.

Watermeyer, B. (2013). *Towards a Contextual Psychology of Disablism.* London: Routledge.

Watermeyer, B., & Swartz, L. (2008). Conceptualising the psycho-emotional aspects of disability and impairment: The distortion of personal and psychic boundaries. *Disability & Society, 23,* 599–610.

Wendell, S. (1996). *The rejected body: Feminist philosophical reflections on disability.* New York, NY: Routledge.

Wendell, S. (1997). Toward a feminist theory of disability. In L. Davis (Ed.), *The disability studies reader* (pp. 260–278). New York, NY: Routledge.

World Health Organisation. (2011). *World Report on Disability. Geneva: World Health Organisation.* [online] Available from http://whqlibdoc.who.int/publications/2011/9789240685215_eng.pdf

Afterword
The Middle Way: Internalizing, Externalizing, and Balance in Life

I believe in choice, freedom, and control—being captains of our ship, as it were. I believe in the power of the situation, the context, and the contingencies—Skinner would say reinforcement contingencies control behavior (Skinner, 1971). I believe in the Middle Way, which Siddhartha Gautama describes as the character of the path that leads to liberation. In Buddhism, it is the insight that transcends the oppositional beliefs about existence, life, and death. Internalizing oppression is real, whether referring to the shame one feels because he is gay, or the guilt a battered woman feels because she fears she may have angered her batterer. Overcoming this guilt or shame, self-hatred, or fear is an enormous challenge for individuals, groups, and societies. My view is that the transcendent awareness of the Middle Way is the foundation for enlightenment, self-awareness, and self-preservation.

MY STORY

One extremely important value of this book is the stories it tells. Dr. David begins in this vein in his preface. A critical element of the oppression story is the other-ness that one recognizes, feels, and internalizes. I recall the ages-ago images of a nascent television industry and my aspirations to be Bud on *Father Knows Best*. And I wanted my mother to be like Margaret Anderson: neat house, with fruit and flowers on the table, Mom in a nice housedress, baking cookies for when I came home from school, and serving them with milk. I (We)—the others—looked at them with aspiration, hope, envy.

We (Blacks) lived on the south side of town, in projects, and we had our own night at the skating rink (Thursdays). We could set pins at the local bowling alley but we couldn't bowl there. We all went to the same high school but came from different directions—Whites from the North side of town, Blacks from the South side. We were different from them—we knew or thought we knew—not as rich, not as smart, not as good. But were we? The answers to uncertain questions were also uncertain! Yes, they had more money, more access, more opportunity, more privilege. In some ways they were smarter, and in other ways, not! However, by all accounts they were not better. This is a tough calculus to compute on a daily basis when your psychological well-being is at stake.

When I was invited to write a book on prejudice in 1970, I reflected on my (our) story as a cultural story, a psychological episode, an example of the race problem, and, importantly, my (our) responses to it. Yes we were segregated, we occupied a low rung of society, and our opportunities were truncated. Yes, at times, we envied them—they became the other, the privileged. However, day to day, we played, we fought, we learned, we loved, we sang and danced, hoped and tried, and we prayed. The problem, for me, was bigger than prejudice, which I felt was limited to the individual attitudes, beliefs, and actions of people. No, it was racism I wanted to illuminate; that systemic blight on culture and psyche that affected and infected all it touched. Thus, *Prejudice and Racism* (Jones, 1972) emerged. However, I also wanted to reflect on the resiliencies, the coping ways we lived ordinary lives. Oppression is two-dimensional, a tale of two psyches called Prospero and Caliban (see Mannoni, 1990, for the application of this Shakespeare story to colonization psyches). Dr. David and the contributing authors in this book take us inside this duality, into the psyche of Caliban—the slave, the beast, the "other" who exists in Prospero's dominion.

Individuals are prejudiced, in part because of institutional practices, values, and contingencies, and in part because of cultural mores and practices (see Paula Dean's fall from the mountaintop because she was a citizen of her culture and "Nigger" was a normative concept). As cultural psychologists argue, "Culture and psyche make each other up" (Shweder & Sullivan, 1993). Cultural contingencies, social hierarchy, and psychological characteristics are counted up, tallied, and used to assign place, purpose, and possibility. No wonder internalized oppression is so complicated—and important. Reality and fiction, belief and fact are intertwined in ways the mind and soul must understand in order to have a balanced and useful sense of self. Dr. David and the chapter authors in this book take this on in a sensitive, personal, scholarly, and comprehensive way.

OPPRESSION AS NARRATIVE

Oppression is a fact: slavery and Jim Crow, Trail of Tears, Japanese Internment, Stonewall, Chinese Exclusion Act, and so forth (see Jones,

Dovidio, & Vietze, 2014, Chapter 3). At the same time, oppression is also a *narrative*—a story about one's individual and collective past. The narrative assembles the facts into a story that gives meaning to one's personal and collective experience. That meaning can vary depending on the personal needs and experiences of a person or a group. The oppression narrative is at once a generalizable connection of the past to the present built from beliefs about the nature and the degree of oppression one's group has faced, and the stories of resistance, redemption, personal and collective worth, and resilience that comprise it. "What doesn't kill me may make me stronger," or, alternatively, weakens me so that I am vulnerable to the bad intentions of others and the lack of intention in myself. My view is not an either/or constriction, but a synthetic amalgamation of danger and threat with purpose and creativity.

Therefore, the collective narrative matters a great deal. The oppression narrative can follow three courses (at least). One course is the externalizing one—the oppressor is evil and must be resisted or eliminated. Another is internal, "I am (we are) who the negative stereotypes say we are." A third is also internalizing, but can be experienced as a self and collective affirmation; "I am (we are) NOT who they say we are." Oppression not only concerns the physical constraints of freedom and control—over one's body, and opportunities for access to life sustaining and affirming assets—but also the psychological meaning of selfhood, collective identity, and self-worth.

The Middle Way requires changing the psychological meaning of the narrative—the third path. We may add a corollary, "We are who WE say we are." A large body of research on racial and ethnic identity, acculturation, and identity development address these issues. Each implicates not only the self, but also the collective ("I am because we are, and because we are, therefore I am" [Mbiti, 1969]).

OPPRESSION PARADIGM

Is there a paradigm of internalized oppression—are the oppression narratives and the psychological responses to them similar across groups? I have argued that slavery—a well-known and massive system of oppression—created not only a system of physical and legal control, but produced two mechanisms of psychological control—loss of freedom and dehumanization (Jones, 2003). In the United States, these are perhaps the two most important psychological characteristics one can have—the feeling or even the illusion of control, and feelings of self-worth. Internalized oppression, therefore, may be characterized by lack of personal control, and feelings of diminished self-worth—a paradigm of internalized oppression. I offer two important caveats to this, however; (1) lack of control is not always a deficiency and spirituality (ceding some degree of control to forces beyond the self) can form a sound basis of human character and personal commitment (see Ani, 1994); and (2) the self, in some cultural systems, may be overrated as a source of psychological well-being (Markus & Kitayama, 1991) and the collective may supersede the self as a basis for personal and collective value, meaning, and organization (Moemeka, 1998)

The paradigm of oppression, then, can be applied to any group with a common identity and an historical narrative bound up in oppression. Therein lays the commonality. The consequences, as noted above, can be internalizing with acceptance or rejection, and externalizing with blame or outrage. Dr. David's book has done a good job of framing these variations and proposing ways of understanding and ameliorating their negative aspects while capitalizing on the resiliencies and strengths they also provide.

The Paradigm of Oppression must also include the variations in the form, content, and historicity of oppression for different oppressed groups. Each narrative of oppression is rationalized by the oppressors along several different lines (whether to justify entering the oppressive relationship or sustaining it). Women are feminine, nurturing, emotional, weak, or precious and therefore are excluded or marginalized from some opportunities, or put on a pedestal and thereby excluded from daily commerce (Glick & Fiske, 1997). Blacks have been viewed as culturally inferior, cognitively inadequate, morally suspect, infantile, superstitious, and impulsive over several centuries. In the 20th century, they "became" aggressive, hostile, and criminal—the current primary contents of black stereotypes. The arc of moral inclusion bends away from gay men and lesbians (see Opotow, 1995). American Indians were savage and uncivilized, and thus removing them from their lands and sending them to Indian Schools to "save them from their uncivilized state" was an amelioration strategy of the United States government, undertaken without compunction. Chinese or Japanese were not like White Americans and thus were initially barred from coming to the United States (see Chinese Exclusion Act of 1876; Asiatic Barred Zone Agreement of 1917; Jones et al., 2014). In 1919, a California legislator even suggested they were less fit to marry his daughter than even the lowest Italian (Jones, 1972). However, we should also note that Italians were lynched in the early 20th century because they were thought to be violent and a threat to the American sense of security and freedom (Jones et al., 2014).

In short, the stereotype becomes the content of the internalized oppression thoughts and feelings. Because the stereotype contents differ between groups, so too the nature of the internalized beliefs, feelings, and emotions differs between and among them. The stereotype content model (Fiske, Cuddy, Glick, & Xu, 2002) provides a useful account of the differential values and emotions that accompany the contents of diverse stereotypes of marginalized and majority groups. So the issue is constructing a system for analysis, understanding, and amelioration that builds on the generalized paradigm of internalized oppression, but tailors this analysis to the particulars of the group being considered, as well as the resiliencies that the oppression context may enable and elicit. This text sets us up for this type of system.

THE HISTORICAL PARADIGM

One important consideration is how oppressive contexts evolve. When people say that racism has ended (see D'Souza's *The End of Racism*, 1993), I ask, what year was that, what day did it happen and how was it commemorated? Voting Rights Act of 1965 maybe? (Hardly, with the recent Supreme Court decision striking down the key Section 5 of the Act). Was it the election of Barack Obama as President (the disrespect and recalcitrance of his opposition is hard to pass off as conventional politics, and much easier to recognize as thinly veiled aversive racism; see Dovidio & Gaertner, 2004)? So racial bias has not gone; it is just gone underground. What are the implications of subterranean oppression for internalized conceptions of self?

OPPRESSION UNDERGROUND

We used to have to cope with abject and unmitigated overt racism, sexism, and every other form of biased sentiment and behavior. In many respects, those times were easier psychologically. Now it is nuanced, subtle, and provides "plausible deniability" for would-be racists (or whatever type of biased perspective one holds). Attributional ambiguity (Crocker & Major, 1989) is a concept that captures one of the psychological dynamics that is quite relevant to internalized oppression in this more nuanced world of oppression. One asks of a particular judgment or outcome: Is it based on my personal attributes, or the biased perspectives and intentions of others? If we attribute it to our own characteristics, then we may internalize the assertion of inferiority or inadequacy and accept a negative self-view. If, however, we attribute the treatment to biases in others, then we can discount the negative implications and keep our positive self-concept intact. Several studies support the esteem-maintaining value of an attributional ambiguity approach.

My point in raising this is to highlight the fact that internalizing oppression is not automatic and inevitable. As Dr. David has noted, people are not born feeling inferior and ashamed of themselves; internalized oppression is learned. Therefore, people can refuse to learn—or to accept—internalized oppression. If people can learn to internalize the oppression they have experienced, then they can unlearn it. If we refuse to let others define our reality and humanity, capability, and potential, then we need not internalize the negative messages that are delivered routinely in our society and ongoing encounters. This is a conduit to the Middle Way.

BEYOND THE BINARY

The psychological attention to otherness has focused primarily on race for over a century (see DuBois' [1903] famous dictum, ". . . the problem of the twentieth century is the problem of the color line"). In my own writing, I have tried to expand that binary, but I have been bound to the psychological research—focused primarily on race, and on Blacks and Whites—that is ensconced in it (see Jones, 1997; Jones et al., 2014). Dr. David and his colleagues have done an admirable job of balancing this out. The breadth and coverage of differences in the United States is a great value of this volume. These comparisons allow us to examine simultaneously the paradigm of internalized oppression and the ways in which it diverges for different groups and around the world. In my view, internalized oppression is a negative psychological state of otherness with self-destructive consequences. Occupying that psychological space has consequences whatever the source of the otherness, or the nature and degree of the negativity it carries. This text, then, expands our thinking into the ways in which one's connections to one's group and the experiences that ensue affect our interpretations and responses to negative otherness. The specificity of the varied experiences brings into focus the generality of the paradigm of internalized oppression.

THE BALANCED PSYCHE

Another important perspective is the idea of bicultural adaptation (LaFromboise, Coleman, & Gerton, 1993). Marginalized and oppressed people necessarily live in two worlds, the world of their existence and the world of the oppressor. Balance is achieved by alternating between two cultural caveats and stipulations. No need to choose, only to master the cultural grammars. I propose the idea of *psychological navigation* to describe the challenges of duality (living in two worlds of polarized affective and value differences) and the need for holism and personal coherence. Internalizing oppression is more likely when the duality is conceived as a zero sum circumstance—instrumental possibilities conflict with self-expressive realism. What to do? LaFromboise et al. (1993) propose a bicultural adaptation of alternation—oppressed and marginalized groups are, by their nature and experience, in a subordinate position on the power and value hierarchy of society. How does the "double consciousness" of being simultaneously inside and outside of mainstream society play out (see Dubois, 1903, for the most well-known enunciation of this principle).

Berry and colleagues offer a balanced perspective on acculturation (Berry & Kim, 1988). Maintaining one's cultural heritage may conflict with becoming involved and competent in a new culture. Berry sees the balanced way as the most psychologically healthy—he labels it *integration*. Research in several countries shows that an integration approach to acculturation leads to the best psychological outcomes (Berry, Phinney, Sam, & Vedder, 2006). In personality terms, we may think of integration as personal coherence (see Cervone & Shoda, 1999). Internalized oppression is most likely when one's heritage culture is diminished, and the mainstream culture is privileged. Those who tip the balance in the direction of the mainstream culture and away from their heritage are characterized uncharitably as an "Oreo cookie"—Black on the outside, White on the inside; "banana" (Asian); "apple" (Indian); or "coconut" (Latino) to round out the list.

WHY INTERNALIZED OPPRESSION?

Cross and colleagues (Cross, 1991; Vandiver, Cross, Worrell, & Fhagen-Smith, 2002) refer to accepting negative stereotypes about your group as *miseducation*, and *self-hatred* identifies internalization of those negative stereotypes. In their analysis of racial identity, it is only self-hatred and miseducation statuses that correlate negatively with self-esteem. The negative stereotypes are well known and the evidence for discrimination is readily available. But the manifestations of internalized oppression vary greatly within groups. Why?

One reason may be system justification—accepting inferior status as normative (Jost & Banaji, 1992). Another label for internalized oppression, in the system justification concept, is *false consciousness*. The issues are coming into focus. All marginalized oppressed groups with an historical narrative of oppression face the psychological navigation challenge. So the problem may well lie in how that narrative is understood, the degree to which it is accepted as accurate for the group, and the extent to which it becomes part of one's personal self-concept. Amelioration of the negative aspects of internalized oppression should focus on all three elements. The first requires systematic education and exploration of group and society history. The second requires knowledge of the group and its value and meaning, as well as one's connection to it. The third requires psychological processes that lead to self-affirmation. History, society, group, and self are all ingredients of the internalization of oppression and each must be part of its amelioration.

IT TAKES A COMMUNITY

We talk about the deaf community, immigrant community, the Black community, and others with awareness that members of these communities may not share physical space, but do reside in similar psychological spaces. The problem of internalized oppression is not one of unique individuals responding to personalized experiences and understandings. It is the connection of those individuals to their communities that makes the oppression narrative psychologically relevant. Thus, it is an extremely important and compelling aspect of this book that the academics and community activists and leaders collaborate in telling the story and analyzing its psychological and behavioral implications.

Academics are often divorced from the issues "on the ground"—theirs may be a view from 50,000 feet. Community activists and leaders address these issues in "real time," and may miss important connections that are revealed from scholarly analysis. By joining these two, Dr. David has provided an excellent paradigm for addressing this complex problem, and taken an important step toward the Middle Way.

THE MIDDLE WAY

In Theravada Buddhist soteriology (study of religious ideas of salvation), the self does not live in eternity, nor does it cease totally at death. The self is a dynamic interplay of origins and endings, living and dying—birth makes death possible. Internalized oppression is death—of the soul, of the self, of the connection to the good in us. Externalized oppression is war—psychological, emotional, and behavioral. The Middle Way leads us on a path that avoids each of these destructive directions.

Internalized Oppression: The Psychology of Marginalized Groups is an important bridge across marginalized groups, oppressed psyches, academic and community contexts, and the universal and the particular. In the age of diversity, human complexity challenges our internal psyches, our intergroup interactions, and our societal and institutional structures and practices. Our ability to understand and transcend the internalization of oppression requires nuance, synthesis, converging perspectives, analysis, and response. This book guides us expertly and compassionately on the path to psychological well-being—the Middle Way!

James M. Jones, PhD
University of Delaware
Author of Prejudice and Racism *and*
coauthor of The Psychology of Diversity:
Beyond Prejudice and Racism

REFERENCES

Ani, M. (1994). *Yurugu: An African-centered critique of European cultural thought and behavior.* Trenton, NJ: Africa World Press.

Berry, J. W., & Kim, U. (1988). Acculturation and mental health. In Berry, J. W. & Kim, U. (Eds.), *Health and cross-cultural psychology: Toward applications (pp. 207–236).* Thousand Oaks, CA: Sage Publications.

Berry, J. W., Phinney, J. S., Sam, D. L., & Vedder, P. (2006). Immigrant youth: Acculturation, identity, and adaptation. *Applied Psychology: An International Review, 55*(3), 303–332.

Cervone, D., & Shoda, Y. (Eds.). (1999). *The coherence of personality: Social-cognitive bases of consistency, variability, and organization.* New York, NY: Guilford Press.

Crocker, J., & Major, B. (1989). Social stigma and self-esteem: The self-protective properties of stigma. *Psychological Review, 96*(4), 608–630.

Cross, W. E. (1991). *Shades of Black: Diversity in African American identity.* Philadelphia, PA: Temple University Press.

D'Souza, D. (1993). *The end of racism.* New York, NY: Basic Books.

Dovidio, J. F., & Gaertner, S. L. (2004). Aversive Racism. *Advances in experimental social psychology, 36,* 1–52. San Diego, CA, Elsevier Academic Press.

DuBois, W. E. B. (1903). *The souls of black folks.* Chicago, IL: McClurg.

Fiske, S. T., Cuddy, A. J. C., Glick, P., & Xu, J. (2002). A model of (often mixed) stereotype content: Competence and warmth respectively follow from perceived status and competition. *Journal of Personality and Social Psychology, 82*(6), 878–902.

Glick, P., & Fiske, S. T. (1997). Hostile and benevolent sexism: Measuring ambivalent sexist attitudes toward women. *Psychology of Women Quarterly, 21*(1), 119–135.

Jones, J. M. (1972). *Prejudice and racism.* Reading, MA: Addison-Wesley.

Jones, J. M. (1997). *Prejudice and racism* (2nd ed.). New York, NY: McGraw Hill.

Jones, J. M. (2003). TRIOS: A psychological theory of African legacy in American culture. *Journal of Social Issues, 59,* 217–241.

Jones, J. M., Dovidio, J. F., & Vietze, D.L. (2014). *The psychology of diversity: Beyond prejudice and racism.* New York, NY: Wiley/Blackwell.

Jost, J. T. & Banaji, M. R. (1992). The role of stereotyping in system-justification and the production of false consciousness. *British Journal of Social Psychology, 33,* 1–17.

LaFromboise, T., Coleman, H. L., & Gerton, J. (1993). Psychological impact of biculturalism: Evidence and theory. *Psychological Bulletin, 114*(3), 395–412.

Mannoni, O. (1990). *Prospero and Caliban: The psychology of colonization.* Ann Arbor, MI: University of Michigan Press.

Markus, H. R., & Kitayama, S. (1991). Culture and the self: Implications for cognition, emotion, and motivation. *Psychological Review, 98*(2), 224–253.

Mbiti, J. S. (1969). *African religions & philosophy.* New York, NY: Praeger.

Moemeka, A. A. (1998). Communalism as a fundamental dimension of culture. *Journal of Communication, 48*(4), 118–141.

Opotow, S. (1995). Drawing the line: Social categorization, moral exclusion, and the scope of justice. In S. Opotow (Ed.), *Conflict, cooperation, and justice: Essays inspired by the work of Morton Deutsch* (pp. 347–369). San Francisco, CA: Jossey-Bass.

Shweder, R. A., & Sullivan, M. A. (1993). Cultural psychology: Who needs it? *Annual Review of Psychology, 44*, 497–523.

Skinner, B. F. (1971). *Beyond freedom and dignity.* New York, NY: Knopf.

Vandiver, B. J., Cross, W. E., Jr., Worrell, F. C., & Fhagen-Smith, P. E. (2002). Validating the cross racial identity scale. *Journal of Counseling Psychology, 49*(1), 71–85.

Index

67896615R00182

Made in the USA
Lexington, KY
25 September 2017